THE
QUEE
RIFLE

GROUP TAKEN AT AGNEZ LES DUISANS, JUNE, 1917

Back Row.—Sergt. H. W. Crossingham, Sergt. G. W. J. Bowden, R.Q.M.S. S. J. Turnbull, C.S.M. J. B. Hill, D.C.M., C.S.M. W. H. Musselwhite, M.M., Sergt. W. B. Green, C.Q.M.S. C. B. Evans, Sergt. H. H. Partridge.

Middle Row.—R.S.M. A. H. Davis, Sergt. P. N. McCready, C.S.M. E. L. Ives, Sergt. L. H. Jenks, Sergt. L. Mabbett, Bugle-Major A. D. Pink, C.Q.M.S. E. P. Loveland, Sergt. M. A. Johnson, C.Q.M.S. A. E. Finbow, M.M., Sergt. A. H. Bowdidge.

Bottom Row.—2nd Lieut. L. P. Harrow, D.C.M., Major P. M. Glasier, Lieut.-Colonel R. Shoolbred, C.M.G., T.D. Captain S. R. Savill, M.C., Lieut. and Quartermaster E. W. N. Jackson.

THE WAR HISTORY
OF THE
1st BATTALION QUEEN'S WESTMINSTER RIFLES
1914–1918

BY

MAJOR J. Q. HENRIQUES, T.D.
(Formerly of the Regiment)

LONDON THE MEDICI SOCIETY LIMITED
7 GRAFTON STREET, BOND STREET W.1 1923

PREFACE

THIS volume contains the history of the 1st Battalion Queen's Westminster Rifles during the War, 1914–1918. A short record of the war service of the 2nd Battalion has already been published, but their full story still remains to be told. A battalion can only be regarded as a cog in a huge war machine, and its war history obviously cannot be a history of the war. The writer has, however, sketched as briefly as possible the general idea of the major operations in which the Queen's Westminsters were engaged. He hopes that, by so doing, he will have shown how the work of a unit, with a fighting strength of under one thousand men, had its appointed place in the work of the larger formations whose fighting strength ran into millions.

A draft history of the Battalion was written shortly after the Armistice by Lieutenant W. F. D. Young, under the supervision of Lieut.-Colonel S. R. Savill. This was kindly placed at the disposal of the writer and he desires to give the fullest acknowledgment of the great use he has made of it. Brigadier-General E. S. D'E. Coke very kindly consented to read through the manuscript, and his comments and suggestions have been deeply appreciated. Lieut.-Colonel R. Shoolbred has taken the greatest interest in the preparation of this history throughout all its stages, and has given the writer every possible help and encouragement. Colonel P. E. Harding and Lieut.-Colonel S. R. Savill have read the portions of the narrative relating to their periods of command and have given much valuable information. It would be difficult to write too appreciatively of the help given by Major A. F. Becke and Mr. E. A. Dixon of the Historical Section (Military Branch) of the Committee of Imperial Defence. Their advice and suggestions have been invaluable, and they have proved a never-failing source of information. The writer also offers his best thanks to all those who have given their help, particularly to Major J. B. Baber and Mr. G. W. T. Horrod for reading the proofs, and to Captain J. H. Kelly for the great trouble he has taken both in seeking information which the writer desired to obtain and in the preparation of the roll of officers who served and of the list of honours and awards. In the preparation of the latter, he

PREFACE

was assisted by members of the Queen's Westminster Retired Members Association. The maps have been drawn by Mr. H. Burge from tracings from official maps made by the writer; and Major Becke has rendered the greatest assistance in advising on the form of the maps and in checking their accuracy. The panorama and the air photograph are reproduced from official photographs, the group was taken professionally and the collotype of the memorial window in Westminster Abbey is reproduced from a photograph kindly given by Messrs. James Powell and Sons (Whitefriars) Limited, by whom the window was designed and carried out. The remaining illustrations are from photographs taken in France by Major J. B. Baber, Lieutenant D. M. Hutchinson and the writer.

Donations towards the costs of publication have kindly been given by Lady Howard Vincent, Colonel G. Haward Trollope and Lieut.-Colonel R. Shoolbred, and the writer greatly appreciates their support of his efforts to produce this History at a price within the reach, it is hoped, of all ranks who served with the Battalion.

Cordial thanks are also due to the publishers, for their advice and assistance while this volume was in the press.

J. Q. H.

November, 1923.

CONTENTS

		PAGE
PREFACE		v
HISTORICAL NOTE		xiii

CHAPTER
- I. MOBILISATION AND TRAINING — 1
- II. THE BATTALION GOES TO FRANCE — 14
- III. WITH THE SIXTH DIVISION — 21
- IV. HOUPLINES — 37
- V. IN THE YPRES SALIENT — 52
- VI. WITH THE 56TH DIVISION—TRAINING FOR THE OFFENSIVE — 74
- VII. GOMMECOURT, JULY 1ST, 1916 — 85
- VIII. THE BATTLES OF THE SOMME, 1916
  - I. THE FIGHTING FOR COMBLES. LEUZE WOOD — 111
  - II. THE BATTLE OF THE TRANSLOY RIDGES — 124
- IX. NEUVE CHAPELLE AND LAVENTIE — 130
- X. ON THE ARRAS FRONT — 139
- XI. THE BATTLES OF ARRAS, 1917
  - I. THE FIRST BATTLE OF THE SCARPE, 1917— THE ATTACK FROM THE WANCOURT RIDGE — 145
  - II. THE THIRD BATTLE OF THE SCARPE, 1917 — 156
- XII. THE SUMMER OF 1917 — 161
- XIII. THE BATTLES OF YPRES, 1917 — 168
- XIV. ON THE CAMBRAI FRONT, 1917 — 177
- XV. THE BATTLE OF CAMBRAI, 1917
  - I. THE CAPTURE OF TADPOLE COPSE — 189
  - II. THE GERMAN COUNTER-ATTACK, NOVEMBER 30TH, 1917 — 201
- XVI. THE FIRST BATTLE OF ARRAS, 1918
  - I. IN THE GAVRELLE SECTOR, DECEMBER, 1917, TO MARCH, 1918 — 209
  - II. GAVRELLE, MARCH 28TH, 1918 — 220

CONTENTS

CHAPTER		PAGE
XVII.	IN THE TELEGRAPH HILL SECTOR, ARRAS	237
XVIII.	THE BATTLE OF THE SCARPE, 1918	247
XIX.	THE BATTLE OF THE CANAL DU NORD	
	I. ON THE VIS EN ARTOIS FRONT	263
	II. THE CAPTURE OF SAUCHY CAUCHY	265
	III. ON THE "NE PLUS ULTRA" LINES	277
XX.	THE ADVANCE TO VICTORY	
	THE BATTLES OF VALENCIENNES AND THE SAMBRE AND THE PASSAGE OF LA GRANDE HONNELLE	281
XXI.	PEACE	300

ITINERARY	307
THE ROLL OF HONOUR	315
REWARDS WON BY OFFICERS, WARRANT OFFICERS, NON-COMMISSIONED OFFICERS AND MEN, 1914–1919	329
LIST OF OFFICERS WHO SERVED IN THE FIRST BATTALION, 1914–1919	335
INDEX	339

LIST OF ILLUSTRATIONS

GROUP OF OFFICERS, WARRANT OFFICERS AND NON-COMMISSIONED OFFICERS, 1917 *Frontispiece*

To face page

PANORAMA OF THE HOUPLINES SECTOR, ARMENTIÈRES, 1915   39

PANORAMA OF THE GOMMECOURT SALIENT, 1916   85

HOUPLINES, 1915
- *"BUCKINGHAM PALACE"*   44
- *THE GERMAN TRENCHES FROM THE BRITISH FRONT LINE*   44
- *"THE MAPPIN TERRACES"*   54

YPRES, 1915
- *MACHINE-GUN SECTION WEARING THE FIRST GAS MASKS*   54
- *THE CLOTH HALL*   64
- *A STREET SCENE*   64
- *DUGOUTS ON THE CANAL BANK*   64

SAUCHY CAUCHY FROM THE AIR, AUGUST 25TH, 1918   279

THE QUEEN'S WESTMINSTER MEMORIAL WINDOW, WESTMINSTER ABBEY   315

LIST OF MAPS

GENERAL MAP OF WESTERN FRONT	*End paper*
	To face page
SECTOR OF ARMENTIÈRES FRONT, 1915	50
HOOGE, AUGUST 9TH, 1915	56
YPRES, 1915–1916	72
GOMMECOURT, JULY 1ST, 1916	108
LEUZE WOOD, 1916	115
THE SOMME, 1916	128
LAVENTIE, 1916–1917	136
ARRAS, 1917	158
YPRES, 1917	174
CAMBRAI, 1917	206
GAVRELLE, 1918	234
BATTLE OF THE SCARPE, 1918	260
SAUCHY CAUCHY, 1918	278
SEBOURG, 1918	291
THE FINAL ADVANCE, 1918	296

HISTORICAL NOTE

AT the end of the eighteenth century, when England was threatened with invasion by the French, a large number of volunteer units were raised for the defence of the country. Amongst them were the London and Westminster Volunteer Light Horse (1779), the Royal Westminster Volunteers (1787), The Armed Association of Westminster (1797–1798) and the Queen's Royal Volunteers (1803). The Queen's Royal Volunteers were the successors to the Pimlico Armed Association raised in 1798. The infantry volunteers were disbanded in 1814 and the cavalry in 1829.

In 1859 and 1860, the old corps of the City of Westminster were reorganised, and the Pimlico Regiment became the Queen's Rifle Volunteers. In 1860, this Regiment amalgamated with the companies raised in nine other parishes in the City of Westminster, under the name "The Queen's (Westminster) Rifle Volunteers," and its commanding officer was Hugh Lupus, Earl Grosvenor, afterwards first Duke of Westminster, K.G.

During the South African War, 1899–1902, many members of the Regiment served at the front with the Imperial Forces, and they earned for the Regiment the war honour " South Africa, 1900–1902." The commanding officer, at the time, was Colonel Sir C. E. Howard Vincent, K.C.M.G., C.B., A.D.C., V.D., M.P., etc. Sir Howard Vincent commanded the Regiment for twenty years, and his energy and enthusiasm were reflected in everything that the Queen's Westminsters were called upon to do. On his retirement in 1904, he became Honorary Colonel, in succession to the Duke of Westminster, and he retained this appointment until his death in 1908, after a life of great public service. Colonel George Haward Trollope, V.D., commanded the Regiment from 1904 to 1909.

In 1908, the Corps was transferred to the Territorial Force and became the 16th (County of London Battalion) The London Regiment, with the special title " The Queen's Westminster Rifles."

Colonel Trollope resigned in 1909, after completing over forty-eight years of service with the Queen's Westminsters, and he subsequently succeeded Hugh Richard Arthur, second

Duke of Westminster, G.C.V.O., D.S.O., as Honorary Colonel. Lieut.-Colonel C. A. Gordon Clark, C.M.G., D.S.O., was in command from 1909 to 1911. He was succeeded by Lieut.-Colonel R. Shoolbred, C.M.G., T.D., D.L., under whose command the Battalion was mobilised and went out to France in 1914.

On the reduction of the establishment of the Territorial Force in 1921, the Queen's Westminster Rifles and the Prince of Wales's Own, Civil Service Rifles, were amalgamated. The Regiment, now known as the Queen's Westminster and Civil Service Rifles, is commanded by Lieut.-Colonel E. G. H. Cox, C.B.E., T.D., and it is privileged and honoured to have for its Honorary Colonel, H.R.H. The Prince of Wales, K.G., K.T., etc.

ADDENDUM, page 90

The following officers went into action with their companies at Gommecourt, July 1st, 1916:

A Company.—Captain F. G. Swainson (in command); 2nd Lieutenants J. J. Westmoreland, E. H. Bovill, E. H. Jarvis, J. Daniel.

B Company.—Captain G. E. Cockerill (in command); 2nd Lieutenants J. A. Horne, F. S. Thomas, W. F. Strange (2nd Londons), H. Luscombe.

C Company.—Captain H. F. Mott (in command); Lieutenant P. Spencer-Smith (Headquarter Bombers), 2nd Lieutenants A. G. V. Yates, A. G. Negus, D. F. Upton.

D Company.—Captain P. M. Glasier (in command); 2nd Lieutenants C. C. Iveson, and 2nd Lieutenants C. A. Stubbs, F. A. Farley and A. M. Manson (of the 2nd Londons).

Corrections:

p. 28, for Sergeant G. E. Fulton read Sergeant A. G. Fulton.
p. 60, for Lieut. D. M. Hutchison read Lieut. D. M. Hutchinson.
p. 93, for Corporal R. T. Townsend read Corporal R. F. Townsend.
p. 118, for Sergeant G. E. Cordery read Sergeant G. C. Cordery.
p. 159, for Sergeant Plummridge read Sergeant Plumridge.

CHAPTER I

MOBILISATION AND TRAINING

ON the 14th March, 1914, a practice mobilisation of the Queen's Westminster Rifles took place at the Battalion Headquarters in Buckingham Gate. This was in no sense in anticipation of the general mobilisation that was to take place less than five months later, but was part of the normal military training of every unit of the Territorial Force.

Before the outbreak of war, the extent to which this force formed an integral part of the national scheme of defence was not realised by the outside public. It was generally considered that military operations were matters for the professional soldier, and public opinion was not alive to the responsibility of the individual citizen to prepare himself for the defence of the Empire.

It is true that wide discussion had been taking place as to the desirability or otherwise of universal military training, but the question was treated by the great majority as one of theoretical rather than of practical importance. The arguments put forward in favour of some form of compulsory service not only resulted in obscuring the steady work that was being done by the Territorial Force, but also unquestionably served to discourage and in many cases actually to deter men from coming forward to join its ranks.[1]

Although military opinions differed widely as to the potential value of the Territorial Force as it existed in the years before the war, every effort was made to render it as efficient a fighting body as was possible under its conditions of service.

The Territorial year commenced annually on November 1st. In the Queen's Westminster Rifles a progressive scheme of training, mainly under company arrangements, was carried out in preparation for the fortnight's field training which took place either under brigade or divisional arrangements at the annual camp in August. During the winter the training of the Battalion as a whole was confined to route marches through the London streets, with occasional miniature range work and

---

[1] See a speech by Lord Roberts to the citizens of Manchester on October 25th, 1912, published by John Murray in "Lord Robert's Message to the Nation."

MOBILISATION AND TRAINING

lectures at Battalion Headquarters, but in the spring and summer months Battalion exercises were carried out in Richmond Park and other open spaces near London. In addition to this there were frequent Sunday and week-end tactical tours for officers, and tactical work of a more elementary description for the N.C.O.'s. Musketry formed a very important feature of the training, and in the years before the war the Queen's Westminster Rifles consistently took a high place in the musketry returns of the District.

At Easter, a large contingent of the Battalion was generally attached to a battalion of the K.R.R.C. in barracks at Aldershot or Blackdown, for musketry and field training. The experience, gained at these short Easter camps, of the routine of a regular battalion and the association with regular soldiers were of the utmost value to the Regiment.

During the year a large number of inter-company competitions were held in nearly every branch of normal military work, and the preparation of the teams did much to stimulate a desire to attain a high general standard of efficiency. This was particularly the case in rifle shooting. Large numbers used to attend the Regimental shoots at Bisley, and the annual Bisley rifle meeting. At this meeting individuals and teams from the Battalion worthily maintained its traditions as a shooting regiment, which had been founded in the early Volunteer days at Wimbledon.[1]

The annual training at camp was designed to cover a wide field of military requirements. Regarded in the light of subsequent experience it is difficult to see how the syllabuses issued by the Division and the Brigade could have been materially improved upon. The training was eminently practical, and it was carried out under conditions approximating as nearly as possible to those likely to prevail in war.

Two notable camps provided experience that was of inestimable value when the Battalion was called upon to take the field less than three months after mobilisation. The first of these was held at Minster in the Island of Sheppey in 1911 when the Queen's Westminster Rifles took part in manœuvres on an extensive scale involving a severe test of marching and endurance. The second was that held at Abergavenny in 1913, when the Grey Brigade marched to Tal-y-Maes, a deserted spot

---

[1] The Queen's Westminster Volunteers won the silver jewel at Wimbledon in 1866 and 1878.
 Sergeant G. E. Fulton won the King's Prize at Wimbledon in 1888, and his success was repeated by his son, Rifleman A. G. Fulton, at Bisley in 1912. Rifleman Fulton went out to France with the Battalion as machine-gun sergeant and was awarded the D.C.M. His brother-in-law, Corporal R. de Roche, who was also a well-known Bisley and international shot, was killed in 1915 while serving with the Battalion.

AUGUST 4TH, 1914

in the Welsh mountains, where it bivouacked for several nights and carried out strenuous training in attack, defence and outposts. The approaches to the camping ground were so steep that, with the exception of some of the Battalion's wagons, none of the transport could get up, and all baggage and supplies had to be man-handled for a considerable distance across the rough ground. Many were reminded of this experience when they were called on in France for the first time to provide carrying parties for the front line.

The above short account of the peace-time methods of training in the Battalion will have shown that military experience of a very varied character had been available, and that solid foundation had been laid for the more thorough preparations for actual war.

On the morning of Sunday, August 2nd, 1914, the Battalion entrained at Paddington *en route* for Perham Down, Salisbury Plain, where the annual camp was to be held. The air was alive with rumours. "War had been declared," "the Expeditionary Force had started," "the Battalion was to be mobilised at once and was to be sent here, there, everywhere." The excitement amongst the men was intense, and when news was received in the evening that French patrols had crossed the German frontier cheer after cheer was heard from every camp.

At about 9.30 p.m. orders were received that the whole of the 2nd London Division was to return to London. By admirable organisation on the part of the railway authorities the move was carried out without a hitch in the course of the night, Major J. Waley Cohen, 2nd in command of the Battalion, acting as railway transport officer. The Battalion arrived at Paddington Station in the early hours of the morning and at once proceeded to its headquarters. The men were then given leave, with orders to be prepared for mobilisation at any moment.

On Tuesday, August 4th, war with Germany was declared, and orders for the mobilisation of the Territorial Force were issued.

The total strength of the Battalion on the day that it was mobilised under the command of Lieut.-Colonel R. Shoolbred, T.D., D.L., was 511.

The wastage caused by the termination of engagements of the large numbers who had joined during the big recruiting boom in 1909 was being made good, but the process was a slow one. The Queen's Westminsters had always made careful selection of their recruits, but with the inauguration of the Territorial Force the Regiment demanded a far higher standard of training than in the old Volunteer days. This involved greater sacrifices on the part of the men who joined its ranks and kept away those who did not intend to take their soldiering seriously. At the cost of a temporary reduction in numbers the Queen's Westminster Rifles had gained enormously in efficiency.

As soon as war was declared the old members of the Regiment flocked to headquarters, almost to a man; and recruits of splendid quality presented themselves for enlistment. In less than forty-eight hours the Battalion was at full strength, and many hundreds had been turned away.

The mobilisation scheme as practised on the 14th March, 1914, worked perfectly. The men reported to their companies in the playground of the Endowed Schools in Palace Street, Westminster, to the authorities of which the Regiment is deeply indebted for their assistance in every possible way. After kits had been examined and a note made of any deficiencies the men proceeded to Battalion Headquarters, where they were medically examined, and particulars of their next of kin were taken. By the evening practically every man on the strength of the Regiment had reported.

The scene in the Battalion drill-hall was a busy one. Recruits were pouring in, mobilisation stores of every description were being collected and arranged under the direction of the quartermaster, Major A. S. Pridmore, T.D. Machine-gun belts were being filled, and ball ammunition was being served out to the men.

The novelty of the situation prevented the men from realising its true significance. The issue of identity discs was treated by them as a touch of melodrama; orders to be prepared for immediate move were received in a spirit of light-hearted adventure. Meanwhile the organisation of the Battalion on a war footing was proceeding with all seriousness. The Battalion transport for the annual camp training had always been composed of vans and horses belonging to Messrs. James Shoolbred & Co., Limited, and the whole of the transport required for the war establishment mobilisation came from the same source. The horses were of magnificent quality and in splendid condition. They subsequently went out to France with the Regiment and rendered long and faithful service to their country. A few of them remained with the Battalion during the whole war.

The duties of transport officer were taken over by S. G. L.

Bradley, who, while a member of the Queen's Westminsters, had served with distinction in the South African War. After his return from South Africa he held a commission in the mounted-infantry company of the Regiment until it was disbanded on the formation of the Territorial Force in 1908. On the outbreak of war he at once applied for and was granted a commission as 2nd lieutenant. His wide and mature experience and powers of organisation were invaluable, and the Queen's Westminsters must ever be grateful to him for his unselfish service. He served in France throughout the whole of the war, and after acting for a time as staff captain to the 18th Infantry Brigade, and later as D.A.Q.M.G. 6th Division, he eventually became assistant-director of labour with the rank of full colonel, which appointment he held until demobilisation.

The Battalion remained in London, billeted at the Endowed Schools, until August 13th. The short fortnight was a busy one, but chiefly to be remembered by the route marches along the tarred roads which reflected from the ground all the heat of a broiling August sun.

The only events worthy of note during this period were the following :—

August 5th. The Battalion was ordered to be "ready for instant move." This meant, amongst other things, "sleeping in boots and puttees," a new experience to many, but one that in later days became almost a habit. The reason for the order was that the Expeditionary Force was then being moved to France and an attempted landing by the enemy on the East Coast was considered a serious probability.

August 7th. Companies marched to the Tower of London to draw rifles from the armoury.

August 9th. The Battalion attended a special service in Westminster Abbey. The very impressive and stirring sermon preached by Archdeacon Wilberforce brought home to all, more than anything else had done up to that time, what was before them.

August 11th. Lieutenant E. G. H. Cox, commanding B Company, was married in King Henry VII's Chapel in Westminster Abbey. This was the first wedding to be celebrated in this chapel for more than three hundred years, and permission for it to take place there was granted by the Dean and Chapter as a mark of special privilege for the Queen's Westminster Rifles.

August 15th. The 2nd London Division was inspected by Major-General T. L. N. Morland, C.B., D.S.O., who had been appointed to command in place of Major-General C. C. Monro, C.B., who went overseas with the Expeditionary Force as G.O.C. of 2nd Division.

At the outbreak of war the Queen's Westminsters formed part of the 4th Infantry Brigade of the 2nd London Division. The Brigade, which was commanded by Colonel F. J. Heyworth, D.S.O., who had succeeded Colonel G. J. Cuthbert, C.B., was known as " The Grey Brigade " from the colour of the uniforms of the units composing it. These were: The Kensingtons (13th London), the London Scottish (14th London), Prince of Wales's Own Civil Service Rifles (15th London), and the Queen's Westminster Rifles (16th London). The Artists Rifles (28th London), which had become an officers' training corps, was attached to the Brigade.

On August 16th the 2nd London Division moved to its war station in the St. Albans district. The Division assembled in Hyde Park and marched, via the Edgware Road, to Edgware, where it bivouacked for the night, and on the following day moved to its final destination. The weather was exceptionally hot, and the men were carrying full packs, ground sheets and 250 rounds of ball ammunition. As the distance covered was 12 miles on the first day and about 10 miles on the second, it was quite a good test of marching even for seasoned troops, but very few men fell out, though it must be acknowledged that there was too much straggling towards the end of the second day's march. Thus early the Queen's Westminsters and their fellow-battalions of London men showed some inkling of their powers of endurance which afterwards were to be so much more highly tried.

On arrival, Battalion Headquarters were established in the village school at Leverstock Green near Hemel Hempstead, the headquarters mess at a house called "Pancake," and the companies were billeted in the following farms in the neighbourhood :—

A and B	Bunkers Farm.	E	Well Farm.
C	{ Westridge Farm.	F	Leverstock Green Farm.
	{ Potter's Crouch Farm.	G	Corner Farm.
D	Westwick Hall Farm.	H	Westwick Row Farm.

A systematic course of hard training was at once commenced both by day and night. A minimum of seven hours' training was carried out every day, with a rest on Sundays and a half-day on Saturdays. The men invariably carried full packs, and during the earlier part of the training 250 rounds of ammunition as well. The work at first consisted almost entirely of section training, during which the N.C.O.'s gained experience in control and leadership which in the short peace-time training it had been impossible to obtain.

The men reached a very high pitch of physical fitness. On the physical development and growth of young men, who had come straight from the sedentary life of a city office, the effect of the open air and hard exercise was extraordinary. Measurements were not taken, but men rapidly outgrew their uniforms, which burst at the seams, and in a short time were unable to get into clothes which they had worn with comfort a few weeks before.

Towards the latter end of the Battalion's stay at Leverstock Green, company and inter-company tactical exercises were arranged, and then men were put through a very short musketry course[1] under Lieutenant O. P. L. Hoskyns, who was appointed assistant adjutant. Battalion or Brigade route marches took place at least once a week, and there were occasional Brigade field days, as well as tactical schemes for officers conducted by the Brigadier.

The Adjutant (Captain H. J. Flower) was the only regular officer with the Battalion during the whole of the training period, and his time was fully occupied with office work. The entire training of the men was carried out by the company officers under the supervision of the commanding and field officers.

It is impossible to overrate the value to the Territorial Force of the work done in pre-war days by the regular officers who were posted to it as battalion adjutants, and by the regimental sergeant-majors and the permanent staff instructors, all of whom were regular soldiers. They formed the link between the regular and the auxiliary forces, they played a large part in the training of the latter, and to the very strong Territorial spirit built up from the older traditions of the Volunteers, they engrafted an appreciation of the standards and ideals of the professional soldier.

The Queen's Westminsters had been particularly fortunate in their adjutants, all of whom, except one, had come from the K.R.R.C. Those who were appointed in recent years were Major C. A. Gordon Clark, C.M.G., D.S.O.,[2] who raised

---

[1] A miniature range was made in the garden of "The Dells," Bennett's End, which was placed at the disposal of the Battalion by Mr. Secretan. This was suitable for use with service ammunition, and was particularly useful for training machine-gunners and for revolver practice.

[2] The ranks are those held at the date of the appointment. Lieut.-Colonel Gordon Clark commanded the Queen's Westminster Rifles from 1909 to 1911. Another former adjutant, Lieut.-Colonel H. C. Legh, K.R.R.C., was appointed the first commanding officer of the 3rd Battalion Q.W.R., which was raised in December, 1914.

the 2nd Battalion Q.W.R. in 1914 and commanded it in France, Salonica and Palestine until February, 1918; Captain R. J. Jelf, who became brigadier-general; Captain M. L. Porter, afterwards Secretary of the Berkshire County Territorial Force Association; Captain G. Makins, who was killed in France in 1915 while serving with the 2nd K.R.R.C., and Captain H. J. Flower, who went out to France as adjutant in 1914, and, after being appointed brigade-major of the 85th Infantry Brigade, was very dangerously wounded in 1915. He died in 1918, never having recovered from the effects of his wound.

A few days after mobilisation the Commanding Officer was asked by the War Office to call for volunteers for service abroad. The authorities had under-estimated or failed to appreciate the strength of the Battalion *esprit de corps*. Officers and men, although as Territorials they had only undertaken the duties of home defence, were loud in their demand that the Battalion should be allowed to serve abroad as a whole, or at any rate that those who volunteered should be allowed to go as a distinct unit. Large numbers of those who responded to the first call only did so on those conditions. In the middle of August, the Battalion was asked to volunteer to go as a unit. No one had any conception of the urgency of the situation, perhaps it was impossible, from military considerations, to let it be known how urgently men were wanted abroad. Whatever the reasons were, officers and men were not told of their country's need, and their complete ignorance of the facts made it doubly hard for those who had family and other responsibilities to come to a decision.

Nearly 90 per cent of the Battalion immediately volunteered. It was pride of Regiment that called them, probably even more than their country's need, of which they were ignorant. If they could have been told that their services were really required it is doubtful whether there was a single man who would not readily have answered to the call.

Lord French, in the following passage, refers in sympathetic terms to those early volunteers from the Territorial Force who, privileged to serve side by side with their comrades of the Regular Army, shared with them the fruits of the sacrifices they had made in the early months of the war:—

" But the time for the employment of troops other than the regulars of the old Army arrived with drastic and unexpected speed. The wastage of war proved to be so enormous that the fighting line had to be reinforced almost before the New Armies were in existence.

"It was then that the country in her need turned to the despised Territorials. The call came upon them like a bolt from the blue. No warning had been given. Fathers and sons, husbands and brothers, left families, homes, the work and business of their lives, almost at an hour's notice to go on active service abroad.

"It seems to me that we have never realised what it was these men were asked to do. They were quite different to professional soldiers, who are kept and paid through years of peace for this particular purpose of war; who spend their lives practising their profession and gaining promotion and distinction; and who on being confronted with the enemy fulfil the great ambition of their lives.

"Equally distinct were the Territorials also from what has been called the New Army, whose officers and men had ample time to prepare themselves for what they were required to do.

"I wonder, sometimes, if the eyes of the country will ever be opened to what these Territorial soldiers of ours have done.

"I say without the slightest hesitation that, without the assistance which the Territorials afforded between October, 1914, and June, 1915, it would have been impossible to have held the line in France and Belgium, or to have prevented the enemy from reaching his goal, the Channel seaboard."[1]

Time at Leverstock Green passed happily and rapidly, the days were fully occupied, the weather was uniformly fine, and the health of the troops was excellent. The kindness and hospitality shown by the local residents was unstinting and will never be forgotten, and it is hoped that they knew how deeply their actions were appreciated.

The following were the chief events of note during August, September and October :—

August 27th. General Sir Ian Hamilton, G.C.B., D.S.O., inspected the Battalion. After each officer had been introduced to him, he addressed the Battalion on parade and told the men that the Battalion would be sent overseas before the end of the year.

September 15th. The Brigadier informed the Commanding Officer that the Battalion would probably be going overseas in about six weeks' time.

[1] "1914." By Field-Marshal Viscount French of Ypres, p. 293.

September 29th. Lord Kitchener inspected the 2nd London Division in Gorhambury Park. As he was riding round the Battalion with the Brigadier he was heard to remark in answer to a question as to when the Brigade would go abroad, "Not a man will leave until your second battalions are fully equipped and ready to take your place."[1]

October 7th. Order issued at 12.15 a.m. "(1). The Brigade will move at once under instructions from Divisional Headquarters and entrain at King's Langley Station as follows: 16th Battalion, 3 a.m. Battalion will parade on Battalion parade ground at 1.40 a.m., 7.10.14. 1st Line Transport will entrain at Watford. . . . (4) Only men capable of doing a long march and recruits who have fired Table A to be taken."

A warning order for the move had been received late on the 6th. Its receipt caused considerable excitement and speculation as to the ultimate destination of the Battalion. As usual on such occasions the wildest rumours went round as to the cause of so sudden a departure. The denouement came when, on arriving at King's Langley Station, the Battalion was ordered to return to Leverstock Green. It then transpired that the whole affair was a divisional practice.

Everyone had been completely hoaxed, surplus kit had been ruthlessly discarded, and the stock of the company canteens had in many cases been distributed amongst the men. Valuable lessons, however, were learnt, with the result that certain weak points were speedily rectified.

October 7th. Extract from Battalion Orders: "(3) Presentation bugle. The Regiment has been honoured by the gift of a silver bugle from Lady Lloyd, wife of Major-General Sir Francis Lloyd, K.C.B., C.V.O., D.S.O., Commanding London District, as a token of her good wishes to the Battalion in anticipation of its proceeding on service abroad.

"The C.O. has assured Lady Lloyd how much her kind present is appreciated by all ranks of the Battalion."

October 11th. "(3) Presentation of new machine-gun tripods to the Battalion. The Commanding Officer desires to offer his grateful thanks to Lady Howard Vincent, Mrs. Wilkin, Mrs. Cohen, Frederick Shoolbred, Esq., and Colonel G. H. Trollope, V.D., D.L., for their kind and generous help by which the Battalion has obtained these new tripods."

October 26th. "Moves. It is notified for information that the

---

[1] The author himself heard this conversation. The Battalion left for France on November 1st, while the 2nd Battalion, which with other units of the second line experienced enormous difficulties in obtaining both arms and equipment, did not leave London until 13th January, 1915.

ORDERS FOR FOREIGN SERVICE

Battalion will move into new billets at Watford on Friday, 30th inst."

This order seemed to dispose of the many rumours that the Battalion was to go abroad, but a dramatic change occurred when on the very next day the order came: " Move. The Battalion having been selected for service on the Continent will embark on Friday, 30th inst."

This information was received with the utmost enthusiasm, the weeks of hard preparation were at an end, the Battalion was to go out as a unit, and the use of the word selected was accepted as a mark of honourable distinction.

Other units of the Grey Brigade were similarly honoured, and the only feeling of regret was that the Brigade was to be broken up.

The next days were spent in final preparations for foreign service. The Battalion was completely re-equipped with new rifles of a pattern officially known as Long Charger-Loading Magazine Lee-Enfield. The rifle with which the Battalion was armed on mobilisation was not adapted to fire the Mark VII cartridge, which had a pointed bullet, while every available short rifle, the weapon with which the Regular Army troops were equipped, was earmarked for the use of the Kitchener Army.

Sergeant A. G. Fulton, his father, Armourer-Sergeant G. E. Fulton, and some of the expert regimental shots tested on the range as many of the newly issued rifles as possible. There was no time for the men to fire them themselves, and thus it came about that the Regiment went to France armed with a weapon which the individual had had no opportunity of putting to a practical test, even to the extent of firing a few sighting shots.

The new rifles, which only differed from the old ones in their sighting and in certain minor modifications in the breach, proved most serviceable and continued in use until the Battalion " made " all its own short ones after the attack at Bellewaarde in 1915.

The khaki uniforms available for issue after mobilisation were of very inferior material, but the Battalion had made arrangements for the supply of some exceptionally good material, and authority had been obtained for an issue of specially made uniforms. These were being made up, but could not be completed in time. It was accordingly decided that it would be wiser for men to keep their pre-war kit, even though it had had long wear and been patched, rather than indent for uniforms of the new material which a short trial had shown to be incapable of withstanding even moderate wear.

A delay in the departure of the Battalion was caused by the receipt of orders that the transport vehicles were to be exchanged for wagons and limbers of Government pattern, and that a field travelling kitchen and new water carts were to be drawn at Deptford.

These arrived on October 31st. On November 1st, 1914, the 1st Battalion Queen's Westminster Rifles, marching to the strains of " Auld Lang Syne " played by the Regimental Band, set forth from Leverstock Green in two detachments, the first leaving at 9 a.m., the second an hour later.

The Battalion numbered all told 892 officers and other ranks, and the following is a roll of the Officers, Warrant-Officers, and senior Non-Commissioned Officers who accompanied it to France :—

Battalion Headquarters

Lieut.-Colonel R. Shoolbred, T. D., D.L., J.P. — Commanding.
Major J. Waley Cohen, T.D. — 2nd in Command.
Major N. B. Tyrwhitt, T.D. — Junior Major.
Captain H. J. Flower (60th Rifles) — Adjutant.
Lieutenant and Quartermaster J. H. Kelly.
Lieutenant H. Murray (R.A.M.C.) (T.) — Medical Officer.
R.S.M. A. H. Davis.
R.Q.M.S. E. W. Jackson.

A Company

Captain S. Low (commanding).
Lieutenant S. R. Savill.
Lieutenant J. A. Green.
Cr.-Sergeant C. Gay.[1]

B Company

Captain E. G. H. Cox (commanding).
2nd Lieutenant R. S. Dickinson.
2nd Lieutenant F. Barwell.
Cr.-Sergeant F. Cane.

C Company

Captain J. Q. Henriques (commanding).
2nd Lieutenant W. M. Henderson-Scott.
2nd Lieutenant M. E. Trollope.
Cr.-Sergeant L. H. Samson.

---

[1] Cr.-Sergeant Gay completed his thirty-fifth year of service in the Regiment on the 21st January, 1915, when the Battalion was at Houplines.

NOVEMBER 1st, 1914

D Company
Captain J. B. Whitmore (commanding).
Lieutenant F. G. Swainson.
Cr.-Sergeant C. W. Froome.

E Company
Captain M. M. Shattock (commanding).
Lieutenant C. de B. James.
Lieutenant S. L. Townsend-Green.
Cr.-Sergeant E. J. Turnbull.

F Company
Captain H. R. Townsend-Green (commanding).
Lieutenant P. E. Harding.
2nd Lieutenant S. G. L. Bradley, D.C.M.
Cr.-Sergeant J. J. Macnamara.

G Company
Captain G. H. Lambert (commanding).
Lieutenant E. G. S. Waley.
Cr.-Sergeant W. F. H. Rosenberg.

H Company
Captain O. P. L. Hoskyns (commanding).
Lieutenant P. M. Glasier.
2nd Lieutenant H. D. Corlett.
Cr.-Sergeant H. M. Masson.

Machine-Gun Section
2nd Lieutenant J. B. Baber, Machine-Gun Officer.
Sergeant A. G. Fulton, Machine-Gun Sergeant.

Signalling Section
Sergeant L. G. Masson.

Transport
2nd Lieutenant S. G. L. Bradley, D.C.M., Transport Officer.
Sergeant H. W. Chapman, Transport Sergeant.

Pioneer Sergeant
Sergeant R. Dunn.

CHAPTER II

THE BATTALION GOES TO FRANCE

AT 11.40 a.m. on November 1st, 1914, the 1st Battalion, Queen's Westminster Rifles entrained at Watford for Southampton Docks. On arriving at the docks at about 4 p.m., they found the Liverpool Scottish, another Territorial battalion whom they were destined to meet again in the Ypres Salient in 1915, waiting to embark. After a short interval the two battalions, with all their transport, embarked on the steamship *Maidan*.[1] She was a fine cargo boat of over 8,000 tons, belonging to the Anchor-Brocklebank line, which had been fitted out as a cavalry troopship on the outbreak of war.

At 6.30 p.m., her decks and rigging crowded with men, the *Maidan* steamed slowly from the deserted quay. Silently and stealthily the nine transports, which formed the convoy carrying reinforcements to the hard-pressed army in France and Flanders, glided through the searchlight zone, past the Isle of Wight, out into the darkness.

Each ship, as she passed through the glare of the searchlights, shone up for an instant like a beautiful silver ghost, and then all that could be seen were the groups of coloured lights hanging from the masts of the transports, and the fitful flashes of the signals from the escorting destroyers.

The *Maidan* arrived off Havre early in the morning of the 2nd November, but for some reason or other she was not allowed to enter the harbour until the following day. The weather was fortunately fine, and to while away the time an impromptu sing-song was organised on the deck. This was the last concert the Battalion was to hear for many months.

The Queen's Westminsters landed in France at 9 a.m. on November 3rd, 1914, and marched through Havre to a camp on the hills above the town. They received an excited and enthusiastic welcome from the inhabitants, who gave bread and fruit to the men as they passed and threw flowers amongst them, while the children ran along the pavements calling for souvenirs in the form of cap-badges and shoulder-titles.

The arrival of fresh units on the soil of France was a novelty

---

[1] A dinner, known as "The Queen's Westminster Maidan Dinner," is held annually on the anniversary of the Battalion's first landing in France.

in those early days, when something of the romance and glamour of war still remained, and great was the contrast with arrivals in later years when the grim business of the war had overshadowed other feelings. Then troops in their thousands passed through the base ports unnoticed, save for an occasional cheer from a lorry-load of girl munition workers passing to the factories, or a muttered prayer from some old man or woman too old to fight or work.

The Battalion only remained in the rest camp for one night. On the following day webbing equipment was issued to the officers in place of Sam Browne belts, swords were discarded and sent home as being useless in modern warfare, walking-sticks being substituted in their stead, and complete sets of maps of Northern France and Flanders were issued to the companies.

Orders to move were received during the morning of November 4th, and in the late afternoon the Battalion marched down the narrow streets of Havre to the Gare Maritime, the inhabitants cheering from their windows, and wishing the troops " *bonne chance.*"

A glimpse of the Kensingtons, who had just landed and were marching towards the rest camp, and an account in the morning's paper of the fight of the London Scottish at Messines, stirred everyone with pride at the thought that the greater part of the Grey Brigade was already in France.

As the Battalion entered the station, a batch of German prisoners, some of them mere boys, others bearded men, was being marched away under escort to a concentration camp. This was the Queen's Westminsters' first sight of the uniform of the enemy.

The train was due to leave at 7 p.m. After a delay of some three and a half hours, when it eventually steamed out of the station, the men found themselves crowded into cattle trucks, about 40 in each, and the meaning of the mystic inscription on the French railway vans " *Chevaux* 8, *Hommes* 40 " became for the first time painfully clear to them.

The first destination was Rouen, which was reached soon after midnight, but on arriving there further orders were received that the train was to proceed to St. Omer. This it did very leisurely and by a very circuitous route, though the journey was enlivened by the cheers and cries of " *Vive l'Angleterre* " from the French peasants who had collected in groups all along the line, and by the presents of bread, fruit and chocolate which they showered upon the troops.

There was a long stop at Abbéville, where tea was issued,

and another long stop had been arranged at Calais for the issue of hot Oxo to the men. The best intentions, however, are apt to be thwarted by the apparent irresponsibility of the drivers of French troop trains, for, without a word of warning, the train quietly moved out of the station and proceeded on its journey, leaving behind on the platform the party of some thirty men who were boiling the " dixies." The rest of the Battalion had to go without their meal, for nothing would induce the train to stop, and the party left behind had to wait until midnight, when they were brought on by a goods train.

St. Omer was reached in the early hours of November 6th. On detraining the Battalion was billeted in some barracks in the centre of the town, the other occupants being the few survivors of the 2nd Royal Irish Regiment which had been badly cut up and had been withdrawn from the line to reorganise and refit.

The Commander-in-Chief (Field-Marshal Sir John French) paid an unexpected and informal visit to the Battalion soon after its arrival. He came into the barracks quite alone, and chatted to several of the men who were standing in the square. None of them recognised him; in fact, after he had left, one of the men said that a " general of sorts " had been in the barracks and had been looking round. Sir John French also paid a visit to the officers' mess and talked with the officers.

The Battalion spent four days at St. Omer, during which it was put through a varied course of training, and, unknown to all, was being carefully tested by General Headquarters as to whether it was fit to be put into the fighting line. On the 7th of November a reserve line of trenches was dug on the high ground about six miles to the east of St. Omer, on the 8th a practice attack was carried out, and on the 9th two companies fired their new rifles, for the first time, on a 250-metre range near the barracks. The pre-war training and the hard work at Leverstock Green bore good fruit, for the Queen's Westminster Rifles were immediately passed for duty at the front. The following passages from Lord French's book are of interest in this connection : " Units were all put through a course of training at St. Omer. There was a great difference between individual battalions as regards their actual condition when they came out, and the time required to prepare them to take their places in the trenches. . . . Seven or eight years' experience as Territorials operated to the greatest advantage when these

BAILLEUL. NOVEMBER 11TH, 1914

Territorial battalions arrived in the theatre of war and commenced their final preparations to fill the gaps in our line, through which, as I have shown, the Germans must have penetrated had the Territorial Army not existed to step into the breach. . . . The Queen's Westminsters and the 8th Royal Scots only embarked on the 1st and 4th November respectively, yet their condition was so good that they were able to be sent to the front immediately after the H.A.C."

The Battalion left St. Omer at 9 a.m. on November 10th, and marched some 15 miles to Hazebrouck, where it was billeted for the night in various schools and buildings. Although the men were in excellent marching condition, they found the slippery setts and the uneven surface of the *pavé* roads of the district most trying, and everyone was glad when the march was over.

On the following morning, when the Battalion was parading after breakfast, a detachment of French cuirassiers, wearing their old-time uniform with plumed helmets and metal breastplates, rode slowly through the square at Hazebrouck. They had evidently just come out of battle, for the men were mudstained and looked haggard and worn, their accoutrements were rusty and tarnished and their horses exhausted. The sight of these allied troops, in such surroundings, was reminiscent of some Napoleonic battle picture, and seemed strangely out of harmony with the British guns and wagons which were parked in the centre of the square.

The second day's march brought the Battalion to Bailleul. The road was crowded with numbers of refugees, the old people riding in carts, the younger ones walking and pushing handcarts and perambulators piled high with a motley assortment of household goods hastily gathered together. Most of them seemed to accept their lot in a curiously matter-of-fact way, though here and there one saw signs of real distress.

At Bailleul the Battalion was billeted in a large convent school in the centre of the town, which had been last used as a hospital for Native (Indian) troops and bore very evident traces of its former occupants. After the companies had been settled in their billets the men were allowed in the town, where they met many old friends in the Artists Rifles. This battalion was on its way down to General Headquarters to take up the duties of an officers' training corps, for which it had been designated on the formation of the Territorial Force.

In the evening the Commanding Officer decided to reorganise the Battalion on the four-company basis, as follows: No. 1 Company (A and B Companies) under the command of Captain S. Low (2nd in command, Captain E. G. H. Cox); No. 2 Company (C and D Companies) under the command of Captain J. Q. Henriques (2nd in command, Captain J. B. Whitmore); No. 3 Company (E and F Companies) under the command of Major N. B. Tyrwhitt, T.D. (2nd in command, Captain H. R. Townsend-Green); No. 4 Company (G and H Companies) under the command of Captain G. H. Lambert (2nd in command, Captain M. M. Shattock).

Companies were split up into platoons by the simple process of renaming half-companies, and the colour-sergeants of the two companies forming the double company were appointed sergeant-majors and company quartermaster-sergeants according to their seniority. By 9 a.m. the following morning the reorganisation was complete.

It is impossible to understand the policy of the authorities at home in refusing to allow Territorial units to depart from the eight-company organisation, while the new battalions of the Kitchener Army were all organised on the four-company system. It seemed so obvious that if a unit was to be employed on active service it should have the same organisation as that of the army in the field. The result of this policy was that the Battalion had to be reorganised at practically a moment's notice, when it was within less than a day's march of one of the fiercest battles recorded in history. It was absolutely essential that it should possess the same organisation as the regular battalions of the brigade of which it was to form part; yet the risk was great, for none of the officers had any knowledge of the tactical handling of a double company.

The night of November 11th was very dark and wet; from the convent school could be seen the flashes of the guns at Ypres which lit up the distant sky, and the sound of heavy artillery fire went on unceasingly. It was on this day that the Prussian Guards had delivered their desperate attack and been heavily defeated, but the issue of the First Battle of Ypres still hung in the balance.

On the 12th November, the Battalion marched to Erquinghem, a small village about a mile and a half to the south-west of Armentières. Large numbers of refugees were again passed on the road; they had mostly come from Chapelle d'Armentières, a suburb of Armentières, which had been heavily shelled during the night. Parts of the town had been set on fire and dense clouds of smoke could still be seen rising from the burning houses. As the Battalion marched into Erquinghem it realised that it was at last within range of the enemy's guns, for a shell burst in a field a little distance away on the left, destroying a small building but doing no other damage.

A notable and, for those who took part in it, an unforgettable event occurred during the afternoon. On arriving at Erquinghem an order was received that the Battalion would be inspected almost immediately by Field-Marshal Earl Roberts. The companies, accordingly, after taking over their billets which were a little distance away, returned to the village and were drawn up in single rank on either side of the narrow street. Next to them were the 2nd Battalion Durham Light Infantry, who were later to become such good friends of the Queen's Westminsters.

After a long wait and an expectant silence, broken only by the distant thunder of the guns at Ypres, Lord Roberts arrived with his daughter, Lady Aileen (now Countess) Roberts, and a number of staff officers.

The inspection was quite informal. Lord Roberts, after a short conversation with the Commanding Officer, walked slowly down the ranks, first of the London Territorial battalion fresh from England and untried in war, and then down the D.L.I., with their long and glorious record of battles fought and won. He paused a moment as he passed each company commander, to shake hands and speak a few words of encouragement or advice.

Two apparently trivial questions he addressed to the writer of this history, and his short comments on the answers stand out vividly in the writer's recollections, for they were full of a deep significance, coming as they did in such surroundings and from so great a soldier. The first question was "Do you hear those guns?"—the comment "There is a *great* battle going on there" (with a grave emphasis on the word great); and the second question was "Can your men shoot?" and the comment "They will do all right." Lord Roberts must have realised fully all that depended on the result of that desperate struggle at Ypres. His strong advocacy of civilian rifle shooting and of its value to the nation in war was more than justified by the events which were to come.[1]

This inspection must have been the last appearance of

---

[1] Reference is made in later chapters to the failure, at certain stages of the war, and as the result of long spells of trench warfare, of the British troops in the field to appreciate fully the supreme value of the rifle as the principal weapon of the infantry soldier.

Lord Roberts on a parade. Alert and, apparently, full of vigour in spite of his great age, no one could have thought, as they saw him move off, that two days later he was to pass away after a few hours' illness. The sight of him at Erquinghem, too old to fight, but ever anxious to be with the troops he loved so well, had sent a strange thrill of pride and imagination through the hearts of all who were present, and the news of his death at St. Omer was received by all with true sorrow.

As soon as the inspection was over the troops dispersed to their billets in the farms round Erquinghem, which only a short time before had been in the occupation of the enemy. All the civilian inhabitants told the same story of harsh treatment by the Germans and of the seizure, without payment, of food, horses and fodder. What wonder, therefore, that they greeted the British soldier with joy and gratitude, treating him as a deliverer and lavishing on him all the hospitality they could provide.

So far the Queen's Westminsters were mere spectators. For hours after dark the men stood outside their billets watching, spellbound, the bursting star shells and the red flames from burning Armentières throwing into black relief the tall factory chimneys. Even the sound of shells as they whistled through the air had a peculiar fascination for those men who now heard it for the first time.

CHAPTER III

WITH THE SIXTH DIVISION

THE Battalion was now in the 6th Division (Major-General J. L. Keir, C.B.), having been posted to the 18th Infantry Brigade (Brigadier-General W. N. Congreve, V.C., C.B., M.V.O.) on arriving at Erquinghem.

The Brigade was composed of the following units :—

1st The Prince of Wales's Own (West Yorkshire Regiment); 1st The East Yorkshire Regiment; 2nd The Sherwood Foresters (Nottinghamshire and Derbyshire Regiment); 2nd The Durham Light Infantry.

On the 13th November a conference of officers was held at Battalion Headquarters at which both the Divisional and Brigade Commanders were present. General Keir made a short speech in which he explained the situation. Every trench was to be held at all costs, and there was to be no retirement without an express order. In pointing out how a company commander in the trenches was like the captain of a ship and must be the last man to leave his trench, he told the story of a captain in the Irish Guards who, when his trench was surrounded, turned round to his men and said, " If any man attempts to leave this trench I shall shoot him ; and if *I* attempt to do so, you may shoot me."

Later in the day the C.R.E. (Lieut.-Colonel G. C. Kemp) described the types of trenches and wire entanglements then being used, laying particular emphasis on the importance of having deep and very narrow trenches, with very short lengths between the traverses.

During the next few days, in spite of the weather, the Battalion was able to carry out a little tactical training under the new double-company organisation, and those companies which had not yet fired their new rifles had some musketry practice on a hastily constructed range on the outskirts of the village. The greater part of the time, however, was occupied in digging and completing a new defensive line to the east of Erquinghem and in cutting brushwood and making fascines for use in the front line. One party was actually detailed to plant roots, for the purpose of concealment, on the parapets of the new trenches, which had been dug in a root field. It was a useful enough expedient when the defences consisted practically of a single line, and photography from the air was almost unknown, but an aeroplane photograph would have shown up the trench at once.

An occasional enemy aeroplane flew over, and was fired at by a " pom-pom,"[2] which was the only form of gun then available for anti-aircraft defence. These guns were quite useless for this purpose, with their limited range and light shrapnel shells; but the bursting of the shells in the air, and enemy aeroplanes flying high out of range, were novel sights in those days and were watched by all with interest.

On November 16th, No. 1 Company (Captain S. Low, Captain E. G. H. Cox, Lieutenant S. R. Savill and 2nd Lieutenants J. A. Green, R. S. Dickinson and F. Barwell) was detailed to report at night at the Headquarters of the 16th Infantry Brigade (Brigadier-General E. C. Ingouville-Williams, C.B., D.S.O.) to act as a support company and to work for the Brigade. Brigade Headquarters were in Calvert Farm, a short distance to the south of Bois Grenier and only a few hundred yards behind the firing line. The work done by the company consisted chiefly in carrying fascines and revetting material from Brigade Headquarters up to the waterlogged trenches.

For the first time in the campaign the Queen's Westminsters were under fire, for there were frequent bursts of rifle and machine-gun fire from the enemy trenches during the night. But there were no casualties, and the company returned at dawn to its billets.

On the 17th, the Battalion moved into billets at Gris-Pot and about La Vesée. The civilian inhabitants who had been evacuated from Gris-Pot had left everything except their few portable belongings behind them. Their homes showed signs of a hasty departure, and their fowls and rabbits were still in the tiny yards of the cottages.

On the night of the 17th, No. 2 Company was in support to the 16th Infantry Brigade, and reported at Calvert Farm soon after dark. One platoon was employed as a carrying party to the front line, and the remainder of the company dug a communication trench forward from Calvert Farm towards La Flamanderie Farm. The company had a very lively time soon after work had started, for the enemy shelled the farm and kept up a very heavy rifle fire for about twenty minutes. The carrying party was got under cover, and the digging party lay down in the trench, which was not more than eighteen inches deep. By a miracle no one was hit, and

[1] 1 Pdr. Q.F. gun.

a useful lesson was learnt as to the value of unaimed fire and the advantage of even a little cover. The night turned bitterly cold, and in the early morning, when the company returned through Bois Grenier to Gris-Pot, the ground was quite white.

Bois Grenier which had been recaptured by the III Corps, on the 18th October, had been very severely shelled, all the inhabitants had been evacuated, and the whole village was in a complete state of ruin.

On November 17th, the front of the 18th Infantry Brigade was extended by seven hundred yards, and on the following night No. 1 Company relieved a company of the 1st East Yorks in the trenches facing La Houssoie to the south of Rue du Bois and about three hundred yards from the enemy's line. The Queen's Westminsters received a very warm welcome from the Yorkshiremen, who had been in the trenches for three weeks, and had been through some of the severest fighting of the past two months. The men were very tired, and the contrast between the war-worn troops and the men just out from England was very marked, but what struck everyone was their wonderful cheerfulness. They did everything possible to help the Westminsters. The duties of the sentries and the routine of the trenches were comparatively easily explained, but such things as the art of keeping a charcoal fire alight in a bully-beef tin, and cooking a dinner over it in a mess tin, were much more complicated. The only fuel available in the trenches for warmth and cooking was a small ration of charcoal that each man took in with him.

The evening of the relief was damp and warm, but during the night there was a heavy fall of snow. The trenches taken over by No. 1 Company had been dug in a root field, and all that could be seen at night was a flat waste of snow with the tops of the beetroots showing above. In the foreground the stout wooden pickets of the wire entanglement showed up clearly and gave a feeling of security, and in the distance could faintly be distinguished a line of willows which seemed to move and change their form. The longer they were looked at, the more certain did it seem that they were endowed with movement.

The first night in the trenches passed quietly. On the 19th, Rifleman Sharp drew first blood for the Battalion by shooting a sniper who was seen moving through the roots. During the night the Germans opened rapid fire on the trenches and kept it up for a considerable time, doing no damage.

The firing extended along a considerable front, and the companies in Gris-Pot " stood to " in view of a possible attack.

No. 2 Company relieved No. 1 on the night of the 20th and had an uneventful spell of forty-eight hours in the trenches, after which they were relieved by No. 3 Company. The weather now turned extremely cold, and it was found that there was a serious tendency for the bolts of the new rifles to stick. This was partly due to the lack of rifle oil at this time and the necessity of having to use bacon fat as an inadequate substitute. In order to minimise the risk of jamming, the sentries were ordered to work the bolts of their own rifles and those of their two reliefs every quarter of an hour, a precaution which proved most effective.

The three companies out of the line remained at Gris-Pot until the 24th, one company going at night to Desplanque Farm, the Headquarters of the 18th Infantry Brigade, to act as Brigade Reserve.

While at Gris-Pot the following letter written in English and addressed to " *Messieurs les Officiers Anglais* " was received from the owner of one of the billets occupied by officers of the Battalion. It is a good example of the welcome accorded to British troops at this time, and it gives a striking impression of the anxieties suffered by an inhabitant of an invaded country :—

" Dear Sirs,—I am glad to hear that our English friends are occupying my house, and beg you to consider it as your home. Would you be kind enough to leave a note after your departure, so that the house be kept in order? I was wounded last month and hope to join our troops at the front as soon as possible.

" Wishing you good luck, I beg to remain, sincerely yours,

" EDOUARD VANDENBUSSCHE,
"(Caporal du 43 ème).

" Blessé au Château de Chabrignai par Juillac (Corrèze).

"I have not heard yet of my wife, nor of my parents, of Bourg de Bois Grenier. You would oblige me very much in asking one of the neighbours where did my wife go when the German troops entered the village.

" Thank you in advance for your kindness.

" What do you think of the wine I have in the cellar? You would oblige me very much in leaving one or two bottles, so that I may be able to shake my glass to the victory of great England and sweet France when I return."

SIR JOHN FRENCH'S DESPATCH

On the 24th November, the Queen's Westminsters went into the trenches for the first time as a unit, relieving the East Yorkshire Regiment. The Battalion had passed through its probationary period, and from this time onwards it was treated on exactly the same terms as the regular battalions of the Brigade, taking its turn with them on the roster for duties.

The regular battalions, both officers and men, were always ready to help in a true spirit of comradeship, and from the first the Queen's Westminsters were made to feel thoroughly at home in the regular Brigade to which they had the honour to be posted.

The following extract from Battalion orders, published at the time, added if possible to the keenness of the Regiment to give a good account of itself. " The G.O.C., 6th Division, has told the Commanding Officer to inform the Battalion of the great pleasure it is to him to have received such excellent reports of the Battalion's work, both from General Congreve commanding the 18th Brigade, and from General Ingouville-Williams commanding the 16th Brigade."

The Queen's Westminsters were specifically mentioned in the following passages of Field-Marshal Sir John French's official despatch, dated November 20th, 1914, as being amongst the first Territorial units to be engaged in the War.[1]

" *The Territorials.*— In the period covered by this despatch Territorial troops have been used for the first time in the army under my command. The units actually engaged have been the Northumberland, Northamptonshire, North Somerset, Leicestershire, and Oxfordshire Regiments of Yeomanry Cavalry; and the London Scottish, Hertfordshire, Honourable Artillery Company, and the Queen's Westminster Battalions of Territorial Infantry.

" The conduct and bearing of these units under fire, and the efficient manner in which they have carried out the various duties assigned to them have imbued me with the highest hope as to the value and help of Territorial troops generally."

The line held by the 18th Infantry Brigade at this time ran from a point due west of La Houssoie to the Boulogne-Lille Road, north-west of Wez Macquart. The trenches taken over by the Queen's Westminsters were in No. 1 section on the right of the Brigade line, and covered a front of over six

[1] This despatch deals with the operations of the Army in France during October and November.

hundred yards. The defences consisted of a single line of very narrow fire trenches about 4 ft. 6 in. deep, with lengths of a lateral communication trench dug in places a few yards behind. There were only two communication trenches at this time: one, a deep one about eighty yards long, linking up Battalion Headquarters with the front line, and another on the extreme right of the Battalion front. The approach to all other parts of the line was across the open.

The support company were accommodated in a series of shelters at the side of a road near Battalion Headquarters.

The shelters for the troops in the front line consisted of a number of hollows scooped out under the parapet, with the roofs supported by wooden struts. The entrance was about 2 ft. 6 in. high, and each shelter held from one to three men. They were universally known in those days as "Funk Holes," "Cubby Holes" or "Bug Hutches." The traverses were short, most of them holding about three men. The trenches were not revetted for there was practically no material for doing so, beyond a certain number of fascines[1]; sandbags were non-existent. The wire consisted of a single curtain fence, with a narrow belt of trip wire a few yards in front. Had the Germans chosen to attack that portion of the line in real strength it seems impossible to think that they could not have got through; but they had already been beaten to a standstill, and weak as the line was, it was sufficient to prevent them making any further attempt to get forward.

The routine of the trenches was simple. The sentries, who remained on duty for two hours at a stretch, were posted in the proportion of one man per section by day, and one man in every three by night. At night, therefore, each man might expect to get four hours' sleep out of every six. But at this period of the war it seldom happened that a night passed without one or more "alarms," when the whole Battalion had to "stand to" with each man standing at his post in the trench ready for any emergency. Rifles, with bayonets fixed, and with five rounds of ammunition in the magazine and none in the chamber, were, at first, left resting on the parapet during the night, but later, when the extreme cold set in, the men were ordered to sleep with them close to their bodies to keep the action of the rifles warm and to prevent the oil from freezing.

The whole Battalion, in accordance with the usual rules of war, "stood to" just before it began to get dark, and every man remained at his post until it was quite dark and the

[1] Bundles of brushwood.

order for night sentries was given. The men " stood to " again at dawn, and were dismissed as soon as it was light. There were rifle inspections in the early morning and in the evening. The officers were always on duty and a roster of N.C.O.'s was kept. It was their duty to patrol the trenches at frequent intervals by day and night and see that everything was in order, and that the sentries were at their posts and alert. The days were spent in working in the trenches, and by night parties were sent out to repair the wire and do any work that was necessary above ground. This routine was substantially the same as that which prevailed throughout the war.

The line was held at this time with three companies in the fire trench and one company in support; the Battalion, during its first tour in the trenches, being disposed as follows:

No. 3 Company on the right in touch with the 1st Shropshire Light Infantry of the 16th Infantry Brigade, No. 4 Company in the centre, No. 2 Company on the left in touch with the West Yorks, and No. 1 Company in support.

A thaw set in on the 25th and there was heavy rain. The trenches which had stood well during the cold weather began to crumble, and many of the shelters fell in without warning. It was through the collapse of one of the shelters that Rifleman R. Brooks of No. 4 Company was killed, and his brother who was sleeping next to him had his leg badly crushed.

This was the first death in the Battalion on active service. Rifleman Brooks was buried near the farm building just in rear of the firing line, the funeral service being read by the Commanding Officer.

At this period of the war there was very little shelling, and what there was came principally from the enemy. Our own guns were strictly rationed as to the number of shells they were allowed to fire, and these were reserved for special targets. On the other hand there was a considerable amount of rifle fire, and sniping on both sides was continuous throughout the day. The parapets, of both the enemy's and British trenches, were provided with loopholes which formed a very favourite target; and any indication of work in the enemy trenches, such as earth being thrown over the parapet or planks showing over the top as they were being carried along, was invariably greeted with a burst of rifle fire. The enemy were not without a sense of humour, for they would signal the results of the shots by waving their shovels above the top of the trench.

A large number of wooden loopholes, for fitting into the

parapet, were sent out from England about this time. These were found to be a considerable source of danger, for they not only provided a target for the enemy, but bullets which struck the inside of the loophole were deflected down into the trench. One of the first men in the Regiment to be wounded was hit in the hand, as he was sitting in the bottom of the trench, by a bullet deflected from one of these loopholes. After several casualties had been caused in this way, the order was given that the loopholes were to be removed, and that the sentries were to look over the top of the parapet instead. A good many of the sentries were hit in the head by the enemy snipers, and it was not until the introduction of steel loopholes and periscopes later in the year that the casualties amongst the sentries really began to diminish. It was seldom that a sniper knew for certain that he had hit his target, but on one occasion Sergeant G E. Fulton, a winner of the King's Prize at Bisley, made a very remarkable shot. Through a telescope, an enemy officer was seen sitting in the windows of a house well behind the enemy's lines. Estimating the range at eight hundred yards, and firing through open sights, Sergeant Fulton picked the man off, with his first shot.

There was always a considerable amount of indiscriminate rifle fire at night, which frequently developed into an outburst of rapid fire from some point of the line. When this happened the firing would extend all along the trenches on both sides, the fronts of as many as three battalions sometimes being involved, and would continue for about twenty minutes and then die down as suddenly as it had started. These outbursts usually commenced from the enemy's trenches. There was no apparent reason for them, and the only effect they had was to disturb the rest of the men who were not on duty, and cause the garrison to "stand to."

On the 30th November, Lieutenant J. B. Baber and Corporal R. de R. Roche captured the first prisoners for the Battalion. They had gone out at night to patrol along a ditch some way in front of the line, when they suddenly found themselves surrounded by three different parties of the enemy who had apparently arranged to meet at a certain spot. Two of the enemy patrols passed by without having their suspicions aroused, but the third consisting of three men were making their way towards the place where Lieutenant Baber and Corporal Roche were crouching. The latter immediately opened fire, and after killing one man rushed the remaining two, who threw down their rifles and surrendered.

THE FIRST CAPTURES. NOVEMBER, 1914

The victors had a very narrow escape as they were returning to our lines with their prisoners. The N.C.O. who was in charge of the machine gun, seeing in the darkness the outlines of more figures approaching our line than had left the trenches, and realising that some, at any rate, were in German uniform, opened fire on the party as soon as they reached the wire. Fortunately an officer who was near grasped what had happened, and gave the order to cease fire before any harm had been done. It seemed impossible that the party could have escaped unhurt, for they were less than twenty yards from the trench, but by an extraordinary piece of good fortune no one was hit, although the bullets cut the barbed wire through which they were passing.

The two prisoners belonged to the 179*th Regiment* of the *XIX (2nd Saxon) Corps*. They were the first prisoners that had been taken on this portion of the front for some time, and the identification of their regiment provided useful information.

On the 2nd December, H.M. the King, accompanied by the Prince of Wales, who had joined the Expeditionary Force on November 16th, visited the 6th Division and held an informal inspection of some of the troops, near the village of L'Épinette. The 18th Infantry Brigade was represented by two companies of the 1st Prince of Wales's Own (West Yorkshire Regiment) and one officer and eight other ranks from each of the other battalions in the Brigade.

Major N. B. Tyrwhitt was selected to command the detachment of Queen's Westminsters, and the party left the trenches early in the morning to march to L'Épinette where the representative troops were lining the road. The inspection was quite a simple ceremony: the King walked slowly down the ranks, each officer in turn being introduced to him as he passed.

The events of the first few days of December are best told in the words of the Battalion War Diary.

"*December* 1*st*.—Enemy (179*th Saxons*) digging two lengths of trench (in front of present line) converging forwards. From two prisoners captured last night (the third of the party having been shot) learn that they were sent out, by order, in turn, as patrols in parties of three at night. One prisoner, eighteen years old, joined six weeks before. The other, who looked like a schoolmaster and wore glasses, was twenty-seven years old and had joined five days before. Enemy machine gun in house 150 yards in rear of trenches. Frightened away by our howitzers. Parapet repaired and trenches deepened.

"*December 3rd.*—Enemy seem to have finished digging, and are now putting out each night very strong entanglements, apparently ready made in sections and staked down.

"*December 4th.*—Enemy snipers busy, but we subdued their ardour by turning on a few good shots.

"*December 5th.*—Enemy sniped[1] left company (No. 2 Company) hard and accurately during last night. Probably to cover putting up of wire. Hope we bagged some, having sighted our rifles before dark and fired salvoes at intervals of half an hour during the night.

"Removed all wooden loopholes. These are found to be a beautiful target from the front, and act as a funnel catching bullets and directing them down into the trench.

"Relieved at 5 p.m. by the West Yorks and went into billets at l'Armée. Some of the men's feet very sore from wet and mud. After getting through narrow trenches fully loaded and marching a mile or so to billets the men were quite beat.

"*December 6, 7, 8.*—In billets. Very peaceful. No bullets and dry warm home to sleep in. Men bathed at 6th Divisional baths and got change of clothes. Much appreciated."

These billets were within a mile of the front line, and the fact that so much comfort was possible is in striking contrast to the conditions which prevailed a few months later.

The Battalion's first tour of duty in the trenches had lasted eleven days. The casualties were three men killed and ten wounded, all from rifle fire. The health of the men was excellent although for the greater part of the time they had been sleeping in the open trench with practically no shelter from the cold or rain. Very little sleep was possible under such circumstances. Water was very scarce, and the daily allowance of one water-bottle full per man had to serve for drinking, cooking and washing. Small parties were occasionally sent out of the trenches for a bath, but the majority of the men had been without a shave or a change of clothes during the whole period.

The night of the relief was very wet and stormy, and the trenches on which all had worked hard, so as to hand them over in a good condition, were speedily reduced to a state of muddiness. The West Yorkshiremen who took over the trenches averaged several inches shorter in height than the

---

[1] The expression " sniped " was used in most war diaries at this period to indicate rifle fire of every description, other than rapid fire. In some cases it is known that the enemy used rifles, fixed in position, which had been accurately sighted on to the opposing parapets.

Westminsters, who as a body were exceptionally tall, and when the former arrived they found that the fire steps, over which so much trouble had been taken, were too low to enable them to shoot over the parapet. It must have meant many hours' work in the pouring rain to alter the trenches so as to adapt them for the shorter men.

The mention of the condition of the men's feet in the War Diary marks the first appearance of that very painful malady known as "Trench Feet." It was the cause of some twenty thousand men being withdrawn from the trenches during the first winter of the war. It was many months before the medical authorities understood its real nature. But during the later stages of the war an elaborate set of precautions was laid down and enforced as a matter of discipline, with the result that this cause of so much wastage was practically eliminated.

The first reference to precautionary measures in the Battalion occurs in the following Battalion order, dated the 20th January, 1915 :—

"*Prevention of swollen feet and frost-bite.*—Before going into the trenches boots to be well rubbed inside and out with whale oil, which will shortly be issued. Feet and legs to be washed and dried and then well rubbed with whale oil or other grease, especially between the toes. A dry pair of socks to be put on, boots to be loosely laced, puttees never to be put on tightly, a pair of spare socks to be carried. On coming out of the trenches the feet to be carefully washed at once with *cold* water."

On the 9th December, the Queen's Westminsters again went into the trenches, relieving the Durhams in No. 3 section of the Brigade line, opposite Wez Macquart. The front held by the Battalion extended from just east of Rue du Bois on the right to the Lille-Boulogne road on the left. The trenches were echeloned forward from the right, where No. 1 Company was in touch with the South Staffords, towards the left where No. 4 Company was in touch with the 2nd Rifle Brigade. Battalion Headquarters were in the Du Biez Farm, in rear of the left of the line. The one communication trench was already half flooded, but the water had to some extent been kept under in the fire trenches, on which a great deal of work had been done.

The Battalion's tour in the trenches lasted for nine days; it was one continual struggle with the elements, and the condition of the trenches got worse and worse. In the low-lying ground drainage was impossible, and baling the water out was an exhausting and ineffective expedient. An experiment was made of using an ordinary village pump fixed to a board and provided with a suction pipe, but this quickly became choked with mud and was found to be useless. No other pumps were procurable.

The Battalion War Diary again gives a very good idea of the life in the waterlogged trenches. It reads as follows :—

"*December 9th.*—Relieved D.L.I. in trenches (4.45 p.m. to 9 p.m.). Only one communication trench in a ditch. Eighteen inches of water and six inches of mud. Men all went in overground. One officer (2nd Lieutenant M. E. Trollope, No. 2 Company) hit on ankle on way in. Very confusing getting into new trenches at night.

"*December 10th, 11th, 12th.*—Heavy rain. Many sections of trench flooded. Some of the flooded parts dammed and water localised. No chance of draining. Try digging new trenches —some in front, some behind; but water level seems to be everywhere about eighteen inches below the surface. Parapets falling in continuously and most of our energy required repairing them, so men spend their time standing in one or two feet of water. . . .

"*December 14th.*—Parapets continually falling in. Men employed day and night digging it out.

"*December 16th–18th.*—Water in trenches rising steadily. Men employed in making dams and digging out falls of parapets, etc.

"During the night of the 11th all units of the 18th Brigade, less the Queen's Westminsters, were relieved and marched north, where they were in reserve to the III Corps for an attack on Ploegsteert Wood on December the 19th.

"The Queen's Westminsters remained in the trenches under the orders of the 17th Brigade (Brigadier-General W. Doran).

"On the 13th the enemy fired about sixty shells, which fell in rear of Battalion Headquarters. They were presumably intended for the 24th Battery, R.F.A., which was in position in front of La Chapelle d'Armentières. The Germans were firing captured French shells, and evidently did not know how to use them, for only about twelve burst, and practically no damage was done."

On the following night Armentières was heavily bombarded. About five hundred shells fell in the town, doing a good deal of damage, but causing practically no loss of life. On the 15th the enemy put about thirty shrapnel shells into our trenches, without causing any casualties.

After being relieved, the Queen's Westminsters went into billets at Chapelle d'Armentières for four days' "rest," one company being sent up each night to be in Brigade reserve at Desplanque Farm. The enemy put a certain number of shells into Chapelle d'Armentières every day, but only succeeded in hitting one house where troops were billeted, killing one man and wounding several others.

Before the Battalion went into the trenches for Christmas, the Reverend N. Talbot (the present Bishop of Pretoria), who was then chaplain of the 2nd Rifle Brigade, conducted a series of services for the companies. These were the first services it had been possible to hold since the Battalion had landed in France, and they were much appreciated.

The Christmas mails and parcels began to arrive about this time. Every friend at home seemed to have remembered the Queen's Westminsters, and food and comforts of every description were sent out in large quantities. The Queen's Westminsters as a whole were more fortunately situated in this respect than some of their comrades in the regular battalions, and they were only too glad to be able to share their luxuries with them.

The Battalion returned to the same trenches on December 23rd, relieving the 1st Royal Fusiliers. The state of the trenches was worse than ever; in places the water was waist deep, and rest was out of the question except for the lucky few who could find a plank on which to get a little sleep.

The enemy snipers were very active on the 24th, and one man was killed and four wounded. Amongst the latter was Sergeant Rogers of No. 2 Company, who was hit in the head and died later in hospital without regaining consciousness. He had been one of the most popular and energetic members of D Company before the war, and his loss was keenly felt.

In the late afternoon our batteries shelled the enemy trenches and the buildings in Wez Macquart, starting a fire in what, judging from the number of small explosions that were heard, must have been an ammunition store.

As darkness fell, lights were seen in the German lines in the Rue du Bois. Our snipers fired at them, and they were put out, but no fire was returned by the enemy. All firing gradually died down and an uncanny stillness reigned. It was thought at first that this was some trick of the enemy, and extra vigilance was ordered in the trenches, but later on lights began to appear all along the enemy trenches, and their whole line was illuminated. It looked as though lanterns had been hoisted at the end of long poles. Presently the enemy began to sing part-songs and carols, and late in the evening they finished up with " *Die Wacht am Rhein* " and the German and Austrian National Anthems. The singing was really very good and produced a wonderful effect in such surroundings. When it was over the Germans became more noisy; cheering, and shouting remarks across No-man's-land. The night, which was very cold, passed without a shot being fired.

Christmas Day, 1914, dawned in a thick mist, with the ground white with frost. The Germans began to sing again at daybreak, and our men could not resist applauding them, and then they began to shout greetings across No-man's-land. At one point they called " Good morning, Englishmen. A merry Christmas—you no shoot, we no shoot." At another point they invited the company opposite them to send a representative half-way between the trenches. Rifleman (later 2nd Lieutenant) A. J. Philip went out and found five Germans who made no attempt to take advantage of their numerical superiority. One of them gravely saluted and announced that he was an officer and came from Catford! Gifts of wine, cake, chocolates, cigarettes etc., were interchanged, and the officer intimated that hostilities on Christmas Day would be considered unnecessary.

The same sort of thing was taking place on the front of the units on either flank, and on the right a formal truce was agreed upon to enable each side to bury its dead.

On the front of No. 2 Company, several of the enemy were seen moving in the mist about two hundred yards in front of the line, and a party was sent out to investigate. It was found that they were burying their dead.

As the mist cleared the enemy were seen in large numbers standing on top of their parapet. The British troops did likewise when they heard that there was a truce on the right. Permission was given for the men to go out into No-man's-land, with orders that they were not to go more than half-way and to see that none of the enemy approached our lines.

Sufficient men were kept in the trenches to make any attempt at treachery on the part of the enemy impossible.

The men all returned to their trenches for their Christmas dinner, but in the afternoon the scene can only be described as astounding. The enemy were standing in dense masses on their parapets, and groups of British and German soldiers could be seen half-way across apparently, as indeed they were, for the time being, the best of friends. Presents and souvenirs of every description, including copies of the cartoons, in the " Daily Mirror," of " Big Willie " and " Little Willie," were exchanged and some curious pieces of information obtained. The troops holding the line were Saxons belonging to the 107*th Regiment;* they were of good military age for the most part, though there were some very young men among them. They seemed happy and healthy, and well fed. Some of them, however, were despondent. Some said that they thought they were just outside Paris, having been brought up to the line in closed railway carriages, and they also believed that the Germans were occupying London!

The Saxons behaved extremely well, and in no way attempted to take advantage of the situation; they freely acknowledged their hatred of the Prussians, and their officers went so far as to warn ours not to allow this temporary truce to influence us in our dealings with Prussians, who, they said, could not be trusted to play fair in similar circumstances.

The troops on both sides were withdrawn to their trenches before dark, and in the evening a note was sent across by an officer from the enemy lines, stating that at midnight he would " fire his automatic pistol, when the war would continue."

Thus ended the most remarkable Christmas Day that any of those who took part in it are likely to experience.

During the day, the Christmas cards sent out by Their Majesties the King and Queen were delivered to every man in the Battalion; and, when the Battalion came out of the line, everyone received Princess Mary's gift of a beautifully designed box containing cigarettes and tobacco, or chocolates, and a pipe. The kindly thought that had prompted the sending of these presents and the stirring message on the Christmas cards gave intense pleasure, and both the card and the gifts remain among the cherished possessions of those who received them.[1]

After an exceptionally quiet night the Battalion was relieved at 4 a.m. on the 26th by the 1st Royal Fusiliers, and rejoined the 18th Infantry Brigade at Houplines, a suburb of Armentières on the right bank of the River Lys.

Between the 24th November and the 27th December, the

[1] The men were allowed to post them to their homes. In one instance, at any rate, the Customs authorities at home showed a singular lack of appreciation, by seeking to levy duty on the tobacco contained in Princess Mary's gift. The box in question, as a matter of fact, contained chocolates.

Battalion had spent 23 days in the trenches, and had lost by casualties six men killed and two officers, Lieutenant P. E. Harding and 2nd Lieutenant M. E. Trollope, and twenty-nine men wounded.

The men were very tired, but there had been practically no sickness and their spirits were excellent. It is difficult when looking back on the conditions under which the men lived during the wet winter months to understand how they could be really cheerful, but they were. It has always been a characteristic of the British soldier that his spirits rise when he has his back against the wall, and things look their blackest. The regular battalions, worn out as they were with months of weary fighting, before the period of trench warfare began, displayed this characteristic in a marked degree. The British temperament, magnificent discipline and regimental tradition all combined to bring this about. The first line Territorials had further and slightly different factors to help them. They were founding the fighting traditions of their regiments and they had the example of the regular troops before them to set a standard. Their discipline was not less strict, but was of a different quality. The driving force which had prompted them to volunteer for service abroad, and the sense of responsibility which had moved them to join the Territorial Force in time of peace, were displayed in the enthusiasm of individual men to undertake any work that was required. To form one of a working party was looked upon as a privilege rather than a duty in those early days. This was the foundation of the Territorial spirit. It persisted right up to the end of the war, although as the months dragged on, with their never-ending fighting and monotonous routine of continuous work, discipline necessarily assumed a sterner aspect.

CHAPTER IV

HOUPLINES

ON arriving at Houplines on the morning of the 26th December, the Battalion relieved the 1/5th Scottish Rifles, who were "resting" out of the line. The billets taken over were mostly large factories, which provided little comfort for the men. The flax factory, in particular, was very uncomfortable, with its floor covered with huge vats and large pieces of machinery. Parts of Houplines had been considerably damaged by shell fire, but the factories were comparatively intact at this time, the only outward indication that they had been shelled being a large nick in the tall chimney of the flax factory which looked as though it would collapse at any moment.

The Battalion occupied these billets until it went into the trenches for the first time in this sector, but when the companies next came out of the line the men were billeted, with the permission of the Brigadier, in cottages which were still occupied by the civilian owners. This was a highly prized privilege, for the owners of the billets never failed to do all they could to make the Queen's Westminsters comfortable.

The Battalion remained out of the line until the end of the year, and the five days' rest effected a wonderful change in the men. As the stiffness and weariness of the trenches wore off, games were started, and an inter-company football competition took place in a field where a howitzer battery was in position. Permission to use the field was given only on condition that the battery aiming posts were not interfered with, and that play should cease if the battery wanted to fire. The last condition was not likely to interfere with play for very long, for shells were very scarce in those days, and the daily ration of ammunition was exceedingly small.

The number of parcels that arrived from home at this time had a wonderfully inspiring effect on everyone. A committee of ladies, under the presidency of Lady Howard Vincent, a never-failing friend of the Regiment, and Mrs. Gordon Clark, organised a supply of comforts for the members of the Battalion, and the gifts of socks, comforters, balaclava helmets and luxuries were very much appreciated. The

Battalion has special reason to be grateful to Lady Howard Vincent and to Mrs. Gordon Clark and the many other ladies connected with the Regiment for their untiring work on its behalf as members of this committee.

Presents came from many other unexpected sources, as for instance a large consignment of toffee and sweets in specially decorated tins from the Grocers' Federation, and a supply of candles sent out as the result of a collection by unknown friends at a dinner at a London restaurant. The Christmas plum puddings distributed to the Battalion from the "Daily News" (Princess Mary's) Fund were specially subscribed for by the Wimbledon Collegiate School and Emanuel School, Wandsworth.

With the exception of finding night working parties to dig a new communication trench, no work was done by the Battalion during the period of rest.

The Queen's Westminsters relieved the Durhams on the left of the 18th Infantry Brigade on the evening of January 1st, 1915. The trenches taken over by the Battalion covered a front of about half a mile, with the left resting on the right bank of the River Lys, opposite the village of Frelinghien. The enemy trenches were about a hundred yards away from the British lines on the left, gradually dropping back to about four hundred yards on the right. The British defences in the centre section, which had been constructed by cutting away part of a bank, were distinctly unorthodox, for there was no parados, and the garrison had an uninterrupted view to the rear. This was pleasant enough in its way, but there was absolutely no cover from shell fire. For some reason or other, however, the enemy never shelled this part of the line, and the Battalion was duly appreciative. The accommodation for the men in this portion of the line consisted of shelters, built in under the parapets, and roofed over with a sheet of corrugated iron and one or two rows of sandbags. A shallow boarded trench and a low breastwork of sandbags (manned only at night) took the line across the Houplines-Frelinghien road, after which it continued down to the river in a series of excellently revetted trenches. A row of wooden shanties at the foot of the bank on the Houplines-Frelinghien road provided accommodation for Battalion Headquarters, and for the two supporting platoons. These were not more than six or seven yards behind the firing line, but, as the trenches were inaccessible by day, no other arrangement was possible. At first they were not protected in any way, for sandbags were scarce in these early days of the war, but eventually sufficient

HOUPLINES SECTO

RMENTIERES, 1915

were procured to place one row on the roofs and a row on the sides and fronts of these fragile shelters. The occupants then let themselves think that they were in quite a safe place. This illusion would speedily have been dispelled if the enemy had started to shell them, but it was not until the Battalion removed to the Ypres Salient that it realised how much it had to be thankful for the enemy's failure to make use of his opportunities at Houplines.

For several hundred yards in rear, the country was absolutely flat and in full view of the enemy. In wet weather it was covered with water; and in dry weather, during the winter, it was little better than a muddy swamp. The one communication trench was flooded to a depth of three or four feet, and all reliefs had to take place after dark, across the open, while the ration parties had to struggle nightly through the water and mud to bring up supplies for the garrison of the trenches.

Familiar names were given to some of the more prominent features of the trench, as for instance : Buckingham Palace (or Buck House), to a cottage close up to the firing line which served as the left company headquarters; Ludgate Hill, to part of the trench which sloped down from the bank towards the road; the Mappin Terraces, to the portion of fire trench that was not protected by a parados; Westminster Bridge, to a rough plank bridge across a small stream and round a very large sandbag traverse; and Margate Pier, to a duckboard path about twenty yards long, leading from the support line on to the flooded country behind.

A lamp was hung at night at the end of Margate Pier to serve as a guide to the ration parties, and anyone coming up to the line at night had the unusual spectacle of quite a bright illumination from the pierhead light and from the lights in the support shelters.

The village of Frelinghien afforded many vantage points for the enemy snipers. The chief one was from a large circular shell-hole near the top of the brewery chimney, and another was an estaminet a little further to the south. From both of these the enemy was able to enfilade the line from the left, and the Battalion suffered many casualties until the artillery had husbanded sufficient shells to bombard the village. The long, straight length of trench in the side of the bank, in particular, was subjected to very heavy and accurate sniping. It was a slow and difficult task to put up sandbag traverses in that portion of the line, and resort was had to canvas screens as a temporary expedient. These proved most effective. The trench to the south of Westminster Bridge was also overlooked from the brewery. An attempt was first made to add further sandbags to the existing traverse, but the swampy foundations were insufficient to bear the additional weight, and the structure threatened to collapse. As an alternative, three rows of sandbags, filled only with straw, were placed on top of the traverse and kept in position by wire. This early form of camouflage deceived the enemy and stopped all sniping in the neighbourhood.

The ordinary routine of trench warfare continued during the first eleven days of January, when the whole Battalion was in the line. The casualties from the enemy snipers mounted steadily, and valuable men were killed or wounded.

On the 8th January, just as it was beginning to get light, Corporal R. de R. Roche was shot as he was crossing the open to get some water for his gun. He was not missed until after daylight, when he was seen lying in the open in rear of the trench and in full view of the enemy, who was not more than a hundred and twenty yards away. It was practically certain death to attempt to reach him; but two very gallant men, Rifleman P. H. A. Tibbs, a stretcher-bearer, and Rifleman Pouchot (both of No. 2 Company), crawled out to him to see if anything could be done. As soon as they were seen, the enemy opened fire on them, but both men went on and succeeded in reaching Corporal Roche, who was found to be dead. Rifleman Tibbs was killed as he was kneeling over his body; but Rifleman Pouchot, who saw that both men were beyond help, managed to get back to our lines untouched. He was awarded the D.C.M. for his bravery on this occasion, and thus won the first decoration gained by the Battalion. Rifleman P. H. A. Tibbs was mentioned in despatches. Corporal Roche was a noted rifle and revolver shot, and a very keen member of the Regiment. At home he had always been ready to give to others the benefit of his experience; he had served in the South African War, and in France he had already done some splendid work for which he was mentioned in despatches. In him the Battalion lost a good soldier and a very true comrade.

On the following day the Battalion suffered another deeply felt loss by the death of Captain M. M. Shattock, who was killed instantly while looking over the parapet to examine a suspicious point in the enemy lines.

Captain Shattock, who was the first Queen's Westminster officer to fall in the war, had been a member of the Regiment for very many years, having joined as a rifleman in 1891.

He had resigned his commission in 1912 on account of age and poor health, but rejoined on the outbreak of war and managed to get passed as medically fit. He had always thrown himself with whole-hearted energy into every form of the Regiment's activities, but he was specially associated with the musketry of the Battalion and with the School of Arms. As musketry officer he was responsible for the organisation of the regimental shooting teams and rifle competitions, and the success of these is sufficient tribute to his good work. The whole Battalion mourned the loss of one who had set the finest example as an officer and whom all regarded with affection.

Some very wet weather set in during the first week of January. The River Lys rose steadily day by day and flooded the surrounding country, making the trenches on the left flank of the Battalion untenable. The following are some extracts from the War Diary for this period:—

"*January* 7*th.*—Heavy rain 6/7th and all day 7th. Parapet and bug hutches falling in a great deal. Ditches much swollen. Dams broken and bridges flooded.

"*January* 8*th.*—Parapets falling in—River Lys rising rapidly, necessitating evacuation of trenches near the river bank. Barricade just south of Houplines-Frelinghien road collapsed and stream, middle of right-centre section, rose rapidly, necessitating evacuation of listening post. Work day and night on repairs. Conditions very bad.

"*January* 9*th.*—Work day and night on repairs to trenches. Parapets collapsing. River rising, necessitating more trench evacuation. . . . Less rain.

"*January* 10*th.*—Fine day after wet night. General work repairing ravages of storm in trenches—water controlled. Enemy seen to be baling water.

"*January* 11*th.*—Enemy still baling and digging. Stormy, wet night."

The entry of January 8th has reference to a night-long struggle with the rising water at Westminster Bridge. The enemy had apparently made an attempt to flood our lines, for there was a sudden rush of water through a culvert leading through the bank at this point. A party under Lieutenant W. M. Henderson-Scott, a mining engineer by profession, worked for hours on end piling sandbags, filled with semi-liquid mud, on the banks of the stream. It was a race between the workers and the water, which the former won, but it was literally a question of inches. Sleep was almost out of the question during this period, for the men were wet through and everyone was kept continually at work to prevent a complete collapse of the defences. Many suffered from internal chills and exhaustion, but, strange to say, there was not a single case of the ordinary domestic cold.

Owing to a shortage of doctors at this time, medical officers were forbidden, by order, to come into the trenches, and the resulting experiences of the Queen's Westminsters were typical of those of other units in France at this period. The sick had to struggle back at night, as best they could, to Houplines. The Battalion was beginning to get very weak in numbers, and only the severest cases were kept out of the line; the remainder were given a night's rest at the dressing station and had to return to the trenches before dawn. Chlorodyne was supplied to the company commanders for issue to the men, and this was the only medical attention that numbers received who were really quite unfit to remain in the line. The arrival of a draft from England was very eagerly awaited.

After the Battalion had been eleven days in the trenches, the right company was relieved by a company of the Sherwood Foresters; and a system of reliefs was started under which one and a half companies went back to Houplines for four days' rest, leaving two companies in the line and two platoons in support.

Being in support meant that there was no sentry duty for the men, but continuous work on the trenches. This system continued until the end of the month when, with the arrival of the new draft, two complete companies were able to be out of the line at a time.

The collapse of trenches during the wet weather had caused the garrison to be still further exposed to enfilade fire from the north; and, on January 12th, it was found necessary to evacuate certain portions of the line by day, pending the arrival of proper revetting material. On the 14th, the enemy shelled the empty lines in rear of the trenches, and in the afternoon of the same day our own guns carried out an effective bombardment of Frelinghien Brewery, doing considerable damage and causing the high roof to collapse. The War Diary for the next day reads as follows :—" Result of shelling yesterday is that snipers much quieter in front of us —our snipers put a pump in enemy lines out of action and claimed to have bagged three of the enemy. Continuous work is at last showing its effect in improving conditions of trenches. Enemy do not appear to have attempted to repair damage done by us."

JANUARY, 1915

The month of January marks the beginning of a rapid development in the methods of trench warfare. On the 5th, an officer was sent to witness experiments with a new " trench howitzer " throwing a 9-lb. shell. This was not considered suitable for the Houplines trenches, and was not approved of generally, owing to the throw-back from the shell which made it unsafe to use at a range of less than four hundred yards. It made a very big flash and much smoke, and required more room than the width of most trenches provided.

On the 16th, periscopes are mentioned for the first time, when the Diary reads : " Considerable advantage derived from the use of periscopes made, by our pioneers, from wood of tea boxes, and looking glasses." Later in the month, a few experimental bombs were issued. These were made by filling empty jam tins with high explosive and shrapnel bullets, and fitting a length of fuse to be ignited with a match. These primitive weapons were in fact not very dangerous to the enemy, but they made a considerable noise on exploding, which probably had its moral effect and certainly caused much satisfaction to the throwers. On the 23rd, a considerable amount of enemy transport of all kinds was heard behind Frelinghien between 4 p.m. and 7.30 p.m. It was suspected that preparations were being made for an attack in honour of the Kaiser's birthday on January 27th. Special precautions therefore were taken against a surprise, but the day passed quietly. On the 28th, however, the enemy was reported as being " decidedly musical under cover."

The casualties of the Battalion during January were one officer (Captain M. M. Shattock) and six other ranks killed, and twenty other ranks wounded.

The long-expected draft of three officers and two hundred and forty-four other ranks arrived from the 2nd Battalion on the 1st February. The draft, as a whole, probably contained the finest men that reinforced the 1st Battalion during the whole war. They had all been very carefully selected, and it must have been a hard wrench for the Commanding Officer of the 2nd Battalion to part with such splendid material, and so delay the chance of his own Battalion getting out as a unit.

A concentration of the enemy was reported on the 30th January in the neighbourhood of Courtrai and Menin, and also towards Perenchies and Premesques ; and, as a precautionary measure, one of the resting companies in Houplines was sent up for the next few days at dawn to reinforce the front line, being withdrawn again in the evening.

On the 3rd February, the Battalion again took over part

of the line on the right, from which it had been relieved by the Sherwood Foresters. The enemy had been exceptionally quiet on the 2nd, but on the following day his artillery was very active, shelling the batteries in Houplines, and also shelling Armentières. Our guns replied with a further bombardment of the sniping posts in Frelinghien. No enemy attack developed, and the ordinary trench routine was resumed on the 6th.

The chief items of interest mentioned in the War Diary for the rest of the month are the following :—

"*February* 13*th*.—Enemy working party discovered on their river parapet. Heavy rapid fire opened. Enemy retaliated by heavy sniping all day on the left company.

"*February* 14*th*.—A hyposcope attached to a rifle provided a useful sniping weapon.

"*February* 15*th*.—River rising very rapidly, causing part of the reclaimed trench to be flooded.

"*February* 18*th*.—A half-company of the 3rd Battalion (Toronto) Canadian Regiment came into the trenches for instruction in trench warfare, the Canadians being alternated with our own men. Six N.C.O.'s and men transferred to the Cadet School at St. Omer.

"*February* 19*th*.—Half-company of Canadians relieved their other half-company.

"*February* 23*rd*.—German observer still noticed in shell hole in chimney.

"*February* 24*th*.—Two platoons, 15th Canadian Battalion (48th Canadian Highlanders), came in to-night and were placed alternately with our own men for instruction. Arrangements made for fifteen miners, from the Durhams, to prepare saps for listening posts against mining.

"*February* 26*th*.—For the first time the enemy harried our usual four-day relief at night—six wounded.

"*February* 28*th*.—Heavy batteries destroyed the big chimney, with shell hole in it, at Frelinghien, from which sniping and artillery observation had been carried out by the enemy. Comfort of our trenches largely increased. Enemy greatly incensed, sniping very heavily for some time."

The officer in charge of this "shoot" was a brother of Captain B. L. Miles, who was for so long the transport officer of the Queen's Westminsters.

The casualties of the Battalion during February were five other ranks killed and eighteen other ranks wounded.

The Canadians, whose arrival had marked a further stage

THE GERMAN TRENCHES FROM BRITISH FRONT LINE, HOUPLINES, 1915

"BUCKINGHAM PALACE," HOUPLINES, 1915

in the progress of the war, gave early evidence of their fighting qualities. Their keenness in the firing line and the easy manner in which they adapted themselves to the conditions of trench life were very marked, and created a great impression on all ranks.

The month of February saw further developments in the "refinements" of trench warfare. The "hyposcope,"[1] which was first used in a primitive form on February 14th, and was subsequently improved, was an ingenious sniping rifle. The ordinary service rifle was placed in a rest on the parapet and had attached to it a dummy butt, bolt and trigger projecting downwards into the trench, which worked corresponding parts of the actual rifle. Aiming was effected by the use of a periscope attachment. By these means it was possible for the sniper to take aim, fire and re-load without showing his head over the parapet; and when it was necessary to recharge the magazine, the whole device was lowered into the trench. The hyposcope was completely successful, and only went out of use when sniping in its primitive form died out and elaborate camouflage and telescopic sights were introduced.

Rifle grenades also began to come into general use about this time. The Germans were well supplied, and did some very accurate shoots with them, but so far as the Battalion was concerned the number was strictly limited, and it was distinctly disappointing not to be able to return the enemy's fire in at least equal volume. The British grenades, at this period, were fired from a rifle fixed into a special wooden rest, the butt being supported against a wooden shoe and the barrel resting against a bar capable of vertical movement, to secure the necessary elevation.

By the end of February the equipment of the trench garrison had been very much improved. Every man was issued with a warm soft service dress cap and a fur waistcoat, and there was a plentiful supply of excellent waterproof capes and gum boots, which were greatly appreciated during the very wet weather.

A small number of Verey lights and pistols was available for use in the trenches. The Germans, even at this period of the war, employed them lavishly, but they were never used to anything like the same extent by British troops.

On the 3rd March, Captain H. R. Townsend-Green, 2nd in command of No. 3 Company, died from wounds received the previous day. He was an exceptionally keen soldier, and

[1] A good example of a hyposcope may be seen at the Imperial War Museum at the Crystal Palace.

one of the best rifle shots in the Regiment. Before mobilisation he had been Battalion machine-gun officer, an appointment which he relinquished to take over command of F Company. His cheerful spirits were infectious, it was impossible to be dull or gloomy when he was present. His loss was very deeply felt in the Regiment. It was a curious coincidence that, within a little over six weeks, the Battalion should have lost three of its members who were so prominently associated with its success as a shooting regiment.

From the beginning of March, hostilities assumed a much more active character. There was a great increase of the artillery fire on both sides throughout the month, and bombardments of the Battalion front, with rifle and heavier grenades, were of almost daily occurrence, causing a number of casualties. On the 6th, for instance, seven men were wounded by the explosion of a German grenade between two shelters, and on the 17th there were six casualties in the Battalion lines as a result of one of these bombardments.

During the operations at Neuve Chapelle, at the beginning of March, a brisk fire fight was maintained on the front of the 6th Division. But, with the exception of a very successful operation on the 12th, when the 1st North Staffords (17th Infantry Brigade) occupied a row of houses in L'Épinette, and advanced their line on a front of half a mile to a depth of 300 yards, no attack was made by the Division.

The policy of harassing the enemy by fire achieved its object of pinning him to his ground while the Neuve Chapelle operations were in progress. The War Diary of the 6th Division states that "signs from the enemy's attitude, statements of prisoners, and evidence contained in papers on the dead showed that the line was strongly held and that the enemy were more than usually nervous."

The following are more extracts from the Battalion War Diary:—

"*March 9th.*—Fairly heavy artillery bombardment—considerable damage done in Frelinghien. At night a huge explosion by the Brewery, and a fire in the enemy's lines on the left, which apparently destroyed some of his ammunition.

"*March 10th.*—Under instructions during night and day a considerable increase was made in our sniping efforts. In the early morning and at intervals during the day artillery bombardment of Frelinghien. Enemy slow to reply. Another heavy explosion in German lines; evidently intended, as it was preceded by two shrill whistles.

"*March* 12*th*.—Sniping heavily as ordered. Reply rather more active. Some grenading by enemy. Reports received of successes at Neuve Chapelle. Effect of sniping is to increase the flares thrown at night by the enemy, especially in parts of the line not firing so heavily and therefore suspected.

"*March* 17*th*.—Enemy very active with a heavy grenade, heavier than ordinary. Only quieted after guns, both heavy and 4.5 in. battery, had shelled buildings opposite Brewery and south of Houplines-Frelinghien road, doing considerable damage.

"*March* 18*th*.—Again considerable bombardment by grenades—not quietened by our grenades, but quietened after a few rounds by our artillery on buildings and trenches.

"*March* 21*st*.—Two platoons 1/5th North Staffords (Territorials) came in at night for instruction in trenches. During the night the sentries heard the enemy shout across to know if we were the 5th Staffords.

"*March* 22*nd*.—At 6.30 p.m. the Germans inquired if we were relieving, and stated that they were. It was our usual relief night.

"*March* 23*rd*.—Early morning practice alarm. Enemy somewhat perturbed, put up many lights. Working party at Le Touquet, at range of about 1000 yards, sniped by our picked shots sufficiently accurately to annoy and make them careful.

"*March* 26*th*.—German captive balloon noticed during the day. We did some long-distance sniping, at working parties at Le Touquet, with Martin telescopic sights issued to us.

"*March* 29*th*.—Heavy counter-mining suspected. Listening at regular intervals did not confirm.

"*March* 31*st*.—Three captive balloons noticed together."

The Battalion's casualties for March were one officer (Captain H. R. Townsend-Green) and eleven other ranks killed, and one officer (Captain S. Low) and twenty other ranks wounded.

The incidents recorded on March 21st and 22nd are an example of what was often thought to be a very effective system of espionage employed by the enemy, but later knowledge makes it very doubtful if he really knew any more or even as much about us as we knew about him. At any rate it is certainly curious that, with the means of knowledge that he appeared to possess, there was practically no interference with reliefs during the whole time the Queen's Westminsters were on the Houplines front. Many a reported " spy " turned out to be a cat still living in its old home.

The month of April was comparatively peaceful. A good deal of work was done on improvements of the defences, and the mining operations, started at the beginning of March by a platoon of miners from the Sherwood Foresters, were steadily continued. This platoon was commanded by 2nd Lieutenant Palmer, who was attached to the Queen's Westminsters for this special work.

On the 2nd April, a company of the 1/7th Warwickshire Regiment, T.F. was attached to the Battalion for (to use the official term) " instruction " in trench warfare.

With reference to the mining operations the Battalion War Diary has the following entries :—

" *April 22nd.*—About 7.15 p.m. two mines exploded north of us near Le Touquet.

" *April 27th.*—In No. 6 mine enemy heard quite clearly working—estimated to be about 30 feet away. All necessary preparations made to blow in or explode if necessary—exact position of enemy not definitely located."

The Battalion's casualties during April were three other ranks killed, and seventeen other ranks wounded.

On the 28th April, the two companies in reserve took over, from the 1/5th South Lancashire Regiment, T.F. (12th Infantry Brigade), the line to the north of the River Lys, from the left bank of the river to the Le Bizet-Le Touquet road, the whole Battalion now being again in the line.

The Battalion was relieved on the 1st May by the Sherwood Foresters. On relief the Battalion went into billets at Houplines and at Le Bizet, and on the following day the whole Battalion was billeted at Houplines, with one company occupying the reserve trenches at night. This was the first time that the Battalion had been out at rest as a whole for four months, and it had the bad luck to come in for a very heavy bombardment of the village on the 3rd May. On this day the mine at Frelinghien opposite the " chicken run " was exploded at 8.30 a.m. ; and the enemy retaliated by shelling Houplines from 11 a.m. to 2 p.m. with 5.9 shells, causing a considerable amount of material damage. The church was wrecked, and some of the debris destroyed one of the Battalion machine-guns. There is little doubt that the enemy was attempting to destroy the bridge across the River Lys. He was probably expecting an attack after the explosion of the mine and thought that the bridge would be used for bringing up troops or guns. There were a good many casualties both amongst the troops and the civilian inhabitants, a large number of whom still clung to their homes. The Battalion lost three killed and eight wounded, one of the killed being C.Q.M.S. E. C. Whiskin, who came out as a member of A Company. He had done good work in France, and the loss of his influence and personality was a great blow both to his company and to the Battalion.

The much-respected Curé of Houplines was killed at the same time, while he was tending civilian wounded. No member of the Regiment, who was billeted in the village, will ever forget his genial presence and the innumerable acts of kindness he did for the Queen's Westminsters. A big-hearted, brave Frenchman, he did his duty unflinchingly to the last. He was loved by all, and when he was buried nearly the whole Regiment attended the funeral. The affection of his parishioners was shown in the memorial chapel fitted up by them in his own house, which they lovingly tended during the whole time that the Battalion remained in the Houplines sector of the line.

The way in which the civilian inhabitants, regardless of danger, refused to leave their homes, was very remarkable, for some of the houses in which they lived were little more than a thousand yards from the firing line. The Queen's Westminsters were always treated with every mark of friendship and hospitality. It was arranged that men, coming out of the trenches after a relief, returned to their former billets, and they generally found that the owner was waiting up to receive them, however late the hour, and that hot coffee and some other welcome luxury had been thoughtfully prepared for them. Even beds with sheets were provided in many cases, and the men's " washing " was invariably done for them, and their clean clothes were ready for a welcome and much-needed change.

The enemy shelled Houplines again on the 4th and 5th, but not so severely. The front line was also shelled and Buckingham Palace, on the Houplines-Frelinghien road, which, it will be remembered, was the left company trench headquarters, was destroyed by shell-fire on the evening of the 5th. The Battalion relieved the Sherwood Foresters in the trenches south and north of the river on the 7th of May, and then remained in the line until relieved by the West Yorks on the 14th. With the exception of a mine exploded by the enemy, between the Frelinghien road and the " chicken run," close under his own wire, the tour was a very quiet one on the Battalion front, and during the whole seven days in the trenches there was not a single casualty.

On the 18th, the Battalion relieved the East Yorks in No. 1 section, from the road north-west of Pont Ballot on the right to Hobbs Farm on the left. Two companies of the 10th Royal Scots were attached to the Battalion for instruction on the 20th, and, on the 22nd, the Battalion was relieved by the East Yorks.

The Battalion returned to the same trenches on the 26th. This was its last visit to the line on the Armentières front, for, on the 28th, the 18th Infantry Brigade was relieved by troops of the 27th Division, the Queen's Westminsters handing over their portion of the line to a battalion of Cambridge Territorials. During the last two tours in the trenches, both of which were quiet ones, a great deal of work had been done in siting and digging a new fire trench from Edmead's Farm towards the left of the 17th Infantry Brigade, to straighten out a re-entrant, and in linking up the new trenches.

The casualties of the Battalion for May were four killed and fourteen wounded, bringing the casualties for the five months on the Houplines front up to a total of 123, of which 2 officers and 29 other ranks were killed and 1 officer and 91 other ranks wounded.

After relief the Battalion marched to Bailleul, where it arrived at 3 a.m. on the 29th. The whole of the 18th Infantry Brigade was now out of the line for the first time for many months, and was billeted in the town.

The Brigade was inspected on the 29th by the Commander-in-Chief, Field-Marshal Sir John French, who made a complimentary speech on the work it had done during the last six months. After expressing his admiration for the magnificent work done by the Brigade, both on the Aisne in September, 1914, and in the very critical days for the Empire when it had assisted in pushing the enemy back and taking up a line between Bethune and Nieuport, he referred to the consistent good work it had done in holding the line throughout the winter months under such very trying conditions. On the same day Major-General W. N. Congreve, V.C., was appointed to command the 6th Division, the command of the 18th Infantry Brigade passing to Lieut.-Colonel H. S. Ainslie, C.M.G., 1st Battalion Northumberland Fusiliers.

General Congreve possessed that characteristic quality of a leader which makes each individual under him feel a personal link between himself and his commander. Such a feeling begets trust, and General Congreve possessed the trust of his

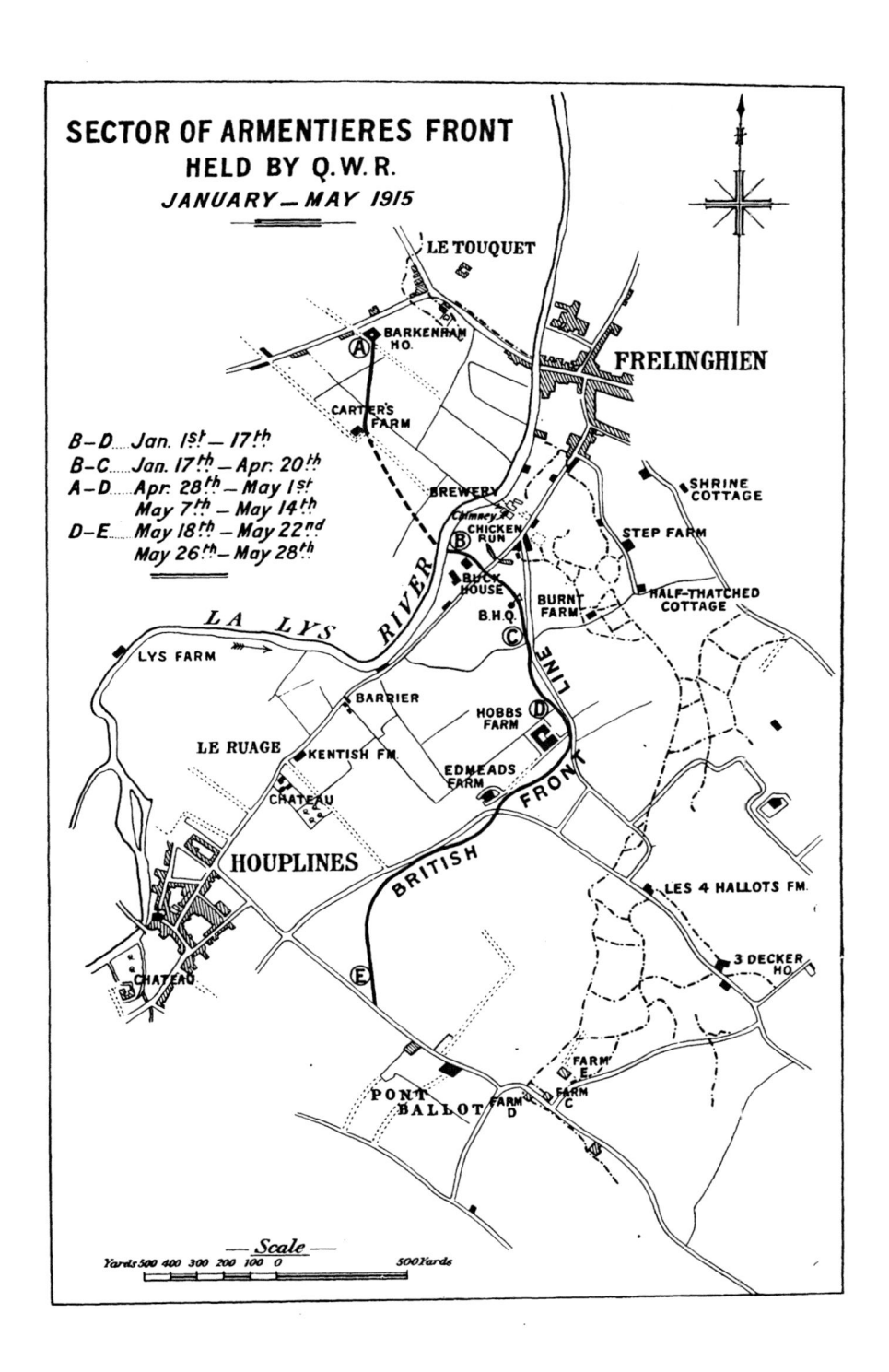

SECTOR OF ARMENTIERES FRONT
HELD BY Q.W.R.
JANUARY — MAY 1915

B–D .... Jan. 1st – 17th
B–C .... Jan. 17th – Apr. 20th
A–D .... Apr. 28th – May 1st
          May 7th – May 14th
D–E .... May 18th – May 22nd
          May 26th – May 28th

troops to a remarkable degree. His frequent visits to the trenches were welcomed, by company commanders and junior officers, as those of a helpful friend rather than a critic; and his advice, especially in the early days, and the manner in which it was given, created a spirit of confidence that was of the very greatest help to Territorial officers, who both realised their inexperience and felt their responsibilities. Who will forget his cheery " good morning " to the men as he passed down the muddy trenches, or his habitual greeting " and how are the Westminsters this morning ? " The same influence was felt at Battalion Headquarters. After the first week, when the companies were attached independently to the regular units in the line for instruction in trench warfare, he treated the Battalion, composed as it was of untried troops, on terms of equality with the experienced regular battalions of the Brigade.

On one occasion, in January, he narrowly escaped being shot by an enemy sniper, when visiting the trenches held by the Battalion, one of the sentries being shot through the head and killed instantly while pointing out to him some of the danger spots in the German lines.

General Congreve continued in command of the 6th Division until November, 1915, when he was appointed to command the XIII Corps, on its formation.

CHAPTER V

IN THE YPRES SALIENT

THE next eight months were spent in the Ypres Salient. They were months of toil, of almost incessant shell-fire, of gas, of mud and water, of death and wounds and sickness.

At one time or another during 1915 and 1916 the Battalion occupied practically every portion of the northern half of the Salient, from the Ypres-Roulers railway in the south to about a mile north of Wieltje in the north, and in 1917 it fought in the Battles of Ypres, 1917, taking part, on August 16th, in the attack on Polygone Wood further to the south.

The ground round Ypres is indeed hallowed to the Queen's Westminsters by the memory of those 126 of their officers and men who were killed and rest there, and of those 441 who were wounded during these eight months, and in August, 1917.

Leaving Bailleul at 5.0 a.m. on May 30th, the 18th Infantry Brigade marched via St. Jans Cappel, Berthen and Boeschepe to the area between Wippenhoek and Poperinghe, where it billeted for the night. On the following day, the East Yorks, Durhams and Queen's Westminsters moved forward in motor buses as far as Vlamertinghe, and then marched through Ypres, which was still smouldering as the result of the German bombardment a week earlier, to relieve the 9th Infantry Brigade which was holding the line between the Ypres-Roulers railway and the Ypres-Verlorenhoek road.

The line was just crystallising after the "Battle of Ypres, 1915," there were frequent alarms and expectations of attack, but although there was constant heavy fighting on the flanks of the 6th Division, in which individual units were called on to co-operate, the Division itself was not actually engaged until August 9th. The line, in May, followed a big curve running approximately from east of Hill 60, north-eastward to the east of Hooge, and thence north-westward to the east of Steenstraate.

The Queen's Westminsters first went into support trenches over the Ypres-Verlorenhoek road, a little to the east of Potijze, but on June 2nd there was a slight change in the dispositions, the Battalion moving further south, relieving the

BELLEWAARDE, JUNE 16TH, 1915

East Yorks and a battalion of Royal Scots in support trenches north of the Ypres-Roulers railway.

For the first fortnight in June, there were no outstanding events to relieve the monotony of trench routine, with its continuous work day and night, or the strain which every unit in the Salient experienced at this period of the war, of having to remain inactive under constant bursts of heavy shell-fire, with no means of effective retaliation.

On June 4th, there was a severe bombardment of the support trenches with H.E. shells. Much damage was done and 9 men were killed and 12 wounded.

During the night of June 4th, B and D Companies moved forward to the fire trenches east of Potijze, two companies remaining in support.

The Battalion was relieved by the East Yorks on the 8th, and, after spending two days in hutments just west of Ypres, moved into dugouts on the east bank of the Yser Canal. The state of the trenches at this time is best expressed in the terse words of the 18th Infantry Brigade War Diary : " Trenches in a disgusting condition. Communication trenches full of water. Parapets and traverses falling in," and during the period of " rest " nearly the whole Battalion was at work every night on the defences of the Brigade front.

On June 16th, the 3rd Division attacked the German lines immediately on the right of the 18th Infantry Brigade, in the direction of Bellewaarde Farm, with the object of straightening up the line across the re-entrant from Hooge to the Ypres-Roulers railway. For this operation the Queen's Westminsters came under the orders of Lieut.-Colonel F. W. Towsey, commanding the West Yorks, who had been ordered to protect the left flank of the 9th Infantry Brigade, and, if the attack succeeded, to support and assist it as opportunity offered.

Two companies of the Battalion were moved up on the night of the 15th, to support trenches immediately north of the railway, and to the west of Cambridge road.

The assault of the 9th Infantry Brigade was made at 4.15 a.m. on June 16th, and the first two German lines and part of their third line, and about 200 prisoners, were captured on a front of about 1000 yards ; but owing to heavy enemy shelling the troops of this brigade were forced to withdraw to the first German line, which was consolidated and held.

The Battalion was not called upon to take any active part in the operation during the day, but was exposed to a considerable amount of shelling, especially near the railway, where a continuous stream of wounded and prisoners poured along the road to the rear. At night, one company was moved forward to occupy the railway barrier and the fire trench south of the railway, relieving a company of the West Yorks.

On the 17th, the Battalion stretcher-bearers and volunteer parties from D Company, then in reserve, were employed all day in collecting and clearing casualties from the battlefield; and during the night, the operations having been completed, the Battalion returned to the canal bank, as Brigade reserve.

The casualties on the 16th and 17th were 4 other ranks killed; and one officer (Captain P. M. Glasier) and 46 other ranks wounded.

On the 18th, the whole of the Brigade went into hutments to the north-east of Poperinghe for a week's rest. At the conclusion of this period the Queen's Westminsters relieved the 3rd and 5th Rifle Brigade (17th Infantry Brigade), in the centre sector of the Brigade, where the trenches ran in front of Wieltje Farm and to the west of Wieltje. The relief was much impeded by the state of the ground, a heavy thunderstorm having done a good deal of damage to the recently constructed roads, rendering them almost impassable for even the lightest transport.

The tour of the Battalion in these trenches lasted for seventeen days. It was uneventful, and the War Diary, beyond recording a two hours' bombardment on June 26th which did little damage, and some gas-shelling on July 3rd, contains little of general interest.

On July 3rd, the Battalion was relieved by the East Yorks, and went into Brigade support.

The Salient had been taking steady toll of the Queen's Westminsters, as it did of all troops operating there. In May and June the net wastage from casualties, sickness, transfers to commissions and Cadet schools, and from other causes was over 200 men, and the total strength of the Battalion had fallen to 656 all ranks. There were even rumours that the Battalion would be disbanded if no reinforcements came out; but anxiety on this point was set at rest by the arrival of a draft of 132 men on July 8th.

The support trenches came in for a good deal of shelling, and on July 9th some gas shells fell on the ground in front, the effects of which, the War Diary states, " were unpleasant but harmless." The Battalion's first experience of gas shells (early in June) was not without a humorous side. An 8-inch shell landed a few yards from the Headquarter dugout, but failed to explode. Application was made to the Royal Engineers to

"THE MAPPIN TERRACES," HOUPLINES, 1915

THE MACHINE-GUN SECTION WEARING THE FIRST GAS MASKS, YPRES, 1915

JULY, 1915

remove or destroy it, and an officer arrived shortly afterwards and placed a charge under it. The fuse was lighted, but no explosion followed. Preparations for a second attempt were then made, and the spectators retired to the dug-out. This time the effort was successful, but instead of an explosion there was a dense cloud of gas, which poured down the dugout steps. No damage was done, but Headquarters had to go without their dinner that night.

The Battalion was relieved by the Leicesters on the night of the 11th and went back for a week's rest in the hutments near Poperinghe.

On the 19th, the Battalion again returned to the front line, relieving the Leicesters in trenches south of the Verlorenhoek road with two and a half companies in the firing line and the remainder in support.

The following extracts from the Battalion War Diary indicate that the men were in very good spirits at this time. No doubt the arrival of the big draft had had an excellent effect on everyone, but the most important influence was the increased output of shells and munitions at home which was enabling the British Army to adopt more aggressive tactics.

"*July* 22nd.—Enemy snipers in neighbourhood of Stink Houses (called Oder Houses on the map) repressed by ours. A few bombs, rifle and hand, thrown at the same place and replied to by us with interest. Our snipers claim to have hit an enemy officer observing, and several men.

"*July* 23rd.—Our snipers again claim successes, especially with the aid of Espitaloir periscope rifles.

"*July* 24th.—Fire and reserve line shelled with high explosives. Our artillery retaliated and quietened the enemy guns. Following message from O.C., C Company, aptly describes to-day:

> 'Twelve little Willies at noon to the tick,
> Got our heads down, and got 'em down quick,
> Peaceful and calm was the rest of the day,
> Nobody hurt and nothing to say.'

"*July* 25th.—Some bombs and grenades at Stink Houses during the night. Replied to, with two or three to one, and few well-placed rifle grenades, which quietened the enemy's aggressiveness."

On the 26th, the Battalion was relieved by the West Yorks and went into Brigade support just north of Ypres, where it remained until August 2nd. Although there was considerable shelling in the neighbourhood, especially on July 30th and

31st, during the German attack at Hooge and the subsequent counter-attacks, the Battalion only suffered a few casualties. On July 17th, Captain H. J. Flower, K.R.R.C., who had been Adjutant of the Queen's Westminsters since November, 1913, left the Battalion on his appointment as Brigade-Major of the 85th Infantry Brigade. Reference has already been made to his work for the Battalion before the War. His services, during the difficult and strenuous times following the order for mobilisation and while he was with the Battalion in France, were invaluable. He had a keen sense of humour, and his unfailing cheerfulness under all circumstances made him an ever-welcome comrade. Colonel Shoolbred writes of him: "It is really impossible to set out what the Battalion, and most certainly the Commanding Officer, owes to his indomitable spirit and sound and soldierly advice. It came to him to be Adjutant of the Battalion during the period of its first war-service, and to no one could it have been possible to give more effectively of his best, nor to give it with better effect. And when he was eventually hit, in the attack on the Hohenzollern Redoubt in 1915, and received a wound from which he never really recovered, the British Army lost a very gallant and very able officer."

HOOGE, AUGUST 9TH, 1915

On July 30th, the 14th Division was attacked at Hooge, liquid fire being employed, and was driven from the extremity of the spur along which runs the Menin road, back to the borders of Sanctuary Wood and Zouave Wood. Battalions which had just been relieved from the line were hurried back to counter-attack. The counter-attacks were unsuccessful, and it became evident that a deliberate and carefully planned attack would be required to recapture the lost position, the vital importance of which lay in the fact that it overlooked a wide stretch of country to the west. Orders were accordingly issued on August 1st, entrusting this task to the 6th Division, and during the two following days the Division was withdrawn from the line to prepare for the attack.

The Queen's Westminsters were relieved on the night of August 2nd by the Liverpool Scottish (with whom they had sailed in the s.s. *Maidan* in 1914), and moved back into billets at Poperinghe. On the 5th, the Battalion moved forward, into support in the ramparts at Ypres, relieving the 6th D.C.L.I. (43rd Infantry Brigade) with three companies in the casemates south of the Menin Gate and one company billeted near the water tower.

HOOGE

Orders were received on August 7th for the attack on the Hooge Ridge, which was to be made by the 18th Infantry Brigade on the right, and the 16th Infantry Brigade on the

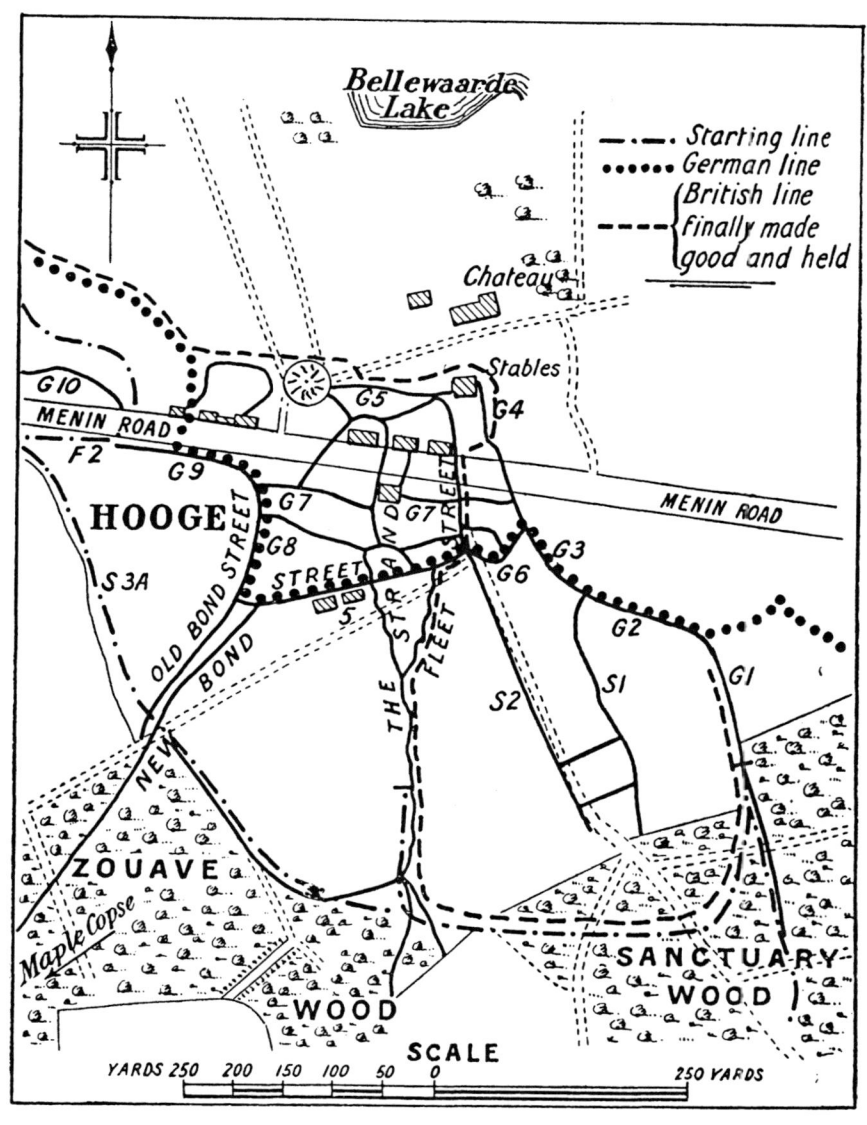

HOOGE, AUGUST 9TH, 1915

left, with the 17th in reserve. The attack on the right was to be launched from Sanctuary Wood, with its right on the captured British trenches known as G1, G2 and G3, and its left on " The Strand " communication trench (see Sketch

Map). It had for its first objective the establishment of a line continuing G3 across the Menin road, and thence north of the houses to the mine crater exclusive. The attack on the left was to start with its right on Old Bond Street communication trench, and was to prolong this line from the crater inclusive; and, as the two attacks converged, touch between the two brigades was to be gained by working inwards from both flanks down G5, G6 and G7.

The D.L.I. were ordered to lead the assault with the Sherwood Foresters in support, the disposition of the 18th Infantry Brigade at the commencement of the attack being as follows :—

D.L.I. in the northern part of Sanctuary Wood facing north-west and about 150 yards from the north-western edge of the wood, their right resting on G1, and their left in touch with the East Yorks, near the junction of Sanctuary and Zouave Woods.

Sherwood Foresters immediately in rear of the D.L.I.

East Yorks in Zouave Wood.

Q.W.R. in reserve in Maple Copse (sometimes called Maple Wood), under the immediate hand of the Brigadier.

On the night of the 8th, the battalions moved up to their assembly positions, the Q.W.R. reaching the dugouts near advanced Brigade Headquarters in Maple Copse about midnight.

The artillery programme for this attack is generally recognised as marking a very great advance in the methods of co-operation between artillery and infantry. The movements of the assaulting troops were regulated by time, the infantry being ordered to advance " exactly at the time ordered, and regardless of what the artillery were doing," and for the first time an organised attempt was made by the British troops to work quite close up to a barrage.[1] It met with conspicuous success.

To continue with reference to the 18th Infantry Brigade. The preliminary bombardment commenced on August 7th, the enemy's position being shelled with evident success during the night and in the morning, both on the 7th and 8th August.

An intense bombardment of the enemy lines commenced at 2.45 a.m. on the 9th, and was continued until 3.15 a.m.,

---

[1] The term " barrage," which had not yet come into general use in the British Army, does not occur in the orders for the attack. In this action the barrage did not creep forward simultaneously with the advancing infantry, but remained stationary on the objective, only lifting at the actual moment of the final assault.

The word " barrage " dates in our Army from the Battle of Neuve Chapelle, March, 1915; but the " creeping barrage " was not employed by us until August, 1916, during the Battles of the Somme.

when the guns lifted. Ten minutes before the finish of the bombardment the D.L.I. got out of their trenches, removed the wire, which had previously been prepared, and worked their way slowly towards the enemy lines. At 3.15 a.m. the men jumped up and dashed into the German trenches which were occupied within ten minutes of the start, most of the occupants surrendering or being bayoneted at once.

On the left, the position was consolidated with little difficulty; on the right, the Durhams pushed on to their objective, and G1, G2 and G3 were also occupied. These trenches were very exposed, the enemy artillery being able to fire on them from the north, the east and the south, and serious losses were incurred by the Sherwood Foresters and the Durhams, and by the East Yorks who had been sent up to reinforce the assaulting infantry.

At 4.45 a.m. orders were received by the Queen's Westminsters to hold two companies in readiness to move, and at 5.5 a.m. C and D Companies were sent forward to Sanctuary Wood to report to the Officer Commanding the Durhams, one company being placed at the disposal of the Durhams to be used only in case of great urgency.

The companies were at first sent up to reinforce the firing line, but they were withdrawn again to the trenches in Sanctuary Wood, from which the attack had been launched, without actually becoming involved in the fighting. They remained in the same position during the remainder of the day and were employed in carrying bombs, ammunition and sandbags forward to the captured trenches. This work was attended with great difficulty, for the enemy maintained a continuous and heavy artillery bombardment throughout the day, and the ground was swept with rifle and machine-gun fire. The upper portion of S2 communication trench was obliterated so that all movement had to take place across the open.

At about 11.0 a.m. the Germans opened an intense bombardment on G1, G2 and G3; and by noon all these trenches had been badly blown in and were held only by isolated groups of the Sherwood Foresters. Later in the afternoon G2 and G3 were completely flattened out, and the southern part of G1 was organised for defence, with a machine gun posted to enfilade its front.

The enemy bombardment on this part of the front continued until about 8.0 p.m. when, after a sudden burst lasting about ten minutes, it died down.

In the meantime, under heavy shelling, the Durhams had been holding on all day to the line they had occupied between the crater and the stables, but they were ordered in the evening to withdraw.

At 9.45 p.m., the Queen's Westminsters relieved the Durhams and Sherwood Foresters in the Sanctuary Wood trenches as far east as G1, and up G1 as far as the northern edge of the wood, linking up with the 139th Infantry Brigade on the right.

The enemy made no attempt to counter-attack, and the Queen's Westminsters sent out bearer parties, covered by patrols, who worked all night collecting wounded in the neighbourhood of G1, G2 and G3. A thick fog in the early morning of August 10th enabled them, unobserved by the enemy, to continue their work until 5.0 a.m., and a great many wounded were brought in.

Early in the morning of August 10th, four officers and about fifty men of the Durhams, who had not previously received the messages ordering them to withdraw, came back to Battalion Headquarters. It was thought that these were the last survivors of those who had gone forward; but in the afternoon a message was received from a further party, of about fifty men, that they were still holding on near the stables and needed reinforcements. These men ultimately rejoined their battalion.

During the whole of the 10th, the trenches occupied by the Queen's Westminsters, the ground in front, and the top of the ridge near the Menin road, were very heavily shelled, but the enemy did not attempt any counter-attack. At night, the Battalion was relieved by the 1st Royal Fusiliers and withdrew to huts in the woods to the north-east of Poperinghe.

The action of Hooge was a very successful operation. The main object of the attack, namely, the capture of the extremity of the Hooge Ridge, was completely attained, and further ground was captured north of the Menin road. In addition to this very heavy casualties were undoubtedly inflicted on the enemy.

Having regard to the fact that the Battalion had been under practically continuous shell-fire for nearly forty-eight hours, the losses were very light. On the 9th, 8 other ranks were killed; and 1 officer and 26 other ranks wounded. On the 10th, 1 officer, Lieut. D. M. Hutchison, was killed, and 1 officer, Captain Henshaw and 5 other ranks were wounded.

Lieutenant Hutchison was killed while in command of the Battalion Machine-Gun Section, which he had only taken over on the day of the attack. His death was felt keenly by all ranks. Posted to B Company at the end of 1914, he had

AUGUST, 1915

been one of the first officers to be sent out by the 2nd Battalion. The qualities of sportsmanship that had made him a distinguished leader in games at Murchiston College had stood him in good stead in France, and he was in every way a most capable and promising young officer. He was one of those to whom was given, in a most peculiar degree, the gift of making himself loved by all.

The Battalion remained at rest near Poperinghe until August 23rd. On the 14th it was inspected by General Sir H. Plumer, K.C.B., Commanding the Second Army, and by Major-General W. N. Congreve, V.C., Commanding the 6th Division, both of whom thanked it for the work done during the attack on Hooge.

On the 20th, another very fine draft of men arrived from the 2nd Battalion. The men are described in the Diary as "equal to the best traditions of the Q.W.R." The hopes of the 2nd Battalion of going out as a unit were once more deferred, but the splendid material being sent out as drafts was deeply appreciated by the 1st Battalion.

On the 23rd, Poperinghe was heavily shelled. One shell landed right into a factory in which two companies were billeted, destroying the staircase as well as a good many kits. Fortunately the company commander had withdrawn the men as soon as the shelling started, and by so doing saved very many casualties. The only casualties caused, were to a party of men who were bathing, 2 other ranks being killed and 2 wounded.

On the same day, eight subalterns from 15th (Service) Battalion of the Middlesex Regiment were posted to the Battalion. In the evening the 18th Infantry Brigade relieved the 41st and 16th Infantry Brigades, taking over the line from a point 200 yards south of the Verlorenhoek road to a point 400 yards north-west of Wieltje Farm. The Queen's Westminsters were in support, with Battalion Headquarters on the canal bank about a mile north of Ypres, and the companies in trenches in various supporting points east of Potijze and at St. Jean. They remained in these trenches until September 2nd, when they relieved the Sherwood Foresters in the front line just north of the Verlorenhoek road.

The enemy's artillery became more active again at the end of August. On the 30th, the trenches occupied by the Battalion were heavily shelled by 5-in. howitzers, parts being completely destroyed. On the 31st, an enemy airman flew over the trenches, firing at them with his machine gun, and also dropping eight bombs, which fortunately fell outside the trench and did no harm.

The Battalion remained in the line until September 9th. The weather turned very wet on the 2nd, and the heavy downfalls of rain so damaged the trenches that the whole energies of the Battalion were barely able to cope with the work of repairing them. All new works had to be abandoned. The only point of satisfaction under such conditions was that the enemy were probably in an equally unpleasant plight.

The following are extracts from the War Diary :—

"*September 2nd.*—Very heavy rain at night making work on trenches almost impossible.

"*September 3rd.*—Wet all day. Communication trenches running streams, fire trenches very wet, knee-deep in places. Stopped raining at night.

"*September 4th.*—Communication trenches like running rivers. Baling, and building parapets. Enemy doing likewise."

St. Jean and its neighbourhood was heavily bombarded every day between the 5th and 8th, and on the 6th the enemy succeeded in bringing down the tower of the village church. In connection with the habitual shelling of St. Jean, the following note by Lieut.-Colonel Shoolbred is of considerable interest :—

" In this matter ' Fritz ' seemed very wanting in ' *nous* ' ; he always shelled this unfortunate church tower and the cross road in the centre of the village where nobody ever stayed. His daily ' strafe' hardly ever touched our positions, which were either well in front of or well in rear of the ruins of the village. Moreover, he always strafed at the same time of day, usually from noon to one o'clock, so that we could quite easily arrange our day's work without being interfered with by his nuisances."

On the 9th, the Battalion was relieved by troops of the 16th Infantry Brigade and moved back to the hutments near Poperinghe, where it remained for a week. On the evening of the 16th, it went into Brigade reserve, relieving the " Buffs " in Brielen. Heavy shelling, both with H.E. and gas, made existence very unpleasant, Battalion H.Q. and some of the billets having to be moved on the 21st. On the same day one company was moved up to the Potijze defences, and one company into the Kaaie Salient. The shelling in these localities grew more intense than before, and on the 23rd the company in the Kaaie Salient was sent out to more healthy surroundings on the canal bank.

On September 25th, the British and French armies assumed the offensive. The 6th Division was not actually engaged, but co-operated in the attack on the enemy positions about Bellewaarde immediately on the right, by fire and by a simulated gas attack, in which various devices for making smoke were used for the first time by the Division. The Battalion came in for a good deal of retaliatory shelling, but otherwise took no part in the operations.

On the 27th, the Queen's Westminsters relieved the Sherwood Foresters in the front line to the north of the Verlorenhoek road. Wet weather again set in, and for the last few days of September the activities of both sides were mainly confined to repairing collapsed trenches, and trying to free them from water.

The enemy artillery increased in intensity at the beginning of October, and the snipers became more active. On October 2nd, Captain R. S. Dickinson was killed by a shell. He had joined the Battalion on the outbreak of war, and came out to France with it in 1914. His happy and cheery character, his fearlessness and his power of leadership, had made him implicitly trusted as well as beloved by his seniors and adored by his company.

For some time the enemy had been directing unwelcome attention to the trenches in the neighbourhood of Stink Houses, and was reported to be sapping towards the British lines; but a patrol sent out on the 1st to search for this reported sap could find no trace of it.

At 8.45 a.m. on the 4th, the enemy started a heavy trench-mortar bombardment on Oder Houses. Lieutenant F. G. Swainson, who had succeeded to the command of A Company after the death of Captain Dickinson, immediately asked for artillery retaliation. Fire was opened at once by the 24th Battery, R.A. The garrisons of the posts were ordered to withdraw into a communication trench, covered by parties of bombers, under Lieutenant Strauss, who remained at the head of the communication trenches to stop any attempt by the enemy to rush them.

The enemy's artillery replied vigorously to the British guns, blowing in the parapet of a saphead and damaging a dugout, and causing the bombers to withdraw further down the trench. British heavies, however, opened fire and silenced the enemy's mortars, after which the enemy guns ceased fire, and the garrison of the trench returned to their posts. Very good work on this occasion was done by Rifleman R. W. Lowman, a signaller, who maintained communication with company headquarters from the destroyed saphead throughout the affair; and by Sergeant S. Tucker who displayed great coolness while in command of the party holding the saphead when it was destroyed, and again, in the evening, when he went out alone and repaired the damaged wire under heavy sniping from the German sap only eighteen yards away.

The promptness of Lieutenant Swainson in grasping the situation and the rapidity with which his call for artillery retaliation was answered, probably saved a further attack that day; for the enemy made another attempt on the same trenches the following morning, after the Battalion had been relieved. After completely flattening out the front trench by his bombardment he effected an entry into the post, but was driven out again later in the day.

The Battalion was relieved on the night of October 4th, by the Sherwood Foresters, and went into billets at Poperinghe. On the 7th, two companies, together with seventy-eight men of the 9th Sussex, who were attached for instruction, moved up into reserve in the neighbourhood of Brielen; and on the 11th, the whole Battalion went into close support in the Potijze defences and at St. Jean. Parties on the way up encountered a considerable amount of shelling on the road, 2 other ranks being killed, and 8 wounded.

On the 17th, the Battalion went into dugouts on the canal bank, leaving one company forward in the Potijze defences; and on the 20th, it relieved the West Yorks in trenches near Wieltje.

The only event of importance during the tour was a useful piece of patrolling by Lieutenant Adams, Sergeant Agate and Rifleman Davidson on the night of October 22nd. After making a reconnaissance of No-man's-land, they lay out in shell-holes until early morning in the hope of being able to harass the enemy. Two German working parties were bombed and sniped by them; the first apparently withdrew, but when the second was attacked reinforcements came up, and the patrol had to return without being able to ascertain the casualties it had inflicted.

On the 23rd, the Battalion was relieved by the East Yorks, and went into billets at Poperinghe, returning to the line in the Potijze section on the 29th to relieve the 11th Essex, who had replaced the Sherwood Foresters in the 18th Infantry Brigade. The month closed with a heavy downpour of rain which caused considerable damage to the communication trenches and a certain amount of flooding, but the fire trenches stood fairly well.

YPRES IN 1915

THE CLOTH HALL

STREET SCENE

DUGOUTS ON THE CANAL BANK, YPRES, 1915

On October 23rd, Captain S. G. L. Bradley took over the duties of Staff-Captain of the 18th Infantry Brigade in succession to Captain C. R. Congreve, D.S.O.

On the 27th His Majesty the King held an inspection of the troops in Flanders, the 18th Infantry Brigade being represented by a company made up of one platoon from each battalion. The following is an extract from an order published after His Majesty had left France :—

SPECIAL ORDER OF THE DAY BY HIS MAJESTY THE KING

Officers, Non-Commissioned Officers, and Men,—

I am happy to have found myself once more with my Armies. . . .

Since I was last among you, you have fought many strenuous battles. In all you have reaped renown and proved yourselves at least equal to the highest traditions of the British Army.

In company with our noble Allies you have baffled the infamous conspiracy against the law and liberty of Europe, so long and insidiously prepared.

These achievements have involved vast sacrifices. But your countrymen, who watch your campaign with sympathetic admiration, will, I am well assured, spare no effort to fill your ranks and afford you all supplies.

I have decorated many of you. But had I decorated all who deserve recognition for conspicuous valour, there would have been no limit, for the whole Army is illustrious.

It is a matter of sincere regret to me that my accident should have prevented my seeing all the troops I had intended, but during my stay amongst you I have seen enough to fill my heart with admiration of your patient, cheerful endurance of life in the trenches : a life either of weary monotony or of terrible tumult. It is the dogged determination evinced by all ranks which will at last bring you to Victory. Keep the goal in sight and remember that it is the final lap that wins.

GEORGE, R.I.

November 1st, 1915.

The Battalion remained in the Potijze section until November 11th. The wet weather which had started at the end of October continued throughout the whole period, and both sides were too busy battling with the water to worry about offensive action. The following extracts from the War Diary need no comment :—

"*November 1st.*—More heavy rain. Trenches become choked by heavy landslides.

"*November 2nd.*—More wet. Water gaining. Notwithstanding heavy fatigues, fire and communication trenches falling in rapidly, being undermined by water.

"*November 3rd.*—Very wet. Heavy work day and night trying to drain trenches, apparently the enemy is equally occupied.

"*November 4th.*—Enemy as busy as ourselves in working on his trenches. Heard and seen baling and pumping.

"*November 6th.*—As a result of continuous work the fire trench is becoming drier, but the parapets keep on falling in. One communication trench has been made passable—not being more than knee-deep anywhere.

"*November 10th.*—Stink House trenches being flooded out; it has been impossible to keep a garrison there as formerly, but a listening post is maintained always ; . . . the level of the fire trench and parapets is being raised above the water-log level."

On the night of the 11th, the Battalion was relieved by the 11th Essex, and went back to the hutments in the woods near Poperinghe.

On November 2nd, Major J. Waley Cohen, who had been second in command of the Battalion since 1911, vacated his appointment on becoming Intelligence Officer to the 18th Infantry Brigade. He joined the Queen's Westminsters in 1893, and from the very first threw himself with characteristic enthusiasm into everything that affected either the efficiency or the welfare of the Regiment. He was specially interested in signalling, and before the war he was Brigade Signalling Officer of the Grey Brigade. His first experience of active service was in South Africa, where he served throughout the war with the City Imperial Volunteers. Of his work with the Battalion in France, Colonel Shoolbred writes : " The Regiment owes him a very deep debt of gratitude for his untiring energy and zeal, which all who served with him, and most certainly myself, fully appreciated."

After leaving the Battalion his record of service was a distinguished one, and he eventually became Director of Communications to the Independent Air Force. He retained this appointment until the end of the war.

The Queen's Westminsters had also lost, by death, two

NOVEMBER–DECEMBER, 1915

valued officers during the last tour in the trenches. In the evening of November 3rd, Captain H. Makins—another one of the first officers of the 2nd Battalion to come out to France, and a younger brother of Captain G. Makins, K.R.R.C., who had been Adjutant from November, 1910, to November, 1913—was killed by a stray bullet while supervising the work of draining a flooded trench. He had joined the Regiment on the outbreak of war and was posted to the Battalion in Houplines at the beginning of 1915. Colonel Shoolbred writes: " He is another of the Sons of the Regiment to whom it owes more than can ever be repaid, and whose memory will always be cherished with affection by all who had the privilege of serving with him, and knowing him. The British Army contained no better officer nor truer comrade." He now rests with his brother, Geoffrey, in the Military Cemetery at Vlamertinghe.

Four days later Lieutenant N. J. Wood was killed by a rifle bullet, in almost exactly the same spot and while employed on similar work. He was one of the eight officers posted to the Queen's Westminsters from the 15th Middlesex in August, and had done good work during the short time he had been with the Battalion.

After a spell of two days in the Wieltje sector, the Battalion was relieved on November 18th by the 6th K.O.Y.L.I., and moved back to hutments near Poperinghe, and on the following day the whole of the 18th Infantry Brigade moved by rail and motor bus to Houtkerque for three weeks' real rest. This was the first rest out of the range of the guns that the Battalion had had since its arrival in France, and it was very much appreciated by everyone.

In December the command of the British Army in France passed to Sir Douglas Haig. The retiring Commander-in-Chief, Field-Marshal Sir J. D. P. French, had paid generous tribute to the services of the Territorial Force in France. His estimate of their value is summed up in the following extracts from his official despatch, dated February 2nd, 1915:—

" In the positions which I held for some years before the outbreak of this War I was brought into close contact with the Territorial Force, and I found every reason to hope and believe that, when the hour of trial arrived, they would justify every hope and trust which was placed in them. . . . I, and the principal Commanders serving under me, consider that the Territorial Force has far more than justified the most sanguine hopes that any of us ventured to entertain of their value and use in the field. . . .

"Army Corps Commanders are loud in their praise of the Territorial battalions which form part of nearly all the brigades at the front in the first line, and more than one of them have told me that these battalions are fast approaching—if they have not already reached—the standard of efficiency of regular infantry."

On December 9th, the period of rest at Houtkerque came to an end, and the Battalion moved forward again to the Potijze section of the Salient. It was first attached for five days to the 42nd Infantry Brigade to furnish parties for digging and work. One of these parties had the misfortune, on the 13th, to be spotted by the enemy as it was on the road, and suffered 11 casualties.

On the 15th the 18th Infantry Brigade took over the line between the Ypres-Roulers railway and Wieltje. The trenches into which the Queen's Westminsters moved were in the centre of the Brigade front; they were known as A5 and A6, and were held continuously by the Battalion until it left the 6th Division in February, 1916. In fact, this portion of the Salient came to be regarded almost as the special property of the Battalion, for the following entry occurs in the Diary of the 18th Infantry Brigade for January: "The Queen's Westminsters continue to hold their own little piece of the line, arranging their own reliefs, having always one company in A5 and A6, one company in the Potijze defences, one company on the canal bank, and one company in Poperinghe." Battalion Headquarters were on the canal bank, and inter-company reliefs took place approximately every three days.

On December 19th, the Battalion had its first experience of a gas attack on a serious scale. Some days previously a German prisoner had disclosed the fact that the enemy, who had dug a large number of gas cylinders into his parapet, was only waiting for a favourable wind before delivering a gas attack on a broad front. The information proved to be correct. Early in the morning of the 19th, gas was discharged on a front of two and three-quarter miles from the Wieltje Salient, on the immediate left of the 18th Infantry Brigade, to the junction of the 49th Division with the French in the north. No gas was discharged on the actual front of the Brigade, but large quantities floated across the Brigade front from the north. No infantry attack developed, though a few Germans left their trenches and followed up the gas cloud. These were probably patrols sent out to investigate the effects of the gas, which was believed to be a new one, consisting of a

GAS ATTACK, DECEMBER 19TH, 1915

mixture of prussic acid and chlorine. Whatever it was, the effects were very insignificant, complete protection being obtained from the gas masks. The gas cloud travelled very rapidly and its effects were felt as far back as Vlamertinghe Château, some three to four miles behind the line.

A Company was then holding the front line, and after the attack the Company Commander (Captain F. G. Swainson) sent in the following report :—

"At 5.15 a.m. approximately, the sentry on the left of our line observed two red rockets in the direction of Wieltje, followed immediately by the throb of an engine. A dense grey cloud was seen rolling towards the trenches on our left. The sentry promptly alarmed the Company, which at once stood to, after adjusting their gas helmets. The Germans then shrapnelled the road and communication trenches behind our lines. The platoon in reserve was sent up to reinforce the front line, and to assist in endeavouring to dispel the gas by rapid fire, should it be directed against us. The gas cloud on our left dispersed in about ten minutes. The enemy then opened general shelling, and the supporting platoon was withdrawn to S.L. (a trench). They shelled the front line, but only succeeded in knocking in one bay. Crump Farm, the Schools on the Verlorenhoek road, and the ground in between the buildings were heavily shelled with heavy, high velocity, H.E. and shrapnel. Aerial torpedoes were used against the left of the road. Our guns retaliated, securing many direct hits on the German front line and the mound. Several of our shells, however, before daylight, dropped short, one H.E. falling in our wire (causing no casualties). The trench howitzer in this trench scored a direct hit in the German trench opposite. At 7.10 a.m. two green rockets were sent up from the direction of Wieltje. This had no apparent effect on the shelling. At 8.30 a.m. the strafing ceased. The only casualty suffered by the Company was one man slightly wounded in the hand."

It is almost inconceivable how this company escaped really serious casualties, for it was heavily shelled for just over three hours. C Company, which was sent up from the canal bank to the trenches in the Kaaie Salient at 6.30 a.m. by order of the Brigade Commander, was less fortunate, and lost 4 men killed and 11 wounded in a very short time. It was withdrawn at about 9.0 a.m. on to the canal bank, which was continuously shelled, more or less heavily, the whole day and during the following night. The garrison of the Potijze defences escaped with one other rank killed and one wounded, although this locality was heavily shelled.

The stretcher-bearers, as usual, displayed self-sacrificing gallantry in tending the wounded under heavy shell-fire and gas. Amongst them were Rifleman W. G. Nicholls, C Company, and Rifleman A. M. Wingfield and Bugler R. Barrow, A Company. Rifleman Wingfield, who afterwards received a commission in the Regiment, had also specially distinguished himself on a previous occasion by running in broad daylight along the parados of the fire trench for over a hundred yards, in answer to a call for stretcher-bearers.

During the night and the following day there were numerous gas alarms, due both to the wind clearing out affected areas and shell-holes, and to the shelling of Ypres with gas and lachrymatory shells. A westerly wind, which set in during the evening of the 20th, followed by rain, removed the possibility of any immediate resumption of gas attacks by the enemy.

For December 25th the following entry was made in the War Diary: " Christmas Day passed quietly. There was no sort of repetition of last year's truce. The Germans shouted across to our men, but receiving no encouragement the conversations ceased. The Germans shelled the school behind S6 about noon and at 1 p.m., and put some twenty whizz-bangs into the Potijze defences. They hit the corner of Glasier's dugout, and knocked a bottle of whisky off the table on to the floor, but by a merciful providence it did not break."

And for the 26th: " In retaliation for a shoot by the British 9.2's, the Germans put about twenty ' crumps,' three-quarters of which did not explode, near Crump Farm, and sprinkled the front trenches with shrapnel and whizz-bangs, without causing any casualties."

The 28th was a very sad day for the Battalion. Major N. B. Tyrwhitt, the second in command, who had gone up to Potijze with Lieut.-Colonel Goring Jones, D.L.I. (temporarily commanding the Brigade), was killed in the big French dug-out there, by a shell which landed right into it. A man of the highest character and a born soldier and leader of men, he was respected and loved by all who knew him. He had been a member of the Regiment since 1891, and had served through the South African War. His work for the Queen's Westminsters cannot be overestimated. He had just been recommended for command of the 3rd Battalion, and it was daily expected that he would be leaving to take up his appointment. No better tribute can be paid to his memory than this entry in the War Diary : " His loss is a very great one to the Regiment, both as tried and trusty officer and comrade in arms in this Battalion in which he had given such loyal and good service for so many years."

The year closed with the usual shelling on both sides ; a special New Year's greeting to the enemy being sent in the form of an hour's bombardment of his lines.

Very active patrolling of No-man's-land commenced towards the end of December, and continued during the remainder of the Battalion's stay in the Salient. The particular objects which interested the patrols most were the Mound and the Stables. Suspicious noises were constantly being heard from these places, and much interest was aroused as to what caused them, and what the enemy was " up to " in the neighbourhood. The work of the patrols and the information gained is best told in the words of the War Diary; but it is well to bear in mind what patrolling actually meant to those engaged in it. First, the object to be attained had to be determined, then the map had to be studied, and the ground over which the patrol was to work had to be examined in daylight, either through a periscope or by glancing over the parapet. At night the patrol, the artillery having previously been warned of the hour of its going and of its return so as to avoid shelling the neighbourhood, would make its way at the appointed hour through the British wire, and proceed as best it could through the mud and slime towards the enemy's lines. On a quiet night the slightest sound was sufficient to arouse the suspicions of the enemy, and in a moment the ground would be lit up by Verey lights from all along the trench, bombs would be thrown, and rifle and machine-gun fire opened ; or a party of Germans would be encountered in No-man's-land. Then, depending on its mission, whether it was to fight or gather information, the patrol would go for the enemy, or lie quietly in a shell-hole hoping to escape observation. The work necessarily had to be done in darkness, and often in driving rain or bitter cold. It was most exhausting, and could not fail to put a severe strain on even the strongest nerves.

The following details of the work of the patrols are extracted from the War Diaries of the 18th Infantry Brigade and of the Battalion, for December and January :—

" *December* 22*nd*.—(18th Infantry Brigade.) Q.W.R. patrol out last night from A6, reports having found, about

9 p.m., twenty or thirty of the enemy engaged, apparently, in putting up wire south of the Mound near the Stables. Enemy seen to be carrying what appeared to be stakes, but nothing suggesting hammering, etc., was seen, or heard. Patrol unable to get close up owing to an enemy covering party fifty yards in front of the working party.

"*December 24th.*—Observation during the day confirms the opinion that the enemy is working—sapping in some way—between the Mound and the old Stables.

"*December 30th.*—During night of 29th and 30th a patrol from D Company, consisting of Sergeant Cooper, Lance-Corporal Farley, and Rifleman Salmon, went out at 9.30 p.m. from A6, and lay for some time within the Stables ; but neither saw nor heard any signs of enemy occupation. It then made its way through a hedge and two ditches full of water, and lay listening for some time. No enemy listening post could be observed. It then crawled through the Stables, and proceeded to the Mound, where it remained for some considerable time. Nothing was heard or seen of the enemy, and when clods of earth were thrown about they attracted no attention. . . . The patrol came to the conclusion that the supposed movements of the enemy in the Stables were really nothing more than the wind among the ruins, as Sergeant Cooper himself noticed the same when he was there. The patrol returned safely at 11.25 p.m., having done a very valuable reconnaissance with great thoroughness and ability, all the more as the Mound was certainly expected to have been found to be occupied at night. It reflects the greatest credit on Sergeant Cooper and the other two men.

"*January 3rd.*—2nd Lieutenant Horne with Riflemen May and Roper tried to get into the Mound, but this time it was found to be occupied. They also saw men in the trench, or ditch, by the fence.

"*January 8th.*—Patrol to the Stables on the night of 7/8th, from 11.0 p.m. to 12.30 a.m. Found no signs of activity in the Mound, though some talking and whistling was heard."

Throughout the rest of the month the Mound was kept under constant observation. Germans were frequently observed there, and several were claimed to have been hit by snipers and by the trench mortars. To vary the bag a partridge was shot one day between the lines. It was recovered and sent down to Battalion Headquarters as a present to the Commanding Officer.

On February 1st, the Queen's Westminsters were with-

YPRES
1915 — 1916

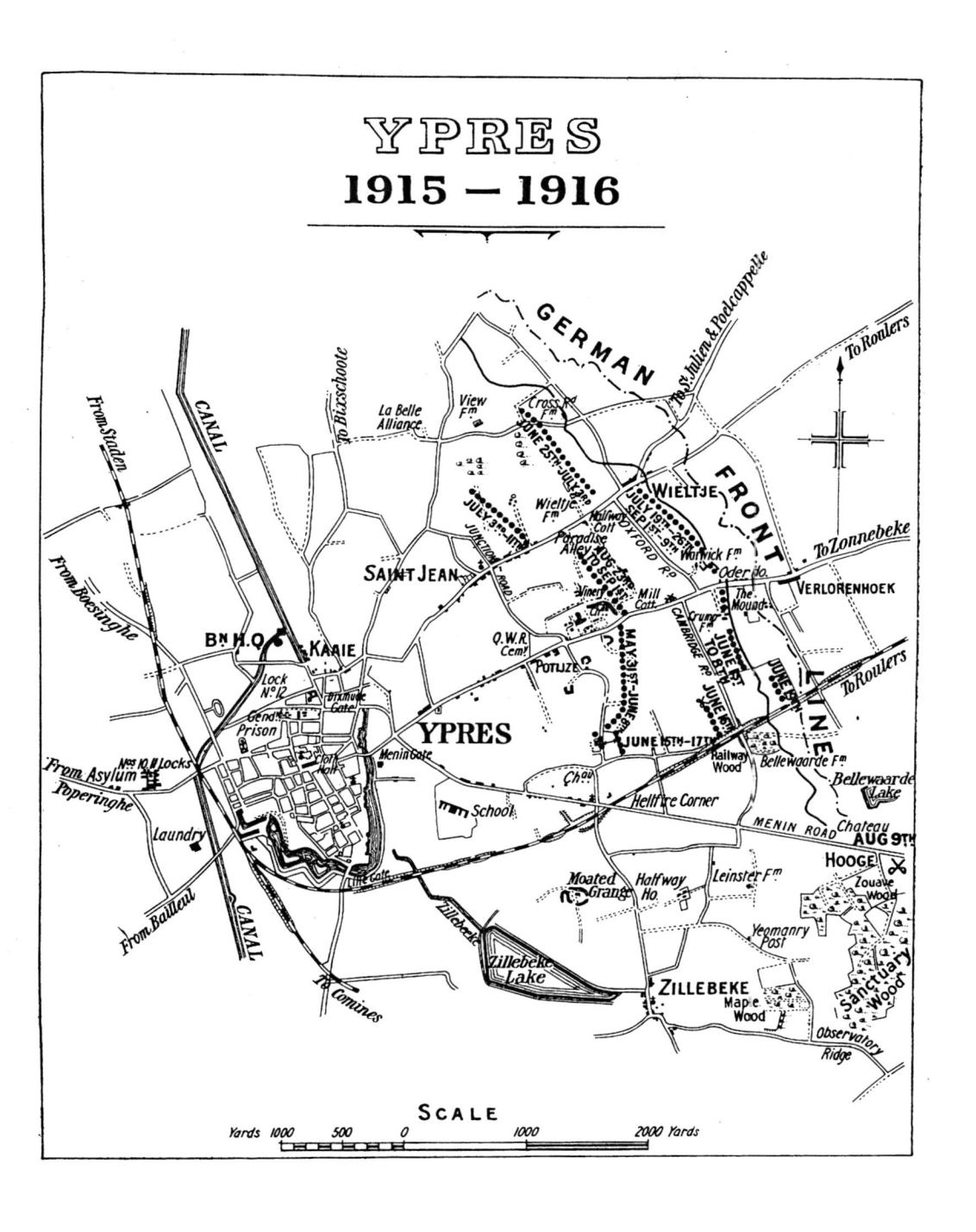

drawn from the front line altogether; and by the 6th the whole Battalion was concentrated at Poperinghe to be refitted in preparation for its transfer from the 6th to the 56th (London) Division, then in process of formation.

On the 8th, General Sir H. Plumer, K.C.B., Commanding the Second Army, inspected the Battalion; and, after thanking it for its work and complimenting it on its efficiency, wished it success, and bade all ranks good-bye.

On the following day, when the Battalion left the Ypres front and the 6th Division, Brigadier-General R. J. Bridgeford, C.M.G., D.S.O., Commanding the 18th Infantry Brigade, came down from the canal bank to bid the Battalion farewell; and at 9.30 p.m. the Queen's Westminsters entrained at Poperinghe to join their new Division.

During the eight months spent in the Ypres Salient the Battalion lost nearly 1100 officers and other ranks from death, wounds and sickness, and over 100 other ranks received commissions or were transferred to Cadet Schools. Of the original officers who came out with the Battalion, Major J. Waley Cohen, Captain H. J. Flower, K.R.R.C. (Adjutant), Captain S. G. L. Bradley, and Captain W. M. Henderson-Scott left to take up Staff appointments in France; Captain G. H. Lambert left for England for instructional duties and was subsequently appointed to command the 3rd Battalion; and Quartermaster and Honorary Captain Kelly was invalided home. Captain Kelly was appointed Adjutant of the 3rd Battalion in 1916, and thus continued, in another capacity, the excellent work that he had done with the Queen's Westminsters in France. Reference has already been made to his work as Regimental Sergeant-Major before the war, and while the Battalion was training at Leverstock Green.

CHAPTER VI

WITH THE 56TH DIVISION—TRAINING FOR THE OFFENSIVE

THE 56th (1st London) Territorial Division[1] was formed in France in February, 1916. The units posted to it were already well seasoned to war, for they were the original first-line Territorial battalions who had been serving in the trenches with the infantry brigades of the first six regular divisions since the latter part of 1914.

The composition of the Division on its formation was as follows :—[2]

Divisional Commander
Major-General C. P. A. Hull.

G.S.O.I. Lieut.-Colonel J. Brind, D.S.O., R.A.
A.A. and Q.M.G. Lieut.-Colonel H. W. Grubb, D.S.O.
C.R.E. Lieut.-Colonel H. W. Gordon, R.E.
C.R.A. Brigadier-General R. J. G. Elkington, C.M.G., R.A.

Infantry Brigades

167*th Infantry Brigade.* Brigadier-General F. H. Nugent :
1/7th Battalion Middlesex Regiment.
1/8th Battalion Middlesex Regiment.
1/1st Battalion London Royal Fusiliers.
1/3rd Battalion London Royal Fusiliers.

168*th Infantry Brigade.* Brigadier-General G. G. Loch, C.M.G. :
1/4th Battalion London Royal Fusiliers.
Rangers (1/12th Battalion London Regiment).
Kensingtons (1/13th Battalion London Regiment).
London Scottish (1/14th Battalion London Regiment).

169*th Infantry Brigade.* Brigadier-General E. S. D'E. Coke, C.M.G. :
2nd Londons (1/2nd Battalion London Royal Fusiliers).
London Rifle Brigade (1/5th Battalion London Regiment).
Queen Victoria Rifles (1/9th Battalion London Regiment).
Queen's Westminster Rifles (1/16th Battalion London Regiment).

[1] The 2nd London Division (the 47th Division) went to France as a unit in March, 1915.
[2] The honours are those held in February, 1916.

Divisional Troops

B Squadron. 2nd King Edward's Horse.
1/1st London Divisional Cyclist Company.
1/1st London Brigade, R.F.A. (1st, 2nd, 3rd City of London Batteries) (12–18 pounders).
1/2nd London Brigade, R.F.A. (4th, 5th, 6th County of London Batteries) (12–18 pounders).
1/3rd London Brigade, R.F.A. (7th, 8th, 9th County of London Batteries) (12–18 pounders).
1/4th London Brigade, R.F.A. (10th and 11th County of London Batteries) (8–4.5" howitzers).
56th Divisional Ammunition Column.
2/1st, 2/2nd London Field Companies, R.E.
56th Divisional Signal Company.
Pioneer Battalion, 1/5th Cheshire Regiment.
56th Divisional Train.
2/1st, 2/2nd, and 2/3rd London Field Ambulance.
56th Divisional Ambulance Workshop.
1/1st London Sanitary Section.
1/1st London Mobile Veterinary Section.

(The initials L.R.B. and Q.V.R. will be used throughout the remainder of this history to designate the 1/5th and 1/9th Londons respectively.)

The only change in the composition of the infantry brigades, throughout the remainder of the war, took place in February, 1918, when all the infantry brigades were reduced from a four-battalion to a three-battalion establishment. To the great regret of all, this reduction necessitated the temporary disbandment of the 1st Battalions of the 3rd Londons, the Rangers, and Q.V.R.

Major-General Sir C. P. Amyatt Hull commanded the Division until July 20th, 1917, and again from May 4th, 1918, until after the Armistice. Except for one month in 1917, when Major-General W. Douglas Smith was in command, the Division was commanded during the absence of Major-General Hull by Major-General F. A. Dudgeon.

Brigadier-General E. S. D'E. Coke remained in command of the 169th Infantry Brigade throughout the remainder of the war, relinquishing his appointment in March, 1919.

The following held the appointments of Brigade Major and Staff Captain to the 169th Infantry Brigade during the war:

Brigade Major:

March, 1916–May, 1917.   Captain L. A. Newnham.
June, 1917–March, 1918. Captain W. Carden Roe, M.C.
May, 1918–March, 1919.   Lieutenant (Tempy. Captain) T. G. McCarthy.

Staff Captain:

March, 1916–November, 1917.   Captain E. R. Broadbent.
December, 1917–March, 1919.   2nd Lieutenant (Tempy. Captain) F. Bishop.

Although there were many regrets on the part of the Queen's Westminsters at leaving the 6th Division, after having served in it for so many months, these regrets were tempered by the thought that the new Division, a London one, was composed of regiments who had served together and trained together both before and after mobilisation, and had known one another as friends and friendly rivals for very many years. These old associations were the foundation of the strong Divisional and Brigade *esprit de corps* which asserted itself from the first, and gave birth to the keen offensive spirit which characterised the Division in every engagement in which it took part.

The Queen's Westminsters joined the 56th Division on February 10th, 1916, when, after detraining at Pont Remy, the Battalion marched[1] to Huppy, and reported to the 169th Infantry Brigade. The 2nd Londons and L.R.B. also joined on the 10th, and with the arrival of the Q.V.R., three days later, the establishment of the Brigade was complete.

No time was lost in commencing training. After spending the 11th in improving the barns and stables in which the men were billeted, the Battalion started preliminary work on the 12th, pending the issue of the Divisional scheme which was to come into operation on the 21st.

The general principles on which the training was to proceed, were set out in an explanatory memorandum issued by the Division, from which the following are extracts :—

" Throughout the whole system of training the vital importance of imbuing all ranks with the offensive spirit will be insisted on, this will be the personal concern of brigade and

---

[1] It is interesting to note that during this march the Battalion crossed the Somme at Pont Remy, where the crossing was reconnoitred in force before the Battle of Crécy in 1346. It was then found to be guarded, and the party pushed on to sound another crossing lower down the river.

other commanders. . . . It is of the highest importance that a good understanding should exist between the artillery and the infantry whom they support. . . . To sum up, all training and schemes should be based on one of the following three phases of war, which are placed in order of importance : *First.*—The attack from trenches of a strongly fortified and prepared position, such as exists all along our front. *Secondly.*—The rapid consolidation and strengthening of a defensive position, with the view of reducing to a minimum the number of rifles required to hold it, thus releasing numbers for offensive action elsewhere. *Thirdly.*—The attack of rearguard positions and pursuit in the open."

Training continued until February 25th, when it was interrupted by a heavy fall of snow, and large working parties were employed on clearing roads.

On the 27th, the Brigade marched to Ailly, about twelve miles away. The roads were covered with snow and the weather was very bad ; but the Battalion was again rapidly getting into good marching condition, and the improvement in the physical fitness of the men showed itself in the way the march was accomplished.

The Battalion remained at Ailly, where three companies were billeted in barns and one company in the schools, until March 12th, when the Brigade moved on to the Fienvillers-Gezaincourt area, the Battalion being billeted at Gezaincourt. On March 16th, the Battalion marched, as part of the Brigade group, to Monchaux, a village in the VI Corps reserve area.

It was known by this time that the Division was being specially trained to take part in an offensive on a very big scale, and special attention was paid to practising the attack on an entrenched position. In the ordinary trench warfare, such as had been experienced for the past fifteen months, there had been little opportunity for the use of the rifle, and practically none for the employment of fire tactics, with the result that the bomb and the bayonet had come to be considered the most effective weapons of the infantry soldier. Colonel Shoolbred writes of the musketry training of the Battalion at this time, as follows : " Although we honestly did our utmost in the Battalion to emphasise the fact that the rifle (primarily to shoot with, and secondarily, but most importantly, with the ' sword ' on it) must and should always be considered the infantryman's real weapon, it must be acknowledged that it was found impossible to carry out all the musketry training that the commanding officer desired. This was due to two causes, namely, limited range accommodation, and lack of time owing to the amount of specialised training which had to be carried out. The most thorough training, however, was carried out in what were the most essential of all the uses of the rifle under the conditions of the war, namely, rapid loading and bayonet fighting. It can confidently be said that not a single man went into action at Gommecourt, on July 1st, 1916, without the confident knowledge that he was master of his weapon in these two respects."

Each battalion in the Brigade had a special bombing officer, who was in charge of the Battalion " grenadier party," and was also responsible for training all bombers. The Battalion " grenadier party " consisted of an officer, a sergeant, a corporal, and three parties of nine men each ; and, in addition to these, each company had a specially trained bombing section. Lieutenant P. Spencer Smith (who was severely wounded and taken prisoner on July 1st, 1916) was the first battalion bombing officer of the Queen's Westminsters.

During the training many demonstrations were given in the use of new devices of war, and in the tactical handling of men under conditions such as were likely to prevail in the approaching offensive. Work, too, of a more or less experimental character, was done in connection with such matters as the use of smoke, and methods of communication between infantry and aircraft.

On April 6th, the Q.V.R. gave a demonstration of infantry advancing in various formations; and as a result of this, it is interesting to note that it was agreed that the most suitable formation for a company advancing under artillery fire was by platoons in fours.

On April 1st, a demonstration was given, at the Divisional School at Givenchy, of an attack on trenches under cover of a smoke barrage created by " P " bombs, and of the production of smoke by the use of smoke candles and Fumite bombs. On the 9th, the chemical adviser of the Third Army gave a demonstration with a captured enemy Flammenwerfer, in the course of which one spray, lasting about forty-five seconds, was put over a trench containing 135 men, without harming them in the least. " The demonstration showed," states the Divisional War Diary, " that a man keeping low in a trench has nothing to fear from liquid fire apparatus. It is a weapon more terrifying than dangerous."

On April 17th, the 169th Brigade machine-gun company was formed, and Captain J. B. Baber, Q.W.R., was appointed second in command of the company.

As a result of the experience gained during the training, and after several conferences of Brigadiers and Battalion Commanders, a memorandum, containing suggestions for the training of drafts for the 56th Division, was drawn up and sent to the draft-producing units in England who furnished reinforcements for the infantry of the Division. The requirements of commanding officers were summed up in the following words: " What commanding officers most want in the drafts they receive are, in the case of officers, those who know how to command men, and to drill and instruct them themselves. In the case of men, those that are thoroughly grounded in drill and discipline and know how to handle and use their arms."

To fulfil the first of these requirements was one of the great difficulties that were being dealt with at home. Officers had to be sent out to France within a few weeks of receiving their commissions; and the only training it was possible to give them was a course, of from four to six weeks, at one of the numerous schools of instruction scattered throughout the country. The presence of recruit officers, with the draft-producing battalions, was a serious handicap to the hurried training of the troops, and the majority of the young officers, after they had completed their course at a school of instruction, were posted to one of the " Young Officer Companies," where, in most cases, they had no opportunities of handling men. A great advance was made in the methods of training the ever-increasing number of new officers in, 1916, when the Officer Cadet Battalions, to which the Queen's Westminsters sent many N.C.O.'s and riflemen for training, were started at home. In these battalions every effort was made to give the cadets opportunities for leadership, but the problem of giving young officers facilities for commanding men before they were sent to France was never satisfactorily solved, and it became increasingly difficult during the later periods of the war.

The Queen's Westminsters have good reason to be proud of and grateful to the young officers who joined the Regiment during the war. The way in which the platoon commanders carried out their duties in France deserves the greatest admiration, and can only really be appreciated in its true significance, when their lack of opportunities of practical experience at home is fully understood.

The weeks of training passed very rapidly, and games and sports of all kinds were arranged to fill in the spare time. The Battalion sports were held on April 25th, when D Company won the Battalion championship; and a week later the

Queen's Westminsters won the 169th Infantry Brigade Championship at the Brigade sports meeting held at Frevent. The meeting was a very great success. The great length and glowing terms in which it is described, in the Battalion War Diary, is striking testimony to the exhilarating effect of sport on the spirits of troops, whether as competitors or spectators.

The account concludes with the following words: " . . . the taped track, refreshment marquees, and band (2nd Londons' drum and fife) combined to produce an effect of home."

There were nine events (out of which the Battalion secured five first places) for which points were awarded for the championship; and at the end of the meeting it was found that the Queen's Westminsters had won with thirty-two points, with the Q.V.R. a very close second, two points behind.[1]

Second Lieutenant F. Barwell, who took part in the relay race, afterwards transferred to the Royal Flying Corps and met his death near Beaumont Hamel, on April 26th, 1917, while fighting single-handed a large number of enemy aeroplanes. The exact details of his last fight are not known, but an enemy report shows that it was a most gallant one. Attacked by (it is believed) six of their aeroplanes he took them all on, and won their expressed admiration by his skilful and daring handling of his machine. Numbers beat him, and he was killed by rifle fire. The same report stated that the enemy had buried his body " with generous honour " in the churchyard at Beaumont Hamel, but no confirmation of this, or his exact resting-place, can be traced. He had joined the Queen's Westminsters on the outbreak of war and came out to France with the 1st Battalion in 1914. Quite a boy, absolutely fearless, and full of the spirit of adventure, he was typical of all that is best in the traditions of our public schools and the young British officer. Anything that " Freddie " had to do was not only done, but done thoroughly; and the manner of his death was typical of him in every way.

On May 7th, the Battalion moved from Monchaux to Halloy, and here training was completed on the 19th. The next fortnight was spent on work of varying descriptions in the VII Corps area, in preparation for the approaching offen-

---

[1] The following is a list of the successes obtained by members of the Regiment, who scored points towards the championship:
100 *yards*.—1st, Lance-Corporal McMillan; 2nd, 2nd Lieutenant N. T. Thurston.
220 *yards*.—1st, Lance-Corporal McMillan; 2nd, 2nd Lieutenant N. T. Thurston.
Hurdle Race.—1st, Rifleman Radcliffe; 2nd, Rifleman Bodenham. *Quarter Mile*.—3rd, Rifleman Griffith. *Obstacle Race*.—3rd, Lance-Corporal Roper. *Relay Race.—Team*: Lieutenant F. L. Barwell, Corporal Knudson, Sergeant Owens and Rifleman Bright. *Tug-of-War*.—The team coached by R.S.M. Davis beat the L.R.B. by two pulls to one in the first round, and the Q.V.R. by two pulls to none in the final. *Open Mile*.—(Not counting towards the championship), 2nd Rifleman Winterbourne.

DIGGING ASSEMBLY TRENCHES, 1916

sive. The first tasks allotted to the Battalion were to fell trees for the making of gun emplacements, to become hewers of stone from quarries for the same purpose, and to unload trains at Mondicourt Station.

On the 24th the Queen's Westminsters were reinforced by a draft of 223 other ranks from the 2/2nd London Royal Fusiliers. Many of them had seen service in Gallipoli, and they were an addition of the very highest value to the Battalion. All ranks appreciated the natural feelings of these men, in having their own battalion broken up and being sent to another regiment. The efforts that were made to make them not only welcome but at home in their new unit, were more than fully responded to by them; and, five weeks later, when the Battalion was about to go into action at Gommecourt, these 2nd Londons, of all ranks and without exception, asked if they might wear the Q.W.R. badge, as they were going to fight with the Regiment.

On the 10th Major P. E. Harding was appointed second in command of the Battalion, and Captain H. S. Price became adjutant, an appointment which he held until the end of the war.

On June 3rd, the Battalion moved to Bayencourt and the transport to Coigneux; two days later, after an interval of four months, the Battalion was once again in the front line.

The 56th Division had taken over the line, facing Gommecourt and to the south of it, on May 5th. The opposing trenches were about 700 yards apart, and orders were received that the line was to be advanced 400 yards and a new system of trenches dug. The whole of the 167th Infantry Brigade was employed for this purpose; and during the three nights of the 25th, 26th and 27th May, nearly 3000 men working in No-man's-land, within 300 yards of the enemy, sited and dug 2900 yards of fire trench and 1500 yards of communication trench at a cost of only 8 killed and 55 wounded.

On the night of June 5th, the Queen's Westminsters supplied working parties of 400 men to work on the new front line to the east of Hébuterne, and to clear sap-heads in preparation for the digging of a new line further forward. On the following night the Battalion, working in three parties each 100 strong, dug a new trench in what was known as " Y " sector opposite the south-west corner of Gommecourt Park, while a further party, covered by a detachment of the 2nd Londons, put up wire in front of it. The result of this operation, which was successfully carried out without casualties, was to advance the front by about 100 yards.

It was remarkable that the enemy should have allowed so much digging to be done by such large numbers with practically no interference.

All these trenches were to form the assembly trenches for the attack on Gommecourt; and it was from this sector that the Queen's Westminsters advanced on July 1st.

On June 9th, the Battalion moved to Hébuterne, relieving the 2nd Londons in Y sector, between Hébuterne and Gommecourt.

During this tour in the line some very hard work was done in completing the new trenches and in investigating the enemy position. The following extract from the War Diary is of interest in this connection :—

"*June 12th.*—Very wet weather. Trenches becoming very bad and work greatly hindered by the wet. Three patrols, consisting of Lieut. Webb and Sergt. Davis; Lieut. Wagner, Corpl. Townsend, and Rifleman Wernham; and Lieut. Westmoreland and Lieut. Page (38th Central India Horse), went out to obtain samples of the German wire and ascertain whether the saps running out from Gommecourt Park had machine-gun emplacements at their head. . . . Each patrol brought in specimens of very thick wire (some was too thick to cut), but no trace of the saps could be found. The night was exceptionally dark and wet, and the patrols were soaked to the skin."

On the 16th, the whole Battalion was relieved by the L.R.B. and moved back to Bayencourt, leaving behind 100 men to act as working parties for the Royal Engineers. Preparations for the offensive were being continued at high pressure. The vast quantities of ammunition, wire and stores of every description that were being accumulated and methodically distributed in various dumps, involved continuous work of a very exhausting nature; and during the five days that the Battalion was at Bayencourt every available man was sent forward to Hébuterne for work.

On the 21st, the Queen's Westminsters moved back to Halloy to complete their final training and to rehearse their part in the attack. Dummy trenches, corresponding exactly with the enemy defences, had been dug to represent the objective of the Brigade, and practice attacks were carried out in them, so that every leader and every man knew in every detail what he would have to do during the actual advance.

On the 25th, the 168th and 169th Infantry Brigades practised the attack on these trenches; and, on the 26th, the final

THE BRITISH BOMBARDMENT, JUNE 1916

practice was successfully carried out in the presence of the VII Corps and Divisional Commanders (Lieut.-General Sir T. D'O. Snow, K.C.B., and Major-General C. P. A. Hull.). A smoke screen was put up, aeroplanes co-operated, and the assaulting troops, who were equipped as far as possible as they were to be when the actual attack took place, carried with them the engineering material for consolidating the captured positions.

On the 27th the Battalion moved to St. Amand, preparatory to taking up its position in the assembly trenches. The attack at Gommecourt had originally been planned to commence in conformity with the general attack on the Somme, zero hour being 7.0 a.m. on the 29th; but owing to the terribly bad weather the two attacks were postponed for forty-eight hours.

Of the postponement, Lieut.-Colonel Shoolbred writes :—

"To our Brigade, at any rate, this postponement was a godsend. The men were quite worn out, and they mostly slept solid for the two days in billets in St. Amand. There was a highly successful concert on the evening of the 29th, and after the rest the Battalion did ' come up dancing ' when it went in, in the evening of the 30th."

Battalion Headquarters, too, were glad of the short respite, for the preparation of the orders for the attack had involved an immense amount of labour on their part.

The preliminary instructions had been issued by the Brigade on the 17th, and the operation orders, founded on these instructions and on the subsequent orders, were of a most elaborate nature, dealing with the minutest details, both in matters of tactics and administration.

The bombardment of the German lines commenced on the 24th, and continued up to the hour of the attack. The enemy's retaliation was comparatively weak, which led to the unfounded belief that there was no big concentration of artillery on the front to be attacked by the Division.

The following extracts from the War Diary of the 56th Division, throw an interesting light on the information available at the end of June :—

"*June 28th.*—... Wire reported satisfactorily dealt with in first and second German lines. In third line gaps have been cut, but require widening. Intense bombardment by Divisional Artillery and VII Corps heavy artillery from 6.45 a.m. to 7.25 a.m. Enemy replied fairly vigorously on our trenches, but the number of guns employed by him did not appear to be large. No fire directed on roads or villages behind our lines.

"*June 29th.*—Enemy make very little reply to intense bombardment from 4.40 p.m. to 5.20 p.m."

On the night of June 30th, the Queen's Westminsters moved up by platoons to Hébuterne, and took up their allotted position in the assembly trenches. The men were in splendid spirits, in excellent condition, confident in their preparedness, and eager to play their part in the great attack. Some indication of the moral of the Battalion may be gained from the fact that, during the whole week immediately preceding the attack, only seven men " went sick " out of a total strength of 966 all ranks, a record rarely beaten in peace time, even under the most favourable conditions.

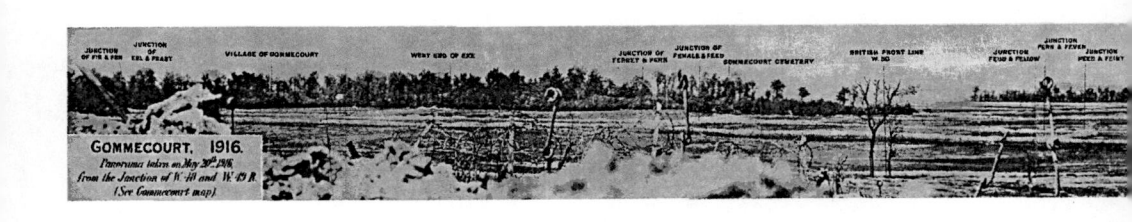

GOMMECOURT, 1916.
Panorama taken on May 30th 1916 from the Junction of W.48 and W.49 R. (See Gommecourt map).

Panorama with labels: LA BRAYELLE FARM — 2TCH — JUNCTION OF FELLOW & FELL — NAMELESS FARM ROAD — QUADRILATERAL — JUNCTION OF FEVER & FETTER — JUNCTION OF FEINT & FELT — JUNCTION OF FELL & FELON — ESRARTS — EPTE — NAMELESS FARM

CHAPTER VII

GOMMECOURT, JULY 1st, 1916

WE have now arrived at one of the decisive turning-points of the war. On July 1st, 1916, the great British offensive was launched on a scale unprecedented in history, and the enemy received a blow from which he was destined never fully to recover. Ever since the close of the Battles of Ypres in 1914, the Germans had been constructing, with all their characteristic thoroughness and industry, an apparently impassable barrier on the Western Front. As a result there lay before the British armies line after line of trenches, provided with every defensive contrivance that a nation bred and trained to war had been able to devise, and protected in front by belt after belt of barbed wire of the densest and cruellest description. The enemy may well have thought that the task of breaking through such defences was impossible of human achievement.

The British attack of July 1st was launched on a front of about twenty miles. On the extreme left of this front lay the village of Gommecourt; and opposite to it was entrenched the VII Corps, consisting of the 36th, the 46th, and the 56th Divisions under the command of Lieut.-General Sir T. D'O. Snow.

The Gommecourt position was a very strong one. About a thousand yards to the east of the village there was a commanding ridge. But the village itself, with Gommecourt Park to the south and Gommecourt Wood to the north, formed a pronounced salient projecting into the British line, and it had been very strongly fortified by the enemy.

The task allotted to the VII Corps was to capture the village and establish itself on the ridge, thus straightening out the British line from a point known as the Sixteen Poplars, about 500 yards east of Hébuterne in the south, to a point known as Z Hedge, about 1200 yards east of Fonquevillers in the north. (This Z Hedge is not shown on the map.)

The plan of the VII Corps, for this operation, avoided a direct advance on Gommecourt village. It arranged that two attacks should be delivered, one from the south by the 56th Division, and one from the north by the 46th Division, and that these attacks should converge on the ridge in rear of the village. If the plan were successful, Gommecourt would be surrounded; and it was expected that the final capture of the garrison would be a comparatively simple matter.

The attack of the 56th Division, from the south, was made on a two-brigade frontage, with the 168th Infantry Brigade on the right, the 169th Infantry Brigade on the left, and the 167th Infantry Brigade in reserve. In order properly to understand the nature of the task with which the 169th Infantry Brigade was confronted, and to follow the course of the day's fighting, it is necessary to consider the German defences in some detail.

They consisted of two systems of trenches separated by a distance of about 400 yards. The front system, which was about 400 yards from the British line, ran in a south-easterly direction from the village of Gommecourt, and consisted of three lines of trenches dug roughly parallel with one another, with a distance of about 100 yards separating the first and second lines, and about 170 yards between the second and third lines. The whole constituted a very strongly fortified zone. Gommecourt cemetery, which was immediately south of the village, and was situated half-way between the second and third line of trenches, had been converted into a very formidable " strong point." The second system, which was inclined at an angle of about forty-five degrees to the first, consisted of two more lines of trenches running nearly due east, in rear of the front system; and the two systems were linked up by a series of communication trenches. The trenches were lavishly provided with deep dugouts, which afforded nearly complete protection from even the heaviest shell-fire.

In the second system, a strong German work had been constructed on the ridge about 250 yards to the east of the village. This work, which was known as the Quadrilateral, was the final objective of the Queen's Westminster Rifles.

To the right of the front to be attacked by the 169th Infantry Brigade, were the remains of a farm, known as Nameless Farm; and the road which ran parallel to the third German trench (from this farm to the village) was known as Nameless Farm road. The ground in front of the British trenches rose steadily in a gentle slope which was somewhat more pronounced towards the right; and to the left were the ruins of Gommecourt village and the shell-shattered tree-stumps of Gommecourt Park.

The panorama, facing page 85, taken before the British

THE PLAN OF ATTACK

bombardment, gives a good idea of the position to be attacked, but the course of the operations during the attack cannot be followed without a close study of the trench map at page 102.

The task of the 169th Infantry Brigade, which was to be carried out in four successive phases, was : (1) to capture the three lines of the first German trench system, and link up with the 168th Infantry Brigade at a point in Fell trench, fifty yards north-west of its junction with Epte communication trench ; (2) to capture Ems and Etch communication trenches and the Quadrilateral ; (3) to join hands with the 46th Division on the ridge to the east of Gommecourt village ; and (4) to clear the village and Gommecourt Park.

The objectives given to the three assaulting battalions of the Brigade were as follows :—

I.—*First Phase.*

(a) *Right attack.*—Queen Victoria Rifles : Fell, Fellow, Feud, Ems (between Feud and the Cemetery) and the Cemetery.

(b) *Left attack.*—London Rifle Brigade : Exe (exclusive of the Cemetery), the Maze, Eel and Fir.

(c) *Centre attack.*—Queen's Westminster Rifles : to follow the right attack from the assembly trenches and to pass over Fern and Feed.

II.—*Second Phase.* (To take place immediately after the First Phase.

(a) *Right attack.*—Q.V.R. : Ems, to its junction with the Quadrilateral, and to consolidate strong points.

(b) *Left attack.*—L.R.B. : to consolidate strong points.

(c) *Centre attack.*—Q.W.R. : to pass over Fellow, and to capture Etch and the Quadrilateral.

III.—*Third Phase.*

Centre attack.—Q.W.R. : to secure the cross trenches to the east of the village, and to join hands with the 46th Division along Fill (not shown on the map), and to consolidate Fillet, facing east.

IV.—*Fourth Phase.*

The clearing of Gommecourt village and Park.

Consequently it will be seen that if the attack went according to plan, the Queen's Westminsters were to follow up the Queen Victoria Rifles as far as the third German trench, and were then to use this trench as a jumping-off line for their attack on the Quadrilateral.

The fact that the second German system was inclined at an angle to the first system, would necessitate a change of direction half-left, as the Queen's Westminsters left the third (Fellow) trench. A change of direction during an attack is at any time a difficult and dangerous manœuvre; and, in an attack on a prepared position, it must inevitably bring the attackers under semi-enfilade fire while the change is being made. In view, however, of what actually happened during the engagement, it cannot really be considered that the contemplated manœuvre had any serious influence on the course of the action.

The disposition of assaulting battalions in the assembly trenches was as follows :—

In Y47—2 companies L.R.B.; 2 companies Q.V.R.

Y47, J and S—B Company, Q.W.R.; A Company, Q.W.R.

Y47, Q and K—2 platoons, C Company, Q.W.R., and Headquarter bombers; 2 platoons, C Company, Q.W.R.

Y47, L—1 company Q.V.R.

R. line, in support—D Company, Q.W.R., and the fourth companies of the L.R.B. and Q.V.R.

The following additional units were attached to the companies of the Battalion and went forward with them :—

1 Section, 169th Brigade Machine-Gun Company; 1 Section, 169th Brigade Trench-Mortar Battery; 2 Platoons, 1/5th Cheshire Pioneers; 16 Sappers, 2/1st Field Company, R.E.

The objectives and tasks allotted to the companies of the Queen's Westminsters were :—

A Company (Captain F. G. Swainson)—(1) North-west corner of the Quadrilateral and Exe trench running into it=1 Platoon.

(2) South-west corner of the Quadrilateral and Ems trench running into it=1 Platoon.

(3) To secure and consolidate Etch communication trench, as a fire trench facing east=2 Platoons.

B Company (Captain G. E. Cockerill)—(1) The north side of the Quadrilateral (exclusive of the north-west corner where Exe ran into it)=1 Platoon.

(2) The north-west corner of the Quadrilateral and the Exe trench running into it from Gommecourt=1 Platoon.

(3) The west side of the Quadrilateral, including its junction with Ems at the south-west corner=1 Platoon; leaving one platoon as a company reserve.

C Company (Captain H. F. Mott) *and Headquarter Bombers*—Fillet trench and to establish touch with the 46th Division, to consolidate Fillet facing east, and to establish a strong point at the junction of Fillet and Indus trenches.

D Company (Captain P. M. Glasier)—in reserve.

The task of the Pioneers was to establish strong points in the Quadrilateral and east of Gommecourt; and the Trench-Mortar Section was to assist in the defence of the Quadrilateral after its capture.

The advance was to be made by lines of companies, in column of platoons in line at eighty yards' distance with the bombing sections on the outer flanks of the platoons, and the Lewis-gun sections on the inner flanks. This meant, in common phraseology, that each company advanced in four lines of men, with a distance of eighty yards between each line.

A compass-bearing was given on which the companies were to advance, to enable them to enter the third German line at the correct points; and further, in view of the fact that the troops in front would be obscured by the smoke screen under cover of which the attack was to be made, the distance was to be gauged by time, the successive waves being ordered to commence their advance at intervals of one minute.

The Queen's Westminsters who, as we have seen, had moved forward during the early hours of the night from their billets at St. Amand, reached their positions in the assembly trenches at 2 a.m. on the morning of July 1st. The attack was not timed to start until five and a half hours later.

Words are not needed to describe either the tense excitement or the nervous strain of that long wait in the narrow, crowded trenches, yet there was a spirit of confidence inspired by the complete success of all the preliminary arrangements. The whole Brigade had been assembled without the loss of a single man, the assaulting battalions had arrived in position according to time table, the wire had been removed from before our trenches, and directing tapes had been laid across No-man's-land to show a path for the advancing troops, scaling ladders and trench bridges were ready, and every man knew thoroughly his task for the day. As the morning broke, fine and clear, a light north-westerly breeze sprang up, which was sufficiently favourable for drifting the smoke screen across to the enemy trenches, and everything promised well for the attack.

The guns, which had been pounding the enemy lines almost unceasingly for the past seven days with shrapnel and high explosive, broke out into a thunderous roar as the final intense bombardment began shortly before 6.30 a.m. It seemed impossible that men could live or trenches stand under the fury of such merciless fire.

Five minutes before zero hour a screen of smoke, from 4-inch trench mortars and from smoke-candles and bombs, was started by the 167th Infantry Brigade all along the front. The smoke steadily drifted towards the enemy. It completely obscured from view the assaulting battalions, as they left their trenches two minutes later and formed up ready to advance at the appointed time.

At zero hour (7.30 a.m.) all was ready, and the advance began. The Q.V.R. and the L.R.B., followed by the Queen's Westminsters, moved forward steadily, as if on parade, across the 400 yards that separated our lines from those of the enemy. At the same time D Company advanced to the assembly trenches, which the assaulting companies had left, and took up its position in readiness to reinforce the assaulting troops and to carry forward material for the consolidation of the captured trenches. At first the enemy's barrage was not excessively heavy, and the advance across No-man's-land was accomplished with comparatively small loss; but when the enemy lines were reached it was found that, in spite of our heavy bombardment, the wire in front of Fern and Fever in the first line, and Feed and Feint in the second line, had been very imperfectly destroyed, and that both these lines were strongly held. Both the Q.V.R. and the Q.W.R. had to wait under galling machine-gun fire, from the right near Nameless Farm, and from Etch trench near the German front line, while the men pressed on in file through such gaps in the wire as could be found.

The enemy now put down a terrific barrage on No-man's-land in rear of the assaulting waves, and increased the severity of the barrage in front of them.

Owing to the heavy casualties none of the trench bridges, that formed part of the attack equipment, reached the first German line (Fern), and all had to jump into the trench and climb out again over the parados before they could resume their advance.

Captain G. E. Cockerill (commanding B Company) was dangerously wounded,[1] Captain H. F. Mott (commanding C Company) and Lieutenant Strange were killed while cross-

---

[1] Captain G. E. Cockerill died of wounds two days later, whilst a prisoner of war.

ing the first German line (Fern), and the losses of the two battalions commenced to mount up rapidly.

In addition to the machine-gun fire, the troops were now under heavy rifle fire from Fellow trench which was strongly held. Parties of the enemy, belonging to the 2nd *Prussian Guard Reserve Division*, had emerged from the dugouts, many of which were quite undamaged, and further delayed the advance. The enemy troops, however, could hardly be expected to put up a spirited defence after the long bombardment they had undergone, and many of them surrendered readily. Owing to the severity of the barrage on No-man's-land, prisoners had little chance of getting back to the British lines, and numbers were sent down into the German dugouts. It appears to be an established fact that many of these prisoners took up the fight again after our men had passed forward, and attacked them from the rear.

In the meantime our own men, pushing doggedly on, struggled through the gaps in the wire in front of the second line,[1] and eventually succeeded in reaching the Nameless Farm road where, mixed up with the Q.V.R., they lined a steep bank about four and a half feet high on the side nearest the enemy. The range of this bank was exactly known by the enemy machine-gunners, and it was under rifle fire at point-blank range from Fellow trench on the left. There were many Germans too on the right, but these were kept at bay by Lewis-gun fire: one Lewis gunner of the Queen's Westminsters,[2] with Corporal L. Ratcliffe, M.M., of the 1/5th Cheshires observing for him, fired his gun for twenty minutes until he fell, hit by a German bullet.

For a time it was impossible to make any advance from the Nameless Farm road. Many tried to press forward, and were killed in the attempt; for instant death awaited any man who showed himself above the top of the bank. The situation at 8.20 a.m. was reported by Rifleman J. H. Orchard, a signaller, who succeeded in getting back across No-man's-land with the news that: " Fellow was still held by the Germans, and the Q.W.R. with the Q.V.R. were lined up on the Gommecourt-Nameless Farm road, thirty yards north-east of Feed, and that we were losing heavily there."

---

[1] From the War Diary of the 169th Infantry Brigade it would appear that the German wire formed practically no obstacle to the advance of the Brigade. This may have been the case on the left flank, but there seems no doubt that, on the front of the Q.W.R. and Q.V.R., it presented a very serious obstacle. The report does state, however, that there was some uncut wire opposite the junction of Fern and Fever which held up a party of Q.W.R. under Lieutenant J. J. Westmoreland.

[2] It is very much regretted that it has been found impossible to identify this Lewis gunner.

This was the only message that came back during the day, although desperate, but unavailing, attempts were made to get signalling communication with the forward troops. Sergeant L. P. Harrow, the signalling sergeant, tried to get a roll of " rabbit-wire " across No-man's-land, as this would be less likely to be destroyed by shell-fire than the ordinary signalling line, but the enemy's barrage was too intense and his effort, like the rest, was fruitless.

Not a single officer, of those that reached Nameless Farm road, and only one sergeant ever came back, and information as to the subsequent course of events is necessarily scarce and in some cases conflicting.

Captain F. G. Swainson (commanding A Company) had been killed shortly after leaving the German second-line trench, near the junction of Feed and Etch; and 2nd Lieutenant J. A. Horne of B Company was the senior officer left, by the time the Battalion was fighting in the Nameless Farm road. This officer and 2nd Lieutenants A. G. Yates, A. G. Negus, and D. F. Upton of C Company, and 2nd Lieutenant E. H. Bovill of A Company, collected their men as best they could and, making their way along the road, dropped into Etch communication trench at the point where the road crossed it. The party then worked forward to the third German line and, led by 2nd Lieutenants Yates and Negus, commenced to bomb their way along Fellow towards their left. 2nd Lieutenant Yates was killed about ten yards down the trench; and 2nd Lieutenant Negus, who had been wounded before he had reached the first German line at the commencement of the attack, was killed a few yards further on.

Second Lieutenant Upton led one bombing party along Fellow and thence along Feud nearly to the Cemetery, where some German bombers held them up for a time. Having cleared these trenches the bombing party put up a Battalion notice board, and on seeing it some of the men, still lining the Nameless Farm road, came over the open and joined them in the trench.

Others,[1] including some of the Cheshires, were led forward by, it is believed, C.S.M. Froome, D.C.M. (B Company), along the trench towards Etch, up which Lance-Corporal D. Newton, Rifleman A. E. Clark, and another bomber were trying to bomb towards the Quadrilateral. The trench, however, was too strongly held, and the bombers were driven back

---

[1] This account is to a certain extent a matter of surmise, but it is supported by an account by Corporal L. Ratcliffe, M.M., of the Cheshires and the information available from other records.

towards the junction of Etch and Fell, both of which trenches were then blocked. These blocks were made and held by a bombing section under Lance-Sergeant H. H. Partridge, and by the Cheshire Pioneers and R.E. sappers who worked most gallantly, covered by the fire of a Lewis gun mounted by 2nd Lieutenant Horne and the only surviving Lewis gunner, who was probably Rifleman Fairclough. The right flank was also protected by parties under an officer of the Q.V.R., but no details are available as to how they were situated.

On the left, parties from B and C Companies, and from the Headquarters bombing section (amongst whom were Corporal F. E. Hayward, 2nd Londons, attached, and Rifleman H. E. Edwards), fought their way towards the Cemetery and then along Ems communication trench, and eventually linked up with the party bombing along the third line from the right, thus securing the whole of Fellow and Feud trenches.

The attempt to reach the Quadrilateral along Etch communication trench on the right had been frustrated, as we have seen; but on the left a young subaltern of the 1/5th Cheshires, with Sergeant W. G. Nicholls, who took over command of the Headquarters bombing section after Lieutenant Spencer-Smith had been wounded, led a party, amongst whom were Corporal R. T. Townsend and Corporal W. C. Ide (2nd Londons, attached Q.W.R.) of C Company, Corporal Hayward of B Company, and Rifleman F. H. Stow of D Company, up Ems communication trench, and actually succeeded in reaching the Quadrilateral. They were met, however, by a strong enemy bombing party, and their advance was checked. They continued fighting until their bombs were exhausted; when the officer, realising that nothing further could be done, ordered the party to withdraw. All further trace of this gallant officer has been lost and undoubtedly he was killed whilst covering the retirement.[1]

The time was now about 9 a.m., and, so far as can be ascertained, the general situation was as follows :—

On the right the Rangers (168th Infantry Brigade) were in Felt, in the second German line ; but it seems that they had been driven back on the left and were not in touch with the Q.V.R., who were now in the third line, in Fell.

The bombing parties of the Q.W.R., who have already been mentioned, and Corporal R. T. Townsend were fighting desperately to prevent the enemy from pressing forward along

---

[1] It is believed that this officer was Lieutenant G. S. Arthur. (See 56th Divisional History by Major C. H. Dudley Ward, D.S.O., M.C.)

Etch, and from driving in the right flank of the 169th Infantry Brigade from Fell.

The Q.V.R. and Q.W.R. were in possession of the third German line (Fellow and Feud), and in the Cemetery; while on the left the L.R.B., who had gained their objectives, had two companies in Fen and Feast, with a party in Gommecourt Park heavily engaged in a bombing fight with the enemy.

The supply of bombs was rapidly becoming exhausted, and large numbers of German grenades were being collected from the dugouts and used by our men.

On the left of the 56th Division, to the north of Gommecourt, the attack of the 46th Division had failed, and its right battalion was held up in one of the British advanced trenches.

It seems impossible even to attempt to describe the terrible character of the fighting that was now taking place and was to continue throughout the rest of the day. Its real nature can only be understood and appreciated by those who have had actual experience of a trench battle during the war.

The enemy had been fully prepared for the attack, and had massed numberless guns of all calibres to prevent the capture of Gommecourt Salient; and, contrary to all expectations, our own bombardment had failed to destroy the enemy's dugouts or to kill the garrison of the trenches, though the trenches themselves were, according to the German accounts, rendered absolutely untenable.

No sooner had the waves of our attack passed forward than the garrison and machine-gunners emerged from their dugouts and engaged our men from the rear. One must at once recognise and admire the bravery of troops who, for a whole week, had been under a continuous bombardment and cut off from all supplies, and were yet able to come out and put up such a fight as they did.

Although the situation in front was only a matter of surmise, the 169th Infantry Brigade realised that the Quadrilateral had not been captured, and issued orders, which were received at 9.20 a.m., for the platoon of D Company to go forward with bombs, and for the assaulting companies to bomb up Ems and Etch to the Quadrilateral, and to report progress. All the officers of D Company had by now become casualties, and the company sergeant-major (H. M. Masson) had been killed. Sergeant H. E. Ironmonger, as soon as the orders had been received, tried to get forward with his platoon, but the enemy was using the whole weight of his artillery in putting down an impenetrable barrage on No-man's-land. At the first attempt the majority of the platoon were killed or wounded as soon as they had left the cover of the trench, but Sergeant Ironmonger collected those who were left, and, after reporting what had happened, made another equally unsuccessful attempt, in the course of which he himself was wounded. There were only four survivors from this platoon.

From this time onwards the enemy attempts to recapture the trenches they had lost, grew steadily stronger. The first counter-attack appears to have taken place on the left, where bodies of the enemy were seen in several parts of Gommecourt Park and the village, advancing towards the trenches held by the L.R.B.

At 10.15 a.m. parties of the enemy were reported to be bombing down Ems towards Feud, and shortly afterwards were seen to leave Ems and to be collecting north of the Cemetery. This must have been the fight in which the party of the Queen's Westminsters, under the subaltern of the Cheshires and Sergeant Nicholls, was involved. By 10.50 a.m. the enemy had pushed forward to the Cemetery, and the whole line to the left of it was heavily and continuously engaged. It was in this neighbourhood that a party of C Company (amongst whom were Sergeant H. A. London, Rifleman Fraser (missing), Lance-Corporal F. E. Wright, Rifleman Lakeman (wounded), Rifleman H. R. Wallis, and Rifleman Pinnell (wounded), having driven the enemy right back to the wood on their left, held him at bay for a full hour and a half behind a barrier which they had erected. This party ultimately became isolated and was forced to withdraw, but not until they had exhausted all their bombs and inflicted heavy losses on the enemy.

The enemy barrage on our old front line and on No-man's-land had continued with unabated violence, and the whole area was swept by machine-gun fire. Although the attempt seemed foredoomed to failure, another effort was made at 11.0 a.m. to get two platoons of D Company forward, across the zone of death, to reinforce the front companies, and to carry up fresh supplies of bombs.

The attempt to get forward was organised by Sergeant W. H. Couper. No progress could be made, for nearly every man who started was hit. By 11.30 a.m. it was clear that it would be hopeless to make any further attempt to get across No-man's-land, unless the intensity of the enemy's fire could be checked by our own artillery.

Aeroplane reports now began to come in, stating that Feud and Fell (in the third German line) were strongly held by

British troops, but that the Quadrilateral was unoccupied by either side. It was of the utmost importance to get this news through to the assaulting troops, and six runners of the 2nd Londons volunteered to make an attempt to get through the barrage with orders for the Queen's Westminsters and the Q.V.R. A few minutes after noon the following written order was despatched by the 169th Infantry Brigade: " R.F.C. observers repeatedly report Ems, Etch, and the Quadrilateral empty of Germans. Push on bombing parties at once and occupy Quadrilateral. Barrage on Quadrilateral lifts at 1.30 p.m."

One runner got through. His message was opened by Sergt. D. G. Hawker[1] who was lying severely wounded and helpless in the German front line. It is impossible to fix the time (Sergt. Hawker states that he believes it to have been about 4.0 p.m.); but at all events it arrived too late to be acted on, for the British troops had already been driven back to the German front-line trench. It seems to be practically certain that the runner, who delivered the order, was Corporal Werner of the 2nd Londons. He was a brave and gallant man, for he volunteered, and made the attempt, to return across No-man's-land carrying a message, asking for support at the earliest possible moment; but the message never reached its destination, and Corporal Werner, who must have been killed on his way back, was later reported as missing.

There are no means, at present, of finding out whether the aeroplane reports that the Quadilateral was unoccupied, were accurate,[2] but it is known, at any rate, that, at the time the order was despatched, desperate fighting was going on on the outer flanks of Fellow and Feud, and it seems quite clear that there could have been no possibility of carrying out the order.

The enemy counter-attacks now began to make headway on both flanks. On the right the strong point at the junction of Felon and Epte (on the front of the 168th Infantry Brigade) had been recaptured, and on the left the bombing parties were being forced back.

By 12.30 p.m. the troops in Feud and Fellow had completely exhausted their supply of bombs, including the large number of German ones which had been taken from prisoners or found in the trenches and dugouts. There was no hope of any further supplies or of reinforcements and, under the cir-

---

[1] See Sergeant Hawker's account on page 101.
[2] The most probable explanation of the report seems to be that the enemy had counter-attacked and were holding our men further forward.

cumstances, 2nd Lieutenant J. A. Horne decided to withdraw to Feed in the second German line.

This very gallant officer remained behind with the Lewis-gun team, which was covering the withdrawal of his men, and died working the gun alone after every member of the team had been incapacitated or killed. He had displayed the utmost bravery and tenacity throughout the day, and in the words of Colonel Shoolbred "his leadership, after the deaths of all his seniors, of the heroic band of Queen's Westminsters and Queen Victorias and Cheshires, who fought for nearly five hours against determined enemy counter-attacks, had more to do than it is possible to attempt to set out in detail, with the gallant stand made in these enemy trenches after the failure of the attack. The honour of the Victoria Cross would not have been more than his bravery and leadership merited. The few survivors spoke of him and his conduct throughout the day in terms of glowing admiration, but indeed there were many also with him, N.C.O.'s and private riflemen, between whom it is impossible to differentiate in the summing-up of a day of deeds whereby a glorious page was added to the records of the Regiment."

After the death of 2nd Lieutenant Horne, only 2nd Lieutenant E. H. Bovill, who had been wounded very early in the morning, and 2nd Lieutenant D. Upton were left from all the officers who had gone forward from our lines at the commencement of the attack. At 1.0 p.m. the signal " S.O.S. Bombs " was sent up by signalling shutter [1] from Ferret in the front German line, and a few minutes later the enemy counter-attacked all along the line between Gommecourt and Nameless Farm.

Another attempt was now made to reinforce the front line with the few survivors of D Company, who had regained our trenches, but the German barrage again prevented them from getting up. The troops who had withdrawn from Fellow into Feed were being hard pressed, and at 1.45 p.m. were forced to withdraw further back to Ferret in the first German line. In the meantime all the Headquarter details, the Headquarter runners and the few stragglers of the three assaulting battalions, were collected and reorganised for the defence of Y Sector, where the troops had assembled before the attack.

From now onward the enemy gradually forced our men

---

[1] Rifleman E. D. Long worked a Venetian shutter (signalling apparatus) for many hours in the captured German lines and succeeded in getting an S.O.S. signal through to the R.F.C. It was believed at the time that this was the only message got through from the other side of No-man's-land after 8.30 a.m., but there is no means of verifying whether the message was the one in question.

along their front line towards Gommecourt Park. In the captured German War Diary of the *55th Reserve Infantry Regiment, 2nd Guards Reserve Division*, we are told that between 3.0 and 4.0 p.m. " the 11th and 12th companies of the regiment pushed forward, after extremely violent fighting at close quarters, with the result that the enemy suffered very heavy losses and took to flight, effectively pursued by rifle, machine-gun and artillery fire." That the losses were very heavy, and that the troops were subjected to the heaviest shelling is perfectly correct ; but the record of the day's fighting is its answer to any suggestion of a hasty retreat ; in fact, the enemy tacitly admits this, when he adds, " Although we had not been successful in entirely clearing the superior forces of the enemy out of the line, by 4.0 p.m. portions of the front trench in B5 (part of Fen and Ferret) had been won back."

We now know that the " superior forces " consisted of barely a hundred men of the L.R.B., the Q.W.R., and the Q.V.R., who were clinging on in Fern, Ferret and Fen with stubborn determination and who held out there until well into the evening, only withdrawing to our own lines under orders of the senior surviving officer.

Shortly before 7.0 p.m. Fern, Ferret and Fen were still occupied by the 169th Infantry Brigade, but between then and 8.30 p.m. the survivors were finally driven back to the old British line. Second Lieutenant Upton,[1] who had led the bombing party along Fellow in the morning, was wounded in the German trenches shortly before the final withdrawal and was unable to regain our lines ; while 2nd Lieutenant Bovill, who had been wounded early in the day and was practically the last man to leave the German lines, was killed on the very parapet of our own trench. These two officers, and the men who had responded so nobly to their leadership throughout a day of continuous fighting, had performed deeds of gallantry that the Regiment will always remember with pride. Gallant seems a poor epithet to apply to what they did, for indeed no words can sufficiently portray their courage, their grit and their devotion.

Of the details attached to the assaulting companies, reference has already been made to the splendid work of the 5th Cheshires (Pioneers) and to the Royal Engineers. Little is known of the fate of the trench mortars ; but the Vickers gun, which was with A Company, got as far as the junction of

---

[1] 2nd Lieutenant Upton was taken prisoner and was subsequently repatriated. He was awarded the Military Cross for his gallantry in this battle.

A TRIBUTE TO THE FALLEN

Etch, Fern and Feed, where it was brought into action by 2nd Lieutenant Engall, who by that time had only one member of his team left. Lieutenant Engall worked the gun single-handed until he himself was killed.

The fight was over, the survivors were collected during the evening in the old British front line, and by 10.0 p.m. the artillery fire had died down, and all was still.

So ended a day of supreme endeavour, a day that will ever call forth proud memories of the officers and men who fought and suffered and died, and who have left behind them an example of heroism and sacrifice that can certainly never be excelled.

Out of 750 officers and men who went into action, 600 were killed, wounded and missing, and it is believed that not a single unwounded member of the Queen's Westminster Rifles fell into the enemy's hands.

Of those who fought and died on July 1st, 1916, Lieut.-Colonel Shoolbred writes with a full heart: "I do not feel able to do justice to them. It is impossible to pay the individual tribute which is their due to the many Westminsters who gave their lives this day in the service of their King and Country and of their Regiment—Captains Swainson, Cockerill and Mott, commanding respectively A, B and C Companies; Lieutenants Bovill, Horne and Yates; and Company Sergeant-Majors Froome and Masson who had given each of them over twenty years' service in the Regiment, are a few amongst those whose memory will always be cherished by their surviving comrades, for their work for and devotion to the Regiment, and by whose blood this glorious day in its history is written."

The attack at Gommecourt was, in fact, a purely subsidiary operation in the great British offensive, and the terrible sacrifices that it involved only serve to emphasise the stupendous scale on which the offensive was planned. To outward appearances the day had ended in failure, but in reality the attack had achieved its main object: namely, to pin the enemy to the ground and to prevent his troops and guns from being employed on other parts of the long battle front, where actual progress was of vital importance.

From the moment that the attack of the 46th Division on the northern face of the salient had failed, the fate of the assaulting battalions of the 56th Division was sealed, for the enemy was at liberty to concentrate the fire of the large number of guns, that he had collected behind Gommecourt, on to the southern areas of the attack. He was, therefore, able, as we have seen, to place an impassable wall of shells behind the British troops who had penetrated into his defences, and to cut them off absolutely from any reinforcements of men or fresh supplies of ammunition. The only course open to the attackers was to fight on until their ammunition was exhausted. This they did to the uttermost limit of their strength, and no men could have done more than did those of the 56th Division.

After the action the following messages were forwarded to the Battalion :—

" The Corps Commander wishes to congratulate all ranks of the 56th Division on the way in which they took the German trenches and held them, by pure grit and pluck, for so long in very adverse circumstances. Although Gommecourt has not fallen into our hands, the purpose of the attack, which was mainly to contain and kill Germans, was accomplished, thanks to a great extent to the tenacity of the 56th Division."

" The General Officer Commanding 56th Division wishes all ranks to know how proud he is of the splendid way in which they captured the German trenches, and of the way they held on to them until all their ammunition and grenades were exhausted. He is satisfied that the main task of the 56th Division, in containing and killing Germans, was most thoroughly accomplished."

" In forwarding the foregoing messages the Brigadier " (commanding 169th Infantry Brigade) " wishes to express to all ranks his praise and appreciation of the excellent work done during the preparations for the attack, and of the gallantry displayed during the day's fighting."

The following account by Sergeant D. G. C. Hawker, B Company, gives a vivid idea of the confused nature of fighting in an entrenched position :—

" I was acting Company Sergeant-Major of C Company on July 1st, 1916, and went over with the company under Captain Mott. The counter-bombardment of our assembly trenches, between 5.0 and 7.0 (a.m.), was not very effective, and C Company, so far as my knowledge goes, suffered little loss on the way. Stretcher-bearer Nicholls, the younger, who was rather badly wounded in the foot before we advanced, insisted on going over with the company.

" We advanced about 7.30 a.m. and progressed steadily, under a heavy smoke cloud, over the first and second German lines, which had then fallen into our hands. Between the second and third lines we were delayed for some moments by uncut wire, and from this point considerable numbers of enemy troops could be clearly seen, evacuating their support positions and retiring hastily to their rear. They presented an irresistible target to our men who got down behind the wire and opened a strong fire. We now came under a heavy shrapnel fire, and the noise was terrific, rendering fire control difficult. Captain Mott, having found and enlarged a gap in the wire, gave the order to cease fire and push on. It was at this juncture, I believe, that he became a casualty. It was for some moments difficult to communicate the order and to control the fire. I collected a party and advanced as far as a slight bank or raised road, which afforded some cover from a withering machine-gun fire, which now enfiladed us from Gommecourt Wood. We had many casualties here; and, while I was walking to a flank to determine our next move, I was put out of action by a shot through the neck and windpipe. Sergeant Courteney of the 2/2nd Londons took over the party, and I made my way towards the rear, hoping to get some medical aid to stop the severe bleeding from my mouth and nose. On my way back I received two more bullet wounds, and on reaching the original enemy front line I lost consciousness. I was aroused later (I think about noon) by a consultation taking place, immediately beside me, between two officers and a C.S.M. of, I think, the Civil Service Rifles (? Q.V.R.). I learned from their conversation that ammunition and specially bombs were running short, that no supports could get up, that the enemy, by counter-attack, had regained his reserve lines, and that all efforts to establish communication with our rear had failed. When I next regained consciousness, about 2.0 p.m., I found that a party of various units, of whom Sergeant Courteney (2/2nd Londons) appeared the senior, were in occupation of the enemy front line where I lay. Sergeant Courteney told me that they had been driven back by successive counter-attacks from the right (where our attack had not established itself). He asked me for instructions, stating that he had about twenty men with him, that they had no small-arm ammunition or bombs, and were expecting a further advance of the enemy from the right. I suggested that they should block a traverse on the right, and endeavour to maintain their position until dusk with any further ammunition they could collect from casualties. At this juncture, however, a runner appeared over the parapet, having succeeded in a most daring venture from our trenches. He brought a message addressed to 'any officer.' As no officer appeared to be in the neighbourhood I took the responsibility of opening the message; it ran approximately as follows: 'Aero reports German 4th line unoccupied. Organise party to occupy and secure same.' The runner volunteered to attempt to return, so I had a message given to him, acknowledging receipt of the Brigade order and urging support at the earliest possible moment. I then instructed Sergeant Courteney to draw his party along to the left and endeavour to get in touch with the L.R.B., who appeared to be still putting up a fight near the wood, and to give the message to the first British officer he saw. I believe it was about 4.0 p.m. when this message came into my hands. The original enemy front line, opposite to the Q.W.R. assembly position, was then evacuated, and shortly after was entered by a German patrol and occupied by enemy troops during the early evening. The positions were shelled by our artillery just before dusk, causing some casualties to the enemy troops in my vicinity."

The night following the battle passed comparatively quietly, and parties were out all night searching for dead and wounded. On the morning of July 2nd, the enemy heavily bombarded Hébuterne, and at about 2.0 p.m. parties of Germans were reported to be in front of their trenches. At first it was thought that a counter-attack was in progress, but later it was seen that the enemy were collecting and tending our wounded. Parties of Queen's Westminsters were at once organised to go out in front of our lines to help in this work, one of the parties being under the command of the Battalion medical officer, Captain A. Ramsbottom, R.A.M.C. When the Germans saw the parties at work, one of their officers, who was in No-man's-land, shouted across that there would be an armistice of fifteen minutes to enable us to collect our wounded and some of the rescue parties were allowed to approach up to the German wire without interference. The artillery were warned as to what was in progress, and the firing was reduced as far as possible on the front involved. The armistice, in fact, continued until after 4.0 p.m., and many wounded were brought into our lines.[1] It is satisfactory to be able to record this act of chivalry on the part of the enemy, but it is a matter of deep regret to know that many of our wounded, who were captured, were very badly treated on their way to the German hospitals.

On July 2nd, the 198 survivors of the Queen's Westminsters

[1] These details, which were supplied by Captain H. S. Price, M.C., the Battalion adjutant at the time, supplement and confirm the official account of this remarkable incident.

marched from the support trenches where they had assembled after the fighting of the previous day, to Bayencourt, where they were billeted for the night. On the following day the Battalion moved to St. Amand. The men were badly in need of rest, but no rest was possible for any troops near the battle front. Every man was needed to take part in the desperate fighting that had only just commenced, and that was to go on relentlessly until well into the winter.

After being reinforced by a draft of 268 men on July 4th, the Battalion, two days later, again went into the trenches, when it relieved the 4th Londons of the 168th Infantry Brigade in the late afternoon. The portion of the line now taken over lay to the north of the Gommecourt Salient, between Fonquevillers and Bienvillers, and was known as "Z" Sector. The trenches here were in a deplorable condition, and for sheer discomfort were as bad as any the Battalion had ever been in. Parts of the fire trench were nearly three feet deep in water and mud, and in the communication trenches water stood waist deep. There was a particularly bad portion on the south side of the Fonquevillers-La Brayelle road, where the trench had been blown in by hostile shelling, and the men holding the line had to remain standing with water up to their waists. A large proportion of the draft that had joined the Battalion at St. Amand consisted of Bantams.[1] These were excellent and very keen and useful men, but they were greatly handicapped by their small stature, particularly in trenches such as those that the Battalion was now occupying. In fact, special arrangements, such as placing ammunition boxes on the fire steps, had to be made to enable them to see over the top of the parapet.

Very heavy rain fell throughout the whole of the 7th; the trenches were flooded even worse than before; and runners, between Battalion Headquarters and the front line, performed their duties stripped from the waist downwards, except for a pair of boots. Everything possible was done to minimise the discomforts of the men in the line; frequent inter-company reliefs took place, and the Medical Officer, Captain A. Ramsbottom, established a drying-room in Fonquevillers where clothes, and especially socks, could be dried. The most thorough precautions against "trench feet" were taken, and proved a complete success; not a single case of "trench feet" was evacuated to the Field Ambulance during the Battalion tour in the trenches, which lasted until July 22nd.

[1] Specially recruited battalions of men below the standard height, but otherwise physically fit in every way. Many of them were miners.

The weather began to improve on July 8th, and pumping was commenced in the trenches. This was kept up continuously, and by the time the Battalion was relieved, the trenches were comparatively dry, and floor boards were being put down.

No events of importance occurred until July 13th, when the Division was ordered by the VII Corps to demonstrate during the night with artillery fire against the enemy trenches and villages, in order to co-operate with the Fourth Army, who were to attack on the following day. Active patrolling was ordered along the whole front of the 169th Infantry Brigade, in response to an order to obtain an identification of the enemy troops holding the line opposite; and a successful minor enterprise, in the nature of a raid, was carried out by a fighting patrol of Queen's Westminsters, consisting of 2nd Lieutenant W. H. Dyson, Sergeant Step, Sergeant Hicks, Lance-Corporal Jones and twenty riflemen.

The Battalion had the luck to secure the desired identification, which proved that no change in the enemy's order of battle had yet been made in this sector, but unfortunately with the loss of the very gallant young officer who carried out the raid at such short notice, and did it with the determination and thoroughness which were characteristic of him.

The following report sent into Battalion Headquarters gives a far more vivid idea of the operation than would a more elaborate account: "*Fonquevillers, July 13th.*—Patrol told off in three parties left our advanced trench at 12.10 a.m. Two parties under 2nd Lieut. Dyson and Sergeant Step reached the German line about thirty yards south of corner of the Z; they found the trench apparently empty. They moved to the corner of the L where there was a dugout and called on the occupants to surrender, but a shot was the only reply. Sergeant Step threw a bomb into the dugout and groans were heard. 2nd Lieut. Dyson was wounded by a shot fired from the hedge. Germans were seen coming down the hedge. The patrol fired at them and Sergeant Step then ordered the party to retire. Lance-Corporal Jones took his party back by the Poplars and then saw two Germans, one of whom he took prisoner [1] and brought in himself—the other got away. 2nd Lieutenant Dyson was too badly wounded to help himself, and Sergeant Step left Rifleman Mullins (2nd Lieutenant Dyson's servant) with him while he himself went back for help. A party went out with a stretcher, but were unable to find 2nd Lieutenant Dyson or Rifleman Mullins, and eventually returned to our lines at 3.30 a.m."

[1] 91*st Regiment.*

The following wire, which was subsequently received from the VII Corps, indicates the appreciation of the good work of this patrol and shows that the loss suffered by the Battalion was certainly not incurred in vain. " The Corps Commander congratulates the 56th Division on the prompt manner in which G.H.Q.'s request for a prisoner, for identity purposes, was responded to. He particularly congratulates Colonel Shoolbred and the Queen's Westminsters for carrying out such a successful raid at such short notice."

The Fourth Army attack referred to was launched at daybreak on July 14th, against the front Longueval–Bazentin-le-Petit, and resulted in the capture of the enemy's second main system of defence on a front of 6000 yards. (See Sir Douglas Haig's despatch of December 23rd, 1916, paras. 12–15.)

On July 19th, a slight change was made in the disposition of units holding the line, and A Company took over some trenches from the 5th Lincolns, on the left of the new Brigade front. Three days later the Battalion was relieved by the Q.V.R. and moved back to St. Amand.

Beyond a certain amount of hostile shelling, the long spell of sixteen days in the front line had been comparatively quiet, and the total casualties of the Battalion had amounted to only twenty-two. As soon as the weather had cleared and the trenches had been drained of water, the energies of the men had been mainly devoted to work on the defences, and a very considerable improvement in their strength and comfort was effected. The Battalion remained at St. Amand for a week, and company training and the training of fresh Lewis-gun teams and bombers was commenced.

On July 28th, Brigadier-General E. S. D'E. Coke inspected the Battalion and presented cards from the Divisional General to the other ranks mentioned for gallantry during the attack at Gommecourt.

The Queen's Westminsters relieved the Q.V.R. on July 30th, in the old trenches at Fonquevillers, and remained there until August 7th.

The Battalion was not engaged in any actual fighting during the period, but there was a considerable increase in the trench-mortar and artillery activities of the enemy, and frequent machine-gun duels took place. The casualties in the Battalion, however, were slight. A great deal of work was done in strengthening the barbed-wire entanglements, and the enemy appeared to be similarly occupied. Patrols, too, were sent out nightly to reconnoitre the enemy's wire and outposts. On August 2nd, one of these patrols, which had crept up to the enemy's wire, discovered a machine gun which opened fire on them at about twenty yards' range. Two men were hit, but the whole party succeeded in returning to our lines.

The following extracts from the Battalion War Diary throw an interesting light on the experiences of the Battalion :—

"*August 3rd.*—Enemy seem to have brought up more anti-aircraft guns, but their aeroplanes scarcely ever cross our lines, and, when they do, they do not venture low enough to be able to see anything.

"*August 4th.*—Enemy started an early morning hate on the Division on our left, presumably to celebrate the second anniversary of the declaration of war. A lot of shells and heavy trench mortars (shells) were sent over, to which our guns made suitable reply.

"*August 5th.*—Enemy trench mortar paid its unwelcome attentions to Z54, but did no damage. . . . The bursting shells, and Verey lights being sent up, can be very plainly seen at night in the direction of the fighting on the north of the Somme, and make a fascinating picture for those who are not in it.

"*August 7th.*—Two enemy staff officers were seen observing our lines. One was wearing white kid gloves, but unfortunately they did not ' stand ' long enough to enable direct attention to be given to them."

In the early hours of August 5th, the Division received some unexpected, but most valuable, information about the fate of many of the men who were missing after the fighting at Gommecourt. About 2.0 a.m. a German, of the 55th *Regiment*, walked into a covering party in front of the right sector of the divisional front, held by the 167th Infantry Brigade. He was found to be in possession of a typewritten list of names of wounded and unwounded prisoners taken on July 1st, which he had been instructed to pin on to our wire. As he had wandered through our wire and across some disused trenches, it was not possible to return this much-appreciated act of courtesy on the part of the enemy, by letting the German go back to his own lines, and he was brought in under escort. Endeavours were made, however, to inform the enemy about what had occurred by means of an aeroplane message, but it is not known whether the message ever reached its destination.

Amongst the names in the typewritten list were those of Captain G. E. Cockerill and Lieutenant P. Spencer-Smith and of fifteen other ranks of the Queen's Westminsters. The fact that every Westminster mentioned in the list was marked as wounded, tends to confirm the proud belief that not a single unwounded member of the Regiment fell into the enemy's hands on July 1st, 1916.

On August 7th, the Battalion was relieved by the Q.V.R. and moved back to Bienvillers, leaving D Company and thirty men of B Company behind in Fonquevillers for work under the Royal Engineers.

Although the Battalion, composed as it was almost entirely of new men, was badly in need of training, particularly as regards bombers and Lewis-gunners, none was possible during the following seven days when it was out of the line. Practically every man was working under the Royal Engineers. The party left behind in Fonquevillers were employed during the nights of the 10th, 11th and 12th in carrying gas cylinders, and placing them in position in the front line, in preparation for a pending gas attack. The carrying party, for a cylinder, consisted of four men, the cylinder being slung on poles and supported on the shoulders of two of them, the third man assisted them, and the fourth was a spare man in case of emergency or casualties. Five hundred and sixty cylinders were thus carried forward in the sector of the 169th Infantry Brigade during these three nights.

The Battalion returned to the trenches on August 15th; and on the 19th, on being relieved by the 7th Lincolns (17th Division), it moved out to St. Amand.

From this date the Division ceased to belong to the VII Corps, and the following message of farewell from the Corps Commander was sent to all battalions :—

" The Lieut.-General, Commanding VII Corps, in saying good-bye to the 56th Division, on their leaving the Corps, desires to record his appreciation of the manner in which the Division has fought and worked, while it has been in the VII Corps. The gallant manner in which the Division fought at Gommecourt will be appreciated in history, but the Corps Commander wishes the Division to know that the less spectacular, but more irksome, work, which the Division has put into the line which they have been holding, has not escaped notice. It is invidious to make distinctions when all have worked so well, but he particularly congratulates those units who have so well repaired that part of the line knocked about in the fighting of the 1st of July. The Corps Commander wishes all ranks good luck, and feels sure that any task committed to the Division in future will be completed in triumph."

The Battalion moved by companies from St. Amand to Sus St. Leger on the evening of August 20th; and, on the 22nd, marched with the 169th Infantry Brigade to Frohen, moving on as a battalion to Villers L'Hôpital, a total distance of about sixteen miles.

The Brigade had had no marching for a long time, and it was largely composed of new drafts who had replaced the casualties of July 1st. The intensely hot weather and the hilly country encountered during the latter part of the march, caused a good many men to fall out from all battalions, but they rejoined their units by the evening. The Battalion moved again the following day to Domvast. This march was longer, but the weather was cooler, and the Battalion stood the march very much better.

On August 25th, the Battalion marched from Domvast to see the battlefield of Creçy. It was met by Professor Delbe of Creçy, who most courteously explained the various points of interest on the field.

On the following day 217 men of the Queen's Westminsters arrived from the 2nd and 6th Entrenching Battalions and 145 men of the 8th, 22nd, 23rd and 24th Londons were sent down to the base. "This exchange," says the Battalion War Diary, "almost makes the Battalion one of the Queen's Westminsters again. The men were delighted to find themselves with their own Regiment, and the Regiment was delighted to get them."

In order to replace the enormous casualties of July 1st, men from a very large number of units had been sent to the different battalions as reinforcing drafts. At one time the Q.V.R. were said to have included in their ranks men from no less than seventeen regiments, including kilted ones.

On more than one occasion reinforcements from the Reserve Battalion at home, who were under orders to join other units in the Division, came up in the same train with drafts from other regiments who had been detailed to the Queen's Westminsters. This system of reinforcing evoked very vigorous protests from all sides, but at the same time it must be borne in mind that the authorities at the base camps were working under very great difficulties. Their most urgent duty was to replenish the ranks of the battalions at the front as quickly as possible, and to do this on an unprecedented scale.

GOMMECOURT
1 JULY 1916

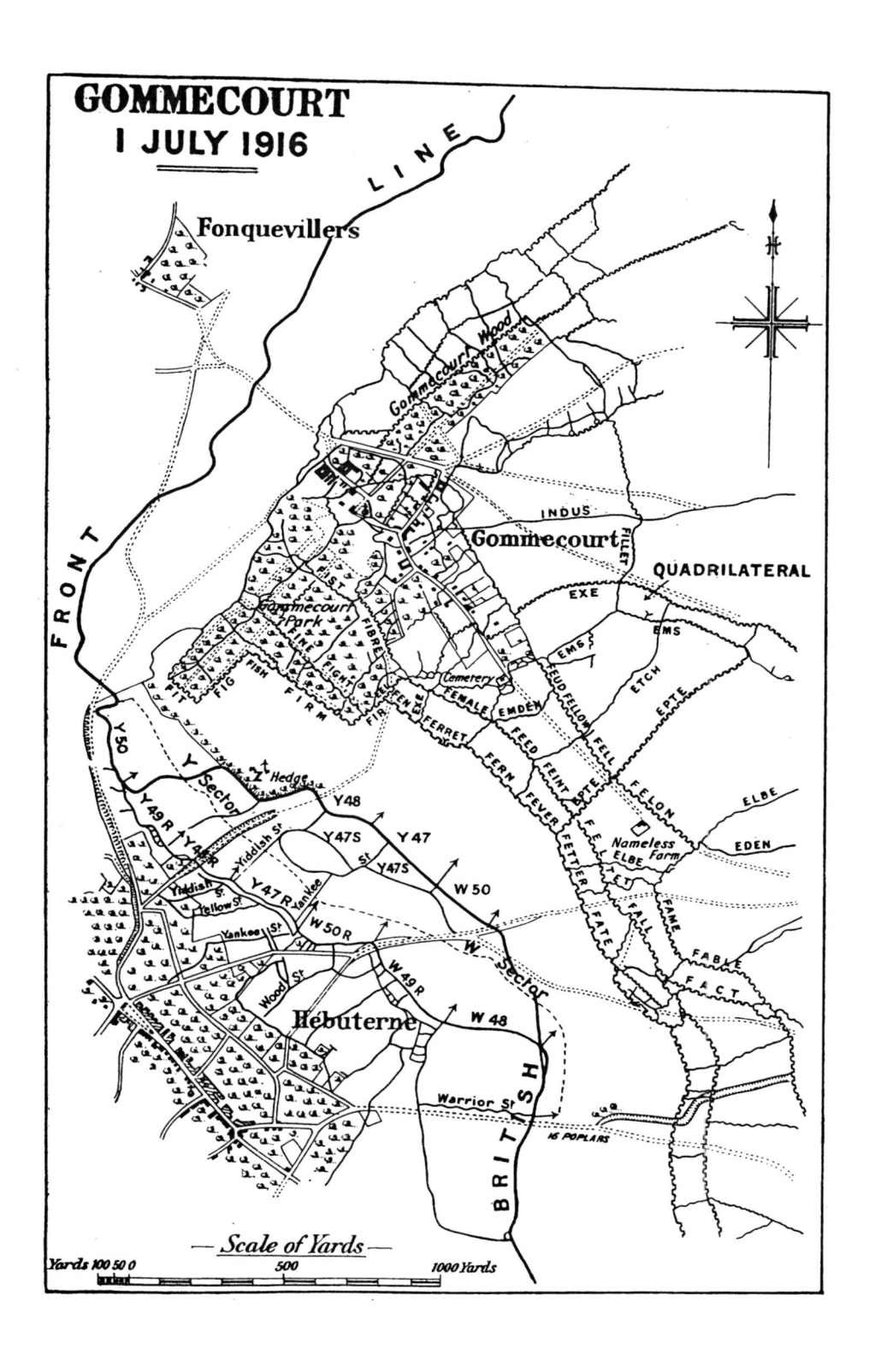

It must be remembered too that entraining arrangements for the various drafts had to be made at short notice, and that once these arrangements had been made it was, in times of stress, practically impossible to alter them without causing delay or even disorganisation of the communications to the front.

It seems probable that, when the enormous demands for reinforcements first arose, there was a certain lack of elasticity in the arrangements for the supply of drafts from the base. Some improvement was subsequently effected, but the system of sending officers and men to units other than their own, continued during the remainder of the war. This state of affairs, however unavoidable it may have been, was regarded very naturally as a hardship, both on the battalions in France and on the reinforcements who had been imbued at home with the traditions and *esprit de corps* of their own regiments.

Perhaps it bore hardest on the officers and other ranks who were sent home wounded or sick, and had very little chance of rejoining their own battalion at the front when they had recovered.

It must not be thought, however, that this complaint of the system casts any reflection on the scores of officers and thousands of other ranks of different units who were sent to the Queen's Westminsters. Although disappointed, at the time, at leaving their own regiments, they loyally served their adopted battalion, and fought in its ranks as worthy and honoured comrades. Many of them transferred later to the Queen's Westminsters, and the Regiment had good reason to be proud of them.

An event which marked the commencement of a revolution in mechanical warfare took place on August 26th. The 56th Division had been specially selected to co-operate with the new Heavy Section Machine-Gun Corps (which afterwards developed into the Tank Corps); and on this date the Division assisted in the first demonstration, in France, of these new engines of war, at which Sir Douglas Haig and many other commanders of high rank were present.

Five tanks took part in the demonstration; two of them broke down, but notwithstanding this, the operation was considered a success.

In spite of some very wet weather, some useful training was done while the Battalion was at Domvast; but far more was needed. Very few of the new draft had had any fighting experience, most of them having come straight out from England after a short, but intensive, recruit training.

On September 3rd, the Brigade moved by rail to Corbie; and on the following day marched to Happy Valley, a mile and a half to the north-west of Bray. The Battalion reached its camping ground after dark, on a cold and miserably wet night. The only shelter available consisted of a limited number of tents. Half the Battalion managed to pack into them, the remainder had to lie out in the open.

The 56th Division was now in the XIV Corps, and within a few hours was to be plunged into the midst of the terrific struggle then raging, which is known as the Battles of the Somme, 1916.

CHAPTER VIII

THE BATTLES OF THE SOMME, 1916

I.—THE FIGHTING FOR COMBLES. LEUZE WOOD

IN order to gain a clear idea of the nature of the operations in which the Battalion was about to take part, it is necessary to trace in some detail the course of the British offensive on the Somme battle front since July 1st. This is fully dealt with in Sir Douglas Haig's despatch of December 23rd, 1916, and the following summary has been derived from that source. The enemy's positions, which were attacked on July 1st, were situated on the high undulating tract of ground which formed the watershed between the Somme, on the one side, and the rivers of south-west Belgium on the other. These positions were defended by two main systems, the first well down the forward slopes of the southern face of the watershed; and the second some three to five thousand yards behind, on or near the southern crest of the highest part of the watershed. This second system extended along a front of 20,000 yards between the rivers Somme and Ancre.

The attack on these positions resolved itself into three phases, the first, which commenced on July 1st and was rounded off by the operations of the 14–17th July, gave the British possession of the southern crest of the main plateau between Delville Wood and Bazentin-le-Petit. The second phase formed a long-drawn-out contest for the main ridge. This was completed by the first week in September, and paved the way for the third phase, during which the advance was pushed down the forward slopes of the ridge and further extended on both flanks, until, from Morval to Thiepval, the whole plateau and a good deal of ground beyond were in British hands.

By July 17th, at the end of the first phase, the right of the British front ran from Maltz Horn Farm, where it linked up with the French, northwards along the eastern edge of Trones Wood, to Longueval; while the French line ran southwards from the farm to Hem on the Somme. The line formed a sharp salient at Delville Wood, on the north-west. It was clear, therefore, so far as the southern face of this salient was concerned, that the British right flank and the French troops in extension of it should swing up into line with the British centre. To do this it was necessary to capture first, Guillemont, Falfemont Farm and Leuze Wood, and then Ginchy and Bouleaux Wood, which was practically an extension of Leuze Wood to the north-east. (See map page 129).

The greatest advantage had been taken by the enemy of the natural strength of these localities, and his main second line of defence ran in front of them from Waterlot Farm, which was already in the British possession, south-eastwards to Falfemont Farm and then southwards to the Somme.

The situation on this part of the battle front is summed up in Sir Douglas Haig's despatch in the following words: " The importance of holding us back in this area could not escape the enemy's notice, and he had dug and wired many new trenches both in front of and behind his original lines. He had also brought up fresh troops, and there was no possibility of taking him by surprise. The task before us was a very difficult one and entailed a real trial of strength between the opposing forces. At this juncture its difficulties were increased by unfavourable weather."

It was most important that any swinging forward of the British right should be accompanied by a corresponding advance of the French left. To ensure this co-operation, it was arranged that the dividing line between the British and the French should run from Maltz Horn Farm due eastwards to the Combles Valley, and thence north-eastwards up that valley to a point between Sailly-Saillisel and Morval. The former village was fixed upon as the objective of the British right, and the latter as that of the French left.

After severe fighting of a preliminary character, which continued throughout the latter half of July and the first half of August, during which gradual progress was made, a combined British and French attack was launched on August 16th. This met with only partial success, and a further attack was made two days later which resulted in the British line being established on the outside of Guillemont. Violent fighting continued until September 3rd, when the British and French again delivered a combined attack.

By the evening of September 5th, the Falfemont Farm position had been captured, and British troops were firmly established in Leuze Wood. Ginchy and High Wood were still in the enemy's possession; but important progress had been made, and the British line had been advanced on a front of nearly two miles to an average depth of nearly one mile.

This, then, was the situation when, on the night of September 6th, the 56th Division relieved the 5th Division on the extreme right of the British line.

On this night, the 169th Infantry Brigade moved forward, and the Battalion went into trenches just south of the Briqueterie and about a mile to the north of Maricourt. The guide, who had been provided, was unable to find the trenches, and the Battalion did not get settled down until 4.0 a.m. The night was very cold, and very little sleep was possible.

On the 7th, the Battalion took over trenches from the L.R.B. about 500 yards north-east of Favière Wood. Although still a considerable distance from the front line, the Battalion lost 7 other ranks killed, and Lieutenant Attenborough and 7 other ranks wounded, from the enemy's shellfire.

On the same day the L.R.B. and Q.V.R. had moved forward to the front line in Leuze Wood. The L.R.B. formed the right battalion on the British front, and the Q.V.R. were on their left. At 11.30 p.m. on September 8th, these two battalions carried out a combined bombing attack, with the object of establishing a line along Loop trench, the sunken road and the northern edge of Leuze Wood. The Q.V.R. succeeded in occupying a trench running close alongside the northern edge of the Ginchy-Combles road; but about 5.15 a.m. on the 9th, the L.R.B., who had made some progress, were driven back into Leuze Wood by a strong enemy counter-attack. This bombing attack was made in preparation for a renewal of the offensive by the 56th and 16th Divisions of the XIV Corps, in co-operation with the XV Corps, on a line running from 500 yards west of Combles to 1000 yards east of Ginchy.

The attack was launched at 4.45 p.m. on September 9th, the 169th Infantry Brigade being on the right of the 56th Division with the L.R.B. on the right and the Q.V.R. on the left, with the Queen's Westminsters in reserve. By 6.15 p.m. the Q.V.R. reported that they had gained their objective outside the north-eastern edge of Leuze Wood. The L.R.B., however, had come under very heavy artillery and machine-gun fire and had been driven back into the wood with serious loss.

The position in Leuze Wood was very obscure, and at 7.30 p.m. the 169th Infantry Brigade issued the following order to the Queen's Westminsters who were in the Maltz Horn Trenches: " Your battalion will proceed straight to Leuze

Wood and drive out the enemy if he has obtained a footing there. You will then follow him up energetically and capture the German trench which runs parallel and to the east of Leuze Wood." (This was the trench which had been the objective of the L.R.B. in the afternoon's attack.)

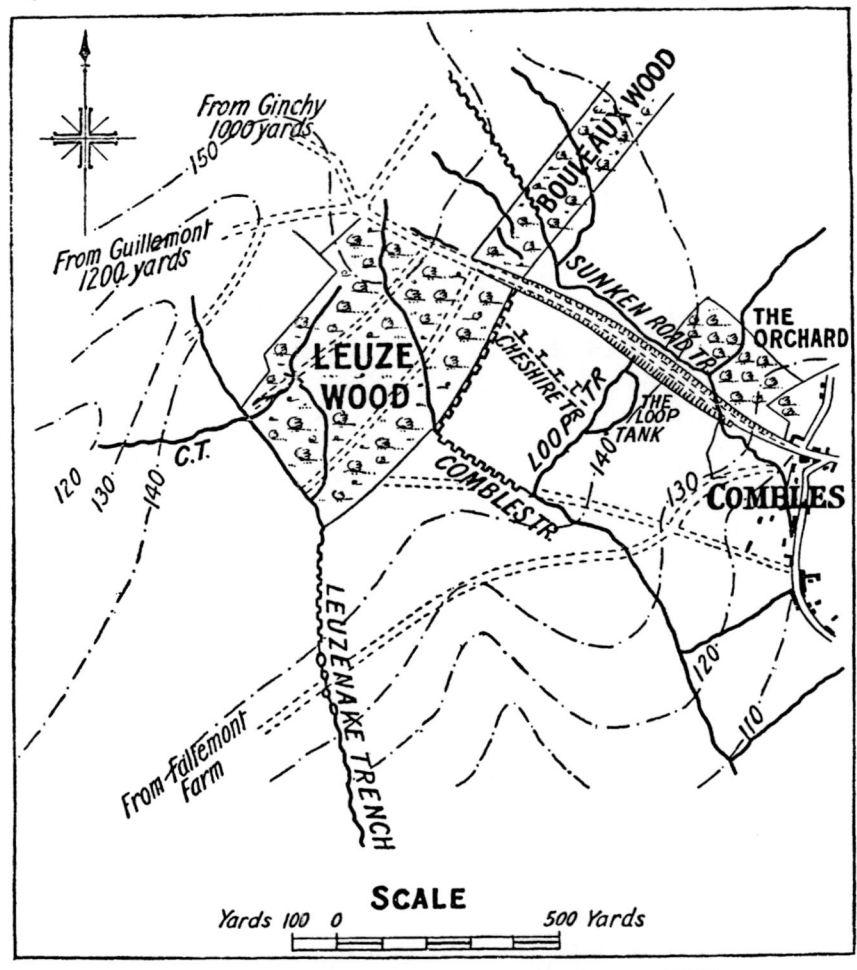

THE FIGHTING FOR COMBLES, SEPTEMBER, 1916

The Queen's Westminsters started at 8.5 p.m. They had to move over very difficult ground, and to go through a severe barrage in passing over the Falfemont Farm line; but they got through with few casualties, and reached Leuze Wood just before 11.0 p.m. Lieut.-Colonel Shoolbred at once got into personal touch with Lieut.-Colonel Dickins (commanding the Q.V.R.), and ascertained that, though the

Q.V.R. were in possession of the wood, they were in need of assistance. A Company (Captain H. Agate) was accordingly sent up to reinforce them on the northern edge of the wood, in rear of the newly captured trenches which were about 200 yards in advance of the wood. D Company (Captain J. A. Green) was sent to line the eastern edge of the wood and B (Lieutenant M. M. Webb) and C (Captain H. F. Grizelle) Companies were kept in reserve.

Leuze Wood was about 700 yards long by 400 broad. No definite information could be obtained from the battalion already there about the enemy's positions outside the wood, or even whether the wood was all clear of the enemy. Parties were accordingly sent out at once from the reserve companies to search it in all directions. The only means of communication between battalions and the Brigade was by runner, and messages took over an hour each way.

At about 1.0 a.m. on the 10th an order, which had been issued by the Brigade at 11.45 p.m., was received, that the trench on the south-eastern side of the wood must be taken before dawn; and that the Brigade was to be informed when the assault would take place, so that a barrage might be arranged. The trench referred to was, in fact, Loop trench.

The night was very dark, the wood was full of barbed-wire entanglements, and the enemy were pouring in heavy shells without cessation. Moreover, the maps were known to be inaccurate, the exact bearing of the trench to be captured and its distance from the wood were unknown, and no reliable reconnaissance could be made in the darkness. All these factors combined to render any organised attack on the enemy trench impracticable before daylight; and, even so, the hour of the assault could not be fixed until some information about the situation could be obtained. This was a problem of extreme difficulty.

The attack having been entrusted to C and D Companies, reconnaissances of the position to be attacked were made, with the result that very valuable information was obtained by a patrol, under 2nd Lieutenant E. F. Johnston of C Company, and by Lance-Corporal H. R. Wallis and Rifleman A. E. Clapham of the same company, the two latter being subsequently awarded the Military Medal for their work.

The following message was despatched from D Company, timed 3.42 a.m.: " Scouts from H.Q. have just gone out in front of my position. Trench faces E.S.E. Have not been able to discover C.T. (i.e. communication trench) in which enemy are supposed to be, and which would be my left in advance. Can only await information from scouts." By this time a thick mist had come on which added to the difficulties of getting the bearings and direction of the objective of the attack. Urgent messages were sent to the company commanders pressing for information that would enable the hour of the assault to be determined. By 5.0 a.m. this had been obtained, and zero hour was fixed for 7.0 a.m.

D Company was ordered to move to the left, so that its left rested on the sunken road at the north-east corner of Leuze Wood; and half of the Headquarter bombers were sent up to be used to protect the left flank of the company, and to bomb back from the flank of the objective towards the trenches held by the Q.V.R. on the left. C Company was formed up on the right of D. Each company was ordered to attack in waves of platoons in line; and the leading platoon of D Company was ordered to swing to the left and to attack the sunken road trench on the north-eastern side of the Combles-Leuze Wood road.

At 6.50 a.m. a message was received from the Brigade, that the artillery barrage had been arranged, and the attack started at 7.0 a.m. The barrage on the right of the attack failed entirely, owing to the destruction of the battery wires by the enemy's shells, but a barrage was put down on the left. This, however, was insufficient to keep down the enemy's fire after the attack had been launched.

Before the assault had started both C and D Companies had suffered severely. 2nd Lieutenants T. S. Apergis and E. F. Johnston had been killed and some 40 other ranks had been killed or wounded. The companies went forward at zero hour under cover of the mist, and nearly reached their objective. C Company, on the right flank, got as far as 120 yards from the wood without finding any signs of the enemy trench. But in a few minutes shots were heard from the enemy garrison, the alarm was given, and an annihilating rifle and machine-gun fire was brought to bear on to the assaulting troops, both from the main objective and from the trench on the left, on the edge of the sunken road.

The defenders, who were not under artillery fire, made good use of their rifles, and the attack was practically wiped out. Eighteen minutes after the start, the following message was received from C Company on the right: "Held up at the edge of the wood by rifle fire. Hopeless task I fear. No artillery." The companies held on as best they could; but when the strength of each of them had been reduced to about twenty-five men they were withdrawn towards their assembly position. At the same time a platoon was sent from B Company to push up to, what was later known as Combles trench but was then believed to be, a sap leading from the centre of the wood to the south-east, in order to guard that flank in case of an enemy counter-attack.

This was the situation at about 8.0 a.m. At 10.30 a.m. the following message was sent from Lieut.-Colonel Shoolbred to the Brigade : " Situation unchanged. I am lining east side of wood and digging in so far as possible, but it is hard digging in the broken tree stumps. If you will arrange an artillery bombardment on the whole trench that was to be captured, I will then try and bomb round it (i.e. through Combles Trench) afterwards. My companies cannot be collected without great delay and difficulty, and I can see no likelihood of a successful attack as at first attempted. The enemy trench, which was our objective (i.e. Loop Trench), is full of enemy, so a good bombardment should do good ; and I hope afterwards to be able to take it by bombing, and then occupy it."

In the middle of the day the Brigadier came up to the wood and, after a personal reconnaissance, ordered a fresh attack to be made at 3.0 p.m. from the south-east edge of the wood, placing one company of the 2nd Londons at the disposal of the Queen's Westminsters. It was to be a purely bombing attack, assisted by Stokes mortars and prepared by artillery.

The bombing attack started, as ordered, at 3.0 p.m. The plan was for A Company of the 2nd Londons to clear the supposed sap, already referred to, and its junction with the enemy trench which was the main objective. From this point the Queen's Westminsters were to push on and capture the main trench. The remaining men of the Headquarter bombers, supported by B and A Companies, were detailed for this purpose. An artillery barrage working up and along the trenches to be captured, at the rate of thirty yards a minute, was arranged and given ; but it did not appear to have had any serious effect in keeping down the enemy's rifle fire.

The 2nd Londons nearly reached their objective, but during their advance all the officers of the company were killed (Captain J. W. Long, 2nd Lieutenant E. W. Lockey and 2nd Lieutenant P. C. Taylor), and the survivors of the company came back bringing the Queen's Westminsters with them. Lieutenant Webb endeavoured to restart the attack, but the heavy and accurate shelling by the enemy was causing severe losses and prevented any progress being made.

The attack was not renewed again, and the survivors of B, C and D Companies were reorganised and formed up along the eastern edge of the wood where they remained until the evening. The Brigade was then relieved by a composite brigade of the 5th Division, and the Battalion was withdrawn to the Citadel (two miles north of Bray). The losses of the Battalion, on the 10th September and on the night of the 9th/10th amounted to 307 all told. Of these 4 officers, 2nd Lieutenants T. S. Apergis, E. F. Johnston, H. Stevenson and M. Spencer-Smith, and 52 other ranks were killed; 5 officers, 2nd Lieutenants G. W. Cranmore, E. G. T. Okill, H. L. Bell, C. E. Moy and W. L. Morgan, and 166 other ranks were wounded; and 80 other ranks were missing. The day had been one of failure. Some of the difficulties connected with the attacks have already been told; but, in view of what was subsequently ascertained as to the strength of the enemy's positions, it appears that the Battalion had only failed to achieve what was a practically superhuman task with the forces available. The sap, to which reference has been made, was not, in fact, a sap at all; it was the remains of a trench that had been nearly obliterated by shell-fire, which led to a strong point adapted for all-round defence. On the left, in the sunken road trench, there was a large fortified crater with a deep mined dugout; this was ultimately captured on September 15th with the aid of a tank. It was from these two points, more particularly the crater, that the enemy had caused so many casualties by a cross fire from his machine guns.

No account of the operation would be complete without a tribute to the extreme gallantry and devotion with which Captain A. Ramsbottom, R.A.M.C. (the medical officer attached to the Battalion), Sergeant G. E. Cordery and all the stretcher-bearers, without exception, attended to the wounded under such shell-fire as the Battalion had never before experienced.

The one German dugout, in the south-west corner of the wood, had been set aside as a dressing-station. This became the centre of the enemy's shelling, and, for practically the whole of the twenty-four hours that the Battalion was in the wood, the work of tending the wounded had to be carried on in the open. The dugout was soon filled with men whom it was impossible to evacuate during daylight, owing to the heavy and incessant fire. Many of the wounded were brought in by deeds of great bravery during the day, and amongst those who particularly distinguished themselves were Rifleman Bishop, of C Company, who gained the Military Medal; Private H. C. Sykes, R.A.M.C. (attached to the Battalion as a candidate for a combatant commission), who brought in many men, including one from practically under the German parapet, and Lance-Corporal J. W. Willcox and Lance-Corporal H. E. Wright, who had been in charge of a Lewis gun during the attack on the sunken road. Lance-Corporal Wright showed conspicuous courage by going into No-man's-land time after time to rescue wounded. Three times his companions were either killed or hit, but he still carried on, getting willing volunteers to help him.

Although the operations to the north-east and east of Leuze Wood had not resulted in any gain of ground on the extreme right of the Fourth Army's attack, yet they were not without effect on the success of the fighting on the remainder of the front. The line of enemy trenches to the east of Ginchy had been captured and further progress had been made to the east of Delville Wood. The French, in the south, had also made valuable progress, the weak salient in the allied line had disappeared, and the way was paved for the further attack by the Fourth Army, in conjunction with the French, which took place on September 15th.

The Battalion spent the 11th and 12th September in huts and tents at the Citadel; and, after an all too short rest of some thirty hours, moved forward on the 13th to the old German trench system near the crucifix, to the north of Hardecourt. On the 15th, the day of the great attack, the Q.W.R. and L.R.B. formed the reserve of the 56th Division. The object of the attack of the Fourth Army on this day was to capture Morval, Lesbœufs, Gueudecourt and Flers, and to break through; while the main task of the 56th Division, on the right of the attack, was to clear Bouleaux Wood and to form a protective flank, covering all the lines of advance from Combles and the valleys running north-east from the village.

The attack of September 15th was a particularly notable one, for it was the first occasion on which tanks were used. Three of these were allotted to the 56th Division, and they are referred to in the Battalion War Diary as "armoured caterpillar motor-cars." One tank was attached to the 169th Infantry Brigade. This was to co-operate with the 2nd Londons in an attack on the trenches, south-east of Leuze Wood, which had been the objective of the Queen's Westminsters on the 10th. The tank travelled successfully as far as the trench running parallel with the edge of the wood, where it broke down; and the crew, who continued firing from it until their ammunition was exhausted, ultimately had no alternative but to set fire to it and make their escape. The tank, however, had served some useful purpose, for it had helped the 2nd Londons to capture the sap and strong point which they and the Queen's Westminsters had been unable to take in the afternoon of the 10th. The 2nd Londons, who continued their progress up to within 100 yards of the sunken road, then made repeated attempts, in conjunction with a party of bombers of the L.R.B., to capture the trench junction at the sunken road; but the enemy held the road in such strength that no progress could be maintained.

This third failure to occupy the trench junction emphasises the strength of the position which had defied all the attempts of the L.R.B., on the 9th, and the Queen's Westminsters, on the following day, to effect its capture.

During the morning the battalions in Divisional reserve were moved up from Falfemont Farm to Angle Wood Valley, just north of the farm, but were not actually employed. In the evening the Queen's Westminsters were placed at the disposal of the 169th Infantry Brigade, but they still remained part of the Divisional reserve.

On the evening of the 15th the situation on the 56th Divisional front was as follows: the 169th Infantry Brigade, on the right, had progressed up Loop trench, to within about a hundred yards of the sunken road; and was in possession of the Combles trench, up to a point about half-way between Combles and Leuze Wood. The 168th Infantry Brigade was holding the main German line, running through the centre of Bouleaux Wood, and was in touch with the 6th Division on its left; while the 167th Infantry Brigade had pushed forward posts into Middle Copse about 200 yards to the north-west of the centre of this wood.

The Queen's Westminsters remained in Divisional reserve until the afternoon of the 16th when they again rejoined the 169th Infantry Brigade, remaining in the Angle Wood Valley until the evening of the 17th. Orders were then received, about 5.0 p.m., for an attack which was to take place on the following day, as part of a general attack of the XIV Corps. The objective of the 56th Division, on the right, was a line from the trench junction on the sunken road to Middle Copse inclusive; while the 6th Division on its left was to prolong this line and gain touch with the 20th Division, at a point some 1200 yards north-east of Ginchy. The 169th Infantry Brigade was on the right of the 56th Division, and its objective was the sunken road trench, from the trench junction to the south-eastern corner of Bouleaux Wood. The 167th Infantry Brigade on their left were to capture the remaining objectives of the Division. The Queen's Westminsters were ordered to carry out the attack of the 169th Infantry Brigade, assisted by bombers of the L.R.B.

During the night, a line of assembly trenches, between Leuze Wood and Loop trench, was dug by a company of the Cheshire Pioneers and a party of the 2nd Londons. These trenches were roughly parallel with the objective, and the Battalion was ordered to assemble in them by 4.30 a.m. on the 18th. The Battalion started at 3.0 a.m. from Angle Wood Valley. Heavy rain had fallen and the going was exceedingly difficult, but the assembly position was reached by the appointed hour.

The plan of attack was for the Queen's Westminsters to move forward to their objective, under cover of an intense artillery barrage north and east of it and of a Stokes mortar barrage on the orchard, which lay to the north-east of the assembly position; and to gain touch as soon as possible with the 167th Infantry Brigade on the left. Meanwhile the L.R.B. were to push on to the trench junction, on the right flank of the attack, and block the trench running south-east from this point in the direction of Combles. Two machine guns were attached to the Battalion for the defence of the objective when gained. In the course of a preliminary reconnaissance for the attack during the evening of September 17th, 2nd Lieutenants G. A. N. Lowndes and Warwick were wounded.

The Battalion which had been organised into three companies owing to its losses, was disposed on the morning of the attack as follows :—

No. 2 (B and D Companies, less one platoon) under the command of Captain J. A. Green on the right, No. 1 (A Company, less one platoon) under the command of a/Captain M. M. Webb on the left, and No. 3 (C Company and the two platoons from Nos. 1 and 2 Companies) under the command of 2nd Lieutenant N. T. Thurston, in support. Nos. 1 and 2 Companies were in the new assembly trench, and No. 3 was in the western end of Combles trench.

At 5.50 a.m. the assaulting waves left their trenches. The enemy barrage was put down almost at once; but the two leading companies worked forward, and had nearly reached their objectives when they came under heavy machine-gun fire. Some men from both companies got as far as the sunken road, and 2nd Lieutenant Eric Jones and Sergeant E. Newnham, who was in command of a platoon, actually reached the German trench. These two were probably the only men who reached the objective. Lieutenant Jones was killed as he was turning round to encourage his men. Sergeant Newnham had nearly reached the enemy trench when he found himself entirely unsupported; he turned back but could not find any unwounded men, so went forward again, through heavy machine-gun fire, to the German parapet and threw bombs amongst the enemy, until he himself was wounded. He then managed to crawl back to the assembly trench, where he reported to an officer later in the day.

Further progress by the companies was impossible; the enemy was found to be holding his position in great strength, and the assaulting troops were suffering very severe losses.

2nd Lieutenant N. T. Thurston, who had moved the support company up to the jumping-off trench as soon as the attack started and had lost many men, was ordered to remain there by Captain Green, who rightly saw the uselessness of throwing away more men in the attack. The survivors of Nos. 1 and 2 Companies were also withdrawn to this trench. In the meantime, on the right flank, the bombing attack of the L.R.B. had failed completely.

The situation at 6.45 a.m. is vividly summed up in the following message from Captain Green: "The first line nearly to objective, and then wiped out. Only twenty left of assaulting company and about fifty of support company. Impossible to advance over the open. L.R.B. cannot get over first barricade; they are trying again with rifle grenades."

On receipt of this message orders were given that the jumping-off trench must be held at all costs; and, if necessary, Captain Green was to ask for help from the L.R.B.

By 10.0 a.m. all that were left of the Battalion were three officers and ninety other ranks; and these, together with the two machine guns, held the assembly trench without further assistance for the rest of the day. The enemy kept the trench under continuous fire, rendering all movement impossible; and the pouring rain and bitter cold added discomfort to the stern task of this gallant band of men.

The renewed attempts of the L.R.B. on the right were assisted by a Stokes mortar, and by 2.45 in the afternoon some sixty yards of the Combles trench had been captured. On the left no progress had been made. Owing to the impossible condition of the ground, the 167th Infantry Brigade had been unable to reach their assembly positions and their attack did not materialise.

During this day the Battalion suffered 104 casualties, 37 being killed. All the officers of A Company were killed. These were a/Captain M. M. Webb, who was wounded during the first advance and was killed later in the day in our own trench;

2nd Lieutenant R. Harrison, a promising officer, who was killed during the advance; and 2nd Lieutenant Eric Jones, whose death has already been mentioned.

Captain Webb was an outstanding example of the many young officers who fulfilled responsibilities of command far beyond their years, and yet retained all the high spirits and light-heartedness of youth. Eric Jones, a son of Major R. T. Jones, formerly of the Regiment, had served during the first year of the war in the H.A.C., and on receiving his commission was appointed to the Queen's Westminsters. Colonel Shoolbred writes of him: " He was one of those happy natures with an infinite gift of seeing the bright side of everything. Not even the dirt and other unpleasantnesses of the Somme checked his overflowing happiness. He spread cheerfulness wherever he was and I myself owe more than one debt of encouragement and help to his ready and eager response to every call. He leaves to the Regiment another example of duty most gallantly carried out."

In the evening the Battalion was relieved by the L.R.B., and moved back to Angle Wood Valley to reorganise.

During the night some seventy men, who had lain out all day in shell-holes in front of the assembly trench, rejoined the Battalion; this brought its strength up from ninety to 160, and the numbers were further increased by a new draft of 180. These latter were nearly all new men with only twelve weeks' training at home, and no war experience.

On September 20th the Battalion returned to the line, relieving the L.R.B. in the left sector of the Brigade front. On the following night they dug a trench at the block established by the L.R.B. in the Combles trench; and on the morning of the 23rd they established a bombing post in a sap, dug by the Cheshire Pioneers from Loop trench to the tank which had been disabled on September 15th.

The Battalion, after being relieved by the Q.V R. on the evening of the 23rd, moved back to the Falfemont line; and on the 24th went into Divisional reserve in Casement trench just north of Maricourt. In the early morning of this day a fifth attempt was made to capture the Combles trench. The attack was made by the Q.V.R., with the aid of bombs, rifle grenades and Stokes mortars; and, although the attack eventually broke down, the Q.V.R. remained in possession of the old German block in the trench.

On the 25th, the Fourth Army delivered a general attack in conjunction with an attack made by the French further south. The task of the 56th Division was to form a protective flank, facing south-east, for the remainder of the XIV Corps. In the course of the day the whole of Combles trench and Loop trench were captured, and the 5th Division on the left took the greater part of Morval, but failed to gain the important spur to the south-east of the village. The enemy, owing to the allied pressure on the north-east and south-east, were compelled to abandon Combles; and, at 5.0 a.m. on the 26th, an officer's patrol of the L.R.B. entered the village and joined hands with French troops who had approached it from the south.

Combles was cleared and occupied in the course of the day, and in the evening the Brigade was withdrawn from the line and moved back into billets at Méaulte.

The capture of Combles, without further sacrifice of men, was a great tactical success. It marked an important stage in the allied advance, and provided a fitting termination to the desperate fighting of the 169th Infantry Brigade in the vicinity of Leuze Wood.

II.—THE BATTLE OF THE TRANSLOY RIDGES

On September 27th, when the 169th Infantry Brigade was withdrawn from the line, and the French front had been extended to the left, it was expected that the 56th Division would be sent back for rest and reorganisation.

The losses suffered by the battalions had, to some extent, been made good by drafts; but the newly joined officers lacked experience, and the men, as has already been pointed out, had only had a few weeks' training at home. Practically all the trained bombers had become casualties, and of the Lewis-gunners very few were left. The situation, however, was such that every available unit was required, to maintain the pressure on an enemy whose resistance was daily weakening; and on September 30th the Division again went into the line on the right flank of the British Army.

Preparations were being made for a renewal of the attack by the Fourth Army on the general line Le Transloy, Thilloy, Warlencourt and Faucourt; and, to ensure its success, divisions holding the line were ordered to gain, by October 5th, certain tactical points from which observation could be obtained of the enemy's main positions commanding the Le Transloy line.

On the night of September 30th, the Queen's Westminsters relieved the 9th Suffolks (of the 71st Infantry Brigade, 6th Division) in trenches about 250 yards to the east of Lesbœufs, where they were in touch with the French on the right and the Q.V.R. on the left. The situation in front was very obscure, the positions of the enemy trenches were entirely unknown, and no air photos or maps were available.

On October 1st certain corps of the Fourth and Reserve Armies made an attack on Eaucourt l'Abbaye. No general advance was attempted by the XIV Corps, which was to the right of the front attacked. Its share in the operations was limited to an intense bombardment of the enemy positions, and, so far as the front of the 56th Division was concerned, to an attempt, under cover of the artillery barrage, to secure a little more ground in front of the existing line.

The Battalion was ordered, as part of this scheme, to send out, at 3.45 p.m. (the zero hour for the attack further north), a patrol of one officer and twenty men to occupy some enemy trenches, the furthest of which was about 600 yards to the east of Lesbœufs; and, after dusk, to send forward an additional party of twenty men to consolidate the furthest trench. The Brigade order intimated that the intention of the operations, on the 56th Divisional front, was " not to become involved in any fighting, but, nevertheless, to take advantage of the artillery preparation, by pushing forward small determined patrols."

2nd Lieutenant T. W. Webster (11th Londons, attached Q.W.R.) was selected to lead the patrol sent out by the Battalion. The objective was marked on the map as a trench, but as a matter of fact it was only half dug and was not continuous, and in many places it had been destroyed by the artillery to such an extent as to render it indistinguishable as a trench at all.

The patrol reached what was thought to be the furthest trench and found it strongly held; and a third trench, not shown on the map, was discovered to the left of what the patrol took to be the first objective. The party came under rifle and machine-gun fire from the front and a heavy enfilade fire from the flank. Lieutenant Webster was killed and several men were hit in front of the enemy trench, and the remainder of the patrol were forced to lie up in shell-holes. They remained in front of the trench until dusk, when a few men, bringing with them the two Lewis guns, returned to our lines.

Twelve of the patrol failed to return, but a party, which was sent out to search for them, succeeded in finding six men. The remainder were posted as missing.

The lack of air photographs undoubtedly contributed very largely to the failure of this enterprise which resulted in the loss of a valuable officer. It appears that the patrol must have overshot its mark and reached a trench beyond the objective, for on the following night, when the L.R.B. successfully located and occupied the required position, it was found not to be occupied by the enemy.

The German guns replied to the British barrage by an extremely heavy bombardment of the front line, but the Battalion casualties were comparatively light, the total losses during the day amounting to 8 killed and 23 wounded, in addition to the 6 men missing from the patrol.

During the night of the 1st/2nd October, D Company moved up to the front line, to relieve a company of the French on the right of A Company. Both A and D Companies were very heavily shelled throughout the day, and it was only the deep, narrow trenches that saved them from very severe casualties. The following extracts from the daily report of the companies in the line speak for themselves :—

"*Right Company*.—The trench was continually blown in by enemy artillery fire during the day, and parties were at work repairing trench, also digging out men buried by shellfire. At night work was done on the incomplete sector of trench between the right company and the left company. Work was carried on until 3.30 a.m."

"*Left Company*.—In the forward trench, work was done on trench to join up with the right company. Parties were also out burying dead and carrying wounded. Work on the trench was rendered almost impossible by the weather conditions ; there was about $1\frac{1}{2}$ foot of mud in the trench. The men worked hard, but they were very tired and had been subjected to extremely heavy shelling."

These extracts indicate the experiences that the Battalion was sharing with the other units of the Division, but the work done did not pass unnoticed by the higher command. The following entry occurs in the War Diary of the 169th Infantry Brigade : " The Corps Commander signified great approval of the work done by the 56th Division in clearing the battlefield with troops already tired out with fighting."

On October 2nd, A and D Companies were relieved in the line by two companies of the L.R.B. ; and on the following night, after handing over to the Kensingtons, the whole Battalion was withdrawn to the Citadel. It was employed for the next two days in track-making, salvage work and cable-burying.

OCTOBER, 1916

On October 7th, the Fourth Army renewed the attack in conjunction with the French. The first task of the 56th Division included the capture of a series of disconnected trenches and emplacements, known as Hazy, Dewdrop, Spectrum and part of Rainbow, which lay somewhat to the north-east of Lesbœufs, and the second task was to establish a line on the forward slope of the ridge from which the Le Transloy system could be seen.

The attack of the Division was made by the 168th Infantry Brigade on the right, and the 167th on the left, while the 169th was kept in Divisional reserve. Major P. E. Harding and ten runners of the Queen's Westminsters were attached to the 167th Infantry Brigade for liaison purposes. Good progress was made on both flanks, but the centre of the attack was held up by machine-gun fire; and later in the day, when the enemy counter-attacked, the whole line was driven back to its original departure trenches.

At noon the Queen's Westminsters moved, by cross-country tracks, to a position to the east of Trones Wood where they remained until evening. The Battalion was then placed at the disposal of the 167th Infantry Brigade; and, after moving forward to a point south of Ginchy, it was employed in carrying stores and ammunition to the forward trenches.

The attack was renewed on the 8th October, but no progress was made. During the night the Battalion relieved the whole of the front line troops of the 167th Infantry Brigade in trenches some 800 yards north-east of Lesbœufs, and on the following evening the line was handed over to three companies of the Lancashire Fusiliers and one company of the Duke's Regiment. The enemy's shelling, which had been very heavy throughout the day, developed into a barrage at about 6.0 p.m., and it looked as though an enemy attack was about to be made. The relief was in progress at the time; and the troops of the three battalions, who were intermingled along the trench, were reorganised by the officers into mixed platoons and "stood to." The S.O.S. signal was sent up by a forward observation officer, and our artillery at once put up a heavy counter-barrage. No attack, however, developed, and in about half an hour the enemy's fire slackened down. The relief, which had been very considerably delayed by this "alarm," was not completed until 3.0 a.m. on the 10th.

On this, the last day on which the Battalion took an active part in the Somme fighting of 1916, the Queen's Westminsters suffered 49 casualties, of whom 7 were killed.

After the relief the Battalion moved back and bivouacked

to the west of Trones Wood, and on the following day it was withdrawn to the Citadel (two miles north of Bray).

The 169th Infantry Brigade marched, on October 11th, to Ville sur Ancre, whence it was conveyed in French motor omnibuses to La Chaussée sur Somme.

The transport moved by road, and on its arrival the transport officer reported that, during the march, two of the Lewis-gun hand-carts had collapsed, and that he had abandoned them. This " catastrophe " was greeted with joy. The hand-carts had been found practically useless; not only did they add to the weight of the Lewis-gun equipment, but they were so ill adapted to rough usage, that hardly a journey was completed without a mishap of some kind. The remaining hand-carts, which had been with the Battalion for over a year, shared the same fate.

The next nine days were spent in resting; and during the period Battalion staff parade was reinstituted for the first time since the Battalion was at Monchaux, in the early summer of 1916.

On October 18th, Lieut.-Colonel Shoolbred, who had brought the Queen's Westminsters to France in November, 1914, and had commanded them continuously ever since, went to hospital. He was invalided to England on two months' sick leave, and the command of the Battalion passed temporarily to Major P. E. Harding, M.C.

On the 21st the Battalion marched to Huppy, a distance of about twenty-one miles. This was a severe test after the recent fighting; but, notwithstanding the lack of march training, the men covered the distance extremely well. A further march of seven miles, on the 23rd, brought the Battalion to Pont Remy where it entrained for Berguette. The Battalion arrived at this place at midnight after being in the train for eight hours. It paraded again at 2.0 a.m. and marched a further nine miles to Calonne sur la Lys, where the troops were billeted in factories and barns.

On October 25th, orders were received for the Queen's Westminsters to be ready to move at one hour's notice, to support either the I or the IV Corps at Givenchy or Cuinchy. They were not, however, called on, and on the 27th the Battalion marched to Lestrem, continuing the journey on October 29th to Bout de Ville, which was its final destination.

The following message from General Sir Henry Rawlinson, Commanding the Fourth Army, was circulated when the 56th Division was withdrawn from the front :—

" I desire to place on record my appreciation of the work

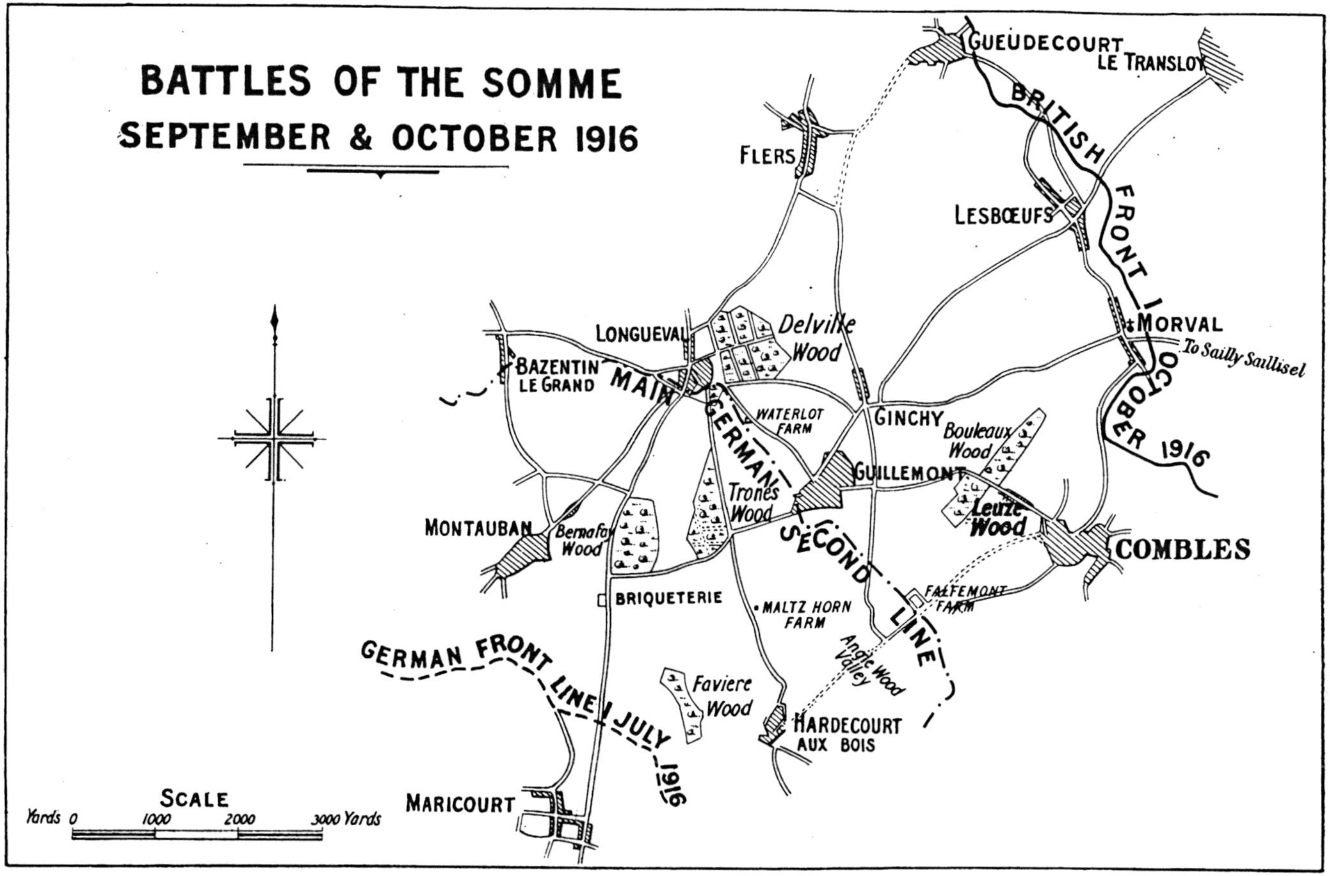
BATTLES OF THE SOMME
SEPTEMBER & OCTOBER 1916
GUEUDECOURT
LE TRANSLOY
BRITISH FRONT 1 OCTOBER 1916
FLERS
LESBŒUFS
MORVAL
To Sailly Saillisel
LONGUEVAL
Delville Wood
BAZENTIN LE GRAND
MAIN GERMAN SECOND LINE
WATERLOT FARM
GINCHY
Bouleaux Wood
GUILLEMONT
Trones Wood
Leuze Wood
MONTAUBAN
Bernafay Wood
COMBLES
BRIQUETERIE
MALTZ HORN FARM
FALFEMONT FARM
Angle Wood Valley
GERMAN FRONT LINE 1 JULY 1916
Faviere Wood
HARDECOURT AUX BOIS
SCALE
Yards 0 1000 2000 3000 Yards
MARICOURT

THE BATTALION LEAVES THE SOMME FRONT

that was carried out by the 56th Division during the Battles of the Somme. The successful operations in the neighbourhood of Bouleaux and Leuze Woods, together with the capture of Combles, between the 9th and 27th September, were feats of arms deserving of the highest praise, and I congratulate the Division on the gallantry, perseverance and endurance displayed by all ranks. When, after only two days' rest, the Division was again called upon to go into the line, they displayed a fine spirit of determination which deserved success. The enterprise and hard work which the Division has shown in sapping forward and constructing trenches under fire has been a noticeable feature in the operations, and I specially congratulate the infantry on the progress they made in this manner at Bouleaux Wood.

" It is a matter of regret that this fine Division has now left the Fourth Army, but I trust that at some future time I may again find them under my command.

" H.Q., Fourth Army, Oct. 27th, 1916."

The part played by the Queen's Westminsters, during the period covered by this message, has been described in the preceding pages of this chapter. No better testimony to the terrible nature of the fighting can be found than in the following summary of the casualties, suffered by the Regiment during the thirty-three days between September 7th and October 9th, 1916 :—

	Killed.	Wounded.	Missing.	Total.
Officers	7	12	1	20
Other ranks	120	334	107	561
Total	127	346	108	581

CHAPTER IX

NEUVE CHAPELLE AND LAVENTIE

THE Queen's Westminsters remained in the Neuve Chapelle and Laventie sectors, in the XI Corps area, from October 29th, 1916, until March 1st, 1917. Life on this front was comparatively peaceful after the violent fighting on the Somme; and, with the exception of about a fortnight, in the latter part of January, when an attempt was made to maintain a series of posts in parts of the German front line which the enemy had temporarily abandoned, the conditions were those of ordinary trench warfare.

After four days' training at Bout de Ville, the Battalion, on November 3rd, relieved the Q.V.R., who were holding the line in front of Neuve Chapelle, the relief being carried out in daylight without interference by the enemy. The Battalion front was held with three companies in the front line and one in support. The two flank companies each had two platoons in the front line, one platoon in a defended post behind the line, and one platoon in support; whereas the centre company had three platoons in the front line and one in a defended post in rear. These dispositions are typical of the whole system of defence in this area and at this period.

The defences consisted almost entirely of breastworks, for, in the low-lying ground, it was not possible to dig for more than two feet below the surface without reaching the water level. The communication trenches on the whole were good; they were well revetted and provided with floor boards; but the fire trenches were in a poor state of repair, and the wire in front was very thin. The sector was provided with a system of trench tramways, which enabled rations and stores to be brought forward as far as the support line without having recourse to carrying parties.

The condition of No-man's-land, and of the German trenches, is dealt with later, but one interesting feature of the enemy defence scheme, described by Colonel P. E. Harding, may be mentioned here. This was a concrete machine-gun chamber constructed a few yards in front of the German front line trench. It was not more than 4 ft. 6 in. high, but was large enough to hold two machine guns. Two narrow slits, one at each end of the chamber, enabled enfilade fire to be brought to bear on an attack against either flank. The chamber was covered with earth and was quite indistinguishable from the rest of the enemy front line, as seen from the British trenches.

Except for recording trench-mortar activity on both sides, the only entry of interest in the War Diary during the Battalion's first spell in these trenches is as follows :—

" *November 7th.*—Very wet. Trenches falling in badly in many places—part of the line flooded. Work continued all night clearing away the landslides and baling and pumping the trenches. A wiring party which was sent out about 6.30 p.m., from D Company, was attacked with rifles and grenades by a strong enemy patrol. Two sergeants who were out in front of the wire, examining the ground, were surprised. One succeeded in getting back to the trench, but Sergeant Hawkins was missing. It is thought that he was wounded and taken prisoner. The wiring party fell back to the trench with two men wounded. The Middlesex on our left then opened Lewis-gun fire on the patrol, who retreated at the double. An officers' patrol was immediately sent out. They searched the ground for an hour and three-quarters, but no signs were seen of the enemy or the missing sergeant."

On the 9th, the Battalion was relieved by the Q.V.R., and went into support billets at Croix Barbée. On the 15th it returned to the same trenches for six days, after which it was again relieved by the Q.V.R., moving back this time to Bout de Ville.

On November 27th, the Brigade was moved out of the front line for twelve days' rest and training, the Queen's Westminsters marching from Bout de Ville to Robermetz, just outside Merville, about seven miles away. Here the Battalion was comfortably billeted in farm buildings and empty houses until December 9th, when it moved forward to reserve billets, at Pont du Hem on the La Bassée road, with two platoons of D Company finding the garrisons of six small posts in the neighbourhood, and the remainder of the Battalion supplying working parties.

On December 15th, the Queen's Westminsters relieved the Q.V.R. in the line, in front of Neuve Chapelle.

All along the Divisional front, No-man's-land was rapidly becoming flooded, and in some places the enemy appeared to be evacuating his front line trenches which were full of water. Patrols were sent out nightly by the Battalion to ascertain the condition of the enemy's trenches, and whether he was occupying them. Sometimes the enemy would be working on his defences. At other times his posts were found to be empty. On December 18th the following entry occurs in the War Diary: ". . . a patrol (2nd Lieut. Rankin and 2 other ranks) went out from the trenches south of Neuve Chapelle. Spotted a wiring party and strong covering party. On return of patrol we turned Lewis gun on the enemy. A second patrol (2nd Lieut. Pickles and 6 other ranks) went out from the trenches north of Neuve Chapelle to examine enemy wire, but was unable to reach it owing to depth of water."

There was a considerable increase in trench-mortar and artillery activity about the middle of December, the entry in the War Diary for the 16th reading as follows: " 30 ' minnies ' over Hell Corner and New Cut Alley at 12.30 p.m. Rifle grenades all along the line "; and for the following day: " The hostile artillery was very active for two hours in the morning and three hours in the afternoon. Two direct hits on New Cut Alley, also shells of various calibre on Hell Corner and Château Redoubt."

On December 21st, the front of the 56th Division was shifted somewhat towards the north; and in the morning the Queen's Westminsters took over part of the line, on their left, held by the 2nd Londons. Late in the afternoon the Battalion was relieved by the Q.V.R. and the 13th Royal Fusiliers, the relief being delayed by a heavy trench-mortar bombardment about New Cut Alley.

After the relief, the Battalion moved into reserve at Pont du Hem; here it remained until the 27th, finding large working parties daily, those on Christmas Day being " rather less owing to the bombardment of our guns."

On Christmas Day the following greeting was received from His Majesty the King :—

" I send you, my sailors and soldiers, hearty good wishes for Christmas and the New Year, and my grateful thoughts are ever with you for victories gained and for your unfailing cheeriness. Another Christmas has come round and we are still at war, but the Empire are confident in you. Remain determined to win. May God bless you and protect you."

The Battalion relieved the Q.V.R. on December 27th, and remained in the line until January 3rd, 1917.

The first two days of the tour were uneventful; but the enemy celebrated the New Year by bombarding the trenches persistently, from 10.30 a.m. to 10.30 p.m., with his artillery and trench mortars. Much damage was caused, but the Battalion suffered no casualties. In reply our guns, trench mortars and Stokes mortars carried out, on the following day, from 12.0 noon until dusk, an organised shoot on the enemy front and support lines. The infantry usually suffer on these occasions from the enemy's counter-shelling, but the bombardment provoked no retaliation, at any rate on the front held by the Queen's Westminsters.

On January 3rd, the Battalion was relieved by the Kensingtons and moved back to billets in Bout de Ville, the relief having to be carried out after dark owing to the damage done to the communication trenches on the 1st.

Three very different events marked the six days' rest that followed. On the 10th, the Battalion was inspected by the Corps Commander, Lieut.-General Sir R. C. B. Haking, K.C.B., who, amongst other things, expressed the opinion that all ranks looked " well set-up, well fed, and happy, and so did their Colonel ! " The next day a ring was borrowed from the Royal Engineers and a boxing tournament was held, in which the events for six weights were keenly contested. The afternoon proved most successful. On January 12th, a bad fire, which lasted from 6.0 p.m. until midnight, broke out in the billets of No. 5 platoon. Most of the men were at the " Bow Bells " at the time and they lost practically the whole of their kits ; but owing to the prompt action of 2nd Lieutenant A. M. Mackle, Sergeant Ing, and Rifleman Buckley and others, the Lewis guns were saved. The building was completely destroyed, but a quantity of paper money belonging to the old civilian owner of the billets, which had been hidden behind the rafters, was saved, as also was a mule who was hauled out of his stable by the combined efforts of six men pulling on his halter and a seventh encouraging him from the rear with a shovel.

The period of rest came to an end on January 12th, and was followed by a very strenuous tour in the trenches. In the first days of the new year, it had been definitely ascertained, by patrols of the 167th Infantry Brigade, that the German front line in the Fauquissart section had been abandoned, and places had been discovered where permanent British posts could be established on the abandoned line (see map).

During the night of January 10th, the 167th Infantry Brigade had established four posts (subsequently named Barnet, Flame, Bertha and Irma) in the German front line, and on the night of the 12th two more posts (Hampstead Heath and Enfield). These posts covered a front of about a mile.

On January 13th, three parties, each consisting of an officer and twenty-three other ranks with a Lewis gun, were sent up to take over Barnet and Enfield, and also Hampstead if it was in British hands. Barnet and Enfield were occupied; but Hampstead had been rushed by the enemy just before the relief took place, and it was allowed to remain in his possession.

In connection with the relief, the following Brigade order had been issued on January 11th: "The posts will be relieved every 24 hours; the points at which they are established have been selected with a view to watching the western exits of the three main German communication trenches. In the event of heavy shelling the garrisons of the posts may move to a flank. It is intended that the posts should be stubbornly defended."

On January 14th, the remainder of the Battalion relieved the 7th Middlesex on the right flank of the Fauquissart section, with three companies in the front and support trenches and one company in Battalion reserve. An extra platoon of B Company was sent up each night to the front line, to stand by in support of the posts which were held by C and D Companies.

Orders had been issued by the Brigade that special attention was to be paid to the strengthening of Enfield post, and that Hampstead post was to be reconnoitred, in order to find out whether it was held by the Germans and in what strength and within what limits. In pursuance of these orders, some excellent work was done by patrols led by 2nd Lieutenant A. M. Mackle, 2nd Lieutenant W. G. Orr (19th Londons, attached), and 2nd Lieutenant B. C. Lewall. These patrols established the fact that the old German front line, opposite the centre and left companies, had been completely abandoned by the enemy, but that he was holding two posts, including Hampstead, which he had captured on the 13th, and also had a sentry group opposite the right company. The Battalion remained in the line until the 20th, and during the tour rapid progress was made with the consolidation of the new posts. The whole of A Company was employed every night in erecting wire, using in six nights no less than 272 coils of barbed wire, 370 pickets, as well as a number of "knife rests."

The following entry in the War Diary gives a graphic picture of the condition of the German lines and of No-man's-land in which the men were working: "Mud knee deep, the country immediately behind the old German front completely flooded, the trenches blown or fallen in."

On the 17th, the enemy opened a very heavy trench-mortar bombardment on Enfield, and the post was temporarily evacuated to save casualties, but it was reoccupied as soon as the bombardment ceased. On the 20th, the Battalion was relieved by the L.R.B. A and B Companies remained in defended posts on the Rue du Bacquerot, whilst the remaining two companies moved back to billets in Laventie.

While the Battalion was at rest the enemy kept the posts under an almost continuous bombardment, and made repeated attempts to rush and capture them. They were, however, gallantly held or reoccupied by the battalions holding the line. On the night of the 21st the enemy raided Bertha post; and so violent was the bombardment that the Queen's Westminsters " stood to " for an hour in Laventie, ready to move forward, but they were not called upon.

On January 26th, the Battalion relieved the L.R.B. in the same sector as before, A and B Companies holding Barnet and Enfield posts respectively. The weather had turned bitterly cold on the 21st, and, in the words of the L.R.B. War Diary, " Instead of the ground being flooded, the whole was now a sheet of ice and all ditches and communication trenches were frozen hard." On the night before the relief, the enemy's artillery had blown away most of the wire on the right (south) of Enfield, but the ground was so hard that it was quite impossible to put in any fresh wiring pickets. The garrisons of the posts suffered intensely from the cold. No fires could be lit, for they only attracted further shelling; and no warm food could be brought up by day from the trenches in rear, as the posts were completely isolated.

On the 28th, orders were issued by the First Army that the posts, as permanent posts, were to be withdrawn; and that the policy to be adopted in future was to render the German front line untenable by the enemy. The order to evacuate the posts and to endeavour to cut all wire anchors holding back the revetments in the enemy trenches, was received by the Queen's Westminsters at 7.0 p.m. By 9.0 p.m. both posts were completely evacuated and all stores brought in. Two strong patrols remained out all night to cut the wire.

The enemy bombarded the evacuated posts all day on the 29th, and a damp fire, lit in Barnet post by a small patrol sent out by A Company, just before dawn on the 30th, attracted further shelling.

During the night of the 29th, when a strong party from B Company was out cutting wire, in front of the abandoned posts, the covering party of six men were surprised by the enemy and forced to withdraw, losing one man. 2nd Lieutenants J. H. Betteridge and T. S. Baker took out a patrol as soon as the party had got in, to try to find the missing man, but they could find no trace of him.

For the next two nights all companies were employed in wiring the original British front line; and on February 1st, the Battalion was relieved by the L.R.B., moving back into Brigade reserve at Laventie.

The decision to discontinue the policy of holding the posts was welcomed, with unmixed feelings, by all who had been entrusted with the task of carrying it out. Colonel P. E. Harding writes : " The water in the German front line trench was deeper than the height of my walking-stick, so that, like sensible people, they left their trenches to look after themselves. The ground was a swamp from which I once pulled a man who had sunk to the knees—we could not save his gum boots, the mud held them too tight. Any question, therefore, of occupying posts ' in the German front line ' was rather beside the point. The garrison of the ' posts ' had to lie still all day long on one side of the German parapet, and, owing to the very wet weather, the parapet was very low. They had practically no cover at all; their only protection was a little barbed wire. I consider it was all quite useless. The ' posts ' were quite untenable positions. We could not dig in, as we came on water at once. I met the Divisional Commander the day after we came out of trenches (after the evacuation of the posts), and he said how sorry he was to have had to issue an order for what he called ' a retirement from our advanced posts.' He told me that the men had got their ' tails up ' as a result of the ' advance.' I assured him in reply that ' no order had ever been obeyed with such alacrity in my own battalion, as had been the order to evacuate those posts.' "

The point of view of the garrisons of the posts is aptly summed up in the words of the War Diary of the 169th Infantry Brigade : " The garrisons feel that they are occupying a shell-trap; battalions are on the defensive and *not* offensive; the moral of the men is suffering, and at the same time our existing defences are falling into disrepair."

The XI Corps' report on the operations of the 56th Division in the Fauquissart sector, contains the following statement :—

" The work done in connection with seizing and holding the Fauquissart posts, and the information gained by the persistent patrolling of the enemy's lines, has been most valuable, and is a fine example of the policy of harassing the enemy by all means in our power."

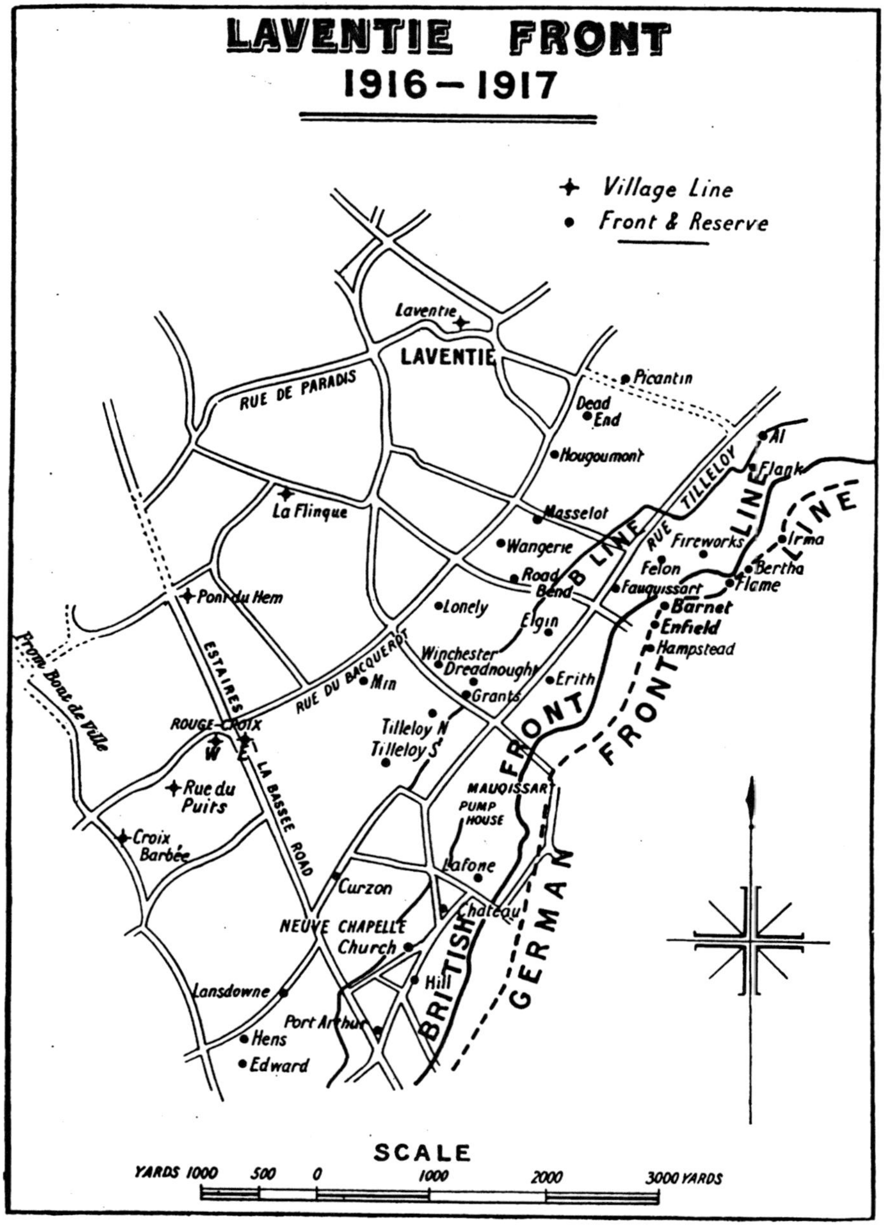
LAVENTIE FRONT
1916—1917
Village Line
Front & Reserve
Laventie
LAVENTIE
RUE DE PARADIS
Picantin
Dead End
Hougoumont
RUE TILLELOY
Al
Flank
La Flinque
Masselot
Wangerie
Fireworks
Irma
Felon
Bertha
Road Bend
Fauquissart
Flame
B LINE
LINE
LINE
Pont du Hem
Lonely
Barnet
Elgin
Enfield
Hampstead
From Bout de Ville
ESTAIRES
RUE DU BACQUEROT
Winchester
Dreadnought
Min
Erith
Grants
ROUGE-CROIX
W
E
Tilleloy N
Tilleloy S
FRONT
FRONT
LA BASSEE ROAD
Rue du Puits
MAUQISSART
PUMP HOUSE
Croix Barbée
Lafone
Curzon
Chateau
NEUVE CHAPELLE
Church
BRITISH
GERMAN
Hill
Lansdowne
Port Arthur
Hens
Edward
SCALE
YARDS 1000
500
0
1000
2000
3000 YARDS

After the evacuation of the posts, the Corps Commander (Lieut.-General Sir R. C. B. Haking) issued the following message:—

"*To G.O.C. 56th Division.*

"I should be glad if you will convey to all the troops of the Division under your command, my appreciation of the operations they have carried out so successfully during the last month in establishing posts in the German front line, and holding them in spite of heavy bombardments and hostile infantry attacks. The effect of these operations is much greater than the troops who took part in them are probably aware of. They have shown the enemy the offensive and enterprising spirit displayed by our troops, and have encouraged other British formations to adopt similar tactics which will have a far-reaching effect. . . ."

It is difficult to see that any useful purpose was, in fact, achieved by the so-called posts. The swampy ground which the enemy had voluntarily abandoned, can have been of no strategical or tactical value to either side; but the bombardment of the British troops who were ordered to hold it, must have afforded the Germans considerable satisfaction.

Colonel Harding writes: "The posts may be compared to bait on a fisherman's line without a hook. They simply provided the enemy with excellent and convenient targets for artillery practice, and the garrisons suffered heavy casualties without any chance of hitting back. The only information the posts obtained was that the enemy's trenches were tumbled to pieces. This information, and much more, had already been obtained by patrols, at a tithe of the cost of the posts. Patrolling did harass the enemy and improve our own moral. The occupation of the posts did neither."

The Battalion was relieved by the L.R.B. on February 1st, and went into Brigade reserve at Laventie. The cold at this time was intense, and on February 3rd the thermometer was down to zero. The frost continued until the 12th, when it was succeeded by a spell of mild and wet weather which caused a wholesale collapse of the trenches and breastworks.

The Battalion was in the line from February 7th–14th, and from the 20th to the 25th, relieving the L.R.B. on each occasion. The tours were uneventful, the Battalion being occupied, almost entirely, in putting up wire and working on the defences. On March 1st, the Queen's Westminsters, who were in Brigade support, in the Rue du Bacquerot and at Laventie, were relieved by the 1/5th West Yorks (49th Division); and the tour of the 56th Division in the Laventie sector came to an end.

The following extracts from Lieut.-General Haking's message of farewell to the G.O.C. 56th Division, show that the work done in the sector was fully appreciated by the Higher Command.

"On the departure of your Division, I am anxious to place on record my appreciation of the excellent work done by the Commanders, Staff, and all ranks throughout the Division during the time it has been in the XI Corps. In the Unit, Brigade, and Divisional Headquarters, I have always found that the basis of work is to help everyone else, and not to make difficulties. . . .

"The fighting spirit of all ranks is excellent; and this has been shown with the greatest success by the prosecution of raids into the enemy's lines; and by the operations, carried out in bitter weather during January, when the front system of the German trenches was held by the Division in a series of posts, and all attacks repelled with success until orders were received to withdraw. . . . I have no hesitation in saying that this Division is one of the best that has been in my Corps, and there have been over twenty in it, since it was first formed. I am convinced that wherever the Division goes and whatever it is called upon to do, the officers, non-commissioned officers, and men will always distinguish themselves. . . . I wish the Division an early victory to add to others it has already gained; and I part with it with the deepest regret, which is shared by all my staff."

CHAPTER X

ON THE ARRAS FRONT

THE COMMENCEMENT OF THE GERMAN RETREAT

IT was expected, when the Battalion was relieved on March 1st, 1917, that the next six weeks would be spent in training in the Willeman area, and all were looking forward to the change from trench life. Events, however, took a very different course, for the Division was recalled to the front before it had even reached its intended training area.

From the 1st to the 8th March the Battalion, with the rest of the Brigade, was continually on the move. During this period it marched nearly 100 miles, only to find itself at the end of its journey some twenty-one miles north of its starting-point. The whole march was a very trying one. For the first three days the weather was bright but cold, but after that, heavy falls of snow made the roads in places almost impassable, and a strong and bitterly cold north wind added to the discomforts of the men. In addition to this the troops were quite out of training for a long march, after a period of three months of trench warfare, during which there had been no marching at all.

The daily itinerary was as follows :—

March 1st.— Laventie to Bout de Ville, 12½ miles.
March 2nd.—Bout de Ville to Cornet Malo, 9 miles.
March 3rd.—Cornet Malo to Floringhen, via Lillers, 14¾ miles.
March 4th.—Floringhen to Œuf, via St. Pol, 16¼ miles.
March 5th.—Œuf to Le Quesnoy en Artois, the original destination of the Brigade, in the Willeman No. 3 area, 9 miles.
March 6th.—Le Quesnoy en Artois to Bonnières, 14½ miles.
March 7th.—Bonnières to Sus St. Leger, 13 miles.
March 8th.—Sus St. Leger to Simencourt, 9 miles.
Total 98 miles.

The Battalion was now once more in the VII Corps, with which it had fought at Gommecourt on July 1st, 1916. On arrival at Simencourt, the 169th Infantry Brigade was placed in Corps reserve, with orders to be prepared to move up to the Corps line in the event of a German counter-attack on the line Bellacourt-Wailly. The Queen's Westminsters and 2nd Londons were placed at the disposal of the 175th Infantry Brigade, but were not called upon.

After five days' training, during which the approaches to the Corps line and assembly trenches were reconnoitred by the officers, the Battalion moved, on March 14th, to Achicourt, a fair-sized village about 2000 yards behind the front line. The village had been subjected to frequent gas-shell bombardments, but had suffered comparatively slight damage up to this time.

On March 13th, instructions had been issued by the Division for the offensive that was about to be undertaken by the Third Army, with the object of capturing Mercatel, Hill 90 (south-west of Wancourt), the German third-line system, from Feuchy Chapel to Feuchy, and the high ground about Monchy le Preux. The VII Corps was to be on the right of the attack, with the 30th Division on the right, the 56th Division in the centre, and the 14th Division on the left. There were to be four successive objectives: (1) the German first-line system, including the village of Beaurains; (2) the German second-line system; (3) two redoubts north-west of Mercatel and Neuville Vitasse; and (4) Mercatel, the German third line north-west of Héninel, and Hill 90, north-west of the latter village.

It turned out, however, that a considerable part of the area to be attacked was captured without fighting.

On March 14th, the 2nd Londons relieved the 6th D.C.L.I. (21st Infantry Brigade) in the trenches facing Beaurains; and for the next three days their reconnoitring patrols were particularly active, in view of reports that the enemy were contemplating a withdrawal.

At 8.30 a.m. on March 18th, patrols of the 2nd Londons discovered that the enemy's front line had been evacuated. The companies in the line were immediately pushed forward; and by 12.0 noon, they were right through the village of Beaurains which had been found to be empty.

In the meantime, at 9.30 a.m., a wire from the Brigade was received by the Queen's Westminsters cancelling all working parties. The men who were out working were recalled, and the Battalion prepared to move forward immediately. At 1.0 p.m. orders were issued for a Brigade advance, on a two-battalion front, towards the German second-trench system, about a mile beyond Beaurains, with the 2nd Londons on the right and the Queen's Westminsters on the left. A and B Companies were then sent forward, and they assembled for the advance in a trench on the south-eastern edge of the village known as Melton Trench, but found that the 2nd Londons, who had met with no opposition, had pushed right on, and to a very large extent had anticipated the Brigade order.

By 6.0 p.m. the 2nd Londons had advanced about 2000 yards in front of the line which they had been occupying at the beginning of the day, and had arrived at what was to have been the second objective of the attack contemplated in the Divisional instructions of the 13th. They were now occupying a very extended front in the German second-trench system covering Neuville Vitasse.

Soon after midnight, the Queen's Westminsters moved up to the left of the 2nd Londons and formed a defensive left flank, along the line of the old German communication trench, known as Preussen Weg, which ran parallel with the Beaurains-Neuville Vitasse road. A Company was on the right, in touch with the 2nd Londons where Preussen Weg joined the German second-trench system ; B Company was on the left, covering Beaurains ; C Company moved forward to Melton trench in support ; and Battalion Headquarters were established in Beaurains. The night of the 18th/19th was very dark, but the moves were successfully accomplished in spite of the great difficulty in maintaining communication in a completely unknown area.

The village of Beaurains had been almost destroyed by the enemy before he left it, the roads had been blown up or obstructed with barbed wire and spikes, and, with the exception of a few bombs and Verey-light ammunition, all stores had been removed. Practically every dugout in the village had been destroyed ; but Lieutenant Harrow, the Battalion signalling officer, discovered an uninjured one that had previously been a German company headquarters.

This was used by the Queen's Westminsters as Battalion Headquarters. The dugout was most elaborately constructed, in two stories. The officers' mess was on the first story, 15 feet below the surface; and at a lower level, 15 feet further down, were additional rooms, four fitted with stoves.

At the main entrance to the dugout, Lieutenant Harrow discovered a fuse, which led to a mine carefully concealed in the wall. Further examination resulted in the finding of similar mines in the two other entrances. Luckily the retiring enemy had not had the time to light the fuses which would have caused the mines to explode. The dugout had evidently been abandoned in great haste, for the former occupants had left a meal all ready laid in the mess room.

The new front line now faced north-east, and ran from a point about 1200 yards north-west of Neuville Vitasse, along Preussen Weg and facing Telegraph Hill, a commanding point about 1500 yards east of Beaurains.

The Queen's Westminsters spent the next five nights in consolidating the position. Lewis-gun posts were pushed forward and linked up with the old German trenches, and patrols actively reconnoitred the enemy's defences. It was found that the Germans were still holding Neuville Vitasse and Telegraph Hill, the latter being an important position and very strongly fortified.

On March 24th, the Battalion was relieved by the L.R.B. and returned to Achicourt. During the relief, which commenced at 6.0 p.m., the enemy heavily shelled the lines, inflicting a good many casualties on the two battalions, and considerably delaying the relief which was not completed until nearly 11.0 p.m.

On the 23rd, the Battalion had suffered a severe loss by the death of Captain J. A. Green who was killed by a chance shell in Beaurains. At the outbreak of war he was "seconded," and was abroad, but he took the first ship home to rejoin. At the time of his death he was attached to the Staff of the 169th Infantry Brigade. A devoted and able officer, he had rendered good service to the Regiment.

After one day's rest, the Battalion relieved the 2nd Londons in support, with two companies in the old German front line, and two companies in the old British front line, northeast of Beaurains. For the next four days, large parties were employed in digging communication trenches and in carrying forward wire and other materials for the consolidation of the captured position.

On March 30th, the Battalion relieved the L.R.B. on the line of the Preussen Weg; and on April 1st, after being relieved by the Rangers (12th Londons, 168th Infantry Brigade), the Queen's Westminsters marched some ten miles to Monchiet (south-west of Achicourt). The Battalion remained at Monchiet until April 7th, giving as much time as possible to the training of all ranks, and in practising the new formations for the attack.

The "platoon" had just been reorganised as a self-contained unit. Its four sections now consisted of a rifle section, a bombing section, a Lewis-gun section, and a rifle-grenade section. Although the rifle still remained the primary weapon of the infantryman, the platoon commander now had under his immediate command four distinct units, each specially trained in the use of a particular weapon, and each capable of fulfilling, under the control of the subordinate leader, a different fighting function. This development necessitated the adoption of small mobile formations, by means of which the platoon commander could employ whichever weapon was best suited to deal with any particular situation.

The new organisation was a great advance on what had previously existed; but it required a great deal of practice and training to enable the platoon commanders to learn the tactical handling of a platoon constituted in this way. The time had been all too short when, on the evening of April 7th, the Queen's Westminsters returned to their former billets in Achicourt.

April 8th was Easter Sunday. No one who was in Achicourt that day can forget his experiences. At about 1.0 a.m. a few shells were fired into the village, and a barn, adjoining one of the billets occupied by A Company, was set on fire. The company immediately turned out and succeeded in preventing the flames from spreading. This fire was the beginning of a series of minor disasters. About midday the town was again shelled; this time B Company headquarters received a direct hit, which caused part of the building to collapse, and inflicted many casualties on a platoon of the company who were inside it.

This bombardment ceased at about one o'clock, but started again an hour later, when a shell fell on a lorry loaded with 9.2" ammunition, forming part of a convoy standing on the Arras road. The lorry immediately burst into flames and the fire spread, until eventually about twenty lorries were blazing. In a few moments the ammunition began to explode, the houses in the square were set alight, and a tremendous fire was raging, baffling all efforts to extinguish it. It requires but little imagination to conjure up a picture of the burning village and the long train of blazing lorries with their loads of high-explosive shells. The square was practically destroyed, many billets collapsed, and large quantities of stores and equipment were buried beneath the ruins. Many gallant deeds were performed in fighting the flames and in rescuing the injured and wounded; mention must be made of a fine piece of work by Major (afterwards Lieut.-Colonel) Guy Campbell of the Kensingtons, who, regardless of the exploding shells, succeeded in getting one of the burning lorries away.

At 8.15 p.m., as the Battalion moved up to the reserve area west of Beaurains, the houses were still burning; and dark figures silhouetted against the flames, could be seen working hard to quell the spreading fires.

The Battalion casualties this day were 2nd Lieutenant A. G. Beville, who was killed during the mid-day bombardment, while looking after some wounded of his platoon, and 16 other ranks killed; and 31 other ranks wounded. Under the circumstances the Queen's Westminsters must be considered to have suffered lightly.

CHAPTER XI

THE BATTLES OF ARRAS, 1917

I.—THE FIRST BATTLE OF THE SCARPE, 1917—THE ATTACK FROM THE WANCOURT RIDGE

WE now come to the commencement of the British campaigns of 1917.

At 5.30 a.m. on April 9th, the Third and First Armies, commanded by General Sir E. H. H. Allenby and General Sir H. S. Horne, delivered a general attack on the front Croisilles-Blangy in the south, and on the Vimy Ridge in the north, the VII Corps being on the right of the southern attack. The 30th Division was on the right, the 56th Division in the centre, and the 14th Division on the left of the Corps front. The 56th Division attacked with the 167th Infantry Brigade on the right and the 168th Infantry Brigade on the left, with the 169th Infantry Brigade in reserve. Its tasks were, firstly, to capture Neuville Vitasse, and secondly, to establish a line of posts just west of Wancourt.

The country in the district was typical downland, affording little cover for advancing troops. Neuville Vitasse itself was very strongly fortified. Part of the Hindenburg line (the Cojeul Switch) ran to the east of the village in a north-westerly direction to Telegraph Hill, just south of Tilloy. Here it linked up with a formidable network of trenches, known from its configuration as the Harp. Another line, running in a north-easterly direction from Henin sur Cojeul to Wancourt, crossed the Cojeul Switch on the top of a ridge about 2000 yards south-east of Neuville Vitasse. This was known as the Wancourt line.

At the end of the first day's attack, Neuville Vitasse had been captured by the 56th Division, and considerable progress had been made by the 14th Division on the left. The 30th Division, however, had not progressed as well as had been hoped; and as a result the right flank of the 56th Division was left exposed to enemy attacks from uncaptured portions of the Cojeul Switch.

On April 10th, a further advance took place. On the right, the 56th Division captured practically the whole of the

Cojeul Switch as far as, but exclusive of, its junction with the Wancourt line; and on the left the 14th Division established itself in the Wancourt line. The latter Division had lost direction to some extent, with the result that there was a large gap between its right and the left of the 56th Division.

On the 11th, further progress was made by the 167th Infantry Brigade, and this cleared up the whole of the Hindenburg line, and the Cojeul Switch to the south, as far as the Cojeul River.

On the evening of April 11th, the 169th Infantry Brigade relieved the 167th Brigade, and the Queen's Westminsters moved up to the Cojeul Switch, east-north-east of Neuville Vitasse, in Brigade reserve. Battalion Headquarters were established in a dugout in Telegraph Lane, on the south-western slope of Telegraph Hill.

The 169th Infantry Brigade was now ordered to make good the whole of Hill 90, which commanded Wancourt and Héninel, and then to push forward patrols into the latter village. The Brigade was further ordered to occupy the high ground, south of Héninel, as soon as the 30th Division, which was attacking on its left, had captured the Hindenburg line, south of the Cojeul River.

At 5.15 a.m. on April 12th, the 2nd Londons on the right and the L.R.B. on the left, attacked. At the end of the day the 2nd Londons had established themselves on the Wancourt Tower Ridge, about 1000 yards south-east of Héninel, and were in touch with the 14th Division, which had reached the western edge of Wancourt.

A further attack was planned for April 13th, and, at 2.30 a.m., the Queen's Westminsters were ordered to move south to the area occupied by the 2nd Londons. While the move was in progress, further orders were received that three companies were to be sent up to the Nepal trench (in the Wancourt line) to the south-west of Wancourt, and that one company was to remain in support in the Cojeul Switch. A, B and D Companies were accordingly sent forward, while C Company, which was employed in shifting an ammunition dump, remained in support.

It had been intended that the 56th Division should advance on April 13th, on Cherisy, keeping in touch with the divisions on either flank; and the Division was ordered to regulate its advance by the progress made by the flank divisions on the high ground. By 1 p.m., however, the 30th Division, on the right, had been unable to make any progress, and the 50th Division, on the left, was held up by machine-gun fire, from the west of Guémappe, and was echeloned back facing east about 500 yards to the east of Wancourt : consequently the attack by the 56th Division did not materialise. At 6.30 p.m. fresh orders were given for the VII Corps in conjunction with the VI Corps to make a general advance on the 14th April. The attack was to be made in a south-easterly direction, with the line of the Sensée River as its objective ; and the advance of the 56th Division was no longer to be dependent on progress being made by the divisions on its right and left. The 169th Infantry Brigade was detailed to carry out the attack on the front of the 56th Division.

At 10 p.m. on the 13th, a warning order was received that the attack would be launched from the Wancourt Ridge, with the Q.V.R. on the right and the Queen's Westminsters on the left, and the 2nd Londons and L.R.B. in reserve on the right and left respectively. It was intimated in the order that the two latter battalions would probably not be required.

The boundary between the two attacking battalions was roughly a straight line drawn from the southern end of Cherisy to the junction of the Wancourt–Fontaine-lez-Croisilles and the Héninel-Cherisy roads.

The Battalion's objectives were, firstly, a ridge, about 1000 yards in advance of the Wancourt Tower Ridge from which the attack was to start ; and secondly, the capture of the village of Cherisy. When this had been effected strong points were to be established on the northern flank of the Battalion's attack, and outposts were to be put out along the line of the Sensée River to the east of the village.

The situation on the morning of April 14th was as follows : The high ground on the right (south) of the Wancourt Tower Ridge had been captured, and the 21st Division had dug a strong-point across the Hindenburg line, which it was hoped would materially assist the advance ; but, on the left, the ridge was still in enemy occupation. Here the British front ran down the north-western slope of the ridge towards the Cojeul River. There was a gap of about 500 yards between the left of the 169th Infantry Brigade and the right of the 50th Division ; and this gap caused the left flank of the Brigade to be exposed from the start.

Beyond the facts that, during the last few days, the enemy had been showing a much stronger resistance than at any period since the beginning of his withdrawal on the front of the VII Corps, and that he was entrenching himself on the ridge, which formed the first objective, nothing was known of his dispositions for defence or of the strength of his artillery.

The final orders for the attack were received at 11.45 p.m. on April 13th, fixing zero hour at 5.30 a.m. the next morning. These orders stated that an enfilade barrage, consisting chiefly of high-explosive shells, had been arranged; and that this barrage would open at zero hour and dwell, for a few moments, to enable the infantry to advance up to it, after which it would move forward at the rate of 100 yards in four minutes. In view of the fact that high-explosive shells were to be used, it was directed that 100 yards was the nearest distance at which the infantry could follow the barrage with safety. Orders were given that the attacking waves must be widely extended, and that there was to be an interval of at least six paces between the men.

In the early hours of the morning, the Queen's Westminsters moved up from the position in the Cojeul Switch, and relieved the L.R.B. on the Tower Ridge, on the left flank of the Divisional front.

The men were thoroughly exhausted, having had not more than one hour's sleep in the twenty-four for the past three days. No previous reconnaissances of the ground over which they were to attack had been possible, and there was no time for any proper explanation to them of what they were to do. In fact, little more could be done than to give them the dispositions for the attack and the general line of the advance on objectives which none of the attacking troops had even seen.

The first objective (the ridge to the west of Cherisy) was allotted to A and B Companies, who formed the first wave of the attack; and the second objective (the capture of the village) was given to C and D Companies, who were to form the second wave. Each wave was to advance in two lines of men extended to six paces' interval, with 200 yards' distance between the lines; and the second wave was ordered to follow the first, at a distance of 300 yards from its second line, in order to conform with the advance of the Q.V.R. on the right.

A few minutes before the barrage was timed to commence, the enemy started a heavy bombardment of the neighbourhood of Wancourt Tower, which was on the ridge, from which the Battalion was preparing to advance, and on the immediate left flank of the Battalion. It appears that the enemy was launching an attack on the position, but the attack does not seem to have been pressed, and in any case it did not interfere with that of the 169th Infantry Brigade.

At zero hour (5.30 a.m.) the attacking waves advanced, A Company on the right, B Company on the left, followed by C and D Companies respectively. It was a beautiful morning and quite bright, with the remains of the moon to help the dawning day. The men went forward with confidence; but as soon as the leading waves had gone over the Tower Ridge, and started to descend into the valley between it and the first objective, they were met by a murderous machine-gun fire from the front and from both flanks. At the same time a number of the enemy appeared on the slopes of the ridge in the left rear of the leading companies. The British barrage was quite powerless to keep down the heads of the German machine gunners or to stop their fire ; in fact, it was described by the survivors of the attacking waves as " seeming to be negligible compared to that put down by the enemy."[1]

The Battalion suffered the severest losses, and in a very short time most of the officers were either killed or wounded ; yet the now almost leaderless men pushed on until they reached the furthest of some shallow enemy practice trenches, about 500 yards down the slope of the Tower Ridge and almost in a direct line between Héninel and Cherisy.

By this time the foremost wave had been nearly wiped out and was consequently disorganised, but the second wave came up to reinforce, and, keeping touch with the Q.V.R. on the right, pushed on to the practice trenches and established itself in rear of the few survivors of A and B Companies.

The Battalion was no longer in sufficient strength to press the attack over ground that was absolutely devoid of cover, and swept by shell, machine-gun and rifle fire of the fiercest description. By 6.30 a.m. not only had the attack been brought to a standstill, but the enemy had delivered a counter-attack. This was successfully beaten off by Lewis-gun and rifle fire, all ranks displaying great courage and resource. Practically no messages got back, and there were hardly any survivors from the leading waves of the attack ; consequently very few details of what happened are available. The following particulars, extracted from the Battalion records, will give some idea of the character of the fighting.

On the right, Rifleman E. F. Barrett and Rifleman G. A. Pelling, both of A Company, found themselves on the right flank of their company, in a captured trench down which the enemy commenced a bombing attack. Mounting their Lewis guns, in the open, under heavy machine-gun fire, they succeeded in driving back the enemy, and then built a block in the trench. At about the same time, Corporal D. Francis,

---

[1] Sir Douglas Haig, in his Despatch of the 25th December, 1917, says, " our advance had now (April 14th) reached a point at which the difficulty of maintaining communication and of providing adequate artillery support for our infantry began seriously to limit our progress."

of D Company, brought up a Lewis gun on the right in a very gallant way. When the advance was held up he found that the man who was carrying the gun had been wounded and was lying in the open some distance back; he immediately ran back a distance of about 150 yards, under heavy machine-gun fire, and returned with the gun. He then mounted it in a good position from which, later in the morning, he helped to repel a counter-attack. He well earned the Military Medal which he was awarded for his conduct.

Battalion Headquarters, which had been in the ruined village of Wancourt, had followed up the last wave of the attack, and, at 6.0 a.m., were established just below the crest of the Wancourt Ridge.

The situation was very obscure. Up to 6.40 a.m. no message had reached headquarters, and all that was known was that all the Battalion were over the ridge, and that the front companies were held up. A message sent to the Brigade by Colonel Shoolbred, at that hour, conveyed the information that a number of 6th Durhams were being driven back by the enemy on the right, and that the Germans were apparently close up to Battalion Headquarters. The message further stated that some 8th Durhams had come up from the right rear.

Reference has already been made to the exposed left flank of the 169th Infantry Brigade. It had been intended to fill the gap which existed on that flank, and hurried orders had been sent, in the early hours of the morning, for the 151st Infantry Brigade (50th Division), which was then out of the line, to establish a defensive flank facing north, roughly along the line of the railway, on the north-eastern slopes of the Wancourt Ridge, with its left on Wancourt Tower.

Wancourt Tower, a conspicuous landmark, had been blown up during the night; and, in the darkness, the troops of the 151st Infantry Brigade got too much to their right, and deployed for their advance in the middle of the Battalion's assembly area. Eventually they crossed the line of the Battalion's advance and, working still more to the right, they came into support of the Q.V.R., instead of being on the left of the Queen's Westminsters; they were then held up on the Tower Ridge. In the meantime two companies of the L.R.B. had been sent up to the left flank, one company to hold the trench from which the attack had started, and the other to form a defensive flank on the left near the river. By 6.50 a.m. the enemy had overrun the left company of the Queen's Westminsters and had worked round the left flank of the attack, where he was held up.

A GALLANT PARTY

The attacks of the divisions on either flank of the 56th Division had also failed, and at 8.0 a.m. the general situation, all along the line, was reported to be the same as before the attack had started.

It is now known that this report was ill-founded, so far as the front of the 169th Infantry Brigade is concerned, for troops were holding out in the neighbourhood of the enemy practice trenches, some 600 yards in front of the starting line of the attack. These troops, under the command of Lieutenant W. G. Orr of C Company, clung on to their position throughout the day.

Lieutenant Orr writes: " The attack started at 5.30 a.m., preceded by a barrage which, however, was merely groping, in the sense that there was no information as to where the Germans had made a stand. Consequently the barrage only had the effect (so it appeared to me) of enlightening the Germans that an attack was on foot. We were mown down by long range machine-gun fire before we got very far, and finally had to give up the idea of advancing, and had to entrench in any little scoop in the ground that offered itself. We were, for the most part, overlooked by the Germans on the higher ground ahead, and we had to remain all day under machine-gun and rifle fire. It was utterly impossible to move from the slight shelter we had, for at the first signs of movement on our part we were greeted with volleys of shots."

It has been possible to fill in some details of this modest account from other sources. Lieutenant Orr had succeeded in reaching the nearest of the practice trenches, which were quite shallow, with about twenty men of his own company; and, with the help of C.Q.M.S. A. D. H. Courtenay, who was acting as company sergeant-major of C Company, had managed to collect about twenty other Queen's Westminsters, together with some of the Q.V.R. He also collected some of the Durham Light Infantry who, having mistaken their direction, had pushed right on over the Tower Ridge, instead of forming the defensive left flank. The position in the shallow practice trenches was consolidated, so far as was possible, and Lieutenant Orr sent a message back to Battalion Headquarters explaining the situation. This message unfortunately never reached its destination. Lieutenant Orr says in his account: " On asking for a volunteer to carry my report, my runner, a lad named Lancaster, immediately volunteered, even though by this time it was fairly evident that there was only an outside chance of getting through (so swept by machine-gun and rifle fire was the ground). He set out, and.

by flinging himself in a shell-hole every few paces, he seemed to me to get clear away." Rifleman Lancaster, however, never got back; and the failure of his gallant attempt had an important bearing on subsequent events later in the day.

By 9.0 a.m. the enemy had worked round both flanks of the defenders of this isolated position. At the same hour observers, near Battalion Headquarters, saw a formed body of the enemy, some 50 strong, about 200 yards to the east of Tower Ridge. They were moving south-west towards a point about 500 yards in rear (west) of the position where the survivors of the Battalion were holding out. It was thought that this party of the enemy formed part of the leading wave of a counter-attack; but, owing to the entire lack of information as to the position of the British troops, it was decided not to turn the artillery on to them unless an attack in force developed. The only troops in the vicinity to resist such an attack were a company of the L.R.B., which was opposite to where the enemy were seen assembling, and some Durham Light Infantry on the right. If the enemy had pressed an attack, at this moment, it seems that he must have got right through, but he did not seize his opportunity. The attempted attack was beaten off by the L.R.B. and no further developments occurred. It seems not unreasonable to suppose that the enemy's attention, at this stage of the battle, was diverted by the presence of Lieutenant Orr's party in the neighbourhood of the captured practice trenches.

This supposition is to some extent confirmed by the fact that Lieutenant Orr was counter-attacked from his left front at about 11.0 a.m. His mixed garrison, consisting of the men of Q.V.R. and D.L.I. in addition to the few survivors of the Queen's Westminsters, successfully beat off the attack. All fought well, and it is a matter for regret that only names of Queen's Westminsters are available from the Battalion records. At one point Corporal J. E. Hales (C Company) took command of all the men near him, in the absence of any officers, and, though badly wounded himself, continued to command them all day. On the left, Rifleman D. J. Gander, with a Lewis gun, inflicted heavy casualties on the enemy who were coming on from the left and from the rear. He then constructed a barricade on which he mounted his gun and drove off all attacks. At another point, Lance-Corporal C. E. Stein did equally good work; during the early stages of the advance he had pushed forward his Lewis gun, in the face of very heavy machine-gun fire and close-range sniping, and, with the only two men of his section who were left, materially helped to repel the counter-attack which developed later. On the right, Corporal D. Francis again distinguished himself by the good use he made of his gun during the counter-attack.

The fighting having died down on the front of the 169th Infantry Brigade, orders were issued for the Battalion to reform in the area in which it had assembled in the morning; and early in the afternoon 2nd Lieutenant A. M. Mackle, the Battalion bombing officer, was sent forward to collect any men he could find in the vicinity of Battalion Headquarters. He only succeeded in collecting about sixty-five men. At 5.0 p.m. a further order was received from the Brigade, for Battalion Headquarters to move back to the position in the Wancourt area where they had been before the start of the attack. Headquarters moved back accordingly; and 2nd Lieutenant Mackle was left behind on the ridge, with orders to go forward at dusk and collect stragglers and wounded from positions that were inaccessible in daylight. When these orders were given it was not known that any troops were still holding out on the ridge; in fact, it seemed impossible for such to be the case. Not only had no message come back, but the enemy was known to have been in rear of the position, where it was learnt later that Lieutenant Orr's party was established.

The enemy must have withdrawn some time during the afternoon, or after dark, for Lieutenant Mackle, during his search, got into touch with Lieutenant Orr, and, not realising that his orders had been intended to be limited to the collection of stragglers, gave Lieutenant Orr the order to withdraw. It is very easy to be wise after the event; and if Rifleman Lancaster had succeeded in getting through in the morning with his message, the mistake could not have occurred.

By now Lieutenant Orr's party, which at one time had numbered between seventy and eighty men, had been reduced to twenty-seven, among the killed being three officers of the Durham Light Infantry. It is regretted that the names of these officers cannot be traced.

Owing to the withdrawal of Battalion Headquarters to Wancourt, it was not until 9.0 p.m. that the Commanding Officer learnt that Lieutenant Orr had been withdrawn from his advanced position. The information was immediately conveyed to the Brigade; and orders were received that Lieutenant Orr was to re-establish himself in the post he had previously occupied, and that he would be relieved by the 4th Londons, when the 168th Infantry Brigade took over the line during the night. Three guides and an officer were left behind to bring up the relieving troops, and Lieutenant Orr, whose party now numbered fifteen men, returned to the post.

Owing to the darkness, the guides were unable to find this advanced position when bringing up the platoon of the 4th Londons for the relief, and Lieutenant Orr was not relieved. He remained in position throughout the night, and only withdrew his men at dawn. Referring to this incident Lieut.-Colonel Shoolbred writes: " During the 14th and the night of the 14th/15th, Lieutenant Orr proved himself a leader of the highest order, and his personality had much to do with the magnificent resistance and tenacity shown by his little band of men." No further attempt was made by the Germans to regain the position which had been vacated, and the London Scottish established themselves in it on the night of the 15th/16th without any fighting or casualties.

The survivors of the Battalion came out of action on the night of the 14th/15th April, and moved back to the Neuville Vitasse area. The casualties of the Queen's Westminsters had been very heavy indeed. They had gone into action with a total fighting strength of 497 all ranks, and had lost, during the day, 12 out of the 15 officers who had gone forward in the morning, and 256 other ranks.

It has not been possible to give any detailed account of the part played by each company during the battle ; for, at the very commencement of the advance, the companies were completely broken up by the very heavy losses sustained. For the rest of the day the fighting consisted, almost entirely, of small groups of men holding out in shell-holes and shallow trenches, until they were killed or wounded.

No praise can be too great for the bravery and devotion of the stretcher-bearers, amongst whom were Rifleman A. C. McCarthy and Rifleman F. J. Watts. Of the former Lieutenant Orr writes : " He did fine work by jumping from shell-hole to shell-hole, to dress the wounds of the men who had been hit, until he himself was wounded by a bullet which first hit the man he was dressing "; of the latter, the Battalion records show that he displayed conspicuous bravery in attending wounded under heavy shell-fire, machine-gun fire and sniping ; particularly on one occasion when he attended a wounded sergeant of the Durhams who was lying in the open. Rifleman Watts, undaunted by the fact that two men had previously tried to reach the sergeant and had been killed, made the attempt and succeeded. After having dressed the sergeant's wounds he brought him back safely to cover.

The following are the names of the officers who went into action with their companies :—

A Company.—Captain H. Agate (in command), 2nd Lieutenants W. Hull, H. Pickles and R. I. Richens.

B Company.—Lieutenant S. C. Yeates (in command), 2nd Lieutenants J. Betteridge and T. S. Baker.

C Company.—Lieutenant W. G. Orr (in command), 2nd Lieutenants B. C. Lewall, W. M. Musgrove and C. A. English.

D Company.—2nd Lieutenant P. Palmer (in command), 2nd Lieutenants S. E. Trotter, V. Bell and C. K. Gray.

With the exception of Lieutenant Orr and 2nd Lieutenants Hull and English, all these officers became casualties during the day.

Of the officers of the two leading companies, A and B, Captain H. Agate, quite early in the attack, received wounds of which he died later in the day, Lieutenant S. C. Yeates and 2nd Lieutenants T. S. Baker and R. I. Richens were killed, and 2nd Lieutenants H. Pickles and J. Betteridge were wounded, leaving 2nd Lieutenant W. Hull the only surviving officer of the two leading companies.

Of C Company, 2nd Lieutenants B. C. Lewall and W. M. Musgrove were wounded. The former had got to comparative safety when he heard a wounded rifleman, who was lying in a shell-hole, cry out for water, and, disregarding his own safety, he jumped out of the trench, got to the shell-hole, and relieved the man's thirst. Coming back he was met by a burst of machine-gun fire and again hit in several places. 2nd Lieutenant Musgrove, who belonged to the 5th Border Regiment, died of wounds on the 15th.

Of the officers of D Company, 2nd Lieutenant C. K. Gray was killed, and the remaining officers were all wounded. 2nd Lieutenant Gray's platoon must have been completely wiped out after they had crossed over the top of the first ridge in advancing to the attack, for not a single man was heard of again.

Lieut.-Colonel Shoolbred writes of the officers killed on April 14th : " Captain Agate came out to France, as a rifleman, with the first draft from the 2nd Battalion. He received a commission in the Regiment in December, 1915, and on rejoining the Battalion after a short time in England, was posted to A Company. By his death the Regiment lost a tried and trusted comrade and a most capable and reliable company commander. Lieutenant Lewall was an outstanding example of pluck and determination, and devotion to duty. Once, when the Battalion was unexpectedly warned to return to the trenches, he absolutely refused to go on leave, although his warrant to England had already been made out. The others were all attached officers and had only been a very short time with the Battalion. Although it is not possible to speak of them with the individual appreciation they deserve, their service with us and their sacrifice with us will always be remembered with affection and gratitude."

Those that were left of the Battalion paraded at noon on April 15th for roll call, and the companies were then amalgamated: A and B forming No. 1 Company, and C and D No. 2. At 3.30 p.m. the Battalion marched back to the old German front line just south of Beaurains.

II.—THE THIRD BATTLE OF THE SCARPE, 1917

After four days' rest the Queen's Westminsters paraded at 9.30 a.m. on April 20th, and marched to Dainville, where dinners were served; and at 5.30 p.m. they continued their journey in omnibuses and lorries to St. Amand, fifteen miles away. Here the men were given two days' complete rest, after which training commenced.

On April 24th, the Battalion marched twelve miles to Wanquetin, via Pommier, Berles, and Beaumetz, marching again on the 26th to Berneville, via Warlus. The Queen's Westminsters left Berneville soon after midday on the 28th, and moved forward to the old German trench system on the south-eastern slopes of Telegraph Hill, known as the Harp.

During the period out of the line the Battalion had resumed its normal organisation of four companies, but it was still very weak in numbers; and, on the 29th, previous to relieving the 1st and 3rd Londons in trenches half-way between Guémappe and Wancourt, it was again formed into two companies.

While in the Harp the Battalion was employed working on the assembly trenches, clearing the battlefields, and burying those who had been killed in the recent fighting. On May 1st, the Queen's Westminsters were relieved by the L.R.B. and moved back to the Wancourt line. The enemy shelling, which had been considerable during the day, became especially severe during the relief, and both battalions suffered heavily. Owing to this the relief, which had commenced at 8.30 p.m., was not completed until 1.30 a.m. the next morning.

A short reference must now be made to the British operations after the opening days of the Battles of Arras, 1917. After an interval for organisation and preparation British troops, on April 23rd, had delivered a further attack, on a front of about nine miles, from Croisilles to Gavrelle. Bitter fighting took place on the portion of the line with which this history is concerned; but by the evening of the 24th the high ground west of Cherisy (which had been the first objective of the Queen's Westminsters on April 14th) was finally secured. The village of Guémappe was also captured, and considerable progress had been made on the rising ground to the east of Monchy le Preux.

Great activity now continued on the Arras front with the object, which was fully achieved, of assisting the French attack on the Chemin des Dames sector which was to take place on May 5th. At 3.15 a.m. on May 3rd, the 56th Division delivered an attack with the object of capturing Factory Trench, north-west of Vis en Artois. This involved an advance of some 2000 yards. The 14th (Light) Division was on the right, and the 3rd Division on the left.

The attack by the 56th Division was made by the 169th Infantry Brigade on the right, and the 167th Infantry Brigade on the left. The L.R.B. and the 2nd Londons were on the right and left of the 169th Infantry Brigade, with the Q.V.R. in support, and the Queen's Westminsters in Brigade reserve in the Wancourt line, west of Guémappe.

The advance started from a line about 800 yards east of Guémappe, and good progress was made on the Brigade front, but the attack failed on both its flanks. By 3.50 p.m. the troops on the right and left were back on their original line, while the 169th Infantry Brigade, having captured Cavalry Farm and Lanyard Trench, was holding a narrow wedge of ground at the bottom of the valley about 1000 yards in front of its starting-point. The leading troops of the Brigade were now in a very exposed position, with both flanks open to attack from the high ground on each side of the valley.

At 7.35 p.m. a very heavy barrage was put down by both sides on a wide front, and it was believed that the L.R.B. and 2nd Londons had been driven back for some distance. At 8.0 p.m. the Queen's Westminsters, who had not been called upon during the day, except to provide small carrying parties, were ordered to move forward and occupy the original front line east of Guémappe.

When Battalion Headquarters arrived at Tank trench, on the north-eastern outskirts of Guémappe, it was reported that the foremost troops had been withdrawn from the line they were holding at the end of their advance, and the situation was very obscure. But when Major Burnell, in command of the L.R.B., went forward to re-establish the line, he found that the garrisons had not withdrawn. In the meantime a wire had been received from the Brigade ordering a withdrawal to the original front line.

This order was not immediately complied with, for it

was believed that the real situation was not known at Brigade Headquarters. It seems that the 2nd Londons and L.R.B. had succeeded in reoccupying[1] all the ground they had won during the day, except Cavalry Farm, where the Germans appeared to be holding the line of the Cambrai road to the south end of Tool trench. This prevented all communication with the troops who were forward, except along the bottom of the valley. General Coke writes : " It was obvious that to continue to hold the farm with the higher flanks in the enemy's possession was to ask for constant anxiety and probable losses without any compensating advantages. Whenever our advance progressed on our flanks, it was equally obvious that the farm must fall into our hands. I therefore ordered it to be given up."

Eventually the Brigade Intelligence Officer arrived at Battalion Headquarters and confirmed the orders received by wire, for the 2nd Londons and L.R.B. to withdraw to the west of the Wancourt line, and for the original front line to be occupied, as a front line, with the Queen's Westminsters on the right and the Q.V.R. on the left. The relief was completed by 3.30 a.m.

The Battalion was relieved on the following night by the 4th Londons, and returned to trenches in the Wancourt line, when it was placed in reserve under the orders of the 168th Infantry Brigade. Here it was employed, during the daytime, in burying the dead and in collecting salvage ; and, at night, in putting up wire and strengthening the defences of the Wancourt line on the Battalion front.

On the night of the 8th, it moved forward to the support positions west of Guémappe and relieved the 3rd Londons. Orders were then received for the Battalion to relieve the Kensingtons in the left sector of the front line ; but, when all was ready for the move, these orders were cancelled, and further orders were issued for the Battalion to be relieved by the London Scottish on the night of the 10th, and then for it to move back to the Wancourt line. These orders were also varied. After being relieved by the London Scottish at dusk on the 10th, the Battalion, instead of moving to the Wancourt line, spent the greater part of the night in shifting forward some dumps. It then went back to some trenches southeast of Tilloy which were not reached until 5.0 a.m. on the 11th.

The 169th Infantry Brigade was now in Divisional reserve, and the next week was spent in reorganisation and training.

---

[1] It would appear from the Battalion War Diary that no enemy counter-attack took place at this time, but that the heavy barrage at 7.35 p.m. was due to both sides having the same S.O.S. signal.

THE BATTLES OF ARRAS 1917

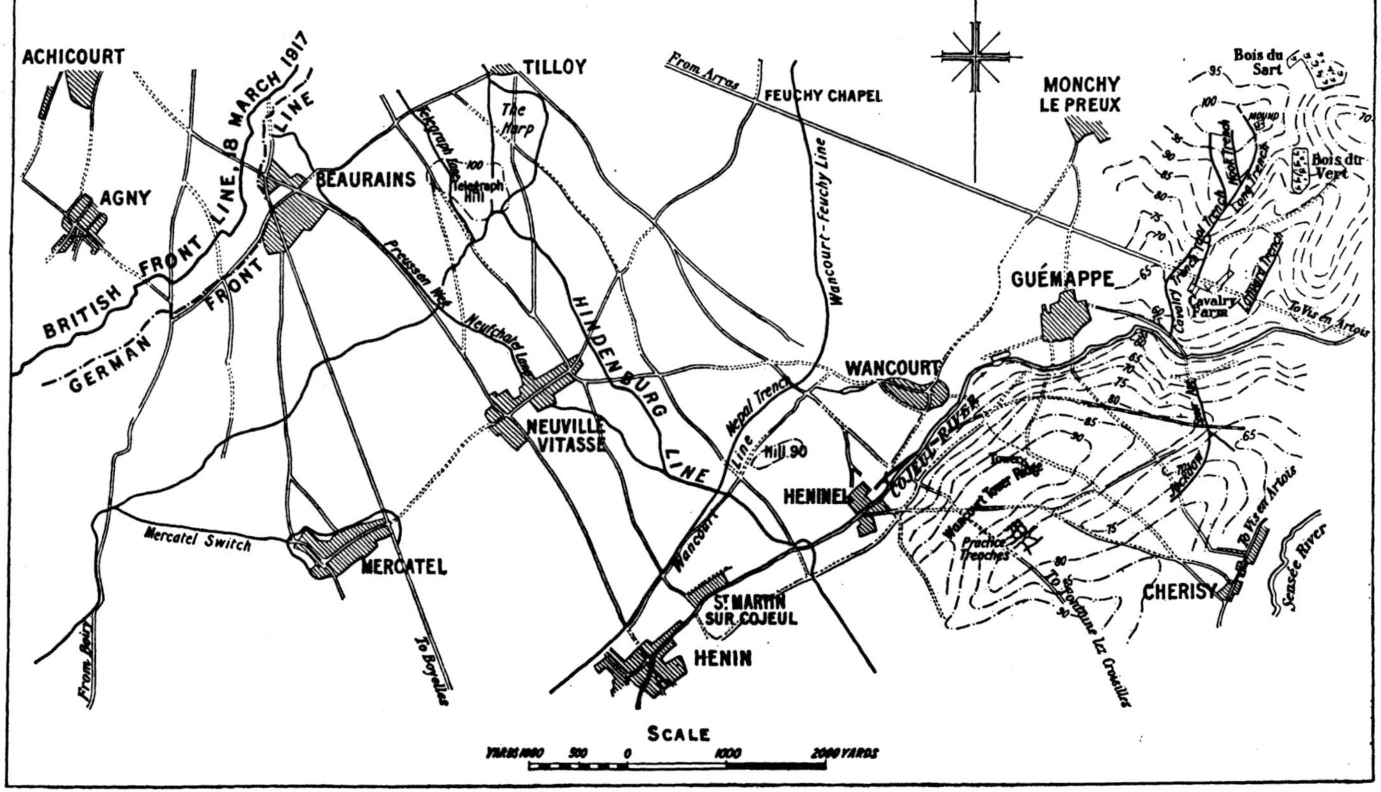

Parties were also employed on salvage work, such as collecting old shell cases. It was now at last possible to provide some relaxation for the men, and 50 of them were sent each day to a performance of the " Bow Bells." This was very much appreciated after the severe strain of the past weeks.

The Battalion was relieved on May 19th by the 8th East Lancashires, and marched by cross-country tracks to Arras, and thence, by infantry tracks, to Duisans, where it commenced a short period of much-needed rest. A further reference to this period will be made in the next chapter.

On June 8th, the Battalion paraded at 5.30 a.m. and marched via Dainville, Achicourt and Beaurains to Telegraph Hill, arriving there at 9.30 a.m. The day was spent in the German trenches in the Harp system, which the Battalion had occupied on April 28th. On the following night the Battalion moved up to the front line, where it relieved the 6th Somerset Light Infantry (14th (Light) Division) in trenches astride the railway about 1000 yards north of Cherisy. The trenches in this area had been named after animals or birds. C Company held the Jackdaw trench, south of the railway, and D Company occupied Spoor and Ape trenches north of the railway. B Company was in support in Boar and Bison, about 400 yards in rear of the front line; and A Company was in reserve in Buck and Lion, another 400 yards further back. These trenches were for the most part old German defences. They had been hastily dug and were in bad order, and there was practically no wire in front of them. A great deal of work was done by the Battalion, during its tour in the sector, in widening and deepening the trenches and in putting up barbed-wire entanglements.

On the night of June 12th, an enemy party, consisting of a corporal and two men, who were patrolling from Cherisy to Vis en Artois, lost their way and blundered into the Battalion lines. A thick mist had prevented the sentries from seeing them, but a working party in the trench fired on them, and the corporal was captured by Sergeant Plummridge and Sergeant Oliver (D Company).

Nothing further of interest occurred until June 14th, when the 3rd Division, on the left, delivered an attack at 7.20 a.m. on a German position, known as the Mound, about 1000 yards to the east of Monchy le Preux. The attack, which was made without previous artillery preparation, was very successful and resulted in the capture of two trenches, known as Hook and Long, some 200 yards from the front line.

Now occurred what, in the words of Brigadier-General

Coke, "deserves to become a classic instance of mutual support by observation. The enemy massed his counter-attacking troops round the south-west corner of the Bois du Vert with the intention of recovering the lost ground. The 3rd Division, who were thus threatened, remained in blissful ignorance of the impending attack, as neither from their lines nor from their observation posts did the lie of the ground permit of the enemy concentration being noticed. The Bois du Vert was about a mile and a half away and well outside the area for which the Queen's Westminsters were directly responsible. But the Q.W.R., who were on higher ground, on the right of the 3rd Division, whence a view of the ground which was dead to their neighbours could be obtained, were keeping the area under close observation, though they had not specifically received any instructions to do so."

At about five o'clock in the afternoon, 2nd Lieutenant J. P. D. Kennedy, who was on duty in the trench occupied by D Company, observed the enemy massing round the south-west corner of the Bois du Vert. This was at once reported to the Brigade, and the information was sent on to the Division concerned. Half an hour later, when the enemy put down a very heavy barrage on all trenches north of the Cojeul River (the left boundary of the Q.W.R.), our own artillery was fully prepared to deal with the situation, and at once opened on the enemy concentration. Captain Relton (commanding D Company) observed for the artillery, whose fire inflicted very heavy casualties on the enemy and caused him to disperse without launching the counter-attack. The prompt action of this officer in sending back the first information as to the enemy's movements, and his subsequent observation for the artillery, contributed very largely to the successful result of the shoot; and in the evening the following message was received from the 3rd Division: "Very many thanks for your co-operation in yesterday's operation. Your assistance materially contributed to our success."

On the night of June 15th, the Q.V.R. took over the front line, and the Battalion, after working on the defences throughout the night, moved back to the support trenches, leaving D Company in immediate support to the front line.

On the night of the 20th, the Battalion was relieved by the London Scottish and marched by cross-country tracks to billets in Achicourt. The march was a trying one owing to the muddy condition of the tracks, but it was the prelude of some of the pleasantest experiences of the Battalion throughout the war.

CHAPTER XII

THE SUMMER OF 1917

WITH the exception of twelve days in June, the Battalion was out of the line from May 20th to August 11th. For nine months it had experienced, practically without an interlude, all the trials and hardships of war in their sternest forms. It had acquitted itself with honour; and pride of Regiment, Brigade and Division was reflected in the spirit of determination, displayed by all ranks, in everything that the Battalion had been called upon to undertake.

One of the characteristics of the British soldier is to be cheerful, even under the most adverse conditions, and the Queen's Westminsters had been no exception to the rule. But a rest from the storm and stress of battle was badly needed and had been well earned. The summer of 1917 was a really pleasant one for the Battalion. The time was mainly spent in training for more serious things to come, but ample opportunity was provided for sport and recreation of every kind. Face to face with the realities of war men learn what life means, and with boundless energy and enthusiasm all ranks threw themselves both into their work and their play.

When the Battalion came out of the line, after the Battles of Arras, it was very weak in numbers, and it had lost the majority of its officers; but nine officers and a large draft of men arrived at Duisans on May 20th. Shortly afterwards the Battalion was up to strength.

From the middle of May to the end of July the Queen's Westminsters underwent a very thorough course of training.

In order to appreciate the object in view, some account must be given of the way in which warfare on the Western Front was changing. We have already seen how, with the general introduction of the bomb, the rifle grenade and Lewis gun, it became necessary to reorganise the platoon so as to enable the platoon commander to make the best tactical use of his men. Reference, too, has already been made to the fact that long spells of trench warfare caused the infantry soldier to forget that the rifle was his most valuable weapon.

In the spring offensive this state of affairs had become very noticeable, notwithstanding the change in the character of the fighting that had taken place during the previous autumn, on the Somme; and many instances were recorded of individuals missing opportunities for the effective use of the bullet. It must be remembered, however, that by this time there were very few men in the ranks, and fewer officers, who had had the advantages of an adequate course of musketry. The greater part of the fighting strength, of the armies in France, consisted of men whose only training had been a short, intensive recruit course in England, during which, with no previous military experience, they endeavoured to become proficient in the use of the bomb, rifle grenade and bayonet, in addition to the rifle.

The experienced soldier realised that, if the infantryman was to fight to the best advantage, he must learn to make full use of the rifle; but it was impossible, in the short time available at home, to give the new recruits any true conception of its possibilities. To remedy this defect was therefore of primary importance, especially in view of the changed defensive tactics of the Germans. The enemy had suffered enormous losses in 1916, and, with a view to economising his man power, had reorganised his methods of holding the line. His new system of defence opened up many possibilities for the effective use, in the attack, of the rifle and bullet. The former policy, of holding a rigid front line with large numbers of men, had proved too costly and had been abandoned in favour of a more elastic system. The enemy defences now consisted of a network of trenches, with groups of fortified posts, or strong points, distributed in depth. Some of these posts were constructed of concrete, and they received the popular name of " pill-boxes," which was a very expressive description. They were manned by small parties of men under the command of a subordinate leader. A further great economy of man power was effected by employing large numbers of machine guns in the forward position.

The principle underlying this method of defence was, first, to disorganise the attacking troops by fire from the posts; and then, having thus broken the initial force of the attack, to launch a counter-attack before the attackers had time to reorganise and push on. The enemy troops taking part in these counter-attacks generally had to advance across the open, and in doing so they provided good targets for well-directed rifle fire.

The training of the Battalion was progressive. At first every man was put through a systematic course of instruction in musketry, bomb-throwing, bayonet-fighting and the use of the rifle grenade; and Lewis-gun teams and bombing and rifle-grenade sections were trained. Later, companies and platoons were exercised as a whole, and the officers learnt how to handle them in every kind of tactical situation that could be foreseen. Brigade route marches formed an important part of the training, and the Battalion, in common with the rest of the Brigade, regained its old standard of marching.

It will be remembered that when the Battalion came out of the line on May 20th, it went to Duisans. It remained there until the 24th and then marched to Agnez les Duisans. On the following day, to the great regret of all ranks, Major P. E. Harding, M.C., left the Battalion, on his appointment as Deputy-Assistant-Director of Labour. On the outbreak of war he had rejoined the Queen's Westminsters, with whom he had previously served for many years, and he came out to France with the Battalion as a platoon commander. He was wounded early in the war and sent home to England; but he came out again and was with the Regiment during the fighting of 1916, becoming second-in-command. He commanded the Battalion during Colonel Shoolbred's absence, on sick leave, from October, 1916, to February, 1917, and resumed his appointment as second-in-command on the latter's return to France. He had rendered splendid and unselfish service to the Queen's Westminsters and was most deservedly regarded with affection and respect by all ranks.

On May 26th, the G.O.C., 56th Division (Major-General Sir C. P. A. Hull) inspected the Battalion, and thanked and congratulated it on the part it had played in the Battles of Arras. In the course of his speech he impressed on all ranks the need for greater reliance on the rifle; and it is of interest to note that, in the fighting in the autumn and afterwards in the spring of 1918, the Battalion specially distinguished itself by the effective use it made of this weapon.

After a brief return to the trenches, from June 9th to June 21st, the Battalion came back to Achicourt where it at once settled down to make the most of its time away from the line.

To begin with, a regimental canteen was started, under the energetic and painstaking direction of Major P. M. Glasier. It became a most popular regimental institution, and did a very flourishing trade. Beer, food, tobacco and other articles were sold at nearly cost price, and the profit was spent in supplementing the Army rations.

At Achicourt the mornings were devoted to training and the afternoons, for the most part, to sports and recreation. One of the chief attractions was the swimming pool near the citadel at Arras, and on July 1st, the Battalion swimming sports were held there. The Divisional band played during the afternoon and the meeting was a great success, in spite of somewhat unfavourable weather.

The next few days were spent in marching. On July 2nd the Battalion marched, via Wailly, Beaumetz and Monchiet, to Gouy en Artois, and on the following day, via Barly and Sambrin, to Sus St. Leger. The weather was exceedingly hot and a good many men fell out on the march. This could not be tolerated in a Battalion which had always prided itself on its march discipline; and the men who had fallen out, most of whom belonged to a large draft which had recently arrived, were sent for a series of route marches during the hours when the estaminets were open. This proved a most effective cure for bad marching, but it must not be thought that the estaminets had been in any way responsible for the men falling out.

The Queen's Westminsters remained at Sus St. Leger until July 24th. Here, as at Achicourt, the mornings were given up to work and the afternoons to play.

The afternoons of the following week provided a striking contrast, both to the bitter days of fighting that had passed, and to the return to the stern realities of war that came in the near future. Officers and men were now fit as the result of hard training, and the Battalion was attaining a standard of efficiency which made it approach that of the magnificent unit which went into action at Gommecourt on July 1st, 1916. All felt prouder than ever of their Regiment.

No account of the life of the Battalion during the War would be complete without some reference to its more cheerful aspects. It may appear somewhat incongruous, in a war history, to devote space to a sports meeting; but such events have a direct bearing on the development of that *esprit de corps* and the will to win which ultimately brought victory to the British arms.

The Battalion sports were held in the grounds of the Château at Grand Rullecourt on July 14th, and these were followed by a Brigade horse show on the 16th, and by a Brigade sports meeting on the next day. A spirit of enthusiasm and lightheartedness, which is difficult for those who have not experienced the ups and downs of war fully to realise, was in the air, and never was a series of entertainments more thoroughly enjoyed. In the Battalion sports, the transport gained the highest number of points, and B Company was second.

The Brigade horse show was a very great success. In one

of the events Lieut.-Colonel Shoolbred secured a most popular win, mounted on " Mary." This game little mare had been presented to the Battalion in August, 1914, by Captain C. Trollope, and had come out with the Queen's Westminsters in November, 1914. She served throughout the war with the Battalion, and returned safely with the cadre in June, 1919, to enjoy the luxuries of civil life in Lieut.-Colonel Shoolbred's stable. Colonel Shoolbred writes of her : " To paraphrase what an eminent divine once said of strawberries, Doubtless God could have made a better pony. He certainly never did."

The climax was reached when on July 17th the Queen's Westminsters, after a very keen struggle, won the Brigade Athletic Championship for the second year in succession.

Amongst the events won by the Battalion were the hundred yards and the mile. The latter provided the finest race of the day, and it was won by Rifleman J. Lee of the Transport, who finished eighty yards in front of the favourite, Lance-Sergeant Winterbourne of D Company, the runner-up in the event in the previous year. Rifleman J. Stanton of the Transport was second in both the high jump and the long jump, and Lance-Corporal Smith won the bomb-throwing. In the tug-of-war the Battalion team was placed second.

The arrangements on the ground were excellent. In addition to the Divisional band, there were numerous side-shows, amongst which the "Bow Bells" entertainment and a "coco-nut shy" were specially popular. Tea was served in the grounds, and a " wet " canteen did a roaring trade. Throughout the day the mounted competitors provided themselves and all spectators with plenty of amusement, and one notable race was won by Captain Mackenzie, the transport officer of the Q.V.R., who rode one of the Battalion's mules. At the end of the meeting the prizes were presented by the Comtesse Kergolay, and in the evening the winners of the championship returned in triumphant procession to Sus St. Leger.

The procession was headed by the bugle band, next came the mounted officers, followed by the regimental sergeant-major and the competitors, who rode in G.S. wagons. Many members of the Battalion brought up the rear on foot. On entering the village the victors were hailed by the rest of the Battalion with cheers and confetti, the guard turned out and presented arms, and the competitors were carried shoulder-high to the transport lines, where celebrations of the day's success were continued until the early hours of the morning.

On July 24th, the Battalion left Sus St. Leger and moved to La Commune, about seven and a half miles north-west of St.

THE SUMMER OF 1917

Omer and in the Fifth Army area. The Battalion paraded at 2.30 in the morning and, after tea had been served out to the men from the cookers of the Q.V.R., marched to Bouquemaison station. Here the Battalion entrained, and, after a five hours' journey, attended by the usual discomforts of cattle trucks, reached Wizernes, three miles from St. Omer, about noon. Dinners were served in a field near Wizernes station, and at 3.15 p.m. the Battalion paraded again and marched to La Commune, where it arrived at ten o'clock at night. The total distance marched during the day was about eighteen miles.

At La Commune more advanced training commenced. The hours of work were from 9.0 a.m. to 4.0 p.m. The companies marched out to the training area, some three miles from the billets, in the morning; the company cookers were sent up for the midday meal and, after a further hour's training in the afternoon, the men marched back to billets. Teas were served on their return, after which those who were sufficiently energetic, and the great majority were, indulged in inter-company games and various forms of sport.

On August 3rd, Lieut.-Colonel Shoolbred paraded the Battalion for the last time as its commanding officer. He had been an officer in the Regiment since 1888, and had succeeded Lieut.-Colonel C. A. Gordon Clark in the command in February, 1911.

During his period of command before the war the Regiment had steadily improved its standard of efficiency; and within only a little more than three months of the outbreak of war, the Battalion was in the front line. This in itself was an achievement of which any commander of a Territorial Battalion might be proud.

For three years, with the exception of a short period when he was home on sick leave, Lieut.-Colonel Shoolbred had commanded the Battalion in the face of the enemy. Both with the 6th and the 56th Divisions, it had been put to the test and had shown itself possessed of great fighting qualities.

Colonel Shoolbred's high ideals, his fearlessness, his solicitude for the welfare of his men and animals, and his devotion to duty, set an example to all ranks which will always be remembered by the Battalion. The Regiment owes him a great debt of gratitude, and the history of the Queen's Westminster Rifles is indissolubly associated with his name. He had a great send-off when he left, on the morning of August 4th, to the accompaniment of the cheers of the whole Battalion and the strains of the Regimental March played by the bugle band.

The command of the Battalion now passed to Major P. M. Glasier, the second-in-command.

On August 6th, the Queen's Westminsters marched to Watten station where they entrained for Abeele (south-west of Poperinghe), and then marched to Wippenhoek. Here the men were accommodated in tents and bivouacs until the 11th, a period remarkable only for the number of nights on which enemy aeroplanes dropped bombs on the adjacent aerodrome.

On August 11th the Battalion left Abeele, and the Divisional rest came to an end.

CHAPTER XIII

THE BATTLES OF YPRES, 1917

AFTER the Battles of Arras, 1917, and the capture of Vimy Ridge, in April, the main operations on the British front spread northwards. The brilliant stroke by which the Messines Ridge was captured, on June 7th, paved the way for a continued Franco-British offensive on a large scale before Ypres. The attack, which marked the opening stage of the Battles of Ypres, 1917, was delivered by the British and French armies on a front of fifteen miles, extending from the River Lys, opposite Deulemont in the south, to beyond Steenstraat in the north. In this attack the main blow was struck by the British Fifth Army, which advanced on a seven-and-a-half-mile front, from the Zillebeke-Zandvoorde road to Boesinghe, with its right flank covered by the Second Army, and its left by the French.

The battle opened at 3.50 a.m. on July 31st, and in the north considerable progress was made; but " the difficult country east of Ypres, where the Menin road crosses the crest of the Wytschaete-Passchendaele Ridge, formed the key to the enemy's position, and here the most determined opposition was encountered." (See Sir Douglas Haig's despatch of January 8th, 1918.)

In this area the German first-line system (which included Shrewsbury Forest, Sanctuary Wood, Stirling Castle, Hooge and Bellewarde Ridge) was captured; but the advance was held up in front of two small woods, known as Inverness Copse and Glencorse Wood. These woods were destined to be the scene of the fighting in which the Queen's Westminsters were engaged twelve days later.

The weather broke a few hours after the attack, and for four days the rain came down in a ceaseless torrent. No words can adequately describe the awful condition to which the ground was reduced. " The low-lying, clayey soil, torn by shells and sodden with rain, turned to a succession of vast muddy pools. The valleys of the choked and overflowing streams were speedily transformed into long stretches of bog, impassable except for a few well-defined tracks which became marks for the enemy's artillery." (Sir Douglas Haig's despatch.)

IN THE GRIP OF THE MUD

Men stepping off the tracks, or attempting to move across country, were held fast in the grip of the mud or sank slowly to their death, while overhead a never-ending stream of shells shrieked through the air to scatter pain or death as they burst. The reader may give full rein to his imagination when he thinks of the experiences of the men who took part in this battle, but unless he had been there he could not conjure up a picture worse than the reality.

An account of one incident must suffice to illustrate what men were called on to endure in those dread surroundings. Weak cries for help were heard by a party of Queen's Westminsters, and a search in the swampy ground was immediately made to discover whence they came. After some time the party came to a large shell-hole, and in it was a man, buried up to his armpits in mud, and quite unable to move. He had been there for four days, sinking deeper and deeper in his struggles to escape, and was in a very exhausted condition. With shells continuously bursting around them, a rescue party made their way, with difficulty, over the soft ground, and succeeded in reaching him. Getting what purchase they could on the yielding mud, they caught him by the arms and tried to drag him out. Their efforts were unavailing, and the man's cries of agony showed that some other means of rescue must be devised. 2nd Lieutenant F. E. Whitby then arranged for a rough platform to be made to give the rescuers a better foothold; and, while this was being done by ready volunteers, a rope was passed under the man's arms, and the ends made fast to a sort of derrick rigged up across the shell-hole. The work was interrupted by the whole company being ordered away for another task; but Rifleman Williams, a C Company stretcher-bearer, was left behind to do what he could to relieve the sufferings of the man. Rifleman Williams, with a devotion that earned him the Military Medal, remained with him throughout the night and all the following day, giving him food and encouraging him, yet wondering all the time whether further help would come. At last some men of the Q.V.R. arrived, and with their assistance the man was got out and sent down the line to safety. By what seems a miracle neither man had been hit, for there was hardly a spot near them which had escaped the bursts of shells.

The man's name was never obtained, but the following message of thanks was received from Lieut.-Colonel Maxwell, his commanding officer, some days later. " I will be grateful if my thanks on behalf of the 82nd (2nd Battalion South Lancashire Regiment) could be conveyed to 2nd Lieutenant

F. E. Whitby and Rifleman Williams for their great gallantry and assistance in rescuing, feeding, and, without question, saving the life of this soldier."

A return must now be made to the story of the Battalion during the Battles of Ypres, 1917.

On August 11th, the Queen's Westminsters moved by train from Abeele to Ouderdom (about seven miles south-west of Ypres), and then marched to Château Segard. Here they bivouacked for the night in a muddy field, with no better cover than could be obtained from their ground-sheets rigged up into rough shelters. In spite of the discomfort and continuous shelling throughout the night, the men were in good spirits and were kept interested by the guns of the 8"-howitzer batteries which were in action all around.

The next afternoon (Aug. 12th), the Battalion moved forward by cross-country tracks to Yeomanry Post, on the west of Sanctuary Wood and about 1000 yards north-east of Zillebeke Lake. It arrived there about 5.0 p.m., and three hours later guides led the companies forward to relieve the 6th Battalion Royal Berkshire Regiment (53rd Infantry Brigade, 18th Division), in the left sector of the front line west of Glencorse Wood. The state of the ground and the incessant shelling had stopped all attempts to consolidate the position; there was no cover from shell-fire, and the British and German dead were still lying out in the open. The " line " was roughly that reached on the first day of the battle and was quite indefinite. It consisted merely of convenient shell-holes, with here and there a disconnected length of trench, and in these the companies with their supports were distributed in two rough lines. A Company was on the right in touch with the Q.V.R., and B Company on the left in touch with the 7th Middlesex (167th Infantry Brigade), with C Company in support north of the Menin Road, and D Company in reserve in a trench north of Yeomanry Post.

On the night of August 13th, the 169th Infantry Brigade attempted to gain a little ground by establishing a line of posts in a ride in Glencorse Wood, one hundred yards in front of the position. The intention was for six posts to be established by the Q.V.R. on the right, and three by the Queen's Westminsters on the left, with an additional post if necessary, in order to keep touch with the 167th Infantry Brigade on the Battalion's left. Each post was to be manned by one section.

The advance was timed to commence at 9.0 p.m. At that

hour A Company and the Q.V.R. on the right were being heavily shelled and their advance was delayed, but on the left B Company succeeded in establishing a post. Seven minutes after the advance started the enemy put down a heavy barrage on the British front line ; and that, together with the counter-barrage which had been called for by lamp signal, had prevented any progress being made by A Company and the Q.V.R.

Continuous and heavy shelling went on all through the night, and, through it all, men hung on to their lonely shell-holes with an heroic endeavour that is beyond all praise. The story of one small band of Queen's Westminsters may be told ; it is typical of what was happening all along the fighting front.

Corporal Skeate and seven men were holding a small post in front of the line, and, cut off from all communication with their company, without rations and exposed to the full fury of the enemy's artillery and machine-gun fire, their position seemed hopeless. Their orders were to hold the post, and for over thirty hours they clung on expecting to be overwhelmed at any moment. The situation was reported to the Brigade, and orders were received that the post was to be withdrawn. Sergeant E. Yarnold, M.M., then volunteered to make an attempt to take the message forward ; and with conspicuous courage he made his way across the open, exposed to machine-gun fire at a hundred yards' range, and succeeded in reaching the post in safety. The party then withdrew, and on their way back to the front line five men out of the eight were hit and lay helpless where they fell. Sergeant Yarnold bore a charmed life, for he got back unwounded, though his clothing was pierced by bullets. Calling for volunteers, as soon as he had regained the line, he went out again with a few brave men and brought in the wounded.

In the evening (August 14th), the Battalion was relieved by the 2nd Londons and moved back to trenches at Half-way House. During the day and the preceding night its losses had amounted to 24 other ranks killed and 51 other ranks wounded.

Two days later, the Queen's Westminsters took part in the second combined attack, delivered by the British and French armies on a wide front east and north of Ypres. The 56th Division, to which was attached the 53rd Infantry Brigade (18th Division), was on the right with the 8th Division on its left. In this attack, as had been the case on July 31st, the main resistance of the enemy was encountered to the east of Ypres, and it was on this portion of the front that the 169th Infantry Brigade came into action.

The line held by the Brigade on the morning of the attack ran just to the west of the shattered remains of Glencorse Wood ; and the task of the Brigade was to advance through the wood, and to capture and consolidate a line running north and south through Polygone Wood, which lay about 1200 yards beyond. There were three intermediate objectives : the first involved the capture of Glencorse Wood, the second an advance to the western edge of Polygone Wood, and the third the establishment of a line inside the wood itself.

Brigade operation orders for this attack were issued on August 14th. These directed that the attack was to be made by the L.R.B. on the right, supported by two companies of the Q.V.R. and by the 2nd Londons on the left, with one company of the Q.W.R. to act as " moppers up," as the advance proceeded. One company of the Q.W.R. was detailed to be in readiness to carry forward materials for the consolidation of the captured positions, and the remaining two companies formed the Brigade reserve.

Each battalion was ordered to advance on a two-company frontage and in four waves, and directions were given that small columns were to be used wherever possible (instead of lines), to facilitate movement over the sodden and shell-torn ground. Each wave was to move straight on to its objective, and there was to be no "leap-frogging," in other words, the leading wave was to move on to the objective furthest away from the starting-point of the attack. The mopping-up company of the Queen's Westminsters was placed under the orders of the commanding officer of the 2nd Londons ; its task was to follow after the second wave, and, when no further mopping up remained to be done, it was to assemble in the reserve line and report to the senior officer of the battalion for which it had been working.

On the morning of the 15th, Lieut.-Colonel Glasier with 2nd Lieutenant R. L. Whittle, who was acting-Adjutant, made a very daring reconnaissance of the ground over which the attack was to be made, going right forward into No-man's-land beyond the advanced line of posts.

In the evening the companies moved up to their allotted positions : the reserve companies to a tunnel under the Menin road, where advanced Brigade Headquarters were established, and D Company (Captain E. Brimelow) to a trench known as Jargon Switch, in the assembly area of the 2nd Londons.

The assembling of troops for an attack is at all times a difficult matter ; but, when this has to be done in the middle of the night, in a position defined by no recognisable landmark, and over ground that is wellnigh impassable even in broad daylight, the difficulties are increased a hundredfold. By 2.0 a.m., however, the troops were in position, but both the Queen's Westminsters and the 2nd Londons suffered heavy casualties from shell-fire during the hours previous to the attack.

At 4.45 a.m., on August 16th, the artillery barrage commenced to creep forward, and the whole line advanced against the enemy's position. On the front of the 169th Infantry Brigade, both the L.R.B. on the right, and the 2nd Londons on the left, made a most promising start; in less than an hour the 2nd Londons had taken Glencorse Wood and were pushing on to the third objective inside Polygone Wood, with the Queen's Westminsters following closely behind; and the leading company of the L.R.B., which had encountered a good deal of resistance from machine-gun emplacements when it had reached the eastern edge of Glencorse Wood, was pushing its way forward. This company eventually reached the final objective in Polygone Wood, but was overwhelmed by a counter-attack and was never heard of again.

In the meantime events on either flank of the Brigade had not proceeded so satisfactorily. It had been arranged that the 4th Londons, on the right, should cover the flank of the L.R.B. as they advanced, but the 4th Londons were unable to get forward. On the left of the 2nd Londons, the leading waves of the assaulting battalions had started well; but an exceptionally heavy enemy barrage had caught the rear waves, with the result that the leading troops were forced to retire under pressure of the enemy counter-attack. These events left both flanks of the 169th Infantry Brigade unsupported.

After the first hour, the resistance on the front of the 2nd Londons began to increase, and the company of the Queen's Westminsters was sent forward to assist the leading waves in their efforts to make further progress. Very severe and confused fighting then took place, and the advance was finally held up in Polygone Wood. By 7.10 a.m. the assaulting troops, who were under machine-gun fire not only from their front, but from their rear on both flanks, were suffering very heavy losses, and at this hour the enemy launched a determined counter-attack. The troops, fighting stubbornly all the way, were gradually forced back into Glencorse Wood, where the remnants of the 2nd Londons, the Q.W.R. and other units of the Brigade were rallied on some rising ground. Here they succeeded in establishing a line of posts; but with this exception the whole Brigade was back in the position from which it had originally started in a little over four hours from the commencement of the attack.

The enemy was kept at bay on the line of these posts throughout the day; but at 4.0 p.m. a further counter-attack drove the defenders back to Jargon trench where they had assembled in the morning. Two hours later the enemy—*49th Reserve Infantry Regiment*—attempted another counter-attack on a strong point on the right, which the Q.V.R. had established during the day. A half-company of the Q.W.R. was sent up to reinforce the garrison, and the attack was successfully beaten off.

The course of the fighting during the day affords a good example of the working of the revised German method of defence to which reference was made in the last chapter. In the earlier stages of the attack the resistance was comparatively weak and ground was yielded; then, when the attackers were weakened in numbers and disorganised, the resistance increased, until at length the enemy launched his counter-attack and regained practically the whole of the ground from which he had been driven.

Although the three remaining companies of the Q.W.R. were not called upon to take any active part in the day's fighting they all suffered severe casualties. One company was employed under very heavy fire in carrying up small-arm ammunition during the attack; and the other two had taken shelter, from the terrific storm of shell which fell all day, in a portion of the tunnel under the Menin road where advanced Brigade Headquarters and the Battalion Headquarters of the Q.W.R. and Q.V.R. were located. The roof was quite thin, and afforded no protection from a direct hit, even from small-calibre high-explosive shells. Every shell that burst in the neighbourhood caused the tunnel to reverberate with the sound and the beams and supports to groan and crack, while the roof threatened to fall in at any moment. To add to this nightmare experience, the floor was covered with several inches of water and the whole place was in pitch darkness, save for a few guttering candles which flickered and threw strange shadows on the walls.

In the portion (about 30 yards long) occupied by the three headquarters and a large crowd of signallers and runners, the same scene presented itself; but the situation was rendered somewhat less tense by the fact that the majority were busily employed on some duty or other.

BATTLES OF YPRES 1917
16TH AUG. 1917

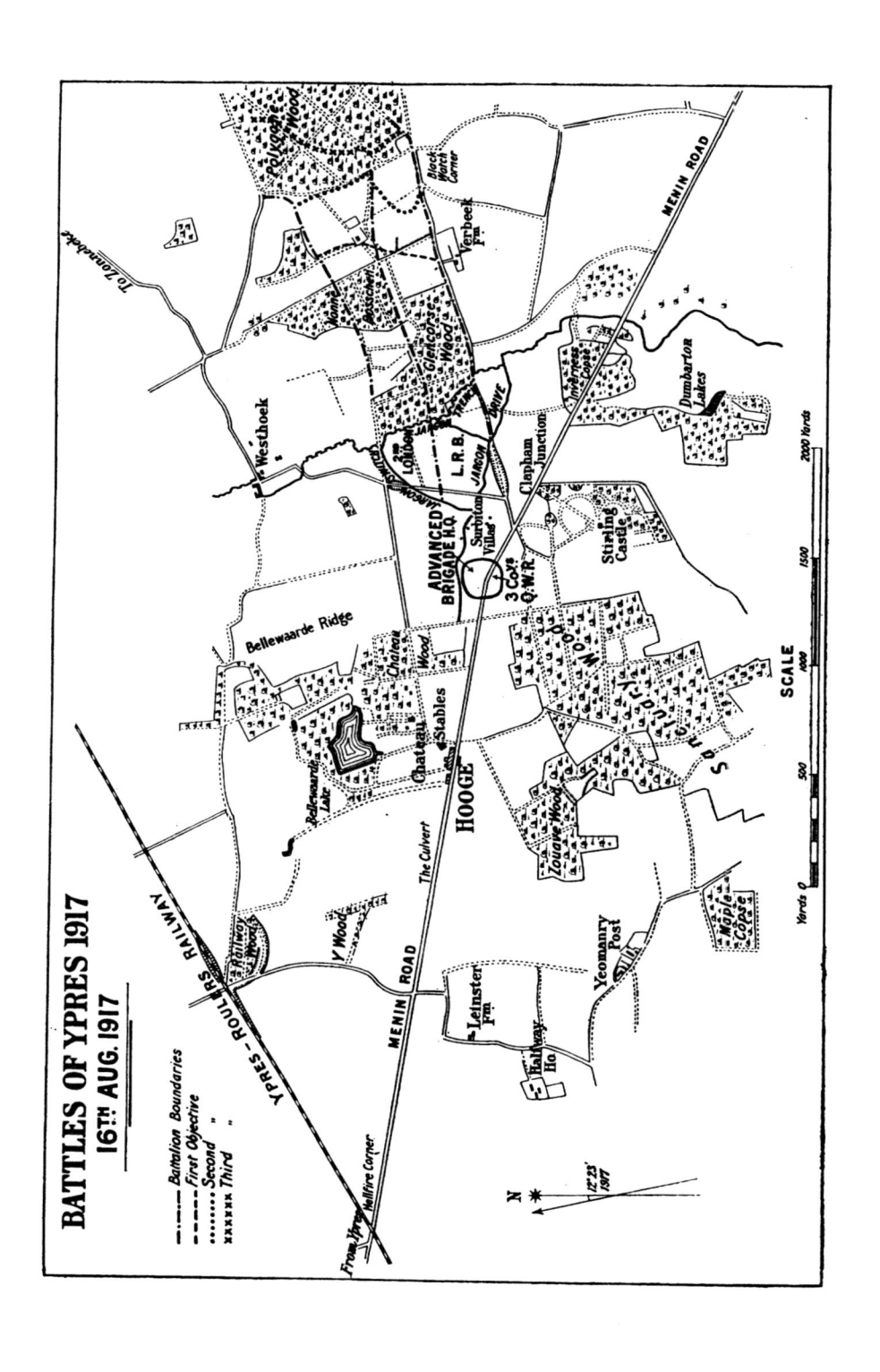

During the day the enemy secured a direct hit on one of the entrances, which consisted of a blown-out portion of the roof, but very fortunately only one casualty resulted from it; another shell broke through the roof above the Queen's Westminsters and a good many men were wounded or hurt.

The losses of the Queen's Westminsters on August 16th were 159 all told. Two officers (2nd Lieutenant S. North, 19th London Regiment, and 2nd Lieutenant A. M. Mackle, 4/5th Border Regiment) and 16 other ranks were killed; and 3 officers (2nd Lieutenant W. D. Smith, 21st London Regiment, 2nd Lieutenant E. E. Ellis, 9th London Regiment, and Captain E. Brimelow) and 109 other ranks were wounded, whilst 29 other ranks were posted as missing.

The stretcher-bearers worked gallantly throughout the day and saved many lives under circumstances which required the highest standard of courage and determination. Rifleman Williams again did splendid work; and Rifleman W. Phelp, who had volunteered to act as stretcher-bearer after all the other stretcher-bearers of his company had been killed, went forward through the enemy barrage no less than seven times and on each occasion brought in a wounded man.

The situation in front was very obscure when, at 7.30 p.m., the Battalion was ordered to relieve the 2nd Londons and the L.R.B. in the left section of our old front line, and to push forward and establish posts in front.

2nd Lieutenant R. L. Whittle took A Company forward to cover an important strong point on the left, the possession of which would have enabled the enemy to render Battalion headquarters untenable; while 2nd Lieutenant F. E. Whitby with the survivors of the three remaining companies succeeded, in the course of the night, in establishing five forward posts on the western edge of Glencorse Wood. During the establishment of these posts, 2nd Lieutenant Whitby could be seen walking up and down the line of shell-holes which he was organising for defence, calmly directing the work of his men and showing an utter disregard of the enemy's fire. He was very deservedly awarded the Military Cross for his work on this occasion, for it was almost entirely due to his skill and initiative that the operation was so successfully carried out.

The enemy's fire continued unabated until the early morning; it died down somewhat during the following day which was comparatively quiet, only to break out afresh while the Queen's Westminsters were being relieved during the night by the 7th K.R.R.C. (14th Division).

The account of the Battalion's experience in the Battles of

Ypres, 1917, would not be complete without some reference being made to the dangers and difficulties connected with the supply of rations and ammunition to the forward areas. The convoys had to come up along the Menin road under a continuous bombardment. Gas shells, high explosives and incendiary shells which lit up the surrounding country as they burst, all combined to terrify the horses and mules; and, on more than one occasion, panic amongst them was only prevented by the coolness and presence of mind of Sergeant Johnson who was in charge of the convoy. The rations were brought as far forward as possible in limbers and on pack animals; they were then transferred to the charge of Sergeant Ashdown, who had the unpleasant duty of guarding them in a much-shelled spot until they were handed over to the parties who had to struggle forward with them through mud and fire to the front lines.

The battle as yet was only beginning; it continued to rage with uninterrupted fierceness until late in the autumn, though Glencorse Wood itself was finally captured by the 42nd Infantry Brigade four days after the Battalion left the line.

The Ypres Salient is full of proud memories for the Battalion. It was here that they had spent those eight grim months in 1915 and 1916, holding on and waiting for the time that an advance would be possible. It was here, too, that they had taken a part, though not a prominent one, in their first attack, supporting their comrades of the 18th Infantry Brigade; and it is some satisfaction to feel that the heavy sacrifices they had just made had contributed in no small degree to the capture of the key to the enemy's position east of Ypres.

The total losses of the Battalion during the six days it had been in action numbered 204 all ranks, of whom 50 were killed.

When the Battalion was relieved, on the night of August 17th, it moved back to Château Segard, where it arrived at seven o'clock the next morning. After a short rest the Battalion embussed for the Wippenhoek area where it had been encamped during the days preceding the battle. It remained here until August 24th, resting and training, and then went by rail from Abeele to Moulle, on the St. Omer-Calais road. The train journey of thirty miles took six hours, and the companies were not settled down in their widely scattered billets until three o'clock in the morning, having left their camp at Wippenhoek at 2 p.m. the previous afternoon.

On August 31st, the 1st Battalion Queen's Westminster Rifles marched to Wizernes and entrained for Miraumont. On this day they left the Ypres front for the last time during the war.

CHAPTER XIV

ON THE CAMBRAI FRONT, 1917

AFTER a very tedious journey from Wizernes, the Queen's Westminsters detrained at Miraumont. Marching via Achiet le Grand, Achiet le Petit and Biefvillers, they arrived in the early hours of September 1st at their destination, a camp near Bancourt, about a mile to the east of Bapaume. They were now in the area of the Third Army, which was commanded by General the Hon. Sir Julian Byng.

The Battalion moved forward on September 5th, and, after spending a night in Brigade reserve near the ruined village of Lebucquière, relieved the 2nd Royal Scots (3rd Division) in the front-line defences astride the Bapaume-Cambrai road.

The new sector was a very quiet one. There had been no serious fighting in the district since the end of the German retreat in April, and both sides had settled down in their trenches, the enemy in the Hindenburg system to the west of the Canal du Nord, and the British on the slightly higher ground some thousand yards away.

The comparative calm which reigned on this front was a welcome change from the bombed transport lines, the shelled approaches and the shell-swept battlefields of the Ypres Salient. The lines here were too far apart for the use of trench mortars, and the shelling of the posts was not very severe ; on the other hand, the broad extent of No-man's-land lent itself to patrol enterprises ; and during the Battalion's stay in the sector a number of most successful encounters took place.

The same portion of the line was held by the Queen's Westminsters alternately with the Q.V.R. until the Battle of Cambrai in November. The defences of the sub-sector consisted of about ten occupied posts, and ran in front of Demicourt and Boursies, from the Demicourt-Graincourt road on the right to the Boursies-Inchy road on the left. The front covered was approximately 2000 yards as the crow flies.

Three companies, each keeping one or more platoons in support, found the garrisons for these posts ; the strength of the garrisons varying from a platoon to a section, according to the size or importance of the post. The remaining company was in close support and was located in other posts a short distance behind the front line. One company of the battalion in Brigade reserve was attached to the front-line battalion as an additional reserve. This company was accommodated in shelters in a sunken road which ran south-east from Doignies about 3000 yards from the front line.

Although the line was very thinly garrisoned, the general scheme of defence was to give up no ground that could be held. In the event of attack, troops were ordered not to fall back, but to continue to defend their posts, whether their flanks were turned or not; and if the enemy penetrated the defences at any point, the posts on the flanks and in rear were to hold him up in a pocket, in which his flanks were open to attack by fire and bombs, until an immediate counter-attack by the troops in support could be launched.

When the Brigade first took over the sector there were no communication trenches between some of the posts, and the trenches between some of the others were not more than four feet deep and were very narrow. A main system of wire ran along the whole front of the sector, and such posts as were constructed for all-round defence were completely surrounded by wire. All the posts had names which consisted either of a number corresponding with the map square in which they were situated, or the name of a fish such as salmon, trout, perch, minnow, roach.

A greater degree of comfort was enjoyed by the Battalion while occupying the line on this front than at any other period during the war. The soil was well adapted for digging; and it was found that if the walls of the trench were properly sloped and kept quite smooth the water ran off them quickly, and that little or no revetting was required, at any rate in the communication trenches. Some amusement was created by instructions received from the Brigade that men " showing special aptitude for the work " were to be specially detailed to keep the trench walls smooth, but as a matter of fact this work was quite a " skilled man's job," and an enormous economy of labour was effected by getting hold of the right men and keeping them permanently at their special work.

The communication trenches, of which many hundreds of yards of new ones were dug during the Battalion's stay in the sector, were all constructed to standard dimensions (7 feet deep, 6 feet wide at the top, and 4 feet wide at the bottom). They were eventually all provided with a duck-board floor, raised upon piles about a foot above the level of the bottom of the trench. This work was done by a permanent party of the 5th Cheshires (Pioneers) specially attached to the Battalion in the line. At least two miles of duck-boards must have been laid in the Battalion subsector alone in a little over two months. The undulations of the ground, on which the posts and communication trenches were sited, made the problem of keeping the trenches dry a comparatively simple matter, and it was very rarely that the garrisons suffered from flooded trenches. Sump pits were dug at intervals of a few yards throughout the whole trench system, into which the water drained underneath the floor-boards and from which it could easily be pumped away. One of these pits, an exceptionally large one, took the overflow from several posts, and was known as " Kingsap's Swimming Bath."

There was only one deep dugout in the front line, and this was used as a platoon headquarters. The remainder of the men were, at first, accommodated in shelters, covered with corrugated iron and sandbags, but later on small " elephant shelters " were erected in short lengths of trench leading out of the fire trenches. The company headquarters were some little distance back from the front line. The right company headquarters were in Trout post in the sunken road running east from the northern end of Demicourt. This post consisted of a deep dugout and a series of shelters dug into the side of the road. The headquarters of the centre and support companies and the regimental aid post were in a chalk quarry, near the junction of two sunken roads about 300 yards south of Boursies ; and those of the left company were in a cellar under a heap of bricks that had once been a cottage, a short distance to the south of the eastern end of the village.

Battalion headquarters were quite a long way behind the line, at Salmon post, in the sunken road some 600 yards east of Doignies. They consisted of two or three deep and spacious dugouts, capable of accommodating a company or more, and a number of elaborately camouflaged iron shelters built against the enemy side of the sunken road. The Headquarters mess was made exceptionally comfortable (luxurious would perhaps be a more suitable description) by the joint efforts of the Q.V.R. and the Queen's Westminsters. The junior members of the mess took a great pride in decorating their home, and displayed considerable ingenuity in making comfortable deck-chairs out of old biscuit boxes, and in upholstering the backs of rough plank seats with old sacking stuffed with grass. The walls of the mess room were hung with art stencilled canvas purchased in Amiens. But the crowning effort was a brick fireplace fitted with a real grate " scrounged " from the ruins of a neighbouring village. This was built under the guidance of R.S.M. Davis, who became quite an expert in making fires burn when no one else could. One of the shelters near Headquarters was fitted up as a Battalion canteen where tobacco, biscuits, candles and other luxuries were stocked. As a rule one man per platoon was sent down from the front line to make the purchases, and a good trade was done, averaging about 300 francs a day during each trench tour. In another shelter a long bath was installed, sent out by friends from home, and officers in the line took turns, when they could be spared, to come down to enjoy the unwonted luxury of a hot bath, and to dine at Headquarters.

Hot meals for all men in the line were cooked at Trout post and the Quarry; and water was laid on to the front line by the Royal Engineers during the Battalion's stay in the sector.

The first spell in the trenches, which lasted from the 6th to the 13th September, was uneventful. The Battalion set to work at once to link up the isolated posts by digging communication trenches, and to put up fresh belts of wire all along the front in accordance with the Brigade scheme. A close study of the ground in front was made by day; and at night reconnoitring patrols were sent out from all companies, to gain information as to the enemy's habits and a knowledge of No-man's-land, with a view to further enterprises.

No-man's-land, which was undulating and sloped down towards the enemy's lines, had at one time been under cultivation, but it was now overgrown with tall rank weeds and wild flowers, with patches of clover here and there. Several roads ran forward from the British lines, the most important being the main road between Bapaume and Cambrai. This had been completely blocked by the enemy by large trees, felled across it during his retreat in April. A ruined house where this road crossed the Demicourt-Inchy road was a never-failing source of interest; it was visited by patrols nearly every night and was found to be occupied occasionally by the enemy. For what purpose this house was occupied was never known, in spite of the fact that it was thoroughly searched whenever it was found to be empty.

There was splendid observation from the British trenches; in the distance could be seen the church spires of Cambrai, while nearer at hand were the red roofs of the villages of Graincourt, Mœuvres and Inchy. These villages appeared to have been little damaged, and there were many envious thoughts of comfortable rest billets for the enemy troops. The enemy's defences, a network of trenches along the Canal du

Nord and a partly dug outpost line some five or six hundred yards in front of them, were barely visible owing to the long grass. The outstanding feature of the landscape was Bourlon Hill; it dominated the country for miles around and gave the enemy observation far behind the British lines.

It is difficult to find words to describe the wantonness of the enemy's destruction when he retreated to the Hindenburg line. The land in rear of the new British trenches was a scene of utter desolation; every village stood in ruins, destroyed with such devilish thoroughness that not even a single room remained intact. The largest heap marked the site of the village church; except at Lebucquière, where the skeleton of the wooden spire rested at a perilous angle, on top of a big mound of broken bricks and rubble, threatening to collapse at any moment. Large craters had been blown at the cross roads in Doignies and Boursies, the civilian cemeteries had been ruthlessly desecrated, graves had been opened and rifled, and tombstones turned over and broken; and, to add to the cruelty of the scene, the large trees bordering the roads had all been cut down, and the fruit trees mercilessly destroyed. All the civilian inhabitants had been evacuated, their flocks and cattle had disappeared, and their neglected fields had relapsed into a state of virgin prairie.

In spite of the difficulties created by such destruction, admirable provision was made for the accommodation and comfort of the troops when out of the line. During September the men were all under canvas; but, as the winter came on, huts were rapidly put up in the fields, and large steel "elephant shelters" were erected in the villages under cover of the ruins. A special hut was set aside as a Battalion recreation room and canteen, a gramophone was purchased with funds supplied by the Regimental Association at home, a plentiful supply of playing cards and a large assortment of magazines and periodicals were sent out by the Oxford and Cambridge Club, and a good stock of liquid and other refreshments was obtained from the British Expeditionary Force Canteen. The Battalion canteen, thanks to the hard work of C.Q.M.S. Loveland and the Regimental Quartermaster, was a very flourishing concern, the daily takings, when the Battalion was out of the line, averaging about 1200 francs.

The Divisional concert party, the "Bow Bells," had fitted up a ruined barn at Fremicourt as a theatre, and ran an excellent burlesque of "The Maid of the Mountains." Day excursions to Amiens were organised, the Division supplying a lorry which took a limited number of men to Achiet le Grand, whence they proceeded to Amiens by special trains. These excursions, by which it was possible to return for a few hours to civilisation, were very much appreciated. The concerts given by the Divisional band, in a large tin recreation hut at Lebucquière, provided another most welcome form of entertainment. One further luxury must be mentioned, namely, a Russian steam bath which had been ingeniously fitted up in the Battalion transport lines. These varied forms of amusement, to which the men could look forward when they came out of the line for rest, certainly kept everyone in excellent spirits and in good health.

The Battalion was relieved by the Q.V.R. on the night of September 13th, and went into Brigade reserve at Lebucquière, leaving A and D Companies in the intermediate line near Doignies and Louverval, in reserve to the battalions holding the right and left subsectors of the Brigade. These two companies were relieved by B and C Companies on September 17th. On the 19th, the Battalion was inspected by Lieut.-General Sir C. L. Woollacombe, K.C.B., commanding the IV Corps, who expressed himself as being very pleased with the appearance and turn-out of the men ; he specially complimented the transport officer (Captain B. L. Miles) on the condition of the horses and mules.

The Battalion returned to the line on the night of September 21st. The two companies at Lebucquière moved by light railway to Louverval, whilst the remainder marched direct to the trenches after being relieved in the intermediate line. The weather was fine and clear, and aeroplanes on both sides were very active. Some very exciting air fights took place on the 24th, in the course of which one of our machines was brought down in front of the L.R.B. on the left. One of the enemy airmen subsequently flew very low over Battalion Headquarters and then up and down the front trenches, firing his machine gun into them. His fire was replied to by every Lewis gun and rifle in the neighbourhood, but apparently with no results.

The hours of daylight in the line were otherwise monotonous and uneventful, but at night patrols were sent out from every company, and it was not long before the Battalion had a fight with the enemy. An aeroplane photo sent to Battalion Headquarters had revealed the fact that the enemy were engaged on some new work at a spot about five or six hundred yards in front of the line, just north of the Demicourt-Graincourt road, and a reconnoitring patrol was sent out on the night of September 28th to investigate. As a result of the information obtained, a fighting patrol from C Company under 2nd Lieutenant W. H. Ormiston, with Sergeant Jenks, Sergeant Ambrose and twenty-eight other ranks, including some Lewis-gun teams, went out on the following night, with orders to engage the enemy if met with, and if possible to capture a prisoner.

The patrol had nearly reached the scene of the enemy's work when suddenly it was fired on from the rear by a party of about seventeen Germans. This force was probably acting as a covering party for those engaged on the new work. The patrol immediately faced about and opened Lewis-gun and rifle fire on the enemy. An exciting fight followed, in the course of which a corporal of the Queen's Westminsters was very nearly captured, being seized by several of the enemy who attempted to drag him back to their lines. The would-be captors, however, were shot, the corporal was rescued, and the patrol returned bringing with them two prisoners, one of them being a wounded non-commissioned officer who had been hit during the engagement. When the patrol got back to our lines it was found that they had suffered six casualties, all fairly slight, but that Sergeant Ambrose was missing. 2nd Lieutenant Ormiston immediately went out again, with a search party, but could find no trace of him; the search party, however, had the satisfaction of counting eleven enemy dead on the scene of the fight. Sergeant Ambrose, who had been wounded in the foot, succeeded in crawling back some little time later. The successful result of the encounter, in which only four Germans out of a party of seventeen succeeded in returning to their lines, had an excellent effect on all ranks; the episode was mentioned in the daily communiqué to the British Press in the following terms: "We also secured a few prisoners during the night as the result of a patrol encounter in the neighbourhood of the Bapaume-Cambrai road"; and the following messages of congratulation from the Army and the Corps Commanders were received by the Battalion:—

"The Army Commander congratulates the Queen's Westminsters on their successful encounter on the 28/29th September. He considers it reflects credit on all concerned."

"The Corps Commander congratulates the 56th Division on the most successful fight of the 28/29 September. He considers it reflects most creditably on the bravery and resource of the officers and men of the 1/16th London Regiment. The identifications were most useful."

The Battalion was relieved by the Q.V.R. on the night of

September 29th, and moved back to the Divisional reserve camp near Lebucquière, the officers and two companies being placed under canvas, and the remaining two companies in Nissen huts. The weather turned very cold about this time, and violent gales and heavy rain made life exceedingly uncomfortable, especially for those under canvas, many of the tents being torn up by the force of the wind. Whenever the weather permitted strenuous training was carried out, and the most was made of the excellent training areas. These were intersected by numbers of old German trenches and afforded facilities for exercises in almost every form of warfare.

The Battalion returned to the trenches on October 7th, and took over the same subsector. Patrolling recommenced at once, and on the 9th another very successful patrol action was fought. The patrols were ordered to rely to the fullest extent on rifle and Lewis-gun fire, and not to use bombs except in cases of great emergency. This policy was fully justified by results; and on this occasion, as soon as the enemy party was discovered, heavy fire was opened by the patrol, with the result that the enemy scattered leaving behind a wounded Würtemberger belonging to the 414*th I.R.* He was brought back a prisoner to our lines.

The Battalion received further congratulations on this successful skirmish, the following wire being sent by the Divisional Commander: " The G.O.C. is much pleased at again having to congratulate the Q.W.R. on the smart action of their patrols. He considers the action of the patrol, under 2/Lieutenants Russell and Harper, on the night of the 9/10th, very creditable, and that they showed the right offensive spirit."

On October 11th, 2nd Lieutenant T. Caudwell and ten other ranks from D Company carried out a thorough reconnaissance of the approaches and wire in front of some craters on the Demicourt-Graincourt road, about 1000 yards away from the British lines. They succeeded in obtaining some very valuable information for a raid which was in preparation by the Q.V.R.

On October 14th, a company of the 4th North Staffords was attached to the Battalion for a progressive course of instruction in the trenches. At first the company was distributed by sections between the various posts, the North Staffords and Queen's Westminsters working in pairs; later whole platoons were attached to companies, and eventually the company took over a portion of the line.

The arrival of a fresh complete unit from England at so late a stage in the war gave rise to much speculation. Could it mean that every available man was to be thrown into the fight, with a view to bringing the war to a speedy conclusion? It seemed hardly possible that there were sufficient reserves still left to keep additional units in the fighting areas up to strength.

The remainder of the tour was uneventful, except for the appearance in the trenches of thousands of small frogs, which came, apparently from nowhere, after some heavy rain.

The Battalion was relieved by the Q.V.R. on October 15th, and moved back to Lebucquière into Brigade reserve. Very little training was possible during this period of rest, as two companies were forward in reserve to the battalions in the line, and the remainder were employed in finding large working parties for the Division.

The Battalion returned to the trenches again on October 23rd, the night after the attempted raid by the Q.V.R. The Q.V.R. had found the posts on which the raid was to be made very strongly held, and the enemy fully on the alert, with the result that they were unable to effect an entrance.

The Battalion lost no time in resuming its patrol operations, the successes of the two preceding trench tours having stimulated all ranks to further efforts.

At least twelve fighting patrols went out during the last weeks in October. The mission of these patrols was to lie in wait for the enemy, either at places where he was suspected to be working on his defences, or near the spots where aeroplane photographs had shown that German patrols had endeavoured to reach our lines.

On October 24th, a patrol from A Company, under 2nd Lieutenant H. A. Kilburn, came into contact with the enemy at the ruined house on the Bapaume-Cambrai road; a fight ensued and the German patrol took to flight. The Queen's Westminsters lost 2 other ranks killed; their bodies were brought back to our trenches and were buried at Louverval. It was known that casualties had been inflicted on the enemy, and observers from our lines reported, on October 26th, that they had seen what appeared to be the bodies of dead Germans near the ruined house. A search party under Captain A. J. M. Gordon accordingly went out in the evening, and brought back two enemy dead belonging to the 120*th R.I.R.* One of them was a sergeant, and on him was found a rough sketch of our lines with what was apparently a patrol route indicated upon it.

Captain Gordon's party heard the enemy moving near the ruined house, but the Germans made no attempt to interfere with the search. The following message from the Divisional Commander was subsequently received by the Battalion: "The G.O.C. is glad to be able again to congratulate the Queen's Westminster Rifles on their successful patrol work. The skirmish on the night of 24/25th October shows that the unit has been taught to depend on fire effect; and although the patrol sustained two casualties, the result undoubtedly ended in its favour, since the enemy abandoned his casualties and ours were brought in, while an identification was obtained."

Further patrol fights took place on the nights of the 27th and 29th October. The Queen's Westminsters' patrol on each night consisted of ten men, that of the 27th being led by 2nd Lieutenant Moulton and that of the 29th by 2nd Lieutenant I. d'A. Stitt. The enemy, on the other hand, was becoming very cautious and only ventured out in strong parties of between forty and fifty men with machine guns. The policy of our patrols was to get in the first blow; and both on the 27th and the 29th the patrol was successful in opening rapid fire on the enemy before it was discovered. The surprise effect thus obtained was decidedly successful, for although the enemy replied with heavy fire, from rifles and machine guns, his fire was wild and caused no casualties. Hits on the enemy were, on the other hand, claimed by the patrols, and it is probable that considerable casualties were caused. It is certain that two at least were killed on the 27th, for their bodies were found two days later, on the scene of the encounter, by a patrol of the 109th Infantry Brigade sent out from the right of the Battalion sector.

The Queen's Westminsters were relieved by the Q.V.R. on November 1st, and went into Divisional reserve at Lebucquière. November 3rd was the third anniversary of the landing of the Battalion in France, and it was celebrated by a Battalion parade in the morning, when Lieut.-Colonel P. M. Glasier addressed the men; and by a very successful concert in the evening, given in the recreation hut by the Sergeants' Mess. A party of "Bow Bells" came out from Fremicourt and contributed several lively items to the programme, to the accompaniment of the sound of a heavy bombardment that was going on somewhere in the north.

Battalion Headquarters had been informed by this time that an offensive was to be launched against the enemy "some time in November," but only the vaguest details had been given, and the rest of the troops were kept in absolute ignorance that anything unusual was to take place. During this spell out of the line great attention was paid to training for open warfare; and reports that the enemy was contemplating a further withdrawal, were accepted as sufficient reason for the active road-making and mending that was taking place in the forward areas, and for the formation of large dumps of ammunition and engineering material near the front line.

The Battalion returned on November 6th for what turned out to be its last trench tour on the Cambrai front. Much work was done in making preparation for following up the enemy " in the event of his retirement." A party from the garrison of Perch Post, which was given the alliterative title of " The Permanent Party from Perch," was detailed to fill in all the shell-holes in the roads near the front trenches; reconnaissances were made of the roads leading forward through No-man's-land, some excellent reports being sent in by Lieutenant G. A. N. Lowndes; and an observation post commanding a good view of the important position known as Tadpole Copse was constructed near one of the front-line posts.

Patrols went out nightly as usual, but no enemy were met with, proof indeed that complete mastery of No-man's-land had been obtained. Brigadier-General Coke, in commenting on what he describes as " the super-excellent patrol work of the Q.W.R. in the Louverval sector," writes: "It is hard to praise too highly the initiative, courage and persistency which enabled your Regiment to gain such an obvious ascendancy over the enemy."

On the 13th, a party was sent out under 2nd Lieutenant J. P. Kennedy to explode a bangalore torpedo (a long metal tube filled with high explosive) under the enemy's wire near the Demicourt-Graincourt road. They successfully accomplished their task, but even this called forth no attempt at retaliation. This was the last offensive patrol to be sent out, orders having been received that the only patrolling that was to be allowed was for the purpose of watching the wire in front. There was always a risk that the enemy might capture a prisoner, who might quite unwittingly give information that would arouse suspicion.

The Battalion was relieved by the Q.V.R. on the night of November 16th, and for the next three days every available man was employed on working parties. All surplus kit was stored in the large tin recreation hut, and it became quite obvious that preparations were being made for offensive action. The nature of the operations was kept a profound secret; and beyond the fact that great numbers of aeroplanes were practising very low flying over the Battalion camp, and that fresh troops had arrived in the neighbourhood, there was nothing to indicate that an offensive on a large scale was imminent.

The weather had for some time been very misty and observation of what was going on behind the British lines was consequently impossible. The secret was well kept; and the enemy had no suspicion of the mighty surprise blow that was to be delivered, against the Hindenburg defences before Cambrai, on November 20th, 1917.

CHAPTER XV

THE BATTLE OF CAMBRAI, 1917

I.—THE CAPTURE OF TADPOLE COPSE

AS day dawned on November 20th, 1917, the thunder of a thousand British guns awoke with startling suddenness the quiet front from Gonnelieu to the Canal du Nord; and nearly four hundred tanks, followed by the infantry, moved forward from the British lines to crash their way through the dense masses of wire in front of the Hindenburg defences. This was the commencement of the surprise attack that will live in history as the Battle of Cambrai, 1917.

The events which led up to the battle are dealt with in Sir Douglas Haig's despatches of December 20th, 1917, and February 20th, 1918. They may be summarised shortly as follows : At a conference of military representatives of all the Allies, in November, 1916, a united plan of campaign was decided on which involved a simultaneous and co-ordinated offensive on all the fighting fronts. This plan never materialised. The Russian Revolution, followed by the collapse of the Russian armies, created a great change in the situation, and the western offensive was launched before Italy was ready to co-operate. A series of brilliant victories in the west had been won by the British and the French, in the course of continuous fighting since the beginning of April, 1917 ; but to a large extent their value was neutralised by the arrival of numbers of fresh enemy divisions no longer required in the east, and also by the disastrous defeat of Italy between October 24th and November 18th, 1917.

By the beginning of November there were but few British troops available for offensive action. Reinforcements were being hurried to the Italian front, and the bulk of the British Army was temporarily exhausted by the fierceness of the fighting in which it had been engaged. On the other hand, the strength of the enemy had been severely taxed, over 100 German divisions having been engaged and defeated by approximately half that number of British divisions.

With large concentrations of the enemy forces pinned down in Flanders and on the French battle-fronts, a favourable opportunity presented itself for a sudden attack at a point where the enemy did not expect it. This opportunity was seized. The Cambrai front had been " relatively inactive " for many months, and it also offered facilities for concealment and the use of tanks; this front was therefore selected as being the most suitable for the purpose.

It was a bold experiment to attempt, at the end of November and without any artillery preparation, a surprise on a front of some six miles and against the formidable defences of the Hindenburg line. But the experiment was fully justified by the results obtained during the opening stages of the battle.

The Germans may well have thought themselves in an impregnable position on the front attacked. Their trenches had been deliberately sited so as to take every advantage of a carefully chosen and naturally strong position; they had been constructed at leisure with consummate skill and with a prodigal expenditure of labour, and were protected by belt after belt of barbed wire of exceptional strength thickened with innumerable coils of loose wire. Some of these belts were said to measure as much as 200 yards from front to rear.

Quite apart from the intricate network of trenches which constituted the Hindenburg line, the dry cutting of the Canal du Nord, varying from fifteen to thirty feet in depth and of considerable width, formed, of itself, a very formidable obstacle. The whole enemy position was made still stronger by the magnificent observation behind the British lines from the tree-clad slopes of Bourlon Hill.

The main Hindenburg line consisted of a front and support system of trenches. It ran through the village of Havrincourt and then followed the western bank of the Canal du Nord as far as Mœuvres. Immediately south of Mœuvres the main line branched in two directions, one portion linking up with the Hindenburg reserve system, where it crossed the canal to the east of the village, and the other running in a north-westerly direction over Tadpole Copse, and thence nearly due west towards Pronville and Quéant. Tadpole Copse itself was a tactical point of considerable importance. The ground over which the Queen's Westminsters fought in the Battle of Cambrai, 1917, lay to the north of the Bapaume-Cambrai road; and here a continuous trench, forming an outpost line, had been dug and wired five or six hundred yards in front of the main system.

The enemy's rear defences were also of great strength. On the east side of the Canal du Nord the Reserve Hindenburg system was about 1200 yards in rear of the main system, and roughly parallel to it. This system also consisted of two lines of trenches protected by belts of wire. It crossed the Canal du Nord due east of Mœuvres, and, after passing through the village, it ran in a north-westerly direction across the lower slopes of the Tadpole Copse Ridge, and then onwards towards the outskirts of Inchy en Artois. On the west side of the canal the distance between the two systems was about 400 yards. Still further in rear was a third system of trenches which ran in front (to the west) of Bourlon Wood and Bourlon village. The village of Mœuvres itself formed a most important pivot in the German scheme of defence, and nothing had been left undone to make it as strong as possible.

To have attacked these positions, by the methods hitherto employed, would have involved an enormous expenditure of ammunition and tremendous casualties; and the warning given to the enemy by a prolonged bombardment would almost certainly have destroyed all chances of success. Only a sudden and unexpected blow could hope to succeed at so late a period of the year.

Some idea of the complete secrecy with which the preparations for the Cambrai attack were made will have been gained from the events recorded in the last chapter. It seems almost incredible that the preparations for an offensive on such a scale could have been completed without the troops, who had spent a long period in the immediate neighbourhood, becoming aware that a really big battle was imminent. Yet this seemingly impossible task was undoubtedly accomplished in the case of the Queen's Westminsters and the other units of the 169th Infantry Brigade. So skilfully were the preliminary work and the massing of the troops and guns organised by the higher command, that the individual was kept in almost complete ignorance of what was going on even a few hundred yards from his camp. There was an almost entire absence of mystery.

To all outward appearance there had been practically no change in the surroundings of the camps behind the lines. A few more huts had been put up, but these were to provide winter accommodation for the troops; the tents which had become superfluous had, however, been left standing. Immediately before the battle these tents were literally packed with fresh arrivals, but they were all kept under cover; and in any case the presence of a few men of new units would occasion no surprise, for a relief might be in progress. Further afield a large canvas camp, which was now similarly packed, had sprung up in Velu Wood, but this was completely screened by trees; and the ruins of the surrounding villages provided further improvised shelter for the battalions that had been brought up. Fresh batteries had been moved up to the forward areas under cover of darkness, and placed in positions at Demicourt, and near Boursies, and between the villages, yet none, except those in their immediate neighbourhood, had any knowledge of their presence.

The following incident typifies clearly what was passing in the minds of men who had been for some time on the northern sector of the Cambrai battle-front. The writer had been detailed as liaison officer with the 109th Infantry Brigade, and was on his way up to advanced Brigade Headquarters, about an hour before zero hour for the attack, accompanied by a telephone operator and a party of runners. These men had all been attached to Battalion Headquarters, and might be expected to know considerably more of what was going on than the rest of the Battalion; yet, when they were asked what they thought was going to happen that day, they all replied that they expected a raid " of some sort " was going to take place somewhere near Boursies (about two miles to the north of the left flank of the first day's attack). They were quite incredulous when told that they were within a few minutes of the commencement of a serious offensive.

Misty weather had favoured the preparations for the attack but, apart from this, the greatest pains had been taken to lull the enemy into a sense of security. During the past weeks the British defences on the Boursies front had been strengthened continuously; and fresh trenches had been dug and fresh wire had been put up as if for a prolonged stay on the existing defensive line. There had been no additional artillery activity, and up to the very commencement of the attack not a single round had been fired from the newly arrived guns, even for the purpose of registration. When the blow fell it came as a complete surprise on an unsuspecting foe.

The immediate object of the attack was to secure a local success. Sir Douglas Haig, in his despatch of February 20th, 1918, writes : " If after breaking through the defence system on this (the Cambrai) front we could secure Bourlon to the north and establish a good flank position to the east, in the direction of Cambrai, we should be well placed to exploit the situation locally between Bourlon and Sensée River and to the north-west. The capture of Cambrai itself was a subsidiary operation, the object of our advance towards that town being primarily to cover our flank and puzzle the enemy regarding our intentions."

The first stage of the operations, therefore, was to establish a line, through Fontaine, Bourlon and Inchy, to join that portion of the line held by the 56th Division on the high spur, midway between Louverval and Pronville. This spur terminated, to the east, at Tadpole Copse.

The plan of operations on the left flank of the attack was for the 36th (Ulster) Division, which was holding the sector on the immediate right of the 56th Division, to work its way along the Hindenburg defences on the west bank of the Canal du Nord, and then for the 56th Division to join hands with it, at whatever point was reached at the end of the first day's attack.

The 56th Division took no part in the initial attack, beyond discharging a smoke screen along practically the whole of its front, and putting out a number of dummy tanks and figures with the object of deceiving the enemy.

Zero hour was 6.20 a.m. on November 20th. The night had been quite quiet on the front of the 169th Infantry Brigade; but, shortly before the hour of attack, the silence was broken by a heavy bombardment by the enemy on the right. For a moment there was a suspicion that he had got wind of what was on foot, but the British guns gave no reply, and in a short time the bombardment ceased. At zero all was peace, and the uncanny silence could almost be felt in the expectant British lines. Suddenly signal rockets went up along the front, and in a moment the German trenches were drenched in a storm of bursting shells, and dense banks of smoke drifted lazily across the landscape, hiding all from view. The smoke, yellow and black at first, was turned to a lurid red as it crossed the path of the thermite shells and was lit up by their molten showers. Overhead aeroplane after aeroplane flew noisily across the lines, each on its appointed mission.

The smoke cleared, and later in the morning a long line of tanks could be seen far across the plain towards Bourlon. They were through the dense masses of wire and over the double line of trenches that formed the Hindenburg line, and were now working their way relentlessly forward. Spiteful tongues of flame issued from their sides as their crews fired their guns. Behind the tanks followed the small columns of infantry. The men appeared to be taking things with the characteristic *nonchalance* of the British soldier : some of them were smoking pipes, but all were ready to leap into the enemy's trenches as soon as the tanks had cleared a path, and to fight their way down them with bayonet and bomb. Never before had British infantry been able to clear the German wire with so much ease and so little loss. A little later large crowds of German prisoners could be seen straggling across the plain towards the British trenches.

The attack met with magnificent success all along the line. On the front of the 56th Division, there was no fighting, but the smoke screen and the dummy tanks drew the enemy's fire, the dummy tanks being shelled throughout the morning.

The 109th Infantry Brigade, on the left flank of the attack, advanced under a splendidly timed barrage. At the end of the day it had captured some 4000 yards of the Hindenburg line and many prisoners, and had reached a line about 200 yards north of the Bapaume-Cambrai road. By 11.55 p.m. the Q.V.R. had established touch with the 109th Infantry Brigade at the barrier across this road, about midway between the British front line and the canal; and during the night they established a number of posts linking up the barrier with the old front line, slightly east of Boursies.

The Queen's Westminsters so far had taken no part in the operations. A and D Companies were in support in the intermediate line near Louverval and Doignies, and the remainder of the Battalion had been standing by in the Brigade camp at Lebucquière. At 3.0 p.m. orders were received for Battalion Headquarters to move forward to Trout Post, on the road running east from Demicourt; and for the two companies at Lebucquière to take over the old front line, between the roads running from Demicourt towards Graincourt and Mœuvres, which had been vacated by the Q.V.R.

The guns moved forward during the night, and on the following morning the 109th Infantry Brigade continued its attack. Good progress was made at first, but the resistance stiffened during the day. At one time this Brigade had actually penetrated right into Mœuvres, but the troops could not maintain their hold on the village, and were driven back. At the end of the day they were holding the front trench of the Hindenburg main line, from the Canal du Nord to Aldgate (the sunken road leading from Mœuvres to Demicourt), and had posts pushed out in front. On their left they were in touch with the Q.V.R. who had bombed up the outpost line roughly as far as Aldgate.

At 2.0 p.m. on November 21st, the Queen's Westminsters received orders to attack Tadpole Copse, and they were informed that Mœuvres was in British hands, but that Houndsditch (the sunken road to the north-west of Aldgate) was under heavy machine-gun fire.

When these orders were received, A and D Companies were still in the intermediate line, and B and C Companies were at work clearing wire and obstructions from the road. It took some little time to assemble the companies and to issue orders, but by 4.30 p.m. all was ready, and the attack started.

B Company (Captain T. Caudwell) led, moving in two lines of platoons, and was followed by C Company (Captain W. G. Orr) in the same formation. A and D Companies, who had a considerable distance to come, arrived shortly afterwards. The former was ordered to follow the two leading companies, and the latter was kept in reserve near Battalion Headquarters. These were now in the old front line, about 200 yards east of Sturgeon Avenue.

On reaching the German outpost line near its junction with Aldgate, the assaulting companies found that the wire was intact. Eventually a patrolling gap was discovered, and 2nd Lieutenant W. H. Ormiston (in command of the leading platoon) and Sergeant R. R. Bulford made a gallant attempt to get their men through it in single file. It was now about 7.0 p.m., and the enemy, who was again in possession of Mœuvres, was raking Aldgate with his machine guns. It became clear that no advance would be possible under these conditions unless very heavy casualties were to be incurred.

The situation was reported to Brigade by wire. Fresh orders were then received that the Battalion was to return to the Boursies-Cambrai road, and was to make another attempt to reach Tadpole Copse, by entering the Hindenburg front line where it crossed the road and working up it past the 109th Infantry Brigade. This order was cancelled. The three attacking companies were then brought back to the old front line, on either side of Sturgeon Avenue, and patrols were pushed well forward in the old German outpost line in front.

By this time the enemy had recovered somewhat from his first surprise, and it was clear that more elaborate preparation was required to effect any useful progress.

It was next decided to make an attempt, in conjunction with the 36th (Ulster) Division, to capture the two Hindenburg systems running north-west from the neighbourhood of Mœuvres ; and the 169th Infantry Brigade was allotted the task of making good the Hindenburg front system, to the west, as far as the Louverval-Inchy road.

At 2.30 a.m. on November 22nd, orders were received by the Queen's Westminsters that they were to attack Tadpole Copse at 11.0 a.m. Entry into the Hindenburg front line was to be made through the communication trench leading from the German outpost trenches just east of Aldgate.

Battalion operation orders were issued verbally to the company commanders. The plan was for A Company (Captain A. J. M. Gordon) to attack up the second line of the system, and B Company (Captain T. Caudwell) up the front line, each being supported by two platoons of C Company (Captain W. G. Orr) who were to relieve sentries over captured dugouts and act as "moppers-up." D Company (Captain F. E. Whitby) was to clear the outpost line and get into touch with the other companies at the point where it joined the Hindenburg line, south-east of Tadpole Copse. The L.R.B. were to follow the Queen's Westminsters in support. A barrage, provided by an enfilade battery of the 36th (Ulster) Division, on the east side of the canal, was to cover the attack and was to move forward at the rate of fifty yards in five minutes.

The Battalion's assembly position was the communication trench already referred to and the outpost trenches on either side of it, and the troops were ordered to be in position by 6.30 a.m. The assembly was carried out without serious loss, though C Company had considerable difficulty in getting up to the position owing to heavy enemy shelling, and was somewhat delayed in consequence.

At zero hour (11.0 a.m.) the guns put down a heavy barrage on Mœuvres and across the Hindenburg line. Half an hour later, the barrage commenced to creep north-west towards Tadpole Copse, with the Queen's Westminsters following it closely and bombing their way down the trenches.

For a short time all went well, then a machine-gun block held up the advance of the infantry at Houndsditch, with the result that the barrage got ahead of the attack. Owing to the uncertainty that existed about the position of the infantry, it was not found practicable to bring the barrage back, with the result that it was of comparatively little direct assistance during the later stages of the attack. Rifle and Lewis-gun fire was opened on the machine guns which were holding up the Battalion, and they were eventually silenced. At this stage of the attack Lance-Corporal S. Rundle greatly distinguished himself by the effective use he made of his Lewis gun.

The advance continued as soon as the machine guns had been dealt with, and Battalion Headquarters were moved forward to the old enemy barrier across the Cambrai road, where the Q.V.R. had joined hands with the Ulstermen on the 20th.

At 12.30 p.m. a runner came back to headquarters with a request for some bombs, and reported that the attackers had passed Houndsditch and were using German bombs. Splendid help was given by the Q.V.R. and the 2nd Londons, the

THE BATTALION CAPTURES TADPOLE COPSE

former with great dash carrying forward large quantities of bombs and rifle grenades, and the latter forming dumps of ammunition in rear.

Severe trench fighting continued through the afternoon; but the enemy's resistance was gradually overcome, and at 2.40 p.m. the Germans were observed to be shelling Tadpole Copse. This indicated that the attack was proceeding satisfactorily.

By 4.30 p.m. D Company had succeeded in clearing the outpost line, and had gained touch with B Company in the front Hindenburg trench by forcing their way through the southern of the two communication trenches south-east of Tadpole Copse. In the course of this operation, these two companies had driven a large number of the enemy into the communication trench. The Germans, penned in on both sides and realising that they had no chance of escape, showed very little fight and were all captured and sent to the rear.

By 5.25 p.m. the Battalion was in Tadpole Copse and was bombing its way forward towards Tadpole Lane, its ultimate objective. At the close of the day it was reported that the leading troops had reached the objective.

The Queen's Westminsters had been fighting continuously for over six and a half hours. It had been pure trench fighting but of a somewhat novel character, owing to the great distance between the traverses in the Hindenburg line. This distance was too great for hand-bombing from traverse to traverse; but the difficulty was got over by the employment of very large numbers of rifle grenades, to cover the advance of the bombing parties as they dashed forward to get within range of the enemy. All fought well, but special reference must be made to the fine leadership of Captain W. G. Orr throughout the day. At the commencement of the attack, when the progress of B Company along the front Hindenburg line had been momentarily checked, this officer, as soon as he had organised his company which was then in support, made his way forward to the head of B Company, where he joined Sergeant R. F. Davis. He himself at once commenced bombing; and, with Sergeant Davis acting as leading bayonet man, led the company, fighting all the way, along practically the whole of the 2000 yards of the Hindenburg front line captured during the day. It was a very fine achievement, and the skill and gallantry exhibited by Captain Orr and Sergeant Davis contributed very largely to the successful capture of Tadpole Copse.

Although less resistance was encountered in the second

line, some very good bombing work was done by A Company, with Lance-Corporal K. M. Marshall in charge of the leading bombing section.

Enormous numbers of bombs and rifle grenades were used during the advance to Tadpole Copse; but a continuous supply to the leading sections was admirably maintained throughout the day, by means of carrying parties organised by C.S.M. Musselwhite, who acted as R.S.M. during the battle, and by C.S.M. Jones of A Company.

The former warrant officer also carried out a most valuable reconnaissance when the situation in front was obscure, and the reports he brought back were of the greatest assistance to Lieut.-Colonel P. M. Glasier in making his arrangements for holding the captured ground.

At the close of the day's fighting, the line held by the Battalion ran from the junction of Short Street and the Hindenburg support trench, to north-west of Tadpole Copse, and the Battalion was in touch, by means of patrols, with the L.R.B. on the right, and the London Scottish on the left.

The day had been a brilliantly successful one for the Regiment. It was firmly established in Tadpole Copse, and had secured 2000 yards of the famous Hindenburg line.

In addition to this it had captured 75 prisoners, including 3 officers; 3 machine-guns, a trench mortar, and very large quantities of stores and ammunition of every description. The casualties of the Battalion on the 21st and 22nd November had been extraordinary light, amounting to 10 other ranks killed or died of wounds, and 12 other ranks wounded.

For their success on this day the Queen's Westminsters were honoured by the following reference in Sir Douglas Haig's despatch of March 4th, 1918 : " Early in the night of the 22nd November a battalion of the Queen's Westminsters stormed a commanding tactical point in the Hindenburg line, west of Mœuvres, known as Tadpole Copse, the possession of which would be of value in connection with the left flank of the Bourlon position when the latter had been secured."

Late in the evening of November 22nd, the London Scottish established a line of posts from the junction of Barbican and Piccadilly along the ridge leading back to the old British front line.

During the night the enemy made repeated attempts to regain some of the ground he had lost, by bombing up the communication trenches that remained in his hands, but blocks had been established in all of these and attack after attack was successfully repulsed. At one block in particular the fighting was exceptionally severe, and a very fine resistance was maintained by a party under the command of 2nd Lieutenant Ormiston, who, although he was slightly wounded and badly shaken by a German bomb, held on to the position until the Battalion was relieved.

The attack was renewed on November 23rd by the London Scottish and the 2nd Londons.

The main idea was for the London Scottish to make ground along the Hindenburg front system as far west as Adelaide Street, while the 2nd Londons endeavoured to gain a footing, in the Hindenburg support line, between Short Street and Tadpole Lane.

Early in the morning of the 23rd (the War Diary of the 169th Infantry Brigade says 3.0 a.m., and that of the Queen's Westminsters " before dawn "[1]), the London Scottish took over the left portion of the front held by the Battalion. The attack was timed to commence at 6.20 a.m., but, in the words of the War Diary of the 2nd Londons : " In spite of all endeavours, it was found impossible to reach the assembly positions by zero hour. The London Scottish were equally late, and, in fact, both battalions moved across the open at daybreak to get to their positions. A new zero was mutually arranged between the commanding officers."

The 2nd Londons were held up by the strong bombing blocks in the communication trenches, and, in spite of all efforts, they were unable to effect an entry into the support system.

When the London Scottish launched their attack, they found that there was a deep valley, not shown on any of the British maps, between them and the Louverval-Inchy road, and that the enemy was holding a strong prepared position on the east of the road. As the London Scottish bombed their way downhill along the trenches, they came into full view of the German machine-gunners and riflemen who were dug into the high bank at the side of the road. After long and stubborn fighting the enemy resistance was overcome, and by 4.30 p.m. the London Scottish had advanced 1000 yards along the Hindenburg line and reached Adelaide Street, their main objective.

Some doubt exists as to the position where the left of the Queen's Westminsters had rested, when they were relieved by the London Scottish. The War Diary of the latter shows that they discovered, after they had launched their attack, that they were to the east of Tadpole Lane ; and the Diary of the 56th Division states that " It appeared as if, during the night,

[1] The sun rises on November 23rd at 7.35 a.m.

some ground had been lost in the support trench, and that the Germans had come back to D.18. d.8.8 (a high bank about 100 yards east of Tadpole Lane, overlooking the deep valley referred to above)." It seems certain that the enemy was still persisting in his counter-attacks when the Battalion was relieved by the London Scottish, but there is no reference in the War Diaries, either of the London Scottish or the Queen's Westminsters, of any ground having been yielded.

There is one explanation which cannot entirely be ignored, namely, that both the London Scottish and the Queen's Westminsters were misled as to their position, by the absence of any indication on the British maps[1] of the valley east of Tadpole Lane. It must be remembered, in this connection, that the Queen's Westminsters had reached their position after dark on November 22nd, and were relieved before dawn on the 23rd; and that the London Scottish did not discover their location until after daybreak.

The London Scottish had barely gained their objective when the Germans delivered a heavy counter-attack. Their War Diary states, " The supply of bombs had by this time (4.30 p.m.) run short in both B and C Companies. B Company, however, received a supply in sufficient time to enable them to beat off enemy counter-attacks and hold their block." The Queen's Westminsters had been working hard all day, forming dumps of ammunition, and were instrumental in getting supplies of bombs forward to the London Scottish at this critical time. Especially good work in this connection was done by a platoon under Sergeant R. R. Bulford.

Bomb fighting, more especially on the front of the L.R.B. and 2nd Londons, had continued throughout November 23rd, and some progress was made up the communication trenches leading to the enemy support system.

On the right, the whole of Mœuvres was at one time in the possession of the 36th (Ulster) Division, who at first made good progress with the aid of tanks, but later in the day the enemy recaptured the village after fierce fighting.

Nothing of importance occurred during the night of the 23rd/24th November. In the early morning of the 24th, the Battalion was relieved and went into Brigade reserve in the old front line trenches north-west of Louverval. C Company, caught by daylight, had to make a long detour

---

[1] This valley is shown by the contours of a captured German map. (See small inset map.) The German map was probably made after the ground had been carefully surveyed for the purpose of siting the Hindenburg line. The British map, on the other hand, depicted ground in the occupation of the enemy.

to avoid the enemy's shelling, and they did not reach the reserve line until after midday.

The next two nights were spent in digging a communication trench along the ridge leading to the junction of Barbican and Piccadilly, near the south-west corner of Tadpole Copse.

During the night of November 26th, the Battalion relieved the L.R.B. in the Brigade right subsector. This consisted of portions of the Hindenburg main system, from midway between Aldgate and Houndsditch on the right, to the bend in the German outpost line south-east of Tadpole Copse.

On the following day the enemy heavily shelled the position and made a determined attempt to recapture Tadpole Copse. This attack was repulsed by the Rangers and the Kensingtons after heavy fighting. During the bombardment the Battalion lost a promising officer in Captain A. J. M. Gordon, commanding B Company, who was killed by a shell. He had only been in France a short time, but had done some very useful work, and had shown himself possessed of a fine fighting spirit. He will be remembered by those who had served with the 3rd Battalion, for the work that he did at home, in organising entertainments and recreation for the men.

The next two days were spent under almost continuous shell-fire, though there was little actual fighting on the front of the Battalion.

II.—THE GERMAN COUNTER-ATTACK, NOVEMBER 30th, 1917

"The story of the fighting on the Bourlon-Mœuvres front is one so brimful of heroism that it deserves to take its place in English history for all time."—Official Pamphlet: "The Story of a Great Fight."

November 30th was destined to be a glorious day in the history of the Regiment.

The night of the 29th had been exceptionally quiet. There was no indication that the enemy was about to employ all his available forces in a desperate attempt, not only to regain the ground that he had lost, but to capture the high ground at Beaucamp and Trescault, and to destroy the whole of the British forces in the Cambrai Salient.

At eight o'clock in the morning, the fighting commenced with an attack on the southern portion of the Salient. This attack met with an unexpected measure of success, for the enemy overran the whole of the recently captured ground, and penetrated right back to Gouzeaucourt, a village behind the original British front line. A dangerous situation was saved by a brilliant counter-attack by the Guards and the magnificent defence of the 29th Division.

This attack was to some extent only a subsidiary operation, and the main German attack developed about two hours later on the front between Fontaine Notre Dame and Tadpole Copse. This portion of the front was held by the 47th (2nd London) Division on the right, the 2nd Division in the centre, and the 56th Division on the left.

The Queen's Westminsters, who, it will be remembered, were on the right flank of the 56th Division, were now holding some five or six hundred yards of the second line of the main Hindenburg system, with their right resting on Aldgate, about 200 yards from the southern outskirts of Mœuvres. The right of the Battalion front was held by B Company (Captain T. Caudwell), which was in touch with the 6th Infantry Brigade; C Company (Captain W. G. Orr) was in the centre and was holding a block pushed forward about 100 yards up Swan Lane communication trench; D Company (Captain F. E. Whitby) was on the left, in touch with the 2nd Londons; A Company (Lieutenant J. H. M. Hooper) was in support; and Battalion Headquarters were in the old German outpost line about midway between Aldgate and Houndsditch.

The first intimation that something unusual was afoot, was a report from the observers that "enormous numbers" of the enemy could be seen moving east through Quarry Wood towards Bourlon, and that there was considerable enemy movement into and out of Mœuvres. This was at 8.0 a.m. At 9.15 a.m. an attack developed on the canal lock to the south-east of Mœuvres, but this was stopped by the 6th Infantry Brigade. Half an hour later the Germans commenced to bombard the trenches on the left of those held by the Battalion; and shortly afterwards the enemy was seen to be advancing, towards the Queen's Westminsters, in two extended lines from the west of the village. Rifle and Lewis-gun fire was opened by a company of the 1st King's, which had moved up to the left flank of the 6th Infantry Brigade, and there were no developments on the actual front held by the Battalion.[1]

[1] It would appear from the War Diaries of the 2nd Division and of the 1st King's that the main attack on the Queen's Westminsters commenced at 9.50 a.m. As a matter of fact no attack was delivered on the Battalion until 10.45 a.m. It is stated definitely in the War Diaries of both the 56th Division and of the Queen's Westminsters that the S.O.S. went up all along the line at 10.45 a.m., and an S.O.S. was reported by the liaison officer of the 169th Infantry Brigade, attached to the 6th Infantry Brigade, to have gone up at the same hour on the front of the latter Brigade. It is somewhat difficult to account for the discrepancy, but what probably happened was that the action of the 1st King's prevented the original attack being pushed home.

In the meantime a large body of the enemy, estimated at one division, had been seen entering Mœuvres and a protective barrage was put down by the Divisional gunners.

At 10.45 a.m., after half an hour's heavy bombardment of the trenches held by the Battalion, the enemy, in very great strength, attacked under cover of a trench-mortar barrage, down the Boursies-Mœuvres road, down Houndsditch, down Swan Lane communication trench, and across the open.

He was met by a devastating fire at point-blank range, from Lewis guns and rifles, and was literally mown down. The attack across the open was completely stopped, and desperate fighting took place in Houndsditch and Swan Lane. The Lewis-gunners were well posted, and they acted with great gallantry. On the right, Rifleman Humphries and Rifleman Harris, both of B Company, inflicted terrible casualties on the enemy as he swarmed down Houndsditch, the former dying bravely at his gun after having accounted for over a hundred [1] Germans. In the centre Rifleman Eveleigh, with a Lewis gun, held up the enemy for a quarter of an hour near Swan Lane, until at last the gun was blown up by a bomb and he himself was wounded.

Under cover of a heavy trench-mortar barrage the enemy now began to press forward down the road and the communication trenches. The latter were very wide and afforded little protection from the barrage, and the Queen's Westminsters suffered severely. The men fought gamely. A dangerous rush down Swan Lane was stopped for a time by a party under Sergeant R. R. Bulford, but his party was eventually driven back towards a bombing block. An advanced post in front of this block was practically surrounded; only two of the garrison were left and these were wounded. Sergeant Bulford then courageously made his way forward alone, and, holding the enemy at bay with his revolver, not only enabled the wounded men to get away, but gained invaluable time for the bombers to reorganise behind the block. The enemy continued to press on with unabated determination, and by sheer weight of numbers succeeded in penetrating the forward line on both flanks. On the right practically the whole of B Company of the 1st King's was killed or wounded; and on the left the 2nd Londons were forced back, as a result of a temporary success gained by the enemy on their left.

The enemy now commenced to work inwards, bombing from both flanks, along the front-line trench of the Battalion; his progress was stubbornly resisted, but the Queen's West-

[1] So it was reported.

minsters were gradually forced back. It was during this stage of the fight that Captain T. Caudwell was killed, while going forward to see that no wounded had been left behind in an evacuated post. By his death the Battalion lost a very gallant young officer. His tastes were literary and artistic, but he possessed a real power of leadership, and whatever he undertook to do he did well and thoroughly.

At 1.15 p.m. the Battalion still maintained a precarious footing in the front line, but the situation was critical and reinforcements were asked for.

By 2.0 p.m. the troops had been driven back to the support line (the old German front line), but blocks had been established in the communication trenches, close up to the front trench, and beyond these the enemy, despite all his efforts, could make no progress.

There seemed no limit to the numbers that were hurled into the attack, they were seen coming on throughout the day in dense masses, in column of fours, and in waves in extended order. The fighting was continuous, and enormous casualties were inflicted on the enemy as he attempted to press on and came under the fire of rifles and Lewis guns from the trenches, and of machine-guns and artillery from the rear. At 2.30 p.m. he advanced in five lines on Mœuvres, moving south from Inchy; and the line threatened to give way. Reinforcements were again asked for, but none arrived.

Fighting of the fiercest character now took place in the communication trenches. In one, a party of bombers[1] under Corporal Harris resisted attack after attack; in another, Corporal G. Bristowe led the D Company bombers and grenadiers in a counter-attack, and drove back the enemy at a most critical time.

For the next two hours, the enemy was unceasing in his efforts to capture the support trench, but the resistance of the troops never wavered. Those responsible for the supply of ammunition, and there were many calls for it, had a hard task, but they worked heroically and never once was the call unanswered. The dump was set on fire three times, and each time Sergeant C. C. Hall and a gallant group of men succeeded, amidst the explosion of bombs and small-arm ammunition, in extinguishing it.

At 4.10 p.m. urgent messages were again sent for reinforcements. The men were quite worn out after nearly six hours of incessant fighting, and it seemed impossible that they could

[1] Amongst them were Rifleman H. Ward and Rifleman S. Eveleigh. The latter had joined the party after his Lewis gun had been blown up earlier in the day.

hold out much longer if the enemy persisted in his attacks. But his effort was spent at last, and his attacks began to die down, although bomb fights still continued at the blocks.

By 6.30 p.m., when the reinforcements at last began to arrive, the day had been won, and all was quiet except for machine-gun fire. The enemy had little gain to show for his tremendous sacrifices ; the support line remained unbroken, and he had only been able to penetrate half-way down the communication trenches leading to it from the front line of the morning. At the bombing blocks, made by the Battalion, his dead lay in heaps. The losses of the Queen's Westminsters, though very light in comparison with those inflicted on the enemy, were heavy, amounting to 126 all told. Captain (2nd Lieutenant) T. Caudwell, 2nd Lieutenant J. H. M. Hooper, and 31 other ranks were killed or died of wounds ; Captain W. G. Orr, and 2nd Lieutenants H. K. Moulton (18th Londons), and G. L. Lloyd (9th Londons, attached Queen's Westminsters), and 66 other ranks were wounded ; and 24 other ranks were posted as missing. It is now known that many of the latter were killed.

A company of the Q.V.R. came up at 6.30 p.m. and relieved the bombers at the blocks, and at 8.0 p.m. two companies of the L.R.B. arrived. Half an hour later orders were received that they were to relieve the Queen's Westminsters who were now holding 500 yards of the old Hindenburg front line, with their right on Aldgate, in touch with the 6th Brigade.

The Battalion did not get clear of the trenches until 1.0 a.m. on December 1st. Wagons had been provided to meet the men near Doignies and take them back to Lebucquière ; but the heavy enemy barrage across the Cambrai road prevented the troops from reaching them, and, exhausted as they were, they had to march the whole way back to Coke Camp. The Battalion was now in Divisional reserve.

Thus ended the Queen's Westminsters' stay on the Cambrai front. There was no further serious fighting north of Mœuvres ; and, except that, for artillery purposes, the bombing blocks were withdrawn to within 100 yards of the new front line, no change occurred for some days on the front vacated by the Battalion.

On December 2nd, the 56th Division was relieved by the 51st (Highland) Division, and four days later a readjustment of the British line was made to conform with the situation further south.

Although part of the ground captured by the Battalion was abandoned in the course of this operation, it is satisfactory to know that the withdrawal was purely voluntary and was effected with practically no interference from the enemy.

The general results of the Battle of Cambrai are thus summed up in Sir Douglas Haig's despatch of February 20th, 1918 : " We had captured and retained in our possession over 12,000 yards of the German front line, from la Vacquerie to a point opposite Boursies, together with between 10,000 and 11,000 yards of the Hindenburg line and Hindenburg Reserve line, and the villages of Ribecourt, Flesquieres and Havrincourt. A total of 145 German guns were taken or destroyed by us in the course of the operations, and 11,100 German prisoners were captured. . . . There is little doubt that our operations were of considerable indirect assistance to the allied forces in Italy . . . and it is probable that the further concentration of German forces against Italy was suspended for at least two weeks, at a most critical period, when our allies were making their first stand on the Piave line."

In dealing specifically with the northern attack of November 30th he wrote : " On the whole of this front a resolute endeavour was made to break down, by sheer weight of numbers, the defence of the London Territorials and other English battalions holding the sector. In this fighting the 47th (London) Division (T.), the 2nd Division and the 56th (London) Division (T.) greatly distinguished themselves, and there were accomplished many deeds of great heroism."

At the close of the fighting on November 30th, Major-General F. A. Dudgeon (Commanding the 56th Division) sent the following wire :—

" The G.O.C. has much pleasure in forwarding following message and congratulations to Brigadiers and their gallant battalions. Please convey to your brigades in the line the appreciation of the Corps Commander[1] for their gallant stand to-day. He feels confident that they will now maintain their positions and thus protect the flank of the IV Corps."

The following messages of congratulation were circulated after the battle :—

From Field-Marshal Sir Douglas Haig (addressed to the Commander of the Third Army, December 1st, 1917) :—

" I congratulate you and the officers and men under your command upon the successful resistance, maintained by the Third Army yesterday, against the powerful attacks deliv-

---

[1] At the opening of the German counter-attack the 56th Division formed part of the VI Corps, commanded by Lieut.-General Sir J. A. L. Haldane.

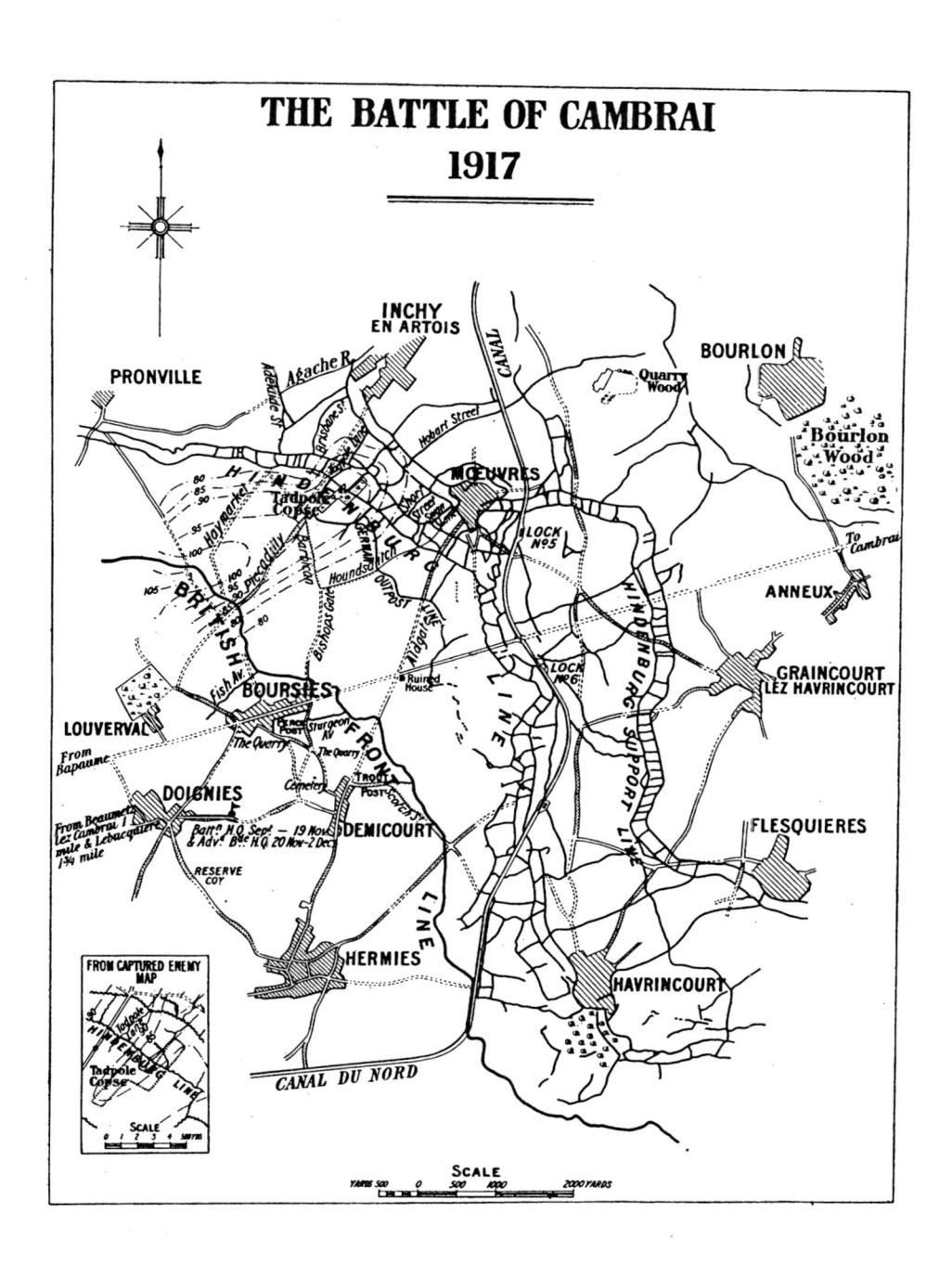

THE BATTLE OF CAMBRAI
1917

ered by the enemy south-west of Cambrai. In particular I desire you to convey to the General Officers Commanding the 2nd, 47th, and 56th Divisions, and to all ranks serving under them my very warm appreciation of their magnificent defence of the important positions entrusted to them. Though exposed throughout the day to the repeated assaults of superior forces, they beat off all attacks with the heaviest losses to the enemy, and by their gallant and steady conduct contributed very largely to the security of the Divisions engaged on the whole front of the attack."

From General the Hon. Sir Julian Byng (Commanding the Third Army) :—

" I cannot allow the 56th Division to leave the Third Army without placing on record my appreciation of its excellent fighting spirit. Both during normal trench warfare and during the active operations connected with the Battle of Cambrai, it has shown both aggression and endurance, which have added greatly to its brilliant record."

Brigadier-General E. S. D'E. Coke (Commanding 169th Infantry Brigade) personally addressed the Battalion on December 4th at Berneville, congratulating it on its work during the operations, and generally on the offensive spirit displayed during its time in the Cambrai area. He paid special tribute to the great amount of work that had been done in perfecting the Brigade defences, and to the exceptionally good trenches that had been constructed by the Q.W.R. and the other battalions of the Brigade.

Some months later an account of the fighting on November 30th was published in a special official pamphlet under the title of " The Story of a Great Fight." The following extracts[1] from it form a fitting conclusion to this chapter :—

" On the morning of November 30th, 1917, the 47th (London) Territorial Division, the 2nd Division, and the right brigade of the 56th (London) Territorial Division were holding a front of about five miles, extending from the eastern ridge of Bourlon Wood to Tadpole Copse, in the Hindenburg line, west of Mœuvres. From Tadpole Copse the left brigade of the 56th Division formed a defensive flank across No-man's-land to our old front line.

" The 56th Division had been in line before the British attack of November 20th, in which its right brigade (169th)

[1] It is regretted that the account is too long to print in full. For the convenience of the reader these extracts have been printed consecutively.

had taken part, and since that date it had captured and held about a mile of the Hindenburg line, west of Mœuvres, including Tadpole Copse. Almost constant fighting had taken place in this area since our attack, and the Division which at one time had been holding a front of 11,000 yards had already been subjected to a very severe strain.

" The story of the subsequent fighting on the Bourlon-Mœuvres front is one so brimful of heroism that it deserves to take its place in English history for all time. The most determined attacks of four German divisions, with three other German divisions in support, were utterly crushed by the unconquerable resistance of the three British divisions in the line. November 30th, 1917, will be a proud day in the lives of all those splendid British soldiers who, by their single-hearted devotion to duty, prevented what would have become a serious situation had they given way. From Mœuvres westward to Tadpole Copse a desperate struggle was taking place for the possession of the Hindenburg line.

" Though much reduced in strength by the fighting of the preceding days, and hard pressed by superior forces, the troops of the 168th and 169th Infantry Brigades beat off all attacks. Queen's Westminsters, London Scottish, and men of the 1/2nd Battalion London Regiment, and 1/8th Battalion Middlesex Regiment, vied with one another in the valour of their resistance.

" At the end of this day of high courage and glorious achievement, except a few advanced positions, some of which were afterwards regained, our line had been maintained intact. The men who had come triumphantly through this mighty contest felt, and rightly felt, that they had won a great victory, in which the enemy had come against them in his full strength and had been defeated with losses at which even the victors stood aghast."

CHAPTER XVI

THE FIRST BATTLE OF ARRAS, 1918

I.—IN THE GAVRELLE SECTOR, DECEMBER, 1917, TO MARCH, 1918

THE next move of the Battalion was to the Arras front. On December 2nd, 1917, when the Brigade was relieved by the 154th Infantry Brigade (57th Division), the Queen's Westminsters, who had been for two days in Brigade reserve at the camp near Lebucquière, marched to Bancourt on the outskirts of Bapaume. Here a bitterly cold night was spent under canvas. On the next day the whole Brigade moved by train from Fremicourt to Beaumetz les Loges, the Battalion being billeted at Berneville. Everyone was hoping for a short rest; but the order came to move on December 5th to Marœuil, previous to going into the line again north of Arras.

Both at Berneville and at Marœuil there was a brief return to civilisation. The sight of people still living in their own homes with whole roofs over their heads, the presence of a few shops where gifts (at a price) could be purchased to be sent to friends at home in time for Christmas, and the comparative luxury of a few nights' sleep on wire bunks in draughty barns, all had a wonderfully inspiring effect on tired men who had lived for several months in the depressing surroundings of a devastated and deserted area. Moreover, the Battalion knew that it had helped to deal a heavy blow to the enemy by its successful stand against the terrific onslaught of November 30th.

On December 8th, the Queen's Westminsters marched, via Anzin and St. Aubin, to the muddy camp of Nissen huts at Ecurie Wood, and came into reserve to the 169th Infantry Brigade which had relieved the 92nd Infantry Brigade in the Gavrelle sector.

The next few months were a trying and anxious time for the armies in France. The whole situation on the Western Front had been changed by the collapse of Russia in the east. Germany, on the one hand, was in a position to transfer large numbers of troops from the east to the west, whilst Britain, on the other, was almost at the end of her resources in men. She was forced for the time being to adopt a defensive policy, and all her efforts in France were needed to build and strengthen defensive positions along her whole front. For France the man-power question was still more acute; and the American Army was not yet present in France in sufficient strength to enable active operations to be recommenced.

The nature of the work that the Queen's Westminsters shared with every other unit in France, during the winter of 1917–18, is indicated by the following summary extracted from Sir Douglas Haig's despatch of July 20th, 1918: " Orders were issued, early in December, having for their object immediate preparation to meet a strong and sustained hostile offensive. In the course of the strenuous fighting in 1916 and 1917 great developments had taken place in the methods of conducting a defensive battle. A vast amount of work was required to be done in the construction of defences, old systems had to be remodelled, and new systems created. The construction of new communications and the extension of old ones involved the building of a number of additional roads. All the available men of the fighting units, with the exception of a very small proportion undergoing training, and all labour units were employed on these tasks. . . . Though the time and labour available were in no way adequate, if, as was suspected, the enemy intended to commence his offensive operations in the early spring, a large portion of the work was, in fact, completed before the enemy launched his great attack. That so much was accomplished is due to the untiring energy of all ranks of the fighting units, the Transportation Service, and the Labour Corps."

The front taken over by the 169th Infantry Brigade, on December 7th, included the village of Gavrelle and the trenches north and south of it. The front-line system of the Brigade sector occupied a frontage of roughly one mile, and was divided into two subsectors. These extended for approximately equal distances on either side of the Gavrelle-Douai road, which ran through the centre of the village.

The Naval-Marine line was about 1000 yards in rear of the front system, and constituted the main support trench; about another thousands yards further back, to the east of Bailleul,[1] the Red line formed the main reserve trench.

The principle of defence, adopted for the front and support systems, was to hold large defended localities in strength, and

[1] Not to be confused with Bailleul near Armentières.

to leave the intervening areas unoccupied; the latter being strongly wired and capable of being brought under concentrated artillery, machine-gun, and trench-mortar fire in the event of the enemy penetrating them. In the front system there were two defended localities, Towy Post in the right subsector and Mill Post in the left subsector, each garrisoned by approximately one company. Between them were Gavrelle and Water Posts, which were held mainly for the purpose of giving warning of any hostile incursion into the area between the two large posts. Orders were given that Towy and Mill Posts were to be held to the last, and that no retirement from them could be justified in any circumstances.

The battalions holding the front line were also responsible for the Naval-Marine line which held the supports. The battalion in Brigade support was responsible for the defence of the Red line; and the battalion in Brigade reserve had to be ready to move forward at the shortest notice to the Red line when the order to " stand to " was given.

The trenches were, on the whole, very poor compared to those that the Battalion had occupied on the Cambrai front; there was a great lack of fire bays, and the wire in front was very thin. No time, however, was lost by the Brigade in getting to work to remedy these defects.

Of the work that was done, Captain G. A. N. Lowndes, who was commanding B Company at the time, writes :—

" In the two months which preceded the fateful March 28th,[1] and after the immediate need for repairing the snow-collapsed trenches had been met, a tremendous amount of steady effort was devoted to strengthening these defences. The untidy belt of wire which protected Towy and straggled across the front of Gavrelle and up the hill to Mill Post was widened, added to, deepened and intersected with hundreds of ' knife rests ' and ' *chevaux de frise*,' while at every turn formidable bombing blocks, bristling with wire, were erected. Thus each separate section, or cross of trenches with a convenient dugout, became a little fortress. At the same time a company of Engineers and a loaned composite company of Westminsters laboured at new dugouts; machine-gun barrages were designed to protect every vital point, and a Stokes gun was planted in the very centre of Towy Post, a serious tactical error no doubt, but one which cost the enemy heavy casualties. Even the officer and twelve men who nightly relieved the ill-omened 'sacrifice' post in the forward outskirts

[1] This was the date of the attack on the sector held by the Battalion. The German offensive was commenced further south on March 21st, 1918.

of Gavrelle village, between Towy and Mill Post, might feel a new sense of protection, when they passed up to a relief through the ever-growing nests of batteries that dotted the reverse slope of Vimy towards the railway cutting of the Arras-Douai line and Roundhay rest camp. The whole front formed one of the most formidable defensive works which the Westminsters had ever held. For once every one of these preparations, except perhaps those round the Corps Headquarters, many miles back, were to be put to the test and abundantly justified."

Captain Lowndes has also supplied the following graphic description of the front held by the Battalion :—

" The Gavrelle front can perhaps best be described by the epithet ' eerie.' So fiercely had the tide of battle ebbed and flowed around the village a year before, that, although it resembled in most respects the other shapeless heaps of rubble which had once been small mining villages on this front, around it had centred all sorts of curious legends. Unburied dead in plenty filled its slimy hollows and ditches, there were rumours of underground waterways, still with boats on them ; a mere whisper of mining would bring up a whole company of Engineers with their listening sets, and the enemy made their contribution to the general mystification by shelling the village daily, though he must have known it to be bare of troops. It was accordingly perhaps not without a feeling of vague uneasiness that the companies, now daily augmented by drafts from home to replace their losses at Cambrai, used to wind slowly up the 5000 yards of Towy trench to their daylight reliefs. The fact that the line was held in depth decreased the individual confidence, though no doubt it increased the general feeling of security. To have fourteen healthy specimens of flesh and blood beside one is far more comfortable psychologically than to know that one is covered by a potential barrage of fourteen machine guns.

" Gavrelle itself lay in a slight depression. On the left a long flat spur, running towards the enemy, terminated in a round knoll upon which stood a derelict windmill. A maze of trenches here formed a post, garrisoned by a company of the battalion holding the left subsector of the Brigade. Down the gentle slope from the mill, and across the flats on the opposite side of Gavrelle ruins, lay ' Towy Post,' the square post which it was always the privilege of the Westminsters to hold. In shape it was almost a perfect square, the sides measuring about 150 yards apiece. To our artillery observation machines it must have looked like a large, much-battered toasting fork with three prongs and Towy trench as the handle. The right and left trenches went by the auspicious names of ' Little Willie ' and ' Invicta,' while the front line—the toast across the prongs—was known as ' Big Willie.' On the right, with a wide, intervening gap across the flat, was a similar post held by the left battalion of the Third Army. Behind Towy there were two further complete lines of trenches, ' Naval Trench ' and ' Bailleul-Willerval ' or ' Red line ' ; while a series of small carefully planned and scrupulously camouflaged platoon strong points, each with a ' model de luxe,' deep dugout, completed the defences between the two."

The Battalion remained at Ecurie Camp until December 14th, 1917, when it relieved the 2nd Londons in the right sub-sector, with one company in Towy Post and one company in Gavrelle and Water Posts, in the front line ; one company in Naval trench, and the fourth company in the Red line.

The tour, which lasted until the 20th, was a quiet one, but there was always a certain amount of shelling, and on occasions the enemy was active with his trench mortars and machine guns. The only incident of special note during the tour occurred on December 18th, when a German plane was brought down by Lewis-gun fire and crashed in the enemy lines due east of Gavrelle Post. On the 20th, the Battalion was relieved by the 2nd Londons. A and D Companies then moved back to the Red line, in support, and the remaining two companies went to Roundhay Camp, about a mile to the east of Neuville St. Vaast. On the 24th the Battalion returned to the line, relieving the 2nd Londons in the right sub-sector ; and it remained in until the 28th. Christmas Day passed very quietly in the trenches, but the Diary states that " Our machine guns and artillery were a little more active than usual." During the 28th December, the enemy put some gas shells on the junction of Naval trench and the Arras-Gavrelle road, but did little damage ; and in the evening, the Battalion was relieved by the 2nd Londons and moved back to Aubrey Camp on the Arras-Souchez road.

Ever since the Battalion had left the Cambrai front the weather had been extremely cold, and the great shortage of fuel and the lack of good accommodation in the forward areas involved considerable discomfort for everyone. At Roundhay Camp, for instance, the men were billeted in rough shelters and unfinished huts which afforded practically no protection against the weather ; and in the line, the men felt the cold intensely, although there was a certain amount of compensation in the fact that the trenches held up well, so long as the frost continued.

The Battalion returned to the line on January 1st, 1918, for two nights; and on the 3rd, after being relieved by the 1/4th Londons, went back by light railway to Marœuil.

This was the commencement of a period of five weeks' "rest." On January 5th, the Battalion proceeded by train from Marœuil to Savy, and then marched on to Caucourt where it was billeted in huts and barns.

From the point of view of training this period out of the line was almost useless. The bad weather continued throughout the "rest." It was very cold, and when it did not rain it snowed. The War Diary constantly refers to the bad conditions. The following are typical entries: "The whole Battalion employed all day in clearing snowdrifts from the roads between the villages." "All training cancelled by reason of rain. Rain ceased later and Battalion went for a route march. Rain fell again, however, and the Battalion got very wet."

The weather naturally affected sports even more than training, but inter-company and inter-platoon rounders and Rugby and Association football competitions were held. There were also competitions in military efficiency, and No. 12 Platoon gained second place in the Brigade inter-platoon competition.

At Caucourt most of the men were accommodated in large French huts which were exceedingly cold and very hard to warm, owing to the shortage of fuel. These were difficult times, both for those at home and those in France. The food question was particularly acute, and as a measure of economy orders were received to under-draw rations so as to make more food available for the civilian population at home. It cannot, however, be said that any real shortage of food was involved by this arrangement. The need for thrift and economy was also brought home to the Battalion by a lecture given by the A.P.M., in which all ranks were exhorted to invest their pay in War Savings Certificates.

The scheme for education and reconstruction after the war was propounded to the men about this time, but, with the enemy massing in greatly superior numbers not many miles away, it could not be expected to appeal as a serious proposition, even to the most optimistic. There was, however, an increasing demand on all sides for opportunities, if not for definite study, at any rate for some form of mental recreation. This demand gave birth to what the late Field-Marshal Sir Henry Wilson described as " the biggest revolution in the

JANUARY–FEBRUARY, 1918

Army since the introduction of gunpowder," namely, the Army Education Scheme.

On January 15th the Battalion had its Christmas dinner, followed by a very successful concert in the evening, these festivities having been postponed as the Battalion was in the trenches both at Christmas and on New Year's Day.

On January 24th, the Battalion (less C Company) moved to Roclincourt and Bailleul, in the forward area, for work (principally wiring) under the C.R.E., XIII Corps. C Company, which had been attached to the 185th Tunnelling Company on the 20th, rejoined the Battalion at the end of the month.

The wiring was a necessary piece of work, but it was rendered very unpleasant by the cold weather and the hard state of the ground. The many changes involved in perfecting the machine-gun defence scheme resulted in much time being spent in dismantling entanglements put up the previous day. But the extra work was more than justified on March 28th, 1918.

On January 29th, No. 2 Platoon (2nd Lieutenant J. C. Goadby, since killed in action) proceeded to Frevillers to take part in a Brigade Army Rifle Association competition, which it won on the following day. A week later the same platoon won the Divisional A.R.A. competition, which consisted of a practice in the combined use of the bullet and the bayonet. The platoon scored heavily both for its rifle and Lewis-gun fire, and its bayonet work on the sacks. The Battalion secured a further success in March, when No. 3 Platoon, under the command of 2nd Lieutenant V. G. Rayner, won a similar competition open to all units of the XIII Corps, each unit being represented by one platoon.

On February 1st, the Battalion marched to Ecurie railhead and entrained for Tinques, whence it marched to billets at Frevillers. Here the Queen's Westminsters were reinforced by a draft of 12 officers and 250 other ranks from the 1st Battalion Queen Victoria Rifles. This fine battalion was amalgamated with the 2nd Q.V.R., when the establishment of all brigades in France was reduced from four to three battalions, under instructions from the Army Council. This involved the splitting up of the unit. The Queen's Westminsters sympathised genuinely and deeply with the Q.V.R., who had to submit to a fate which they themselves had narrowly escaped.[1] The two battalions of riflemen had landed in

[1] The Queen's Westminsters, as the highest numbered battalion in the Brigade, had originally been noted for amalgamation; and it was only the fact that the 2nd Battalion was not then in France, that enabled the two Battalions to retain their identity until the end of the war.

France at about the same time, had served together in the same Brigade for two years, and were both equally proud of their Territorial and Regimental traditions.

The Queen's Westminsters gave the draft a very hearty welcome; whilst the Q.V.R. officers and men, although naturally very sore at heart at the breaking up of their own battalion, entered their new one with a magnificent spirit and did their duty by it nobly. Many became casualties during the fighting that was to come, but quite a number were still with the Battalion at the conclusion of hostilities.

Probably the Queen's Westminsters never received a better draft. Three of the officers subsequently commanded companies, and two were awarded the Military Cross. The N.C.O.'s and riflemen, too, did exceptionally well in all branches of Regimental work. Each individual helps to build up the traditions of his regiment, whether serving with his battalion or away from it; and for the splendid manner in which their officers and men worked for the efficiency and good name of a battalion to which they were compulsorily posted or transferred, the Queen's Westminsters owe a debt of gratitude to the Queen Victoria Rifles which it would be hard to repay.

After a week's training of an advanced character the Battalion, on February 7th, moved by train and march route, via Savy and Marœuil to St. Aubin. On the following day, after proceeding by train to Chantecler siding, it relieved the 2/4th Duke of Wellington's (186th Infantry Brigade) in the Gavrelle right sector of the Divisional front, which included Towy Post and Gavrelle Post.

The Brigade sector was now held by one battalion in the line, one in support and one in reserve. The front battalion had one company manning the two posts; one company in Naval trench to the north of Towy Alley, from which the garrison of Water Post was supplied; two platoons in Naval trench to the south of Towy Alley; and two platoons in the Bailleul-Willerval line, responsible for manning Keillar, Pelican and Halifax Posts. The remaining company was in Ditch Post. Except for an hour's bombardment with " mustard " gas shells, which caused no casualties, the tour which came to an end on February 13th was a very quiet one.

After being relieved by the 2nd Londons, the Battalion went into Brigade support at Roundhay Camp and in the Red line. On February 17th, the Queen's Westminsters went into Brigade reserve at St. Aubin, where the Divisional Commander inspected the Battalion on the 19th. The entry in the

WAITING FOR THE GERMAN OFFENSIVE

Brigade War Diary for this date is as follows : " Turn out and march past very satisfactory. G.O.C. thanked the Q.W.R. for their excellent work done in the fighting at Cambrai."

The next two trench tours were of little general interest. The Battalion was in the line for the periods February 21st–27th, and March 11th–19th, having relieved the L.R.B. on both occasions. The time out of the line was chiefly spent in strengthening the defences, more particularly in putting up wire. Some training, however, was done ; the taking up of battle positions was rehearsed, and counter-attacks on a large scale were practised under a Corps tactical scheme.

The activity of the enemy's artillery and trench mortars was now gradually increasing, and there were frequent bombardments of the front and back areas with gas shells. There were many rumours, too, that the expected German attack on this part of the line was imminent. On February 27th, the battalion in support was ordered to be ready to move at half an hour's notice, the Brigade having wired that " from information received, from a German deserter, a hostile attack was expected at Gheluvelt." Again, on March 12th, a warning was issued that an attack was expected on the morning of the 13th between Arras and Cambrai, and possibly on the Battalion sector, and patrols were ordered to lie out all night in front of our wire. Our artillery was specially active throughout the night 12th/13th March, and the whole Division was ordered to be in a state of immediate readiness. No infantry attack, however, developed.

On March 14th, the enemy bombarded the support lines at frequent intervals with mustard gas. On the evening of March 15th, a patrol of eight other ranks of the Queen's Westminsters, under an officer of the L.R.B., went out to examine the enemy's wire in front of Chaff trench, which was to be raided by the L.R.B. on the following night. The wire was found to be cut and a tape was laid out from our wire to the gap. The raid took place at 10.0 p.m. on the 16th, but the enemy trenches were found to be strongly held and the L.R.B., although they accounted for many of the enemy, were unable to effect an entry. The following passage affecting the Battalion occurs in the account of this raid, appended to the L.R.B. War Diary : " The Lewis-gun teams of the Queen's Westminsters fired continually at the head of Chink, and sprayed the German wire from dusk to shortly before zero. This firing was done from the open in front of our wire at Willie Trench."

On March 18th, the Battalion was relieved by the 2nd Londons and moved back to Roundhay Camp. It was out of the line for a week, working hard at the defences of the Red line and the Naval line. On the 21st March, the enemy offensive started to the south of Monchy and met with unexpected success; the distant roll of heavy gun-fire could be heard far away to the southward, rumours of British reverses spread quickly to the north, and every preparation was made for immediate action. Another week, however, was to pass before any attack was made on the front of the 56th Division. There was at this time every indication that an attack could not be long delayed. The posts, especially Towy Post, were subjected to heavy bursts of shelling by artillery and trench mortars, the enemy aeroplanes displayed great activity, and very considerable movement was observed behind the enemy lines.

When the Queen's Westminsters relieved the 2nd Londons in the Gavrelle sector on March 25th, it was fully expected that the enemy's attack would be launched the next morning. The following report had been received in the afternoon from the First Army: " Prisoners state that an attack is to be made on the morning of the 26th, and that the 219*th and* 23*rd Reserve Divisions* have been brought up for the purpose." Further information was gained from a prisoner captured by the L.R.B. This was to the effect that an attack might be expected the next morning at Oppy, the object of which was to press on forward about four miles and then swing right, behind the Vimy Ridge. All ranks were warned, and every preparation was made for what must assuredly be a determined enemy effort to push forward.

The situation on the Battalion front became electrical when the relieving party of the Queen's Westminsters, under the command of 2nd Lieutenant I. d'A. Stitt, arrived at Gavrelle Post after dark, and found that the garrison had disappeared. This little post, as has already been mentioned, was maintained for observation purposes, and to give warning of any infiltration of the enemy into the unoccupied area. It consisted merely of a dugout and a short length of trench blocked at each end with wire, and its garrison of some fifteen men was completely isolated by day. It offered itself readily to a raid by the enemy, for there were ruins on one side and hedges on the other, and a ditch ran into it from the German lines. The dugout of Gavrelle Post was searched. In the dim light from an electric torch 2nd Lieutenant Stitt discovered, at the bottom of the steps, the huddled bodies of two of the garrison; both had been bayoneted. It was of course clear that a raid had been carried out; and, with this post of observation gone, it was quite possible for comparatively large bodies of the enemy to have penetrated into the village just behind. The battalion on the north was accordingly warned; and patrols were despatched from the Naval line and from Water and Towy Posts to form a cordon round the village and search the ruins. However, the whole area was found clear of the enemy and Gavrelle Post was reoccupied. As extra measures of precaution, a strong patrol lay out in front of the village all night and our artillery kept up a continuous bombardment of the enemy lines east of the village, until daylight.

It was now decided that, in the event of counter-attack, Keillar Post was tactically a better place for Battalion Headquarters than the junction of Naval trench and Towy Alley. Headquarters were accordingly moved to Keillar Post during the night, but a few signallers were left at the trench junction.

No attack developed on the morning of the 26th, although a party of forty or fifty Germans attempted to approach our wire. These were dispersed, with casualties, by Lewis-gun and rifle fire, and the rest of the day passed " quietly."

During the afternoon orders were received for three simultaneous raids to be carried out that night, by the L.R.B. on Cup trench, by the 2nd Londons on Chaff communication trench, and by the Queen's Westminsters on Chink communication trench, in order to discover if possible the intentions of the enemy. Zero hour was fixed for 10.30 p.m., and the enemy's wire was bombarded by the 4.5" and 6" howitzers until late in the evening. No. 3 Platoon, under the command of 2nd Lieutenant V. G. Rayner, formed the Battalion raiding party. At 10.55 p.m., the hour to which the raid had been postponed, this officer, who had previously reconnoitred the route, led his party over in two waves. The first wave stopped some fifty yards short of the enemy's wire, many men being seen in the trenches. The enemy discovered the raiding party and opened on it heavy granatenwerfer, machine-gun and rifle fire. Verey lights were also fired from a sap and from the inner belt of wire, and Sergeant Broadbent, who got through the outer belt, observed some of the enemy between the outer and inner belts. Unable to find a gap in the wire, and shot at by trench mortars and machine guns, without any means of retaliation, the party returned after lying out in No-man's-land for one and a half hours. The other two raids were equally unsuccessful, and patrols all along the Divisional front reported the line strongly held and the enemy alert.

The German lines were again subjected to a heavy bombardment during the early morning of March 27th, but without evoking retaliation on the part of the enemy. Throughout the day many low-flying enemy aeroplanes flew over our positions, and much movement was seen in the German lines. Orders had been received in the morning to clear all ammunition from the forward posts and from the Naval line, preparatory to a withdrawal from them which was to take place that night. This order was cancelled in the early afternoon; and fresh orders were issued for the company in the Red line to move forward and take over the Naval line as far as Belvoir Alley, in order to prolong the Brigade front towards the north. This move was carried out during the night of the 27th/28th, the 2nd Londons, who were in Brigade reserve, taking over the Red line from C Company. In a few short hours the Battalion was destined to be engaged in what was, perhaps, its most memorable and successful fight during the whole course of the war.

II.—GAVRELLE, MARCH 28TH, 1918

On the night of the 27th/28th March, the 56th Division took over, from the 3rd Canadian Division, an additional 1500 yards of front on its left flank. This entailed an extension of the front held by the 169th Infantry Brigade; and, in conformity with the altered dispositions of the Brigade, C Company was moved up from the Bailleul-Willerval line to take over a further portion of the Naval line, up to a point just south of Belvoir Alley (a trench to the north of the Arras-Gavrelle road). The Brigade front was now held by the Queen's Westminsters on the right, in touch with troops of the 4th Division; and the L.R.B. on the left. The latter were holding Mill, Bradford and Bird Posts and portions of the Naval line. The 2nd Londons were in the Bailleul-Willerval (Red) line, and one company of the Cheshire Pioneers was in the Farbus line.

On the morning of March 28th, the dispositions of the Queen's Westminsters were as follows :—

B Company.—Captain G. A. N. Lowndes (commanding) with 2nd Lieutenants I d'A. Stitt and J. C. B. Firth in Towy Post, and Lieutenant L. W. Friend in Gavrelle Post.

A Company.—2nd Lieutenant H. T. Harper (commanding)

with 2nd Lieutenant W. A. Stillwell in Water Post, and 2nd Lieutenant V. G. Rayner in Naval trench (south).

C Company.—Captain R. L. Whittle (commanding) with 2nd Lieutenant F. L. Chamberlain in Naval trench (north), 2nd Lieutenant A. A. M. Eaton in Thames Post and also holding Pelican Post.

D Company.—2nd Lieutenant F. W. Russell (commanding) with 2nd Lieutenant C. H. Raven in Naval trench (central), 2nd Lieutenant F. Fisher in Keillar Post and also holding Castleford Post.

C Company had barely taken over its new trenches in the Naval line, when the enemy, at 3.30 a.m. on March 28th, opened a heavy bombardment on that line and on the posts in rear, pouring gas shells on the rear defences and following these up with high explosives. Some two hours later the enemy commenced to drench the forward defences with gas and to pound them with high-explosive shells from heavy guns and from trench mortars.

At 5.35 a.m. artillery retaliation was asked for by power-buzzer from Towy Post. No infantry attack developed, but the bombardment all along the front continued with unabated violence. The forward posts were blotted out and their garrisons for the most part were annihilated. On the front of the Queen's Westminsters the small garrison of Gavrelle Post, which was only an observation post, was withdrawn to Towy Post as soon as it became clear that an attack was imminent, sentries being left behind to give the warning when the enemy left his trenches. The troops in Towy Post were ordered to remain in the dugout while the bombardment continued. A few minutes after 7.0 a.m., S.O.S. signals were sent up in quick succession all along the line, from the 4th Division on the right, from Mill Post on the front of the L.R.B. on the left, and from Gavrelle Post, and Towy Post.[1] Shortly afterwards a pigeon message from Towy Post was received by the Brigade, to the effect that the garrison was being attacked.

The enemy had launched his attack; and in a very short time he was swarming round both flanks of Towy Post and was pressing forward to the Naval-Marine line. Towy Post, and, on the left of the Division, Wood Post (manned by the 4th Londons (167th Infantry Brigade)), alone of all the forward posts had escaped complete destruction. Their garrisons held out and inflicted enormous losses on the enemy. What remained of the front trenches of Towy Post was

---

[1] Captain G. A. N. Lowndes states that the signals went up in this order.

speedily overrun, for there were practically no survivors from the bombardment to put up any resistance ; but round the Company Headquarters in the support trench there were still some fifty men, and these, as had their comrades in the front trench, carried out to the letter their orders to hold on at all costs. Their gallant stand, and the steady withdrawal of the few survivors when all their ammunition was spent and all but three of their bombs had been thrown, constitutes one of the proudest achievements of the Queen's Westminsters in their many stern fights.

Captain G. A. N. Lowndes has supplied the following account of the stand of B Company in Towy Post on March 28th, 1918 :—

" Just before 7 a.m. the barrage lifted. Up went the S.O.S. from Gavrelle Post where two men had been placed to watch. Up went three S.O.S. signals on our right. ' Here they come, sir ! ' rang out from the dugout sentry. Up went the Towy S.O.S. On the instant the sentry had dived down the dugout steps to get the men up. For a few seconds—they were perhaps the longest seconds of my life—I stood on the fire-step, watching alone.

" The sight was curiously fascinating. Whether it was the smoke of our barrage or an attempted enemy smoke screen I cannot say, but at first I could only pick out one or two grey forms. Quite suddenly the smoke cleared ; and there, barely 200 yards in front, were the enemy in full view bearing down on us in a compact huddled mass that somehow, for its lack of colour, in the cold grey of the dawn, reminded one forcibly of a cinematograph picture. A thing I particularly noticed, even above the still deafening roar of the lifting barrage, was a low snarling growl, which seemed like some bestial hunting cry. I have never been able to estimate the numbers opposite Towy ; but, as the smoke lifted, up the slope towards Mill Post I counted five lines, each, I calculated, five deep, so deep, in fact, that I had to rub my eyes to make sure that they were not new belts of wire grown up in the night !

" Out of the dugout poured the thirty or forty survivors of B Company. In an instant the rattle of rapid fire, a fire sustained almost continuously for an hour till rifles were red hot and bolts jammed, broke out from every fire bay around the cross formed by the junction of ' Towy ' and ' Little Willie ' trenches ; and it was heard with thankful hearts by the groups of watchers up on the Point du Jour. ' The Post will be held to the last ; no withdrawal from it will be justified under any circumstances.' Those were the orders under which that heroic little band manned the parapet, to settle their last account with the makers of the war. That the enemy suffered heavy casualties, in front of Towy, was evident from the gaps which we saw opening in his massed ranks : later it was confirmed by prisoners. Rapid fire, intense, concentrated, sustained, never before had I realised so vividly its terrific potentialities !

" It is hard for an officer under such circumstances to confine himself strictly to his duties as an officer. The three officers, Lieutenant L. W. Friend and 2nd Lieutenants Stitt and J. C. B. Firth, spent their time keeping up the ammunition supply, seeing to the distribution of the bombs, and directing fire on any special targets which presented themselves. Meanwhile, Sergeant Yarnold and Corporal Pettit led a small party to the left to cover Gavrelle village, already penetrated by masses of the enemy. C.S.M. Welling, with Sergeants Miller and Jones, saw to our rear ; but an unlucky shell inflicted a terrible wound on the sergeant-major and killed Miller and Jones.

" By 7.45 a.m. we were completely surrounded. The enemy had passed through Gavrelle village on our left and pushed back the Lancashire Fusiliers on our right. Worse still, strong enemy bombing parties were working down Invicta to the right and Towy trench in front. A body of the enemy with a machine gun was established behind us, the distribution of ammunition was becoming disorganised and, saddest of all, each corner one turned there was yet another crumpled heap of khaki that had been a friend. There were no wounded.

" The end came suddenly ; so suddenly that Sergeant Yarnold and his gallant little party were cut off, though some of them rejoined us across the open. The enemy bombing party, working down the fire bays on our right, reached, and, after a few minutes' delay, passed our bombing block. Stick grenades began to fall thickly, three or four at a time around us. I remember noticing that the roar of the battle almost completely drowned the crash of the bombs, but each heavy concussion seemed to jar the base of one's skull. We returned bomb for bomb, at the same time straining every nerve to keep superiority of fire. A young German officer showed his head over the parapet for five seconds, his last ! We might have held them ; but, at about eight o'clock, I suddenly realised that there were only three bombs left.

" Our position was desperate enough, three bombs, a thousand yards, a machine gun, and an indefinite body of the enemy between us and safety, or such safety as 'Naval trench' could afford. But we were quite unbeaten; I am confident that the thought of giving up never crossed a single mind for an instant. Reluctantly I gave the order 'Withdraw slowly' (the word 'retire' was banned) 'fighting down Towy.' The main group, there were about twenty-five all told, got about fifty yards, when the enemy, perhaps realising our position, tried to rush us over the open, cheering wildly. It was Innes Stitt, poet, dreamer, Scholar of Balliol, who stopped them! That was the last time I was with him, my greatest school friend; a short figure, silhouetted in my mind for ever against the growing dawn, up there on the parapet, revolver in hand covering the withdrawal, his one fear to be thought afraid.

" The rush stopped, we had a moment's breathing space in which to gather our energies to deal with the enemy behind us. Water Post was rushed and recaptured, together with a few survivors of its garrison. There was still the German machine gun, comfortably ensconced on the parapet with the full twenty yards of a fire bay before it, waiting for us! The providential capture of one of the enemy who perhaps masked his comrades' fire slightly as he made his way down the trench, no doubt helped us; but then we were mad, wild with the lust of battle, uttering sounds which I still shudder to think of! Corporal Pike leading, we rushed the gun, crew and all. Its defenders turned and ran, dragging the gun, but leaving the ammunition.

" Soon after 8.30 a.m. we rejoined the remnant of A Company desperately clinging to a few battered fire bays in 'Naval trench': 2 officers and 17 men out of a garrison which, including the trench-mortar battery, must have numbered nearly 110."

Towy Post had amply fulfilled its rôle in the scheme of defence. The enemy, unable to advance over it, was driven round its flanks; and on the left, in the neighbourhood of Gavrelle, he found himself confronted by the masses of wire that had been put up with so much industry during the past months. Here he was exposed to Lewis-gun and rifle fire from Towy and Water Posts and from Naval trench, and to an indirect barrage from the fourteen machine guns which had been arranged to bear on this area. His casualties were terrible, but yet he still pressed on.

To the north of Gavrelle the enemy penetrated the Naval-Marine line, just north of Belvoir Alley, and was fought with

THE DEFENCE OF THE NAVAL LINE

magnificent courage by the headquarters' personnel of the L.R.B., under Lieut.-Colonel R. H. Husey, D.S.O., until they were ordered to withdraw slowly, down Thames Alley to the Bailleul-Willerval line. On the right the enemy was kept in check for a time by the Lancashire Fusiliers.

So long as the enemy was held on their flanks, the Queen's Westminsters were able to hold on to Naval trench between their southern boundary and the Gavrelle road; and the enemy, who was coming on in great numbers, shoulder to shoulder, offered a splendid target to the rifles and Lewis guns. When the L.R.B. had been forced to give way on the left, Captain R. L. Whittle with C Company manned a line along Thames Alley and thence along the Naval line, to cover the left flank of the Queen's Westminsters, and A Company came along Towy Alley to help them.

A little later the Lancashire Fusiliers were driven out of Humid trench on the right, and fell back over the open to Towy Alley and the Bailleul-Willerval line. The enemy now came on in great numbers on both flanks of the Battalion, and orders were given to the garrison of the Naval line, south of Towy Alley, to swing back and form a defensive flank in the latter communication trench.

The Queen's Westminsters were holding their own well; and a determined stand was being made by Sergeant J. Atkins and a party of men at a block in Towy Alley in front of the Naval line. But an unlucky shell from our own artillery[1] destroyed the block, and the enemy, who up to now had been kept well in check, swarmed into Naval trench from the south.

On the northern flank of the Battalion, Captain R. L. Whittle with C Company had been putting up a splendid fight. C.S.M. H. Lintott, by bombing with great boldness, had enabled the company Lewis-gun teams to get into action after the left flank had been turned, and they did great execution. One gun in particular was placed by Lance-Corporal J. Clamp so that a most effective enfilade fire was brought to bear on the masses of the enemy who were coming on over the higher ground. But the Germans were too numerous to be held back indefinitely, and numbers were working round the left rear of the company. The men on the left were then ordered to with-

---

[1] It was known before the commencement of the battle that some of the howitzers were very worn, but there was no means of replacing them. The situation was so critical that it was impossible to withdraw the batteries, even though some risk was necessarily incurred in using them. The artillery support this day was magnificent. The blowing-in of the block was a pure mischance for which the gunners were in no way responsible.

draw, fighting, down the communication trench; and, for a time, Lieutenant Chamberlain and C.S.M. Lintott, fighting at close quarters with revolver and bomb, covered the withdrawal. Lieutenant F. L. Chamberlain was blown off the firestep by a high-explosive shell; but he climbed up again at once and emptied his revolver into the advancing Germans, shooting five of them dead. He carried on most gallantly until wounded in the head and arm. Lance-Corporal Clamp's gun was put out of action; but he picked up a rifle and remained at his post, firing hard at the enemy, who by this time was working round the flank. When eventually he had to come back, he succeeded in bringing Lieutenant Chamberlain with him.

With the destruction of the block on the right, and the resistance on the left overcome, the enemy was able to enter the Naval line from both flanks. Very few of either A or C Company succeeded in withdrawing down the communication trenches, the majority were killed where they fought, only a handful had been captured. There still remained D Company, under Lieutenant F. W. Russell, a few of the survivors of B Company, and the majority of Battalion Headquarters, as yet practically fresh. The enemy now (about 8.45 a.m.) linked up all along Naval trench; but further progress was barred by bombing blocks in Towy and Thames Alleys close to their junction with the Naval line.

When the Germans had broken into the Naval line from the right, Lieut.-Colonel Glasier referred to the Brigadier as to the advisability of holding on to Keillar Post. " The General at once consulted the Divisional Commander who agreed that, in the circumstances, it would be wise for the Westminsters to withdraw fighting down Towy Alley, and then to reinforce the Bailleul-Willerval line." [1]

Almost at the very moment that Lieut.-Colonel Glasier was communicating with Brigade Headquarters, the situation suddenly underwent a further change. The enemy advanced across the open, north of Thames, between Thames and Towy, and south of Towy Alley, in a desperate attempt to reach the Bailleul-Willerval line; but he could make no real progress. His dead lay in heaps, and his wounded crawled painfully back to cover.

Captain N. T. Thurston, who was acting-Adjutant, writes: " To show you how quickly everything happened, I ran up from the dugout in Keillar Post to see how things were going, and had a quick look round. I then went down again and

---

[1] War Diary, 169th Infantry Brigade, which also contains the following entry: " It is to be noted that, during this critical time, perfect telephonic communication was kept up between Keillar Post and Brigade Headquarters."

reported by 'phone to Brigade Headquarters. I returned to the trench at once; and by this time the troops from the right flank were being driven back down Towy Alley, past Keillar Post. The trench was crowded with men. I got up on the parapet and saw the Huns erecting their machine guns out in the open, and several snipers at work. I picked up a rifle and posted men along the parapet of Towy Alley, and the enemy were driven to take cover in the trenches. I then tried to 'regulate the traffic' in Towy Alley, as it was by this time a solid block of humanity; and we gradually 'filtered' them down to the Red line where we could take up a strong position. The Huns came on, bombing down Towy Alley; and they fought their way past Keillar Post where they captured Captain R. Barnwell Rhett of the Medical Reserve Corps, U.S. Army (the acting Battalion Medical Officer), the complete Aid Post Staff, and Sergeant Mabbett the signal sergeant. By this time, we had a good force of men holding the Red line, and the congestion in Towy Alley was relieved. I then gave orders for a party of men to break in the trench and make a strong block in Towy Alley, about 150 yards in front of the Red line. Whilst this was being done our bombers managed to hold up the Huns, who must have suffered very severely; for, by this time, they seem to have had most of the fight knocked out of them. When the block was complete we retired behind it and posted Lewis-gun teams in the sap near by. They only had two drums of ammunition between them, but we were bothered very little more."

As a matter of fact, Captain Thurston's cool judgment and quick initiative had prevented a critical situation from developing into a very dangerous one. With a complete disregard for personal danger, he had run up and down the parapet posting men in fire positions chosen on the spur of the moment; and, while not hesitating to fight rifle in hand when the circumstances demanded, he never lost his grasp of the situation, and throughout he kept his commanding officer fully informed as to the progress of the fight. By his personal example he rallied the men, who were being pressed back down a crowded and heavily shelled trench, with the enemy close behind them; and it was his promptness, in organising the bombing blocks, that had made possible an orderly and successful withdrawal to the next line of resistance in the Bailleul-Willerval line.

On the left of the Battalion front, Castleford Post, commanded by 2nd Lieutenant F. W. Russell, was held throughout the day and until 1.0 a.m. the following morning. The garrison was then ordered to withdraw. 2nd Lieutenant Russell had been knocked over by a heavy shell early in the day, but he managed to " carry on " ; and, by making bombing blocks in the communication trench, he and his company stopped the enemy's further advance after the Naval line had been captured. One of these blocks was held by C.S.M. C. L. Ives for some six hours, against all attacks down the trench and from the flanks. Riflemen and Lewis gunners all helped to swell the losses which were being inflicted on the enemy by the splendidly directed shooting of the 56th Machine-Gun Battalion. The performance of one Lewis gunner on this flank, Corporal H. Lewis, stands out above the rest. The casualties he alone caused must have been enormous. For two hours he fired his gun into the enemy at close range, expending over two thousand rounds of ammunition ; and then, when his gun was destroyed and his team killed or wounded, he got back into the trench, found another gun whose team had become casualties, and returned with it to his exposed position in front. He then continued his deadly and accurate fire.

At 10.30 a.m. the Corps Commander (Major-General Sir F. W. N. McCracken) visited Divisional Headquarters and gave orders for the 169th Infantry Brigade to withdraw to the Bailleul-Willerval line, which was to be held at all costs. By this time, the Queen's Westminsters' right flank had been pressed back and Keillar Post had been lost ; and at 11.0 a.m. the position on the Battalion front was as follows : the main body of the Battalion, which could not have numbered more than 150 all ranks, had reinforced the 2nd Londons in the Bailleul-Willerval line, and bombing blocks were held about 300 yards east of this line in Thames and Towy Alleys. Castleford Post on the left flank was still intact.

The situation on the right of the Brigade had been very obscure throughout the morning. But by 12.0 noon touch was obtained again with the 4th Division in the Bailleul-Willerval line, and the right flank of the Battalion was secured.

The force of the first attack had been definitely broken ; but up to about 2.0 p.m. various groups of the enemy continued to make tentative, but abortive attacks on the Red line. Lieut.-Colonel J. P. Kellett, M.C. (commanding the 2nd Londons), states that the enemy's method in many cases was to throw their rifles forward into the nearest shell-holes, throw up their hands, and then drop into the shell-holes alongside their rifles.[1]

[1] 169th Infantry Brigade report, dated 2nd April, 1918.

At 2.0 p.m. another severe bombardment broke out all along the Bailleul-Willerval line, and low-flying aeroplanes " caused much trouble to the garrison " by the fire of their machine guns. The bombardment continued with varying intensity all the afternoon, the wire in front of the Bailleul-Willerval line was being destroyed, and it appeared that preparations were being made for a further attack. At one time, too, light guns were brought up into the open under cover of smoke. Dragged out of Gavrelle village by maddened horses, then bravely man-handled by teams of men, they came into action near Bradford Post and opened fire point-blank at the Bailleul-Willerval line; but before they had fired many rounds they were silenced by a heavy barrage from our own artillery.

At 5.0 p.m. a heavy attack developed on Bailleul East Post on the left. It was a final desperate attempt by the enemy to penetrate the line. For a short time the issue was doubtful, but once again the concentrated fire of artillery and machine guns, and of rifles and Lewis guns and bombs from the Bailleul-Willerval line, wiped out the attacking lines, and the enemy at last acknowledged defeat.

Early in the afternoon the Division had circulated the following message: " Corps Commander has informed First Army, 56th Division fighting splendidly. Stick to it."

By 6.0 p.m., for the time being at any rate, the work of the Division had been done, and the front was comparatively quiet. The troops *had* " stuck to it," and the line was unbroken. Half an hour later, orders were received that the commanding officers of the Battalions of the Brigade were to divide the Brigade frontage, so that it could be held according to the strength of the Battalions.

The Queen's Westminsters took over the line from the light railway, in touch with the Essex Regiment (4th Division) on the right, to the Gavrelle road on the left, where the Battalion was in touch with the 2nd Londons. The Battalion also held Castleford Post and the block in the communication trench to the east of it. During the night this post was evacuated under orders. Blocks were established in Towy Alley and Thames communication trench, about thirty yards in front of the Bailleul-Willerval line, and each of these trenches was filled in for a length of about a hundred yards in front of the blocks.

In the evening of March 28th, the following messages of congratulation were received :—

From the G.O.C. Third Army (General the Hon. Sir J. Byng) :—

"The Army Commander desires me to convey to the 56th Division his high appreciation of the gallantry and tenacity shown by them during to-day's fight against greatly superior odds."

From the G.O.C. XIII Corps (Lieut.-General Sir F. W. N. McCracken), addressed to the G.O.C. 56th Division :—

"Will you please convey to the troops under your command my great appreciation of the splendid fight put up by them against greatly superior numbers. They must look on to-day's action, however, as being a preliminary to a possible further attack in the morning. In no case must any portion of the Red line be given up."

From the Divisional Commander (Major-General F. A. Dudgeon) :—

"I congratulate all ranks of the 56th Division on the magnificent fighting qualities which they have displayed to-day. The Division has been given a hard task, and the splendid manner in which it is being carried out is having an important effect on the general situation at a critical time. The Corps Commander has wired to the Army Commander an account of the splendid defence which is being put up by the 56th Division."

The Red line never was given up; in fact, it was never again seriously threatened, for the enemy had received such a defeat that he abandoned his offensive on this part of the front.

The Queen's Westminsters were relieved soon after daybreak on April 29th, by the 8th Middlesex, and the weary, but triumphant, survivors marched back to Roundhay Camp.

The casualties suffered by the Battalion amounted to 227. Of these 143 other ranks were posted as missing, and 8 other ranks as wounded and missing, but nearly all the former were killed or wounded. Two officers, 2nd Lieutenant I. d'A. Stitt and 2nd Lieutenant C. H. Raven, and 18 other ranks were killed, and 56 other ranks were wounded.

Reference has already been made to the death of 2nd Lieutenant Stitt. He was quite a boy, of brilliant promise, and imbued with the highest ideals. His firm belief in the justice of the cause for which he was fighting, and his almost over-sensitive ideal of personal duty were perhaps his chief characteristics. He had only been in France for a little over six months and when he died the Battalion lost a very gallant officer.

THE REGIMENTAL STRETCHER-BEARERS

In every action in which the Queen's Westminsters fought, glowing tribute has invariably been paid to the magnificent courage and self-sacrifice of the regimental stretcher-bearers. At Keillar Post, when practically surrounded by the enemy, and with fierce bomb-fighting taking place all round them, Lieutenant Barnwell Rhett and the whole of his staff worked heroically to succour the wounded and to prevent them from falling into German hands. They succeeded, although they themselves were captured. Amongst those who specially distinguished themselves in this gallant work, were Lance-Corporal H. Pattenden and Rifleman A. H. Taylor.

The signallers, too, had worthily done their duty. Sergeant Mabbett and Lance-Corporal Samuels were both captured at their instrument, the former at Keillar Post and the latter in Towy Post.

Sergeant Mabbett had come out with the Battalion in 1914 and his good work had contributed largely to the efficiency of the Battalion signallers. Lance-Corporal Samuels also had done splendid work, particularly during the Battle of Cambrai, when he was attached as telephone operator to the right liaison officer of the 169th Infantry Brigade. He was then continuously on duty for twelve days and maintained communication with the Brigade throughout the whole period. During the German counter-attack on November 30th he went out time and again and mended, under heavy shell-fire, the lines which were being repeatedly cut, and thereby enabled valuable and timely information to get through.

The following further congratulatory messages were circulated in connection with the fighting on March 28th :—

"*March* 30*th*, 1918.—The Corps Commander (XIII Corps) wishes to convey to the troops of the 56th Division his appreciation of their gallant conduct and resolute action in the defence of Vimy Ridge on the 28th March, 1918. Though greatly outnumbered and opposed to overwhelming ordnance, they maintained the line intact until ordered to withdraw to the main line of resistance, where the attacks of the enemy were completely repulsed with heavy losses. This fine work has greatly added to the high reputation already gained by your Division."

"*April* 1*st*, 1918.—The Army Commander personally expressed to the G.O.C. Division his appreciation of the good work done by the Division, and of its tenacious defence during the enemy attack on March 28th. The G.O.C. Division also had the honour of being received by His Majesty the

King, who was graciously pleased to express his approval of the gallantry displayed by all ranks of the 56th Division."

From a tactical point of view the defence of the 56th Division on March 28th is most instructive. It illustrates very clearly the principle of holding a defensive position in depth, and at the same time demonstrates the disadvantages as well as the advantages of holding the forward line by a series of practically disconnected posts. The prime object of such posts is to break the initial force of the attack, and to direct the attackers into an area where they will be subjected to previously organised fire from the artillery and machine guns, and to small-arm fire from a continuous trench line in rear and from neighbouring posts in front. Where, however, a position is held in this manner for any length of time, the enemy must generally be able, by means of previous reconnaissance and from his aerial photographs, to ascertain accurately the location of the defended posts. He can then economise fire, by concentrating his artillery and trench mortars on those portions of the defence that are likely to cause him trouble, during the first stage of his advance.

This is exactly what happened on the 56th Divisional front. With the exception of Towy Post,[1] the enemy succeeded in obliterating the forward posts during his preparatory bombardment; and he was therefore free, except so far as he was impeded by carefully arranged obstacles, to advance against the continuous trench line with the full impetus of his first organised attack. The result was that he was quickly able to drive the defence back to the main line of resistance.

But on the front of the Queen's Westminsters, owing to the escape from complete destruction of the defences of Towy Post and of a proportion of its garrison, the elasticity of the defensive system was preserved. Towy Post acted as the buffer, which, in its recoil, absorbed a considerable part of the initial energy of the attack; and it also served as a directing wedge along the sides of which the enemy was forced into an area covered by the fire of all arms. The attack was consequently disorganised and breathing space was gained by the garrison of the Naval line, thus freed from the danger of an unbroken frontal attack.

When Towy Post fell and the enemy had worked round both flanks of the portion of the Naval line held by the Queen's Westminsters, that portion of the line itself became the buffer-head to receive the already weakened force of the

---

[1] The size of Towy Post probably alone saved it from complete destruction.

THE RESULT OF THE FIGHTING

enemy's blow. Once more the buffer recoiled, and again time was gained for the line in rear to organise against a further enemy advance. But the buffer-spring was never fully compressed, and the enemy's strength was exhausted before he reached the main line of defence.

In many respects the defence north of Arras resembles the northern defence, on November 30th, against the German counter-attack in the Battle of Cambrai, 1917. On each occasion the " ambitious plans of the enemy were foiled " : at Cambrai, to destroy the whole of the British forces in the recently captured salient; and at Arras, to capture the city and the Vimy Ridge and cleave a way forward towards the Channel ports. On both occasions the enemy attacked in greatly superior numbers and received casualties which it would be hard to exaggerate, and in each case his losses were swelled by the magnificent handling of the machine guns and the well-directed fire of the artillery.

The experiences of the Battalion, too, were curiously similar, for on each occasion the forward line, after allowing for the different methods of defence, gave way only when both flanks were turned; and, when ground had to be yielded, the enemy was held up well in advance of the rear line of defence, by bombing blocks pushed well forward in the communication trenches leading back to it.

The main incidents of the day's fighting are concisely stated in the following extract from the XIII Corps Intelligence Summary for the period 6.0 p.m., March 27th, to 6.0 p.m., March 28th, 1918 :—

"*Operations.*—After a heavy bombardment, commencing at 3.30 a.m., the enemy launched a determined attack on the front of the right division as far north as Oppy. Heavy fighting took place in the front system, many positions changing hands several times. Enemy attack was made in greater strength north and south of Gavrelle, but was held on the main line of resistance in this system for several hours, troops displaying great courage and tenacity. About 10.0 a.m. the enemy pierced the front system at several points, and the garrison was forced to withdraw to Battle Zone, inflicting heavy casualties. Enemy reserves pressed forward in strength to attack Bailleul-Willerval line and continued until 5.0 p.m. when the enemy again advanced in large numbers to attack, and was again repulsed at all points in hard fighting. Machine guns did great execution against his advancing waves. Result of day's fighting is that front line of Battle Zone is intact at all points, and outposts are well to the east of it. With the exception of a few posts withdrawn from the forward zone, to conform with the right division, the left division line remains unchanged.

"*Situation at* 7 *p.m.*—Our troops hold the Bailleul-Willerval-Hirondelle line and down Mississippi and Missouri trenches.

"Identifications.—41*st Division,* 83*rd Division,* 187*th Division,* 75*th Reserve Division, and* 240*th Division."*

It will be seen, from the above summary, that no less than five enemy divisions were employed on the front held by the XIII Corps, and definitely held.

It appears that a complete break-through was not only anticipated by the enemy, but considered a very serious probability by the British higher command. On the 56th Divisional front every precaution was taken against the consequences of an enemy success. Lieut.-Colonel (then Major) S. R. Savill, who was with the nucleus personnel, writes:—

"The defence appears to have been unexpectedly successful; for, as soon as the attack developed all infantry first-line transport, Divisional details, and units not strictly speaking of a combatant nature were ordered to the rear; and the area behind Brigade Headquarters speedily became emptied of troops. There appeared to be no troops for miles in rear of the Brigades in the line. Presumably the higher authorities thought that the risk of the infantry being unable to hold the enemy in check was so great, that the safest move was to clear what would probably soon be the battle zone as quickly as possible, and thus allow freedom to manœuvre as the battle progressed."

It is not within the scope of this history to attempt any appreciation of the results of the fighting on March 28th, 1918, but the following extracts indicate in general terms the views of the high command on both sides.

Field-Marshal Von Hindenburg,[1] commenting on the German failure, writes: "The hopes and wishes which had soared beyond Amiens had to be recalled. Facts must be treated as facts—our strength was exhausted." General Ludendorff's comments are still more significant. He writes: "The 17th Army had already attacked, in the last days of March, in the direction of Arras, making its principal effort on the north bank of the Scarpe. It was to capture the decisive heights east and north of Arras; the next day the 6th

[1] "Out of my Life," published by Cassell & Co., Ltd.

GAVRELLE
28 MARCH 1918

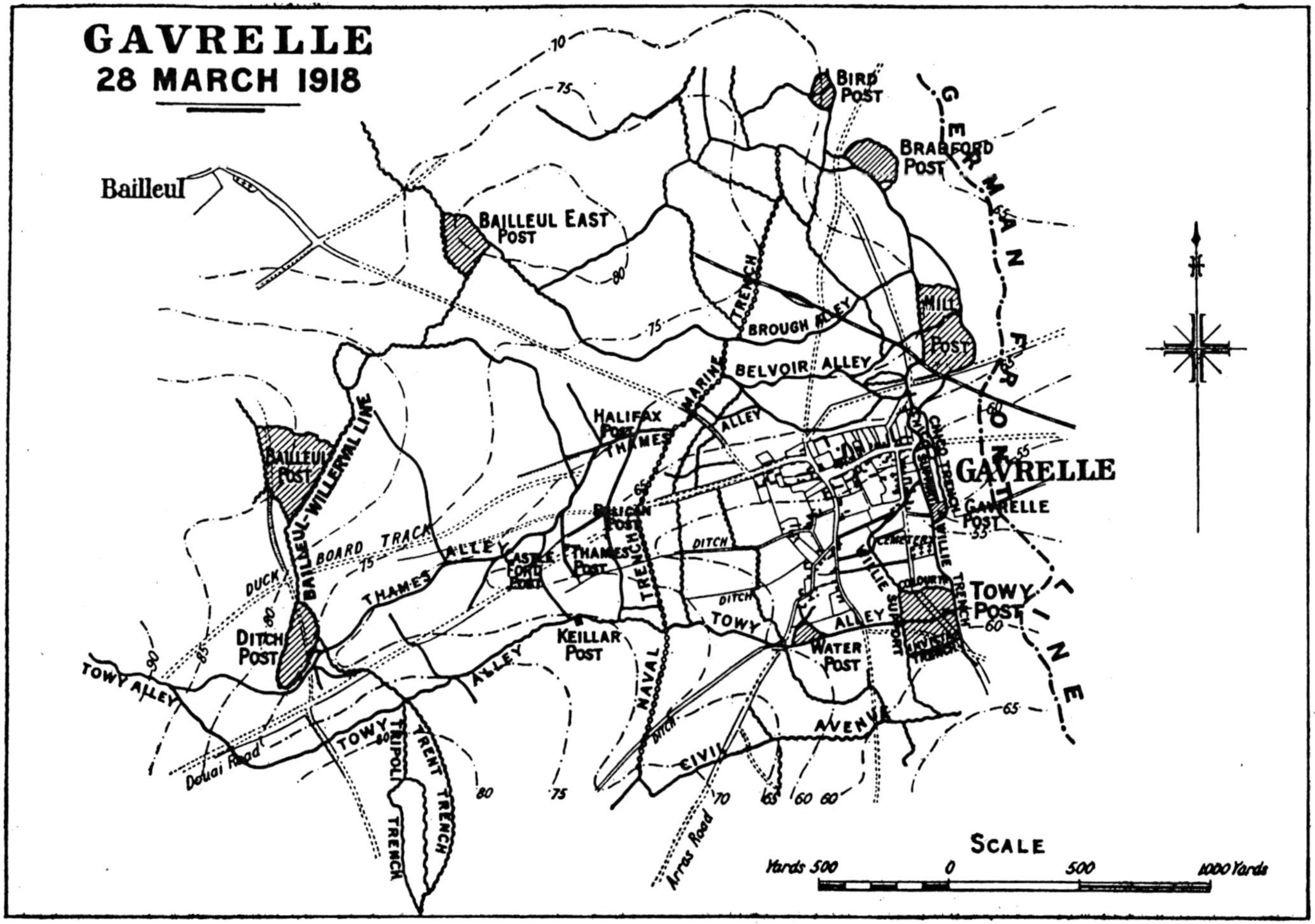

Army was to prolong the attack from Lens and carry the high ground in that area. I attached the greatest importance to both these attacks. To have the high ground in our possession was bound to be decisive in any fighting in the plain of the Lys. In spite of employing extraordinary masses of artillery and ammunition, the attack of the 17th Army on both banks of the Scarpe was a failure."[1]

Sir Douglas Haig, in his despatch of July 20th, 1918, writes: " There is little doubt that the enemy hoped to achieve great results by this new stroke, and that its failure was a serious set-back to his plans. After a bombardment of great violence, three fresh German divisions advanced to the assault all along the north bank of the Scarpe River against the position held by the 4th and 56th Divisions, under the command respectively of Major-General T. G. Matheson and Major-General F. A. Dudgeon and were supported in their attack by the two German divisions already in the line. . . . According to captured documents, the enemy's immediate objective was to gain the general line Vimy-Bailleul-St. Laurent-Blangy, when three special assault divisions were to carry the Vimy Ridge on the following day. With this day's battle, which ended in the complete defeat of the enemy on the whole front of his attack, the first stage of the enemy's offensive weakened, and eventually closed on the 5th April."

On April 9th, the Germans launched their offensive in Flanders, and met with immediate success, particularly on the front held by the Portuguese. The situation became most critical and it called forth the following stirring Special Order of the Day, addressed by Field-Marshal Sir Douglas Haig to all ranks of the British Army in France and Flanders :—

" Three weeks ago to-day the enemy began his terrific attacks against us on a fifty-mile front. His objects are to separate us from the French, to take the Channel ports, and destroy the British Army.

" In spite of throwing already 106 divisions into the battle, and enduring the most reckless sacrifice of human life, he has, as yet, made little progress towards his goals. We owe this to the determined fighting and self-sacrifice of our troops.

" Words fail me to express the admiration which I feel for the splendid resistance offered by all ranks of our Army under the most trying circumstances.

" Many amongst us now are tired. To those I would say

---

[1] "My War Memories," by General Ludendorff, published by Hutchinson & Co., Vol. II, p. 604.

that victory will belong to the side which holds out the longest.

"The French Army is moving rapidly and in great force to our support.

"There is no other course open to us but to fight it out. Every position must be held to the last man; there must be no retirement. With our backs to the wall, and believing in the justice of our cause, each one of us must fight on to the end.

"The safety of our homes and the freedom of mankind depend alike upon the conduct of each one of us at this critical moment."

It fell to the lot of other troops to take part in the bitter conflict known as the Battle of the Lys, that continued throughout the month of April. The Battalion's task in repelling the German onslaught was accomplished on March 28th.

The city of Westminster has recognised the services during the war, of the Regiment with which it is so closely associated, by "adopting" Gavrelle, and it is rendering material aid towards the reconstruction of the shattered village.

CHAPTER XVII

IN THE TELEGRAPH HILL SECTOR, ARRAS

ON March 30th, 1918, the Battalion moved off from Roundhay Camp at 9.0 a.m. *en route* for St. Aubin. As the last companies left the camp the enemy commenced to shell it, but fortunately caused no casualties.

On arriving at St. Aubin the Staff Captain met the Battalion with fresh orders to proceed to Mont St. Eloy. A halt was made for dinners and, just as the Battalion was falling in, to continue the march, two Artillery officers arrived and reported that they had a draft of 321 other ranks for the Queen's Westminsters. These men were splendid fighting material; the majority of them had been fighting with various north-country regiments during the preceding week, and had been wounded and sent to the base; many had several wound stripes, service chevrons and good-conduct badges. They had detrained at Mont St. Eloy and had marched to St. Aubin in very hot weather, and had had nothing to eat for twenty-four hours. Luckily there was a little food and tea for them on the regimental "cookers," and, after they had had a short rest, they followed the Battalion back to St. Eloy.

On arriving at Mont St. Eloy, it was found that a Canadian battalion was still in possession of the camp, and that this unit was not moving for some hours. The Canadians, who had heard of the strenuous fighting in which the Battalion had been engaged, gave the Queen's Westminsters a rousing welcome, and turned out their band to greet them. Lieut.-Colonel Savill writes: " The Canadians vacated their huts several hours before they need have done, made teas for our men on their cookers, and did everything possible for our comfort."

On April 4th, the whole Battalion was employed, near the Arras-St. Pol road, in digging and improving the trenches in one of the numerous switch lines, known as the Haute Avesnes Switch; but the greater part of the week was spent in reorganising, in absorbing the new draft and in the usual routine involved in getting straight after a battle.

The military situation was still giving cause for the greatest anxiety; but notwithstanding this a Corps band competition, open to all units in the Corps, took place on April 6th. The Battalion bugles under Sergeant Lethern gained the second place. This was a good result, for amongst the competing bands were those from three battalions of the Guards.

On April 8th, the Battalion moved to Dainville, in the area of the XVII Corps (commanded by Lieut.-General Sir C. Fergusson, Bart.), preparatory to a long stay in the Telegraph Hill Sector, south-east of Arras.

The billets of the Battalion when " resting " out of the line were usually at Dainville and occasionally at Berneville, where the transport lines were situated. Battalion Headquarters, at Dainville, were at the château near the church, and the joint headquarters of C and D Companies were near the junction of the Arras-Doullens and the Achicourt-Dainville roads. The enemy shelled Dainville and the neighbourhood so frequently with high-velocity guns and 5·9's, that there was a standing order that all those who had cellars should go into them, and that the remainder should go into the crypt under the church as soon as the shelling commenced. There was a heavy bombardment throughout the night of April 10th, which lasted until 11 a.m., in the course of which D Company officers' mess received a direct hit with a high-velocity shell. This shell wounded three of the company officers, a sergeant and two other ranks.

The Battalion remained at Dainville until April 14th, training and working hard at the rear defence systems. It then relieved the 1st Londons in the Ronville caves on the southern outskirts of Arras.

These and the St. Sauveur caves were a very remarkable feature of the Arras defences. They were of vast extent and of great age, having been excavated, it was said, to provide material for building the original cathedral, the Hôtel de Ville and most of the older houses of the city.[1]

Some forty entrances, one of which was through the main sewer of Arras, admitted to a labyrinth of galleries, with large caves opening out of them at depths of from twenty to fifty feet below the ground. The whole system was lit by electricity, and a light railway ran down the main corridor. Both of these had been installed by the British. The accommodation was good, many of the men being provided with wire beds; and the size of some of the caves was so great that it was possible for the Divisional band to give concerts to the occupants. From a military point of view, this subterranean honeycomb was of great value, for a whole division could be

[1] The caves on the Aisne originated in the same way.

assembled there in perfect safety. Extensive use had been made of it prior to the opening day of the Battles of Arras. But from the men's point of view the caves were extremely unpopular. They were damp, dark and dirty; there was a continuous dripping of water from the walls, and the stuffy atmosphere, laden with dust, had a bad effect on the throat. The men were not allowed to go outside during the daytime, and the life underground had a depressing effect. It was bad, too, for moral. To come out of such a place, where the heaviest shells could scarcely be heard, to face any kind of fire, was a transition too complete not to be extremely trying to the nerves.

Until April 19th the Battalion remained in the caves, usually resting by day and working at night. It then went into the line in the Telegraph Hill Sector, relieving the London Scottish, who had just carried out a highly successful raid.

The defences of the Telegraph Hill Sector consisted of two main systems of trenches, the Blangy and the Tilloy systems, each with front, support and reserve trenches. The two systems were linked up by many communication trenches, two of which (London and Scottish Avenues) ran right back into Arras itself, a distance of nearly two miles. The Blangy lines lay in front of ruined Arras and in rear of a long rise known as Observation Ridge. The Arras-Cambrai road formed the dividing line between the right and left sub-sectors. The front line of the Tilloy system was a great trench running nearly due north and south, on the forward slope of Observation Ridge. The line bent back to the south, forming a salient, where the Canadians were holding the trenches facing Neuville Vitasse; and to the north a series of switch trenches (the chief of which was Feuchy Switch) carried the line forward in a north-easterly direction to the marshy banks of the River Scarpe, which formed approximately the left flank of the sector. In front there was a valley with many disused trenches in it, and on the far side of the valley there was a ridge which culminated in Monchy Hill. From this hill the enemy's observation balloons commanded an excellent view of the British lines. The main avenues of approach to the front line, used by the Battalion, were Cemetery and cavalry tracks; the former, through which the reliefs marched on the way to or from Dainville, ran by the cemetery on the eastern outskirts of Arras, and the latter led to Achicourt where it joined the Achicourt-Dainville road.

The Battalion remained in the line from April 19th to April

28th, with three companies in the fire trenches and one company in support. During the tour, which was on the whole uneventful, much work was done on the defences, and patrolling was energetically carried out. On April 21st, the enemy's aeroplanes were exceptionally active, flying in very large formations and sometimes swooping very low over the trenches.

On the 24th, a patrol, of an officer and thirty other ranks, discovered that the enemy had pushed forward his outposts about a hundred yards and had established two new machine-gun positions. At midnight the following night another patrol, of fifteen other ranks under 2nd Lieutenant V. G. Rayner, went out to make a further investigation of the position. They encountered a party of about thirty of the enemy who were advancing towards our line with a machine gun. The patrol opened fire on the Germans at a range of between ten and twenty yards, and several of the enemy were seen to fall; it then withdrew across a trench and waited for the enemy to come on. The Germans, however, had been taught a lesson, and instead of making a further attempt to advance they opened heavy machine-gun and rifle fire on our trenches, and threw bombs down a communication trench.

On the night of the 28th/29th April, after relief by the Kensingtons, the Battalion marched back to Berneville. A and B Companies moved two days later into the St. Sauveur caves at Arras and were attached to the 167th Infantry Brigade for work. During the period of rest a Brigade education class, for all ranks, was started at Berneville.

On May 4th, the Battalion relieved the 8th Middlesex in Brigade support in the Blangy system. It remained here until the 21st.

The enemy's offensive was still in progress, and there was always a possibility that he might renew his attacks on this front. The troops were ordered to be specially alert, and the Battalion stood to arms for a considerable time every morning and evening. Life in these support trenches was monotonous and uneventful; there was little to do during the day, and at night large working parties paraded for work under the Royal Engineers or with the 5th Cheshires.

On May 15th, 16th and 17th, working parties were sent up to the front line to dig a new trench and some posts in No-man's-land. The trench led out of Feuchy trench and was just south of the Arras-Douai railway. The first working party had a warm reception, being shelled by 77-mm. guns, heavy trench mortars, and rifle grenades as well as being heavily gassed. It was fortunate in only having 6 other ranks wounded ; but the majority of the party suffered from the effect of the gas and comparatively few men were available for work the next night. The other two parties got off more lightly, and the three posts started on the 15th, were occupied by the L.R.B. at " stand to " on the 17th.

The Queen's Westminsters were relieved by the London Scottish on May 21st, and then spent two days in billets in Arras. At night working parties were sent forward to dig and wire the Tilloy reserve line in front of Devil's Wood (just west of Tilloy). On May 24th, the Battalion moved back to Dainville, and on the 30th it relieved the 1st Londons in the Telegraph Hill (left) Sector, with three companies in the front line and one in reserve. This tour in the trenches lasted until June 16th. Raids were carried out on nearly every night, by troops of either the 56th Division, the 15th (Scottish) Division on the left, or the 2nd Canadian Division on the right. The enemy's artillery usually opened about three minutes after the raids had started ; but in almost every instance the German barrage was put down on some part of the front line other than that from which the raiding party had jumped off. There were no counter-raids on the part of the enemy, for on this particular portion of the front the British infantry were masters of No-man's-land.

The casualties in the Queen's Westminsters were light at this time ; but on June 2nd, the Battalion, to the intense sorrow of all ranks, suffered a grievous loss by the death of its Commanding Officer, Temporary Lieut.-Colonel P. M. Glasier, D.S.O. The entry in the War Diary is as follows :—

" *June 2nd.*—At 11.0 p.m. the enemy put down a light barrage, soon after which an S.O.S. was sent up by the Battalion on our left. No infantry action followed. The Commanding Officer went up the stairs of the headquarters' dugout to discover the situation and was killed by a direct hit on the entrance by a 4.2 shell."

Lieut.-Colonel P. M. Glasier had joined the Queen's Westminsters in 1911, and had come out to France with the Battalion as a subaltern of H Company in 1914. He had taken part in nearly every action in which the Battalion was engaged, and had been twice wounded, first at Hooge in 1915, and again at Gommecourt in 1916, when he was in command of D Company. He commanded the Battalion during the Battles of Ypres, 1917, the Battle of Cambrai, 1917 and at Gavrelle, 1918 (First Battle of Arras, 1918) ; and no better

IN THE TELEGRAPH HILL SECTOR

tribute can be paid to his leadership than the story of the Queen's Westminsters during these battles, and also during the intervening periods of trench warfare. He was awarded the D.S.O. and was four times mentioned in despatches.

"Phil," as he was affectionately called by his contemporaries, was the soul of kindness and chivalry. No commanding officer could have been more solicitous for the welfare of his men than was Phil Glasier, and he was trusted and loved by all ranks of the Battalion.

The Second-in-Command, Major S. R. Savill, M.C., now assumed command of the Queen's Westminsters. He led the Battalion with great success until the end of the war, and he was awarded the D.S.O. for his services. He returned with the Cadre to England in 1919; and, when the Queen's Westminsters were reconstituted on a peace footing, he was appointed to be their first Commanding Officer.

During the remainder of this tour in the trenches, the enemy displayed a certain amount of activity; his artillery was aggressive at times, considerable movement was observed behind his lines, and his aeroplanes frequently came over, sometimes flying very low along the trenches by day, and on other occasions bombing at night. On June 16th, there was great aerial activity on both sides; two enemy aeroplanes were brought down in the neighbourhood of the Battalion lines, one the result of an air fight, and the other by Lewis and machine-gun fire. In the evening, bombs were dropped close to Battalion Headquarters. The enemy infantry, on the other hand, showed no desire to fight. On June 14th the War Diary states that "a hostile patrol of thirty men approached our left outpost, and, on being fired at, they ran back to their own lines," and there are several other entries of a similar character.

Our own patrols were active. On June 7th, a very successful daylight reconnaissance, of some gun pits, was made by Lance-Sergeant Nelson and three other ranks of D Company. This company had been detailed to carry out a raid on part of the German defences known as Airy Work, and the information gained on this occasion was of considerable value in forming the plan of attack. The raid, however, was cancelled by the Brigadier on June 10th.

The Battalion was relieved by the Kensingtons on June 17th; and after eight days' rest at Dainville it returned to the line, taking over the left subsector from the 8th Middlesex. The tour, which lasted until July 2nd, was a quiet one. The Battalion was then relieved by the L.R.B. and went into

RAID BY "A" COMPANY. JULY 8TH, 1918

Brigade support in the Blangy system, where all companies, except A which had been detailed for a raid on July 8th, were employed on work under the Royal Engineers.

A Company was kept busy at Dainville training for the raid. The objective was some gun pits opposite the left flank of the Divisional sector. The preliminary work was thorough. Firstly the objective itself was very carefully reconnoitred by all the officers and non-commissioned officers forming part of the raiding party, and all ranks made a minute study of the air photographs specially taken from a low altitude. Very valuable information was also obtained from some Artillery officers of the 15th Division who had actually built the gun pits. A plan of the objective was then taped out on the ground, at Dainville, and the actual assault was rehearsed several times both by day and night.

The company was inspected by the acting Brigadier, Lieut.-Colonel Jackson, D.S.O. (London Scottish), on July 6th, and by the G.O.C. 56th Division on the 7th. The final rehearsal took place on the morning of July 8th. In the afternoon the company moved up to the assembly position in Broken Lane, the new front-line trench which the Battalion had helped to dig in the middle of May. The raiding party, under the command of Captain H. F. Grizelle, M.C., consisted of three officers (2nd Lieutenants J. C. Goadby, V. G. Rayner and S. L. Mann) and ninety other ranks divided into nine sections, each consisting of one non-commissioned officer and nine riflemen. Zero hour had been fixed at 9.50 p.m., in the hope of surprising the enemy while in his dugouts and before he had taken up his night dispositions, but this hope was not fully realised. After a two minutes' intense bombardment of the objective by the artillery and light trench mortars, the latter ceased fire ; and a protective barrage round the objective, in which smoke was freely used, was put down by the guns and machine guns. The sections of the raiding party left their assembly trench at zero and had, according to plan, moved forward about seventy yards by the time the guns lifted. They then moved at the double on to their respective objectives and reached them within a few seconds of one another.

The enemy attempted to come out of a deep dugout as soon as the raiding party had reached their objective. The first German to show himself was an officer, who fired his revolver at our sentry who was posted at the entrance. He missed, and was at once shot by the sentry, and fell backwards down the stairway of the dugout. A mobile charge of 12 lb. of ammonal was thrown after him. This duly exploded and blocked the entrance of the dugout. The second entrance was found, and this was also effectively dealt with, firstly by " P " grenades and " M.S.K." grenades, and finally by another mobile charge.

The gun pits, which had been almost obliterated by the bombardment, were quickly cleared, and three prisoners, belonging to the 358 *I.R.*, 214*th Division*, and a light machine gun were captured in the most southern pit.

The enemy's artillery were very late in replying. His barrage was by no means heavy, and his machine guns, which opened fire two minutes after zero, fired so erratically that no inconvenience was caused to the raiders. Fifteen minutes were sufficient for the raiding party to accomplish their task, and twenty minutes after zero they withdrew from the enemy's trenches. Their casualties were only 11 other ranks wounded, 10 of them slightly. It is practically certain that the enemy's casualties were heavy ; for the three prisoners stated that the dugout, which had been well bombed before the entrances were blown in, was accommodating at the time of the raid two officers and between fifty and sixty men.

All ranks testified to the excellence of our own artillery and machine-gun support, and this contributed materially to the complete success of the raid.

The Corps Commander subsequently wired his congratulations to the Battalion in the following terms : " My best congratulations to Lobee (i.e. the Queen's Westminsters) on their raid last night. The information is very useful."

On July 9th, the Battalion returned to the line for a few days relieving the 2nd Londons in the right subsector. It handed over its trenches on the 13th and 14th July to companies of the 10th and 20th Canadian Infantry, on the relief of the 56th Division by the 1st Canadian Division.

The Queen's Westminsters marched to Warlus on July 15th, and then proceeded by motor omnibus to La Comté. Intensive training was carried out for the next fortnight ; the mornings being devoted to drill, specialist training and tactical schemes, while the afternoons were generally given up to games or sports. There is no doubt that the efficiency of the Battalion was successfully improved during the period at La Comté. For the first time, for nearly a year, opportunities were available for real training for open warfare. Many battalion practice attacks were carried out, and all ranks gained experience which was to prove most valuable in the concluding phase of the war. Several battalion drills were held, and great pains were taken over guard-mounting and other ceremonial parades.

An address by General Sir H. S. Horne, the Commander of the First Army, who attended the Battalion church parade on July 21st, created great enthusiasm, and proved a great stimulus to hard work. In the course of his speech, the General congratulated the Queen's Westminsters on their past achievements, and expressed, in feeling terms, his sympathy with all ranks in the loss of " that gallant soldier, their late Commanding Officer " (Lieut.-Colonel P. M. Glasier). He then indicated that the time had nearly arrived when the British Army would be able to turn from the defensive war it had waged since the beginning of the year to an offensive from which much was hoped.

The Battalion was in high spirits, and its feelings were reflected by its bearing and turn-out on parade, and by the energy it displayed both in work and play. On July 28th, the Brigadier was present at a most successful Battalion sports meeting, at which the Battalion championship was won by the Transport with Battalion Headquarters a good second. Everyone had hoped that the Brigade sports would be held soon, for there seemed to be a good chance of winning the Brigade championship for the third year in succession. Some disappointment, therefore, was felt when the Battalion moved at short notice to Caucourt on July 30th.

On August 2nd the Battalion proceeded, in the morning, by light railway from Mingoval to Devil's Wood, and on the same afternoon it relieved the 16th Canadians in the left subsector on Telegraph Hill. The accommodation in this part of the line was extremely uncomfortable. Only a few scooped-out bivouacs were available; these were not revetted and showed signs of collapse, with the result that the men had to be turned out of them. A shortage of engineering material prevented any substantial improvement being made in the shelters for the troops. The front line was knee-deep in water, none of the trenches were duck-boarded, and they were all a foot deep in mud. It rained heavily on August 3rd, which made matters worse, and the men suffered much discomfort through the absence of gum boots. But the weather eventually cleared up; and, by dint of very hard work, the trenches were much improved when the Battalion handed them over to the L.R.B. on August 7th.

After six days spent in Brigade reserve in the Blangy system, the Battalion returned once more to the line, relieving the 2nd Londons in the left subsector. During this tour in the trenches, sixteen officers and thirty-two non-commissioned officers of the 2/213th Infantry Regiment of the American Expeditionary Force spent one night with the Battalion for "instruction." It was intended that the whole of the American battalion should come into the line with the Queen's Westminsters on August 15th for forty-eight hours, but this plan was cancelled.

On August 16th, the Battalion was relieved by the 6th Cameron Highlanders (15th Division) and proceeded to Berneville. The trench tour had been a very quiet one, with the exception of a fairly heavy barrage on the front of A Company on the 14th, while the enemy was making an unsuccessful attempt to raid the Kensingtons on the left. The only other event of interest at the time was the entry of a Battalion team, under 2nd Lieutenant A. H. Chaplin and Sergeant Hurst, in a First Army musketry competition. The Queen's Westminsters gave a good account of themselves, coming out first among the teams entered by the units of the 56th Division.

For the next few days the Brigade was continually on the move. On August 17th, the Battalion moved by train to Liencourt; and on the 19th it proceeded by motor omnibus to Berneville, and thence by march route to Arras. The enemy bombarded the city for the greater part of the night, with gas and H.E. shells; and, as there was only cellar accommodation for 100 men, the majority of the Battalion had an unpleasant and unrestful experience. On August 20th the Queen's Westminsters marched by night to Noyelle Vion, arriving at their destination at 3.30 a.m., and moved on again in the evening to Bavincourt where they arrived at midnight. On August 22nd, the Brigade Commander held a conference of Commanding Officers, and final preparations were made by the Battalion for active operations. On the following evening the Queen's Westminsters had a very trying march to Bailleulval. The road was crowded with artillery and cavalry and progress was slow and difficult. The Battalion arrived at Bailleulval at 9.0 p.m., and within twenty-four hours was engaged in what is now known as the Battle of the Scarpe, 1918.

CHAPTER XVIII

THE BATTLE OF THE SCARPE, 1918

CROISILLES—HENDECOURT—BULLECOURT, AUGUST 23RD–30TH

IN order to appreciate the situation when the 56th Division attacked on August 23rd, 1918, it is necessary to trace shortly the course of events, on the part of the British front with which this history is concerned, since the German defeat before Arras at the end of March.[1]

In spite of this defeat the situation remained, as has already been mentioned, a very serious one. Although the British armies still preserved an unbroken front, the Battles of the Lys in April had strained the line almost to breaking-point, and it was fully expected that the enemy would make a further attempt to separate the French and British armies by an attack on the Arras-Amiens-Montdidier front. The attempt was never made. During May and June the British maintained an active defence, and by harassing operations " of gradually increasing magnitude and frequency " they prevented the enemy from completing preparations for a renewal of his offensive on the Lys front. Meanwhile, the enemy had launched his offensive on the Aisne front. The first attack was made on May 27th, on the Chemin des Dames, and the fiercest and almost incessant fighting followed until June 6th. This thrust, like the thrust in Flanders, in April, was within an ace of success, but the stubborn resistance of the French and British forces brought the German attacks to a standstill. The enemy had shot his bolt, his strength was exhausted. On July 18th the allied counter-stroke on the Soissons-Rheims Sector definitely wrested the initiative from the enemy, and by the end of July the British armies were ready themselves to pass to the offensive.

As part of the allied strategical plans, it was decided that the first step to be taken was to free Amiens and the Paris-Amiens railway, and the British offensive, launched on August 8th, had this end in view. The initial blow was a

[1] See Sir Douglas Haig's despatch of December 21st, 1918.

brilliant success. By August 12th Amiens was freed, the British had advanced twelve miles, and vast quantities of prisoners and guns had been captured.

The spirit of the British armies was raised by this *coup de maître* to a pitch which augured well for the future; while the Germans, hitherto confident of victory, received a blow to their moral from which they never recovered. The fighting which followed was fierce and bitter, but the Allied Offensive continued unchecked until the end of the war. It resolved itself into two phases. The first consisted in the struggle for the enemy's long-prepared defensive positions and in smashing the Hindenburg line; and the second in the pursuit of the enemy, who was striving to hold out in semi-prepared or natural defensive positions sufficiently long to " organise his retreat and avoid overwhelming disaster."

After the Battle of Amiens the British offensive was extended northwards to the area between the rivers Somme and Scarpe. A preliminary attack on August 21st, by which the general line of the Albert-Arras railway was gained, paved the way for the principal attack, two days later, on a front of thirty-three miles, from the junction of the French and British armies north of Lihons to Mercatel. In this neighbourhood the Hindenburg line, from Quéant and Bullecourt, joined the old Arras-Vimy defence line of 1916.

On the front of the 56th Division, which was now in the VI Corps (Lieut.-General Sir J. A. L. Haldane), the 168th Infantry Brigade attacked, on August 23rd, from the west of Boyelles and Boiry Becquerelle. After capturing these villages, this Brigade advanced a further thousand yards and occupied Boyelles Reserve trench. The attack was continued, on August 24th, by the 167th Infantry Brigade, with the object of enveloping the village of Croisilles from the north, whilst the Guards Division, which had made considerable progress on the previous day, on the right, was to envelop it from the south.

The attack started well, and by 11.0 a.m. Summit trench, which lay about eight hundred yards to the west of Croisilles and was the first objective, was captured; but Croisilles was strongly held by machine guns and the attack on the village failed. Summit trench was accordingly organised as the line of resistance. The 167th Infantry Brigade made repeated attempts, on the following day, to penetrate Croisilles, but could make no progress owing to heavy machine-gun fire.

THE FIGHTING FOR CROISILLES

The 56th Division was now transferred to the XVII Corps (Lieut.-General Sir C. Fergusson). Some progress was made on August 26th by the 167th Infantry Brigade, posts being pushed forward to the north-west of Croisilles and touch being maintained with the Guards Division in Leger Reserve. This trench was a continuation southwards of Summit trench. On the left, the 52nd Division was pushing down the Hindenburg line towards the high ground north-west of Croisilles, known as Henin Hill. At 4.0 p.m. on the same day, the 169th Infantry Brigade was ordered to relieve the 167th Infantry Brigade in Summit trench, and to press the attack vigorously, round the north of Croisilles, towards the Hindenburg line, down which the 52nd Division was to continue its advance.

In the evening of August 26th, after the relief of the 167th Infantry Brigade had been carried out, the situation so far as the 169th Infantry Brigade is concerned was as follows : the Brigade had pushed on about 400 yards east of Summit trench and was holding 3000 yards of front, organised in depth, with Summit trench as the line of resistance. Its right flank was in touch with the Guards Division in Leger Reserve opposite the south-west corner of Croisilles. The Queen's Westminster Rifles were on the right, the L.R.B. in the centre, and the 2nd Londons on the left, where, although the position was somewhat obscure, they were in touch with the 52nd Division. Croisilles itself was still strongly held by the enemy with machine guns ; and Fooley trench, opposite the front of the 2nd Londons, was still in the enemy's possession.

The above short summary must suffice as an introduction to a detailed account of the experiences of the Queen's Westminster Rifles in the Battle of the Scarpe, 1918.

The Battalion had hardly settled down to rest, after its trying march to Bailleulval on August 23rd, when orders were received to move to Blaireville. The troops were on the march shortly before 5.0 a.m. on the 24th, and, as on the previous day, the roads were practically blocked with guns, troops and transport moving forward to the fighting area. On arriving at Blaireville at 7.0 a.m., battle equipment, ammunition and rations were drawn and water-bottles were filled. The march was continued at 1.30 p.m. to Boisleux au Mont ; and at 5.45 p.m., after a meal and a short rest, the Battalion moved forward to Boyelles Reserve trench which was reached just as it was beginning to get dark. During the latter part of the advance, which was made in artillery formation, the Battalion was spotted by enemy observers and shelled, but it arrived at its position in the trench with little loss.

Complete ignorance prevailed about the situation on the battle-front. The country was quite strange, and neither the names of the units in the forward area nor the positions they were supposed to be holding were known. It was not even known whether the high ground in various directions was held by British or enemy troops. To give a typical example of the general uncertainty : a battery commander called at Battalion Headquarters after dark to inquire whether his battery, which was just in front, was under observation.

Boyelles Reserve trench was shelled at frequent intervals during the night, and the Battalion suffered several casualties from gas, of which the whole area reeked in the morning. Soon after daybreak on August 25th, touch was gained with the 8th Middlesex in Leger Reserve trench, and it was then discovered that Croisilles, which until then was thought to be in British hands, was still in the enemy's possession. Later in the day, on receipt of a warning order for an attack on the village, Lieut.-Colonel S. R. Savill, with the company commanders and as many other officers as could be spared, made a personal reconnaissance of the position and its approaches, the men in the meantime being practised in the use of German stick-grenades, of which many were lying about. At noon on the following day (August 26th) orders were received for the Battalion to relieve the 8th Middlesex at dusk. But these orders were cancelled, as a result of a successful advance of the 52nd Division on the left which it was hoped might cause the enemy to withdraw from Croisilles.

At about 4.30 p.m. the 169th Infantry Brigade was ordered to relieve the 167th Infantry Brigade, and to press on towards Croisilles throughout the night, giving the enemy no rest, and to follow up immediately any withdrawal as far as the Hindenburg line north-east of the village. The L.R.B. were accordingly ordered to advance in artillery formation from Boyelles trench ; and, if no serious opposition were encountered, to push on to the above-mentioned objectives. Meanwhile, the Queen's Westminsters were to gain touch with the brigade on the right and were to guard the right flank of the L.R.B. and to " mop up " Croisilles after they had gone through the village.

When the Queen's Westminsters received their orders many of the officers were reconnoitring in the forward area and the men were away drawing rations, water and ammunition. But the companies were got on the move as quickly as possible, and orders were issued verbally, while going forward, for C and D Companies to advance in the front line.

All went well until Summit trench was reached; but, on topping the crest just beyond it, the companies were met by heavy machine-gun fire from Croisilles. Fortunately it was now dusk, and the casualties were not so heavy as they would have been if the visibility had been good. Colonel Savill ascertained from the 8th Middlesex that the village was strongly held, and immediately got into communication with the Brigade. The Battalion was then ordered to press on and capture the village without waiting for the L.R.B., who had suffered severely and were held up just beyond Summit trench on the left. C and D Companies now advanced with two platoons each in the front line, but they were held up by the dense barbed wire in front of Croisilles trench on the western edge of the village, and by the heavy fire from the numerous machine guns which were emplaced in the trench. Stubborn attempts were made throughout the night to get forward. The leading platoons suffered many casualties, but no progress could be made; and eventually, just before dawn, the Battalion took up a line in Summit trench with posts pushed forward about three hundred and fifty to four hundred yards to the east of it, in approximately the same position as those established previously by the 167th Infantry Brigade. The Battalion remained in these positions until the afternoon of the 27th August, on which day there was heavy fighting both north and south of Croisilles. On the north, the 2nd Londons, assisted by a company of the L.R.B., attacked in the morning with the object of gaining part of the Hindenburg line north-west of Croisilles, and the 2nd Londons succeeded in reaching the general line of Farmer's trench, due north of Croisilles, where they were held up by very heavy machine-gun fire from the village and its neighbourhood. Later in the day, however, the 52nd Division on the left having captured Fontaine lez Croisilles, the 2nd Londons and the L.R.B. were able to make progress, and by 10.0 p.m. the two battalions were in the Hindenburg line to the south-west of this village, where they were in touch with the 52nd Division.

On the south the Guards Division was very heavily counter-attacked and forced back behind its original line in Leger Reserve trench, with the result that the right flank of the Battalion and the left flank of the Guards became dangerously exposed. Captain F. E. Whitby, M.C., and Lieutenant

R. R. Calkin, commanding D and A Companies, which were in the front line, succeeded in collecting a number of men of the Guards; and partly with the help of these, and partly by moving up their own support platoons, they helped to fill the gap and re-establish the line. The following letter was subsequently received by Lieut.-Colonel Savill from the Commanding Officer of the 2nd Battalion Coldstream Guards, who were on the right of the Queen's Westminster Rifles on this occasion: " Dear Colonel,—I must write and thank you for the very kind assistance which your battalion gave us on the 27th August. The stretcher-bearers from your battalion were perfectly splendid, and I cannot adequately express to you my gratitude for their splendid help. Also the assistance which Captain Jacomb rendered, by bringing up two platoons to help us in holding Leger Reserve when our numbers became so reduced, helped us very much in the rather difficult position in which we were placed."

During the day the Battalion suffered 60 casualties, including 2 officers, Lieutenant F. W. Russell, M.C. (killed), and 2nd Lieutenant O. M. Power (wounded). Lieutenant Russell was a gallant officer and had rendered distinguished and devoted service to the Battalion.

In the late afternoon the London Scottish commenced to take over from the Battalion in Summit trench; but, while the relief was in progress, the orders were cancelled, and the 8th Middlesex took over instead. After the relief, the companies moved off to Brigade Headquarters near the Hindenburg line and nearly two miles north of the trenches they had been holding. This move was made under particularly difficult conditions, the Battalion having to make its way not only in the dark and over completely strange country, but through a sector crowded with troops, including two battalions of infantry in artillery formation.

On their arrival at Brigade Headquarters the Queen's Westminsters were met by Lieut.-Colonel Savill and ordered to move on at once down the Hindenburg line, which had been captured in the morning, to a point about a mile to the west of Fontaine lez Crosilles. As soon as the companies had reached this point, the company commanders were assembled in a "pillbox" where operation orders, for an attack on Bullecourt the next day, were being drafted. This pillbox was the only available cover where a light could be used. Its dimensions were about 8 feet by 3 feet, and in this narrow draughty space were crowded the Commanding Officer and the Adjutant and four Company Commanders. The only illumination was a flickering candle which was with difficulty kept alight, and the Commanding Officer had to lie on the ground with the Company Commanders literally lying on top of him, in order to explain to them the plan of attack. The issue of orders was completed about midnight.

Meanwhile the troops, who had been put to a very severe strain during the past fortnight, were trying to get a little rest.

Ever since August 12th, when the Battalion left Tilloy, the men had not had a single unbroken night's sleep, and during the past ten days they had moved practically every twenty-four hours. The moves were generally made at night, at first along roads blocked with traffic and afterwards across country pitted with shell-holes and traps for the unwary, and for the last forty-eight hours the Battalion had been subjected to very heavy and constant bombardments with gas and high-explosive shells. The last move from Croisilles had been, in the words of the 169th Infantry Brigade War Diary, " fatiguing and difficult owing to the darkness of the night, and to the fact that the tracks near the Hindenburg line could not be used owing to the activity of the enemy's machine guns from the north-eastern outskirts of Croisilles."

But the enemy, who was beginning to give way, could be allowed no rest; at any time his line might crumble and he would then be compelled to retreat with the British infantry in hot pursuit. Under such circumstances it is one of the first principles of war that relentless pressure must be maintained without regard to the exhaustion of the men.

The Queen's Westminster Rifles and their comrades in other battalions understood what was expected of them; physically worn out as they were, the offensive spirit remained and all ranks were imbued with a grim determination to carry on and to complete the destruction of the enemy. The record of the continuous fighting on August 28th and 29th shows what tired men can accomplish when put to the test.

As soon as it was light enough, on the morning of August 28th, for the Queen's Westminsters to see their way, they moved forward, about twelve hundred yards down the Hindenburg line, to relieve the L.R.B. and 2nd Londons and then take up their assembly position in the trenches known as Nellie Avenue, Burg Support, Mole Lane and Janet Lane. After moving forward with great difficulty, through trenches packed with troops of the 56th and 57th Divisions, the companies, with the exception of B Company, were in their final assembly position by 8.0 a.m. B Company, however, found its assembly trench already occupied by the 9th King's (Liverpool) Regiment and was ordered to assemble in the only other trench available. It was most unfortunate that this trench was practically at right angles to the line of advance, for it meant that, when the attack was commenced, the company would have to swing round instead of moving straight forward. This was a difficult and risky manœuvre, but one that was unavoidable under the circumstances.

The ultimate objective of the 169th Infantry Brigade was the capture of Bullecourt and the establishment of a line about 500 yards to the east of the village, while on their left the 57th Division was to move on Hendecourt and Riencourt lez Cagnicourt.

The attack of the 169th Infantry Brigade was to be made under a creeping artillery barrage. The general plan was as follows : the Queen's Westminsters were to lead, with two companies in the front line, one company in support, and one in reserve, and were to fight their way over the open, and not through the trenches, right through to the final objective. There was to be no pause on the first objective, which was about 1500 yards from the assembly position, on the line Queen's Lane-Jove Lane. The L.R.B., followed by the 2nd Londons, were to move forward immediately in rear of the Queen's Westminsters and in close support, and they had orders to intervene without hesitation so as to prevent any delay which might cause the barrage to be lost.

The artillery barrage was timed to open ten minutes before zero, on Factory Avenue and Juno Lane, two trenches some distance in front of the assembly position. Here it was to dwell until zero, to enable the troops to leave their trenches and approach close up to it. It was then to move forward at the rate of one hundred yards in four minutes.

When the order was given for the Battalion to attack over the open, parallel with the line of the Hindenburg trench system, it was of course expected that there would be open spaces between the protecting belts of wire along which the attackers could move ; but, when the troops left their trenches shortly before zero, it was found that, instead of having the usual series of belts, the enemy had completely filled the space between the trenches with wire. This wire was quite uncut ; but in any case, inasmuch as the attack was to take place longitudinally along, and not across it, it must have provided a complete obstacle to any advance. This state of affairs could not possibly have been foreseen either by the Division or the Brigade, when the arrangements for the attack were made, but it had a very important influence on subsequent events.

The companies were assembled for the attack as follows: A Company (Lieutenant A. J. Philip) on the right in Nellie Avenue (south); B Company (Lieutenant C. R. Jacomb) on the left in Nellie Avenue (north); C Company (Lieutenant R. R. Calkin) in support, in Janet Lane (south); and D Company (Captain F. E. Whitby, M.C.) in reserve in Janet Lane (north).

Zero hour was 12.30 p.m. on August 28th. The moment the companies left their trenches, they were met by extremely fierce and accurate machine-gun fire from Guardian Reserve trench on the right and from the high ground about 1000 yards in front. Many of the officers were shot down almost at once, and very many casualties were sustained by the other ranks. C Company alone lost all its officers and 85 per cent of its men as they struggled to get through the wire.

This wire undoubtedly caused the leading troops, in their efforts to advance, to edge away towards the left where the ground was more open; but there were other important factors which influenced the direction of the advance. Firstly B Company, for the reason stated above, had to change direction when jumping off from their assembly trench; secondly "the weight of the attack was on the left, where the 52nd Division was attacking, while no advance was taking place on the right"[1]; and thirdly, but probably only to a small extent, some shells of the British barrage were falling rather short on the right. In connection with the second factor, it must be remembered that there is always a natural tendency for troops to be drawn in the direction of heavy fighting.

Meanwhile, Battalion Headquarters, unaware of the extent to which the companies had swung to the left, pressed forward down Burg Support as previously arranged, in order to get in touch with them. After advancing about 500 yards Battalion Headquarters, together with the remnants of C Company and the headquarters details of the L.R.B. and 2nd Londons (the latter were bombing up Tunnel trench), were held up by hostile machine guns from the front and from both flanks. The enemy was found to be immediately ahead in Burg Support and also in Stafford Lane on the right, where bombing was in progress. Messages were sent back that the system was not "mopped up," and asking for reinforcements

[1] 169th Infantry Brigade report on the operations.

to enable touch to be gained with the companies who were supposed to be ahead. Owing to the difficulties of communication help was a long time in coming, but in the meantime the headquarters details, by strenuous trench fighting, pushed on as far as the junction of Hump Lane and Burg Support.

At one point, seeing an enemy machine gun coming into action on the right front, Lieut.-Colonel Savill lay down with Lieutenant Harrow (the acting-Adjutant) on one side of him and R.S.M. Musselwhite on the other, and opened rifle fire on the team, in the hope of knocking them out before they could bring their gun into action. The gun was eventually silenced; but the very first burst from it killed Lieutenant Harrow and wounded the R.S.M. in the thumb, leaving Colonel Savill untouched. Eventually three platoons of the 4th Londons (167th Infantry Brigade) arrived and were sent forward up Burg Support. They made but little progress; and, after they had reported that they could not get on, they were given instructions to work westward along Knuckle trench. On the right the enemy machine-gunners in Guardian Reserve and its neighbourhood, had put up a brave fight and caused heavy casualties. But by 6.0 p.m. companies of the L.R.B. and Kensingtons (168th Infantry Brigade) had captured this trench, and were holding Stray Reserve trench which led out of it, up to Stafford Lane. They had also rounded up a machine-gun nest on the right which had been causing a great deal of trouble. By 8.0. p.m. the resistance in Stafford Lane and the Hump had been definitely overcome; and by 5.0 a.m. the next morning (August 29th) a strong point in the Hindenburg line, known as the Knuckle, which had formed part of the first objective, was reported clear of the enemy. In the course of the day's fighting on this part of the front a large number of machine guns and prisoners were captured.

Nothing had been heard of A, B and D Companies throughout the day. These companies, as has already been mentioned, swung to their left as soon as the advance began and eventually arrived in front of the ruined remains of Hendecourt instead of the ruins of Bullecourt. But, strange as it may seem when the situation is considered in the calm atmosphere of peace, the mistake was not discovered by the troops on the spot until quite late in the evening. Hendecourt at this time was described as " an indistinguishable jumble of bricks and trenches," as indeed were all villages in the neighbourhood. Quite apart from the fact that villages, as such, were barely recognisable from the map, there was in this case an extraordinary similarity in the situations of Bullecourt and Hendecourt, and in the network of trenches about them. Neither village had been visible from the jumping-off trench for the attack, owing to the higher ground immediately in front; and, from the top of the rise, Hendecourt alone could be seen, Bullecourt being situated in a hollow.

When the leading troops reached the crest of the hill they had already lost direction to some extent, and, seeing a village in front of them, they imagined it to be Bullecourt and immediately made for it. Good progress was made, in spite of heavy hostile machine-gun fire, and by about 3.0 p.m., the attackers had advanced nearly two miles and were in the village. Only three officers, Captain F. E. Whitby, M.C., Lieutenant C. R. Jacomb and Lieutenant J. A. N. Webb, were left of all those who had started with the Queen's Westminster Rifles, the L.R.B. and the 2nd Londons. These three officers collected every man they could and succeeded in establishing a line to the east of the central road running through Hendecourt. They were completely isolated; the 57th Division had not come up and its whereabouts were unknown, and no touch could be gained with any troops on the flanks. The party hung on where they were from 2.15 p.m. to 5.30 p.m.; but their position was precarious, for they were under heavy machine-gun fire and fire from enemy snipers from both flanks and from the rear; and from their front a field gun opened on to them over open sights. Captain F. E. Whitby was wounded in the neck at about 5.0 p.m., but carried on, and the party which was already very weak was gradually being annihilated. Half an hour later, there being no other troops in sight, it was decided to withdraw slowly until touch could be gained with other units. The retirement was carried out very gradually indeed, through the village in a north-westerly direction, until Cemetery Avenue, a long trench about 500 yards north-west of the village, was reached. In this trench touch was gained with troops of the 9th King's (Liverpool) Regiment and the 2/4th Battalion South Lancashire Regiment, both of the 57th Division, and Lieutenant C. R. Jacomb (after Captain F. E. Whitby was wounded) at once organised a line of defence facing Hendecourt. His dispositions were as follows: L.R.B. on the right, King's (Liverpool) Regiment in the centre, and the Queen's Westminsters on the left. A small party, under Sergeant E. W. Gillett, was sent to Crux trench, which led in a north-westerly direction out of Cemetery Avenue, to establish a protective right flank. Small posts of the South Lancashires guarded the left flank, and some other posts were established by the same battalion on the line of the railway in front. The elements of the 169th Infantry Brigade remained on this line until early the next morning (August 29th), when fresh troops of the 52nd Division came up to assemble in the trench, as their jumping-off line for a further attack on Hendecourt. Lieutenant Jacomb was then ordered by Captain D. J. Mearns of the South Lancashire Regiment, the senior officer present, to withdraw his men to the rear in order to make way for the relieving troops.

Captain F. E. Whitby, as he was on his way to the dressing station, had reported to Brigade Headquarters that his party had reached Pelican trench. This trench occupied a position, relative to Bullecourt, curiously similar to that of Cemetery Avenue to Hendecourt. The information was, of course, incorrect; but it was not until nearly midnight that Lieutenant Jacomb discovered that he was in front of Hendecourt, and not Bullecourt. He immediately sent messages to Battalion Headquarters, by Sergeant W. R. Berry and Riflemen W. H. Maslin, reporting his correct position. These two men had the greatest difficulty in getting forward, owing to the heavy machine-gun fire. They eventually arrived at Battalion Headquarters at about 5.30 a.m. on August 29th, having captured a prisoner on the way. At this hour, Lieut.-Colonel Savill was making a personal reconnaissance forward, under circumstances that must now be explained.

The erroneous report, that the 169th Infantry Brigade had actually penetrated Bullecourt before 4.0 p.m. but had withdrawn to Pelican Lane, reached the 56th Division at 6.15 p.m. on August 28th. At 7.45 p.m. the Division issued Operation Orders for the attack to be resumed the following day, and the Brigade Operation Orders reached the Queen's Westminsters in the early hours of August 29th. These orders directed that the L.R.B. were to lead the attack, and were to use Pelican Lane as their jumping-off line. The Queen's Westminsters, in support, were to assemble in Borderer Lane and Gog and Magog trenches, a short distance in rear.

Inasmuch as fighting had been in progress during the evening of August 28th, at the Knuckle (several hundred yards in rear of Pelican Lane), Lieut.-Colonel Savill could not understand how the troops could assemble as ordered. He therefore went forward to ascertain for himself what the true situation was and then discovered that the enemy had retired during the night.

On his return to Battalion Headquarters Colonel Savill received Lieutenant Jacomb's message, and he at once reported the whole situation to the Brigade. He was then ordered to withdraw Lieutenant Jacomb's party from Hendecourt, via Trident Alley (a trench leading south-west from the village), to Gog and Magog trench, where the party was to assemble for the attack. Sergeant Berry was immediately sent back to carry these orders to Lieutenant Jacomb; but, when the orders reached him, he was already withdrawing down Crux trench, well away to the north-west. It was then too late for Lieutenant Jacomb to use Trident Alley, and he proceeded down Fag Alley, towards the position occupied by the Queen's Westminsters in the Hindenburg line on the evening of August 27th. His men had been fighting continuously for some eighteen hours, and they were, in the words of the Battalion War Diary, "dead tired, with a great hunger and thirst and for the time being quite unfit for any further fighting. They were therefore given a short rest, and water and rations were issued to them."

Lieutenant Jacomb's party and parties from the other units of the Brigade, numbering, all told, approximately 2 officers and 185 other ranks, then moved forward to take up their assembly position; but their progress was blocked by troops of the 168th Infantry Brigade, which was to attack on the right of the 169th. In consequence of this the party was unable to reach the assembly position by zero hour, and the attack had to proceed without them.

In this attack, the rôle of the 56th Division was to make good a spur about 1200 yards to the south-east of Bullecourt, and to establish a line, on a front of about 2000 yards, running nearly due north from the extremity of the spur. The 169th Infantry Brigade, on the left, was responsible for about 900 yards of the northern portion of this line; and the 168th Infantry Brigade was to capture Bullecourt, and was also responsible for the remainder of the line.

When Lieut.-Colonel Savill discovered by his reconnaissance in the early hours of August 29th that the enemy had withdrawn during the night, he ordered the two companies of the 4th Londons which had come up the previous day to push on down the two trenches of the Hindenburg line (Burg Support and Tunnel trench) and make good Pelican trench for the assembly of the L.R.B. This they did.

The assembly of the 169th Infantry Brigade, whose total available strength was now only 325 all ranks, was completed during the morning. The strength of the Queen's Westminsters was 2 officers, Lieutenant W. H. Gatfield and 2nd Lieutenant L. C. Pollard, and 40 other ranks. These were organised into one company, under Lieutenant Gatfield, and went forward in close support to the two available companies of the L.R.B. The 2nd Londons, who numbered 102 all ranks, were ordered to follow and act as " moppers up." At 10.25 a.m. a heavy bombardment was opened on Bullecourt, and at zero hour (1.0 p.m.) the attack started. On the right the London Scottish swung into Bullecourt; and, by 3.0 p.m., it was reported that the village was captured but that there were insufficient troops to hold it. On the left the attack went rapidly for the first 500 yards ; but it then slowed down and the L.R.B. were held up, to the north of Bullecourt, by very heavy machine-gun fire. The 57th Division was attacking Riencourt on the left, but had not yet gained touch with the 169th Infantry Brigade. The left flank of the Brigade was consequently left uncovered ; but on the right, touch was maintained with the London Scottish.

Lieutenant W. H. Gatfield now led his small company forward to the left flank of the L.R.B., but was unable to gain touch with any troops of the 57th Division. His Lewis gunners engaged the hostile machine guns, but were unable to silence them. The leading troops of the L.R.B. were now without officers, and all the forward troops were suffering very heavy casualties from the accurate fire of the enemy's machine guns. The line threatened to give way. Lieutenant Gatfield, however, acted with great initiative. Collecting all the leaderless men he could find of any unit, he organised them into parties, and posted them in a position to protect the left flank of the attack. He then got into touch with the reserve company of the London Scottish, and asked for assistance in order to extend the line to the left ; but this company had definite orders to keep touch with their other companies, and his request could not be complied with.

Lieutenant Gatfield held on to his position throughout the afternoon. Eventually he succeeded in finding some more men of the 2nd Londons, and by 6.30 p.m., in accordance with orders received from the Brigade, he had arranged for a line of posts to be established astride a sunken road running north-east from Bullecourt. Touch had not yet been gained with the 57th Division, but Lieutenant Gatfield was able to arrange with an officer of the Machine-Gun Corps for the protection of his left flank.

Throughout the day Lieutenant Gatfield had acted with great daring and promptness, and he had displayed military

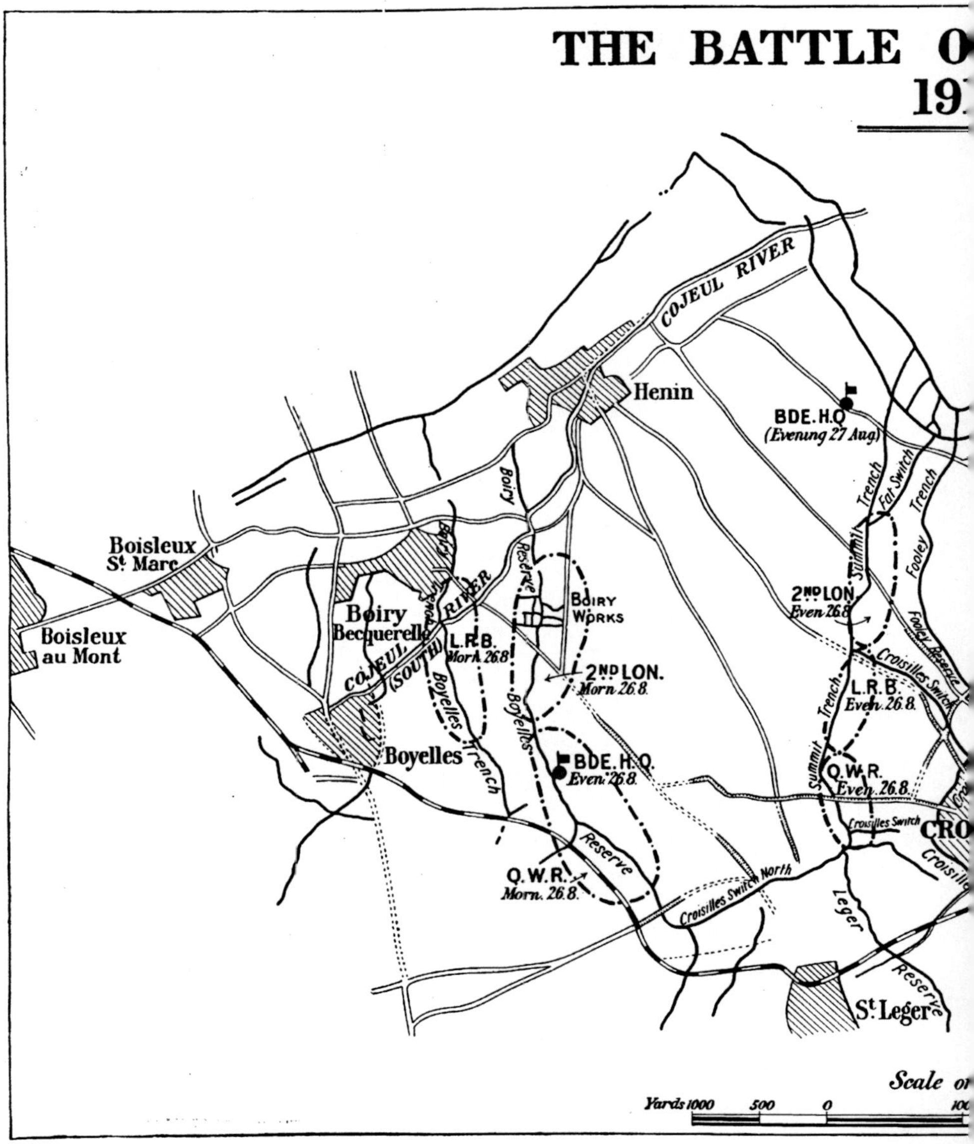
THE BATTLE
COJEUL RIVER
Henin
BDE. H.Q.
(Evening 27 Aug)
Boiry
Boisleux
St Marc
Boiry Becquerelle
Boisleux au Mont
COJEUL (SOUTH) RIVER
Reserve
BOIRY WORKS
L.R.B.
Morn. 26.8.
2ND LON.
Morn. 26.8.
Boyelles
Boyelles Trench
Boyelles Reserve
BDE. H.Q.
Even. 26.8.
Q.W.R.
Morn. 26.8.
Reserve
Croisilles Switch North
Summit Trench
Fat Switch
Fooley Trench
Fooley Reserve
2ND LON.
Even. 26.8.
Croisilles Switch
L.R.B.
Even. 26.8.
Q.W.R.
Even. 26.8.
Croisilles Switch
Leger
Reserve
St Leger
Yards 1000 500 0

THE SCARPE

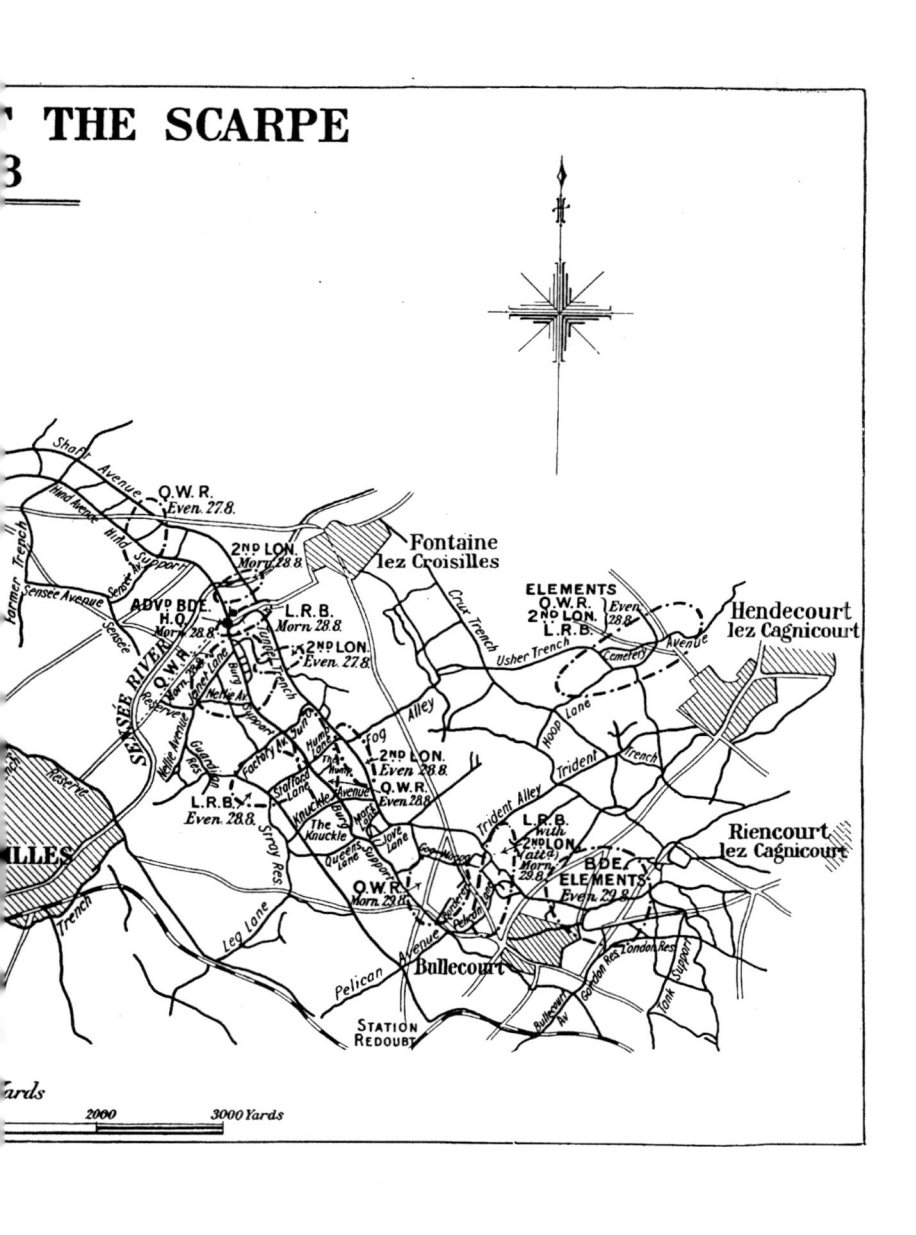

qualities of no mean order. He was very justly awarded the Military Cross for his fine work.

No fresh developments occurred during the night, and Lieutenant Gatfield was relieved just before dawn on August 30th, by troops of the 7th Middlesex (167th Infantry Brigade). The Queen's Westminsters now assembled in Nellie Avenue, in the area from which they had launched their attack on August 28th. Here they were in Brigade reserve.

On their way back to Nellie Avenue, Lieutenant Gatfield's party had to pass through a very heavy barrage of gas and high-explosive shells. This was the prelude to an enemy counter-attack in strength on the line Hendecourt-Bullecourt-Ecoust, which resulted in the recapture of these villages. The 56th Division made a further attack on Bullecourt on August 31st, and the greater part of the village was retaken. After this, the Division was relieved, on the night of the 31st August/1st September, and the Queen's Westminsters withdrew to the area north-west of Boyelles.

The trench strength of the Battalion was now reduced to 200 other ranks, the casualties from all causes since August 24th having been approximately 400 all ranks. Although there was to be much hard fighting ahead, the only further reinforcements received by the Battalion were returned wounded men, and the Battalion was never again up to strength.

On August 28th, the losses of the Queen's Westminsters amounted to 164 all told; of these 3 officers, Lieutenant L. P. Harrow, D.C.M., 2nd Lieutenant J. C. Goadby and 2nd Lieutenant C. G. Warren, and 37 other ranks were killed, and 8 officers and 116 other ranks were wounded, whilst 17 of the wounded were posted as missing.

Lieutenant Harrow, D.C.M., whose death is recorded above, was the Battalion Signalling Officer and had landed in France with the Battalion, with which he had already served for many years as signalling sergeant, and he had received his commission as the result of his excellent work in the early part of the war. For nearly four years he had taken a prominent part in nearly every action in which the Battalion was engaged, and on many occasions he had shown conspicuous courage and resource. He took the greatest interest in the signal section which he had organised and trained, and the splendid services rendered by the Battalion signallers were, to an inestimable extent, inspired by his devotion and example. In Lieutenant Harrow the Queen's Westminsters lost a very gallant officer and a good comrade and friend.

2nd Lieutenant J. C. Goadby was caught under our own barrage whilst taking forward a Lewis gun, the "No. 1" of which had been killed. He had fought with magnificent courage, and by his death, and that of 2nd Lieutenant C. G. Warren, the Battalion lost two very valuable and devoted officers.

The immediate results of the battle appeared to be quite out of proportion to the heavy cost in killed and wounded (the losses of the Division were 123 officers and nearly 2700 men); but it was the smashing of this system of the Hindenburg defences which made it possible for the Canadian Corps to deliver their magnificent and successful assault on the Drocourt-Quéant line further to the east. This was pointed out by the Divisional and Brigade Commanders when, on the 2nd September, they thanked the Battalion in very complimentary terms for its splendid efforts.

The following letter from Lieut.-General Sir C. Fergusson, Commanding the XVII Corps, was circulated on September 4th : " I wish to express to all officers and men in the XVII Corps my congratulations on their achievements in the recent fighting. The task which fell to the Corps was difficult, and was only accomplished by the gallantry, devotion and co-operation of everyone in the line and behind it, in his own particular sphere of duty. The success gained in the culminating operation of the 2nd September, to which all previous work led up, had considerable effect on the situation outside the Corps front. I thank all from the bottom of my heart for their loyal support, and am proud and delighted that their good work has been recognised."

CHAPTER XIX

THE BATTLE OF THE CANAL DU NORD

I.—ON THE VIS EN ARTOIS FRONT

THE Queen's Westminsters now enjoyed a short respite from active operations. They needed it. The men were temporarily exhausted and the losses had been so heavy, especially in Lewis-gunners, that a thorough reorganisation of the Battalion was required. No time was lost in commencing the training of fresh Lewis-gun teams, but at first it was found possible to man only seven guns instead of the normal thirty-two.

On September 5th, orders were received that the Brigade was to relieve part of the 52nd Division in the evening, preparatory to taking over the line from troops of the 63rd Division in the Inchy-Mœuvres area. The Battalion accordingly moved forward to the neighbourhood of Hendecourt and Bullecourt, only to learn on its arrival that the relief had been cancelled, and that it was to return to the area from which it had started in the morning.

The broiling sun, the frequent halts rendered necessary by the congested traffic on the roads and the march through the dust-laden air were in themselves sufficiently trying for tired men, but their discomfort was increased by the fact that many of them had just been issued with new boots. It does not require much imagination to realise the feelings of the men on reaching camp at 6.0 p.m., after having been continually on the move for nearly eight hours.

On September 6th, the G.O.C. XVII Corps (Lieut.-General Sir C. Fergusson) inspected the Battalion, and bade it farewell on its leaving, with the rest of the Division, to join the XXII Corps (Lieut.-General Sir A. J. Godley).[1] On September 8th, the Battalion marched northwards to Vis en Artois, moving on again the following day to the newly captured Drocourt-Quéant switch line, north-west of the village of Dury. Here, in the old German front line, it relieved the 1st Loyal North Lancashire Regiment (1st Division) and was in Brigade reserve. The accommodation

---

[1] From this date until the Armistice, the XXII Corps formed part of the First Army (General Sir H. S. Horne).

was very scanty, and only rough bivouacs could be erected to protect the men from the continuous rain. A week was spent in these trenches. The days were occupied partly in training the whole Battalion in the use of the Lewis gun, and partly in collecting salvage and burying the dead. At night parties were sent forward to help in the consolidation of the new line.

On September 16th, the Queen's Westminsters relieved the 2nd Londons in the outpost line. This was their first experience of open warfare outposts. The sentry groups were posted at wide intervals, along the edge of two large lakes (the Serpentine and Lecluse Lake); and the pickets were established some six or seven hundred yards in rear, on the outpost line of resistance. This line followed the sunken road between Ecourt St. Quentin and Lecluse. The Battalion was so weak in numbers that there was considerable difficulty in covering the frontage allotted to it. Companies mustered only about fifty men, and platoons could barely raise a single section to man a Lewis gun.

The Battalion spent forty-eight hours on outpost duty, being relieved by the 7th Middlesex during the night of September 18th. There had been a good deal of shelling at night, and by day the enemy's aeroplanes had been active against the British observation balloons, but otherwise the time had passed quietly. On being relieved the Battalion moved back to Guémappe, just north of the Wancourt Ridge, where it had suffered so severely in April, 1917. After two cold and stormy nights, spent in rough bivouacs, the Queen's Westminsters, on September 20th, made a welcome move to the trench system known as the " Vis en Artois Switch," about a mile south of Vis en Artois. The Battalion was now in the anomalous position of occupying captured trenches, when at rest, and being in the open when holding the line. This was a sure sign that the days of trench warfare were ending, and one that added zest to the small open-warfare schemes that were carried out during the next few days.

On September 21st, a conference of commanding officers was held at Brigade Headquarters. The outline of the scheme for a further attack in the direction of Cambrai was explained, but orders were given that the matter was to be kept an entire secret for a few days. Operation orders for the attack were issued on September 24th. These were very complete, and, with the help of a plentiful supply of maps and many very excellent aeroplane photographs, it was possible to explain fully to every man the nature of his task. With the exception of the attack at Gommecourt, in 1916, the Battalion was probably never better prepared, so far as information is concerned, for offensive operations. At Gommecourt the odds had been all against the attackers, but now the moral of the enemy had been badly shaken, and the Queen's Westminster Rifles, whose fighting strength numbered only 15 officers and 318 other ranks, made good use of their opportunity.

II.—THE CAPTURE OF SAUCHY CAUCHY

The Battle of the Canal du Nord forms one of the series of battles that have been grouped together under the general title of the Battles of the Hindenburg Line. It opened, on September 27th, 1918, with an attack by the Third and First Armies in the direction of Cambrai. This attack was made, on a front of about 13 miles, from Gouzeaucourt to the neighbourhood of Sauchy Lestrée. It was followed, two days later, by another attack further south delivered by the Fourth Army. These two attacks formed part of a brilliantly conceived plan, and they resulted after nine days' fighting in a brilliant and decisive victory.

The Battle of the Canal du Nord completed the first phase of the British campaign of 1918, and it marked the commencement of open warfare and the final phase of the war.

When the first attack was launched, the Hindenburg line north of Gouzeaucourt was still in the enemy's hands; and to the north of Mœuvres, on the left flank of the attack, the British were still being held on the west bank of the Canal du Nord. It was in the latter area that the Queen's Westminsters were engaged.

The general plan of the attack, north of Mœuvres, was for the Canadian Corps to force the crossing of the Canal du Nord, on a frontage of nearly two miles in the neighbourhood of Marquion, and then to spread out fanwise. The rôle of the left flank of the Canadians was to capture and " mop up " the trench system, north of the Arras-Cambrai road, up to a line (called " the Blue Line ") running roughly east and west just south of Sauchy Lestrée. Under cover of this operation, the 11th Division (on the left of the Canadians) and the 56th Division (on the left of the 11th Division) were to pass over the canal and deploy facing north. They were then to launch their attack from the " Blue Line," so as to take the enemy in the flank.

The objective of the 11th Division took it beyond the

village of Oisy le Verger, whilst the task of the 56th Division, for the first day of the attack, was to capture Sauchy Lestrée and Sauchy Cauchy, two villages on the east of the canal; and then to push on to a sunken road running in a north-easterly direction about two miles in front of the " Blue Line."

The general plan for the 169th Infantry Brigade was for it to deliver two simultaneous but distinct attacks on each side of the Agache River; the immediate objective of the right attack (2nd Londons) being Sauchy Lestrée and the portion of Sauchy Cauchy to the east of the river, whilst that of the left attack (Queen's Westminsters) was the rest of Sauchy Cauchy.

The dispositions of the Brigade on the " Blue Line " were as follows :—

2nd Londons on the right, with their left on the east branch of the Agache River.

Queen's Westminsters on the left, from the point where the railway crossed the west branch of the river up to and including the Canal du Nord.

L.R.B.—One company between the two branches of the river, whose duty it was to clear the ground between the branches up to their junction south-east of Sauchy Cauchy, and to prevent any movement between the village and Sauchy Lestrée; whilst two companies were to move in immediate support to the 2nd Londons; and the fourth company was to cover the construction of bridges across the canal by the Royal Engineers, and later the crossing of the canal by the two assaulting battalions.

The 2nd Londons were directed to push on promptly to Cemetery Wood, and then to attack the eastern portion of Sauchy Cauchy, in order to assist the Queen's Westminsters to take the main part of the village.

The task of the Queen's Westminsters, whose boundaries were the Agache River on the right, and the Canal du Nord on the left, was : (a) To furnish one platoon to move northwards along the west bank of the Canal du Nord in close touch with troops of the 168th Infantry Brigade ;

(b) To search thoroughly the bed of the canal and both banks ;

(c) To clear all woods within its boundaries ;

(d) To ensure that the cemetery, south of Sauchy Cauchy, was clear, and to clear thoroughly that portion of the village which lay to the west of the Agache River.

(e) The final objective of the Battalion was the line of the sunken road about 1,200 yards beyond Sauchy Cauchy.

The dispositions and tasks of the companies were as follows :—

First phase (the capture of Sauchy Cauchy) : (a) D Company (Lieut. G. W. Avens, M.M.) on the right, and A Company (Captain C. R. Jacomb, M.C.) on the left, to lead the attack on a two-platoon frontage, and to clear all woods within their boundaries. A Company had in addition to search the bed and both banks of the canal, and to clear the cemetery.

(b) C Company (Lieut. J. J. Westmoreland) to move in close support to the leading companies ; to assist them, either on demand, or on the initiative of the Company Commander, and to detail one platoon to move along the western side of the canal, in close touch with A Company on the right, and the Kensingtons on the left.

(c) B Company (Captain J. B. Baber, M.C.) was in reserve ; it was to move under the orders of Battalion Headquarters in rear of C Company.

Second phase (to commence immediately after the capture of Sauchy Cauchy) : B Company was to advance through the leading companies and occupy the line of the sunken road already mentioned, gaining touch with units on the flanks, and pushing forward posts to obtain observation.

A and B Companies were to reform quickly and consolidate the broad curve of the railway to the south-west of Oisy le Verger. C Company was to reform and remain in Battalion reserve near the northern extremity of Sauchy Cauchy.

It will be remembered that, on the morning of September 26th, the Queen's Westminster Rifles were at Vis en Artois. During the evening the Battalion moved up to its assembly area in the valley just east of Villers lez Cagnicourt, arriving there at 9.15 p.m.[1] This area had an evil reputation for shelling, but its occupation was rendered necessary by the scarcity of dead ground in which troops could assemble unseen by the enemy. Luckily the shelling on this night only consisted of a few rounds, which fell near A Company, but did no damage.

Heavy rain fell all night, and the troops, who lay out in the open in shell-holes, were soaked to the skin. Tea and porridge were issued from a " cooker " at 3 a.m. followed by a wel-

[1] An account of the Battalion's experiences in the battle, written by Lieut.-Colonel S. R. Savill, forms the basis of the narrative that follows.

come ration of rum at 5.20 a.m. When the sun came out at dawn all felt that some amends had been made for an uncomfortable night. The men's clothes soon dried, and everyone was in the best of spirits. At 5.20 a.m., September 27th, the Canadians launched their attack from the Arras-Cambrai road to Sains lez Marquion; and in a little less than three hours they were reported to have reached the Marquion-Sauchy-Lestrée road.

At 10.20 a.m. the Battalion moved forward, in artillery formation, to " Point K," about three-quarters of a mile west of Marquion. So far the shelling had been slight, although one shell had fallen among a platoon of D Company, killing one man and wounding Acting C.S.M. Toovey and two other ranks. The lack of shelling was unexpected, as the advance of the Battalion was under direct observation from many points on the high ground east of the canal. It was due to the fact that the enemy's best observation point (Oisy le Verger, the objective of the 11th Division) was kept under a smoke barrage by our artillery. On the other high ground the enemy appeared to be too much occupied by the Canadians to pay much attention to the Queen's Westminsters. As the Battalion drew near " Point K," the Commanding Officer went forward and learnt from the Infantry Brigade Major that the situation was by no means satisfactory. The Canadians were apparently meeting with a stiff resistance on the left; aeroplanes, flying low over Marquion, had been heavily fired at by the enemy, and the enemy was also holding out in the marshy ground to the south-west of the village.

Owing to the stand made by the enemy at Marquion, the Canadians were unable to form the left portion of the " fan." It had been intended that they should clear the canal to the north of Marquion, and thus enable the Royal Engineers to bridge it for the passage of the 56th Division. The Royal Engineers had been ordered to prepare two crossings, one, south of the Arras-Cambrai road, for the 2nd Londons, and one, north of this road, for the Queen's Westminsters. But when the bridging parties approached the selected places, they found that both were occupied by the enemy. Heavy fire was opened on them, and Lieut. J. R. Plunkett (the Battalion Intelligence Officer), who had gone forward with them to report on their progress, was hit in the shoulder.

The area in which the Battalion was halted now became very " unhealthy." The rate of hostile shelling increased, and " Point K " and the Arras-Cambrai road were receiving particular attention. A consultation was held, between

Lieut.-Colonel Savill and the Commanding Officer of the 2nd Londons, and it was decided that each battalion should go forward and force a crossing for itself. Officers of the Royal Engineers, who had already been forward, volunteered to accompany the battalions as guides. The Queen's Westminsters moved off at 1.10 p.m. They passed over the Arras-Cambrai road as quickly as possible, under heavy shell-fire, and moved forward towards a point on the canal about 700 yards north of the road. It appeared certain that the crossing would be stubbornly resisted and heavy casualties seemed inevitable, but for some reason or another, the enemy retired on the approach of the Battalion. There was, however, a certain amount of long-range machine-gun fire from the north, and also from Marquion, which was still uncleared by the Canadians.

By 2.0 p.m. the Queen's Westminsters had actually crossed the canal without a single casualty; A and B Companies crossing by a lock, whilst C and D found a crossing a little further to the south. The men crossed in single file and in the case of B Company, when they were all over, the platoon commanders merely had to give the command "left turn" to get their platoons in the correct formation for the advance. It is difficult to understand why the enemy should have allowed the Battalion to pass over unmolested. An abandoned enemy machine gun was found later, some fifty yards from the lock, in a position from which the crossing could have been enfiladed, and there seems very little doubt that if the team had stuck to their gun, the Battalion could never have succeeded in crossing the canal.

The companies now assembled for the advance to their jumping-off position for the attack; D Company on the right, A on the left, C in support, with one platoon on the west bank of the canal, and B Company in reserve. They were now over 1,000 yards south of the "Blue Line," on which the 56th Division was to have relieved the Canadians; and it will be remembered that the original intention had been for the Canadians to "mop up" the area as far as this line. No Canadians, however, were met with, and almost at once the leading companies came under heavy machine-gun fire, while the companies in rear were subjected to some desultory hostile shelling. To meet with opposition 1,000 yards before reaching the jumping-off line was distinctly disconcerting, especially as it was quite impossible to get assistance from the artillery without considerable delay.

Zero hour was originally timed for 2.48 p.m. But when, at

a little after 1.0 p.m., it had become clear that there would be delay in assembling the assaulting troops of the 56th and 11th Divisions, it was decided, by the Divisional Commanders concerned, to delay the hour of the attack by forty minutes. This timely decision reached the Battalion shortly after the crossing of the canal had been effected, and every effort was made to reach the jumping-off line by the new zero hour. Both the leading companies fought their way forward without a barrage. The advance of A Company on the left was, for a time, held up by machine guns; but Lieutenant Avens (D Company), showing great initiative, succeeded in outflanking and capturing them. A number of machine-gun nests were rushed and captured by A and D Companies with great skill and with slight loss; and the jumping-off line was eventually reached just in time to advance with the prearranged barrage. Some fifty prisoners were captured before zero hour.

In the meantime the platoon of C Company on the west bank of the canal had been unable to gain touch with the Kensingtons (168th Infantry Brigade), but it had advanced in line with A Company and, in proportion to its strength, had made a good haul of prisoners.

The advance from the " Blue Line " was made under an excellent creeping barrage from artillery and trench mortars. This barrage moved forward at the rate of a hundred yards in eight minutes, and henceforward progress to Sauchy Cauchy was uniformly successful. The enemy certainly did not make the most of his opportunities; he had splendid fields of fire, but he was only too ready to cease fire when the infantry came within close range, and to hold up his hands. Added to this, his shooting was poor, and our troops, keeping well up to the barrage, dashed in and overpowered him before he had time to pull himself together after the barrage had passed.

Never had the Battalion met the enemy in worse spirit, and the obvious deterioration in his moral acted conversely on our own troops. Prisoners stated afterwards that this attack, on their flank, completely disorganised them. They had been told by their officers that they were in the best possible sector and in a very secure position, as the canal made a British attack absolutely impossible.

The enemy were mostly found in small camouflaged slit trenches on the west tow-path of the canal; and, as our troops rushed each locality, entire parties of Germans came out with their hands up, only too eager to get away from the barrage as quickly as possible. The dirty and insanitary condition of their trenches and dugouts spoke eloquently of their loss of moral and discipline.

A powerful stronghold in the cemetery, on the east bank of the canal, had been expected to give considerable trouble. It consisted of a large dugout, with a plentiful supply of machine guns splendidly placed for firing south as well as west. The garrison offered no resistance, and the Queen's Westminsters pressed on to the capture of the western and main portion of Sauchy Cauchy.

If the enemy had been given any time to pull himself together, there is no doubt that the village would have proved a very formidable obstacle to the very weak companies that were attacking it. But the troops went forward with magnificent dash, and they were on to the enemy and past him before he had time to recover from the effects of our artillery. By 4.20 p.m. they were on the southern outskirts of the village; twenty minutes later they were right through it, practically without loss, and were pressing on to their first objective. Meanwhile the 2nd Londons, on the right, had captured Sauchy Lestrée and were advancing against the eastern end of Sauchy Cauchy. The enemy's resistance now began to stiffen. The platoons, with an average strength of 12 other ranks, had been too weak to " mop up " the village, and the enemy, having recovered somewhat from the first shock of the attack, commenced to snipe from the houses. At the same time the German " heavies " began to drop in the village, and machine-gun fire was opened from the canal bank. On the right, touch had not been gained with the 2nd Londons; and on the left, the Battalion had outdistanced the Kensingtons on the west of the canal, and it was under the fire of machine guns and snipers from that flank. The attack was momentarily checked and Lieut.-Colonel Savill threw in his reserve company. The narrowness of the frontage on which the Queen's Westminsters were advancing rendered intercommunication very simple, in fact the Commanding Officer and the four Company Commanders moved all together in rear of the front companies. The situation could thus be dealt with rapidly.

There were, in the Battalion sector, only two avenues of approach to the first objective, one along the bank of the Agache River, and the other along the canal tow-path, the ground between being an impassable marsh. The action taken was as follows: Two platoons of B Company were despatched to the right flank to push on along the bank of the Agache River, and the remaining two platoons were sent round to the canal to rush the enemy on the tow-path.

The two former platoons were held up almost at once, and the Commanding Officer with C.S.M. Plumridge (the acting R.S.M.) went to the right flank to find out what was happening. The Battalion was now lining the road running east and west across the northern end of Sauchy Cauchy with its right on the Agache River. Here touch should have been gained with the 2nd Londons, but, on reaching this point, the Commanding Officer and C.S.M. Plumridge collided with Germans who were running into a house at the corner in search of a fire position. C.S.M. Plumridge remained covering the house with his revolver, while a platoon of D Company was fetched up to deal with the house and its occupants. This they did effectively, severely damaging the former, and entirely destroying the latter.

Lieutenant G. W. Avens, M.M., then reinforced B Company on the river-bank with every available man of D Company. With great dash, this officer, enfiladed at close range from either flank, led his men up the bank in single file towards the objective, the semicircular railway embankment ahead. The difficulty of this operation was accentuated by the fact that, fifty yards short of the railway, a tree had fallen across the river-bank. This obstacle caused large intervals between the men, but, although only a handful had crossed the tree, Lieutenant Avens, realising that indecision or delay would be fatal, raised a cheer and led a charge against the Germans on the embankment. The men he led were still in single file and widely separated, but the assault met with complete success. Although the Germans were still holding the tow-path 1,000 yards in rear of Lieutenant Avens, and in spite of the fact that they enjoyed a numerical superiority of more than two to one, they appeared to be completely paralysed by his sudden action, and surrendered at once without showing any further fight. Lieutenant Avens, who had already been awarded a Military Medal, gained, by this gallant exploit, a well-earned Military Cross.

Sergeant Frost, not satisfied with the capture of the embankment, by himself pursued the enemy up the tow-path, and returned with thirty additional prisoners. For this feat he received the Distinguished Conduct Medal. Later a platoon of C Company, which had been detailed to clear this exposed flank, rounded up and captured some thirty more prisoners.

On the left flank matters had not been progressing so well. The two platoons of B Company, with a platoon of A Company which had been sent up to reinforce them, were still unable to secure the approach up the tow-path, chiefly owing to very hot fire at close range from the west bank of the canal. It was here that Captain W. C. M. Macrae, A.S.C., who had only been with the Battalion five days, and had had practically no previous experience in leading troops in the field, and Lieutenant C. Sheppard were killed by machine-gun fire in an attack on some machine-gun nests that were delaying the advance.

The action which led to Captain Macrae's death was particularly gallant. The attack, which he had hastily organised, was to be made by the simultaneous advance of three parties, one from each flank and one along the line of the tow-path. One of the parties had been unable to get into position for the attack by the prearranged zero. Captain Macrae saw that, without the distraction of the third attack, the remaining two parties would have to bear the full brunt of the enemy's fire, and he quickly decided that he himself with his runner[1] should take the rôle of the third party. As soon as the attack started, the two charged along the tow-path, but only for a few yards, for they both fell riddled with bullets. Their sacrifice was not in vain, as the nest of enemy machine guns was silenced by the remainder of the Company.

It was now dusk, and A Company was ordered to establish a post on the canal bank and to send a platoon back to cross the canal and clear the bank, while the rest of the Company held the tow-path at its junction with Sauchy Cauchy. By this time the Kensingtons had worked round on the left and gained touch with D Company, and the enemy holding out on the tow-path had no chance. After about a dozen of them had been killed by our Lewis-gun fire, the remainder surrendered, and A Company was able to advance up the tow-path and join D Company.

By 9.0 p.m., the task of the Queen's Westminsters was not yet fully accomplished. At that hour the situation was as follows: C Company on the right and D Company on the left were holding the railway embankment, on a frontage of about 700 yards measured from the canal; touch was established with the Kensingtons, via the bridge over the canal 700 yards north of Sauchy Cauchy; the Kensingtons had cleared the west bank of the canal up to that point, and B Company was endeavouring to advance to the sunken road. A Company was now ordered to withdraw into reserve.

Although the main objective had been captured, the post

[1] It is greatly regretted that the name of this runner cannot be ascertained.

T

at the bridge over the canal, some 500 yards ahead, had not yet been established. The tow-path, leading to this bridge, sloped up gradually and was covered by machine guns manned by the enemy at the bridge itself. There was one other approach, namely, the road leading to the bridge from the semicircular railway embankment, on which the Battalion was already established. The task of capturing the bridge was allotted to B Company, and 2nd Lieutenant A. A. W. Ritchings, M.M., who had also joined the Battalion with Captain W. C. M. Macrae only five days previously, led a party of ten men up the tow-path, under such cover as they could get from the bank of the canal. They had got to within about twenty yards of the machine guns, when a multitude of Verey lights was sent up, and a murderous fire was opened on them at point-blank range. In gallantly trying to rush the guns, 2nd Lieutenant A. A. W. Ritchings and six of his men were killed, and three others were wounded. Sergeant Frost and Rifleman R. Cotton miraculously escaped unhurt.

2nd Lieutenant Ritchings had shown consistent disregard of danger all day, and he was seen calmly strolling about, eating apples, while encouraging his men during some of the severest of the fighting. Although both he and Captain Macrae had been so short a time with the Battalion, their conduct and leadership during this battle will always be remembered by the Queen's Westminsters with pride and admiration.

By this time the night was far advanced. The vigilance of the enemy, and their exceptionally strong position, foredoomed to failure any immediate further attempt to rush the bridge. But at dawn on September 28th, six months after the Battalion had fought for its life at Gavrelle, B Company made a fresh advance against the machine-gun nest which had played such havoc with 2nd Lieutenant Ritchings' party. On the approach of B Company the enemy fled, leaving behind a wounded rifleman of 2nd Lieutenant Ritchings' party whom they had bandaged and placed under cover.

With the capture of the bridge, the whole of the original objectives of the 169th Infantry Brigade for the first day of the attack were attained, and the 168th Infantry Brigade on the left had also reached its objective on the west bank of the canal. In the meantime orders had been received that a further attack was to be made by the 56th Division, under cover of a creeping barrage, with the object of clearing the enemy out of the ground as far as the Sensée River, about a mile ahead.

THE RESULTS OF THE BATTLE

Accordingly, at 10.30 a.m. on September 28th, C Company of the 2nd Londons, with B Company of the Queen's Westminsters in close support, to " mop up," advanced on to the objective on the east side of the canal. Little opposition was met with, and by 1.30 p.m. the 2nd Londons had established a line of posts from the north of the Bois du Quesnoy to Palluel, covering the Sensée River. In the meantime, to the west of the canal, the 168th Infantry Brigade had cleared the banks, and the 167th Infantry Brigade had captured Palluel and was pushing on towards Arleux. This village was entered by the 8th Middlesex late in the afternoon. B Company was now withdrawn, and the Battalion was reorganised near the cemetery, south-west of Sauchy Cauchy, where it remained in Brigade reserve until October 2nd.

So far as actual results were concerned, the crossing of the Canal du Nord, on September 27th, was the most successful operation in which the Queen's Westminster Rifles took part during the whole war. For the first time they had seen with their own eyes the moral collapse of the enemy, of which so much was being written in the daily papers and in the official communiqués, and the troops were in fine spirits after their success. In addition to crossing the canal and seizing large tracts of country the Queen's Westminsters, with a fighting strength of 333 other ranks, had captured prisoners in excess of their own numbers, together with a great quantity of booty.

Orders had been given before the attack that, owing to the weakness of the companies, as few men as possible were to be employed as escorts to prisoners of war, and that prisoners were to be handed over to any unit who could get them away to the rear. No receipts were taken at the collecting posts for many of the prisoners captured by the Battalion, but receipts were actually obtained for 4 officers and 242 other ranks. The prisoners sent down without an escort, taken at the lowest possible estimate, would bring the total captured to about 350.[1] Very heavy casualties in killed and wounded were also inflicted on the enemy. In addition to personnel, receipts were obtained for 21 light machine guns, 11 heavy machine guns and 6 trench mortars. These were all claimed by the Battalion as trophies of war, and many of them may now be seen at the Regimental Headquarters at Buckingham Gate. Besides this number, D Company had wisely thrown

---

[1] In the War Diary of the 169th Infantry Brigade the number of prisoners captured by the Queen's Westminsters, for whom no receipts were obtained, is estimated at one hundred.

four heavy machine guns into the canal. They were holding their objective with very few men; and, embarrassed by the number of their prisoners and partly surrounded by the enemy, there was considerable risk of the guns being captured in the event of an enemy counter-attack. The enemy himself had also thrown many guns into the canal and into the marshes, before giving himself up, and the whole of the captured area was littered with enormous quantities of material.

The Battalion casualties, having regard to the results obtained, were remarkably light, but, unfortunately, the percentage of killed was high. The total losses amounted to 4 officers and 16 other ranks killed, and 1 officer and 47 other ranks wounded. The bodies of all the dead were brought in and reverently buried together in the cemetery at Sauchy Cauchy.

The heavy and accurate artillery bombardment, the surprise effect of an attack from the flank, and the excellent staff work, but above all the work of the section commanders and their men, one and all contributed to the success of the attack.

Colonel Savill's account concludes with the following tribute to the men : " On all sides individuals shewed the greatest energy, initiative and courage in dealing with any situation that arose. It was largely due to the entire absence of hesitation on their part that the enemy so quickly made up his mind that 'Fritz the prisoner was better than Fritz the corpse.'"

It is impossible to give more than a few names, but however good was the work of the men, there can be no doubt that it was inspired by the leadership and example of their Commanding Officer. The following incidents are typical of many of those of which Colonel Savill writes :

Two machine guns and seventeen men were rushed and captured by three Riflemen (W. Sheldon, Trowbridge and Lea) while the Battalion was moving up to its jumping-off line. Another machine gun was captured by Lance-Corporal A. W. Lance, D.C.M., and Rifleman Barlow, who crawled round the rear of it, shot two of the crew, and put the remainder to flight. On two occasions Lance-Corporal Hale and Rifleman Bennett (the latter was afterwards killed) dashed forward into our barrage and on each occasion captured about twenty prisoners. Twenty prisoners also were captured by a platoon, led by Lance-Sergeant W. J. Davis, before the jumping-off line was reached. On the right flank splendid work was done under heavy machine-gun fire during the advance, by Rifleman J. Dennison, D.C.M., and Rifleman L. G. Smith in patrolling the area between the Battalion and the 2nd Londons, before touch had been gained with the latter Battalion. The stretcher-bearers acted with their customary gallantry, one of them, Lance-Corporal W. E. Dealy, successfully rescuing a wounded man thirty yards from ak active machine gun.

On the evening of the 27th September, the following wire, addressed to the 56th Division, was received from Lieut.-General Sir A. J. Godley :—

"Please convey to General Coke and all ranks 169th Infantry Brigade my heartiest congratulations on their most successful and gallant attack this afternoon, and to your artillery and 168th Infantry Brigade for their excellent support and co-operation."

III.—ON THE "NE PLUS ULTRA" LINES

The few days spent in Brigade reserve at Sauchy Cauchy were full of interest. Besides clearing the area of salvage and captured material, of which there were enormous quantities, it was possible to walk all over the battlefield of September 27th. Everyone wondered how it was that the enemy's resistance had been overcome with such comparative ease, for there were many strong positions that were given up without a struggle.

On October 2nd, the Battalion relieved the L.R.B., who were holding the line along the southern edge of the marshes north of the Bois du Quesnoy. The sector was a very quiet one, movement in the open being possible at all hours. After an uneventful tour, lasting three days, the Battalion was relieved by the 7th Middlesex and moved back into Divisional reserve south-west of Rumaucourt. By a curious coincidence the sector held by the Battalion, from the 5th to the 7th October, had formed a portion of the "Ne Plus Ultra" lines held by Marshal Villars in the war of the Spanish Succession. Arleux, on the Battalion's left, had been the scene of what has been described as "perhaps the most remarkable and certainly the most entertaining feat" of the Duke of Marlborough during the whole war, when, by brilliant strategy, he caused Villars to destroy his own forts ; and it was at Aubencheul au Bac, on the Battalion's right, that Marlborough crossed the marshes of the Sensée River in August, 1711, and followed the Marshal back to Cambrai.[1]

The Queen's Westminsters remained in the Rumaucourt area until October 11th. The companies were so widely scattered there that it took a runner over two hours to get from Battalion Headquarters to the four company commanders, and as for accommodation, it simply did not exist. The men managed to make themselves tolerably comfortable in a few old trenches, with the aid of their ground sheets, and nothing could damp their spirits, for the breath of victory was in the air.

On October 7th, the following message from Sir Douglas Haig was circulated among the troops :—

" The Central Powers are approaching the President of the United States on the subject of Peace. In view of the great call that has, and is still being made on the endurance of the troops, it is only natural that such news should attract their attention in a very high degree. The F.M. C.-in-C. therefore warns all ranks against permitting their efforts to be influenced by Peace talk, of which the sincerity is not assured, and wishes it to be impressed upon them that now, when the enemy is visibly weakening, and when there has never been fairer promise of great results, the need of relentless effort is paramount. The Army will concentrate its entire energy in bringing the operations in the field to a successful and decisive issue."

The tone of this message is in striking contrast with the whining hypocrisy of a German Peace-propaganda pamphlet which had been picked up two days earlier near Rumaucourt. The pamphlet, which was printed in English, contained a proposal for a confidential and " *non-obligatory* " conference of delegates from all belligerent nations upon the main principles of a Treaty of Peace ; and expressed the pious hope that " By an exchange of ideas, heaps of all misunderstandings could be cleared away, lots of knowledge might be gained, streams of pent-up human feelings would break through, in whose glorious warmth all questions of material value would maintain their weight, while many contradictory points, which are at present given undue importance, would vanish."

On October 10th, the 56th Division was holding an extended front of 8,000 yards along the line of the Sensée Canal,

---

[1] For a short account of the Duke of Marlborough's exploits on this front see the Hon. J. W. Fortescue's "History of the British Army," Vol. I, p. 540.

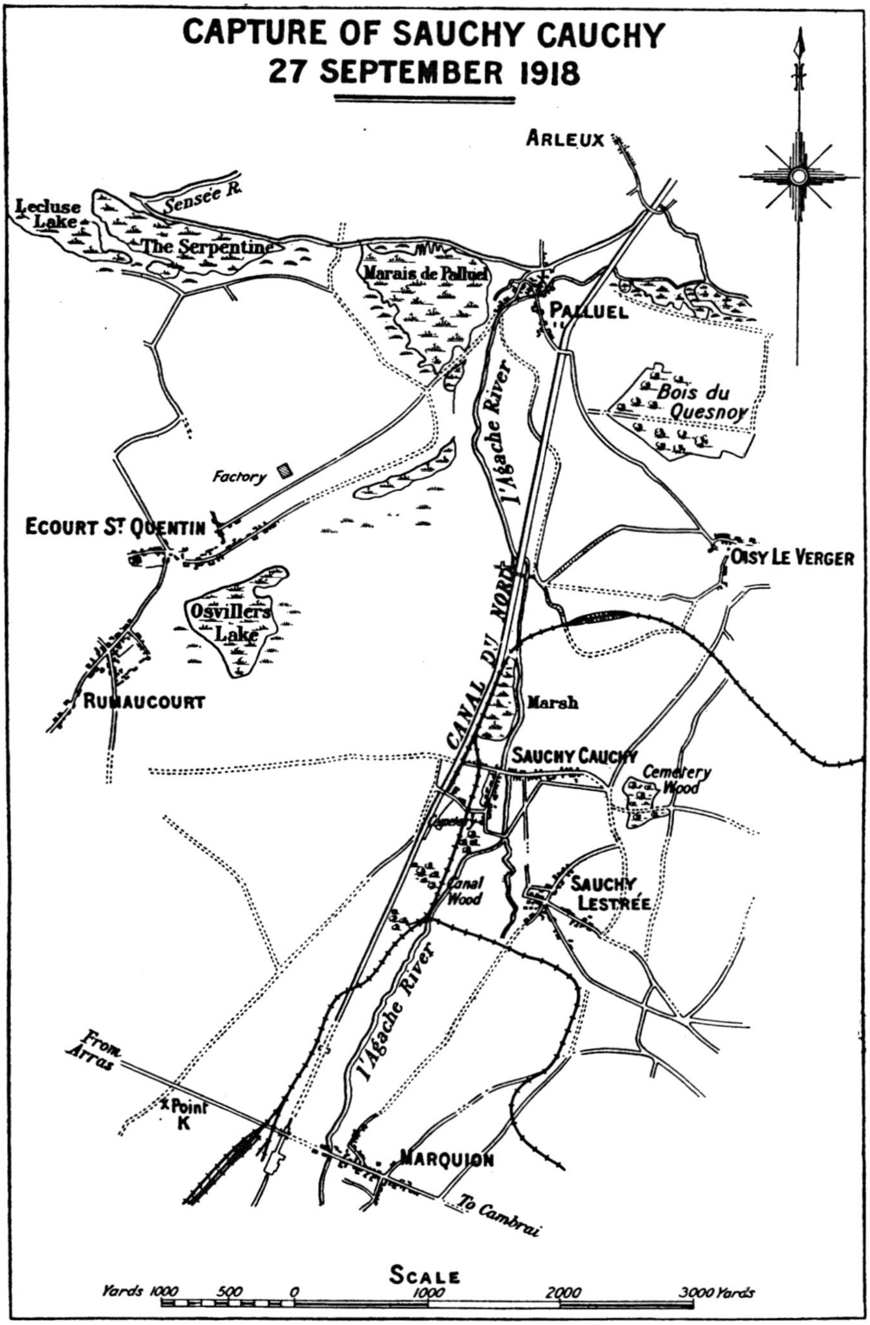
CAPTURE OF SAUCHY CAUCHY
27 SEPTEMBER 1918
ARLEUX
Sensee R.
Lecluse Lake
The Serpentine
Marais de Palluel
PALLUEL
Bois du Quesnoy
l'Agache River
Factory
ECOURT ST QUENTIN
OISY LE VERGER
Osvillers Lake
CANAL DU NORD
RUMAUCOURT
Marsh
SAUCHY CAUCHY
Cemetery Wood
Canal Wood
SAUCHY LESTRÉE
l'Agache River
From Arras
Point K
MARQUION
To Cambrai
SCALE
Yards 1000
500
0
1000
2000
3000 Yards

SENSÉE CANAL BRIDGED. OCTOBER 13TH, 1918

just south-east of Fressies on the right, to and including Palluel on the left, covering the left flank of the Canadians during their advance on Cambrai. On the following day Fressies was captured by the 168th Brigade Infantry, and in the evening the Queen's Westminsters relieved the London Scottish in the left sector of that Brigade's front, with their left near the railway bridge north of Aubencheul au Bac. On October 12th, the Canadian Corps and the 167th Infantry Brigade occupied Arleux and the line of the Canal du Nord to the north of the village.

The enemy was making a minor stand on the west bank of the Canal de la Sensée, and it seemed probable that he would withdraw. All battalions were warned to be specially alert. No signs of withdrawal, however, were observed, and orders were given for a strong bridge-head to be established across the Sensée Canal around Aubigny au Bac, and that, if this operation was successful, endeavours were to be made to cut off the enemy's rear-guards to the west of the village, and disorganise his plans for retreat. The attack was entrusted to the 2nd Londons, who were then in reserve, and the Queen's Westminsters were ordered to send a patrol to the north bank of the canal to cover their crossing. All bridges over the canal, which was about 70 feet wide and 30 feet deep, had been destroyed. South of Aubigny au Bac there were two of these damaged bridges, about 1,250 yards apart, but as they were each guarded by a German post, it was decided that the 416th Field Company, Royal Engineers, should construct a bridge about midway between them (north-east of Aubencheul au Bac).

The night of the 12th/13th October was abnormally dark, and rain was falling steadily, but, although these conditions made the work of bridging very slow, they were to a certain extent advantageous from the point of view of surprise. The Royal Engineers worked magnificently throughout the night under Lieutenant A. E. Arnold, who, unfortunately, was killed on October 13th. By 3 a.m. on October 13th, the bridge was completed without interference from the enemy, and a patrol of the Queen's Westminster Rifles, consisting of a platoon of D Company under 2nd Lieutenant H. R. Smith, passed over the canal to the northern bank. The patrol having reported that they could not move ten paces without being challenged by the enemy, were ordered to make a bold attempt to capture the sentries without raising the alarm. Two prisoners were captured, and the patrol moved forward and formed a protective screen. Under cover of this a company of the 2nd Londons, under Captain D. Sloan, crossed the canal and formed up for the attack. The 2nd Londons, with the artillery co-operating, advanced at 5.15 a.m., and took the enemy completely by surprise. By 6.30 a.m. they had captured Aubigny au Bac and 4 officers and over 200 prisoners—more than their own number. In the meantime the Queen's Westminsters had sent a platoon of C Company across the canal to relieve 2nd Lieutenant Smith's platoon. At 10.30 a.m. the enemy counter-attacked in great strength, under cover of a very heavy artillery barrage, and drove the troops back on to the canal by sheer weight of numbers. A small party of the Queen's Westminsters remained on the north bank of the canal, and the bridge-head was re-established at dusk. A Company, who were in support, in a railway cutting southeast of Aubencheul au Bac, were heavily shelled with gas and high explosives throughout the day, but escaped with comparatively slight loss. The total casualties during the operations were 5 other ranks killed and 1 officer, 2nd Lieutenant H. J. D. Talling, and 14 other ranks wounded. Many others suffered considerably from the heavy gassing, but were not posted as wounded.

The night passed quietly. Patrols went out at dawn on October 14th, but they found the enemy still in position, and no signs of a withdrawal. In the night the Battalion was relieved by the 5th Battalion Canadian Infantry (4th Canadian Division), and marched back to Sauchy Cauchy. On the following night the Queen's Westminsters marched to Marquion, where they entrained for Agnez les Duisans. Their stay on the Canal du Nord front had come to an end, and a well-earned rest, to which all were eagerly looking forward, was about to commence.

CHAPTER XX

THE ADVANCE TO VICTORY

THE BATTLES OF VALENCIENNES AND THE SAMBRE AND THE PASSAGE OF LA GRANDE HONNELLE

THE ARMISTICE

ON October 16th, after a lengthy train journey from Marquion, the Queen's Westminsters detrained at Agnez les Duisans and marched to Haute Avesnes, just off the Arras-St. Pol road, and about six miles north-west of the city of Arras.

It was expected that the Divisional rest would be of some length, and every effort was made both to make it as pleasant as possible for all concerned, and to derive the fullest possible benefit from the change from active operations. The accommodation was comfortable and compact. Recreation rooms, a canteen, officers' and sergeants' messes were soon in full working order, and an excellent field provided a parade and football ground.

Great attention was paid to turn-out and to the general smartening up of the Battalion. During the recent fighting the casualties amongst officers and men had been so heavy that the platoon, as a self-contained unit, had almost ceased to exist. But now every encouragement was given to the platoon commanders, to work up their own small commands, and to take their proper responsibilities, both as regards the training and the welfare of their men. To foster the " platoon spirit," a series of inter-platoon competitions was arranged in such widely different branches of military life as musketry, the Lewis gun and football. All ranks showed the greatest keenness, and in a very short time the Battalion felt that it was able to acquit itself satisfactorily on the parade ground as well as on the battle-front. The bugle band was supplied with drums, and although, as Colonel Savill wrote, this was a transgression against Rifle traditions, yet one seemed to get " more money's worth " out of the band and the assistance in marching justified the break with tradition.

On October 19th, Brigadier-General E. S. D'E. Coke inspected the Battalion, and, in a speech to the men, congratulated them on their excellent appearance and steadiness on parade. He also paid tribute to their work during the last three months, and he expressed the opinion that the reputation of the Brigade had never stood higher than it did at that moment, a result that was most creditable after four years of continuous warfare.

During the " rest " two excellent lectures were given, one by the Intelligence Officer of the 56th Division on " The Present Situation," and one on " The Work of the Royal Air Force," by an officer of that Arm. Whist drives, organised by Sergeant Bowden, took place nearly every night, and the " Bow Bells " and the Divisional Band gave frequent entertainments and concerts. Elaborate preparations were made for a big entertainment and for a dinner for the men, to celebrate, on November 3rd, the fourth anniversary of the landing in France of the 1st Queen's Westminster Rifles; but orders to move, received on October 30th, put an end to these anticipated festivities.

At 8.20 a.m. on October 31st, the Battalion " embussed " near the billets and proceeded to Lieu St. Amand, a little over nine miles south-west of Valenciennes, arriving there about 3 p.m. A rest of thirty-six hours was spent in cleaning up the billets, which had been left in an indescribably dirty and insanitary condition by the enemy; and in clearing away debris caused by the British bombardment, and in making general preparations for a move forward to the battle area.

Open warfare had commenced, on the British front, immediately after the capture of the Hindenburg defences, at the end of September and the beginning of October. By a series of successful blows, delivered in strategic co-operation with the French and American Armies in the south and the Belgian Army in the north, the enemy, on the front with which this history is concerned, had been driven back, by the end of October, on to the general line to Le Quesnoy-Sepmeries-Artres-Famars. Turkey and Bulgaria had capitulated (Turkey on October 31st, 1918, Bulgaria on September 30th, 1918), Austria was verging on a collapse, and Germany's military situation had been rendered ultimately impossible. But, as Sir Douglas Haig wrote in his despatch, " If her armies were allowed to withdraw unmolested the struggle might still be protracted over the winter. The British armies, however, were now in a position to prevent this by a direct attack upon a vital centre, which should anticipate the enemy's withdrawal and force an immediate conclusion."

The capture of Valenciennes was regarded as a necessary preliminary to the launching of the principal British attack, and, if the British plans were to succeed, no time must be lost. Accordingly, at 5.15 a.m. on November 1st, 1918, when the Queen's Westminsters were at Lieu St. Amand, the XVII Corps of the Third Army, together with the XXII and Canadian Corps of the First Army, attacked on a front of about six miles south of Valenciennes. By the evening of November 2nd, the Rhonelle River had been crossed, and the high ground east of Maresches and Préseau had been occupied on the right. On the left the Canadians had captured Valenciennes, and made some progress beyond the town.

Meanwhile the Queen's Westminsters had received orders to move forward to the battle-front in the neighbourhood of Famars. The Battalion roused at 4.30 a.m. on November 2nd and, after stacking packs, blankets, valises and all but absolutely essential fighting stores, moved forward to the Brigade starting-point, which was reached at 9 a.m.

The army was now advancing at a rapid rate, and the necessity for travelling " light " will readily be understood. The vast quantities of ammunition, stores and supplies required on the Western Front, the huge forces engaged, and the difficulties of transport over roads partly destroyed and with every bridge blown up by the enemy, all contributed to magnify the work of an organised advance, and to hamper rapid movement. Notwithstanding these difficulties, the British had advanced some thirty miles since the Battalion had left the Telegraph Hill Sector in August. This was a wonderful achievement, although compared with the progress, measured in miles, in other theatres of war, the actual distance may not seem great.

The Queen's Westminsters, under Captain J. B. Baber, M.C. (the acting second-in-command), marched to Caumont Farm to the south of Famars, halting for a rest and dinner at 12.30 p.m. at Maing. The distance as the crow flies was a little over seven miles, but the actual march was considerably longer. The roads were reserved for motor transport only, and the Battalion had to move across country, using the old German tracks which, even in the early morning, were in a deplorably muddy condition. With the heavy rain which fell throughout the day they grew steadily worse, until ultimately they became practically impassable for transport. The Lewis-gun limbers were continually " ditched," and they were only extricated from the mud with the greatest difficulty. During the latter part of the march, between Maing and Caumont Farm, the transport, which had had to be sent round by road to avoid a particularly bad piece of track, had the misfortune to encounter a stray shell, or " booby trap," no one seemed quite to know which, with the result that the transport N.C.O. and some of the field-cooker horses were wounded.

Meanwhile the Commanding Officer and Lieutenant W. H. Gatfield (the acting Adjutant), who had ridden forward from the starting-point early in the morning to reconnoitre and arrange for the relief, were experiencing their share of the difficulties. The point fixed for their rendezvous with the Commanding Officer of the troops to be relieved, was supposed to be the Headquarters of the Brigade in the line. But on arriving at the spot indicated, not only were no headquarters found there, but no one even knew where they were located. Some confusion of this nature is almost inevitable during the rapid changes resulting from a substantial advance and heavy fighting. Nothing, however, could be done until sectors had been allotted to the incoming troops, with the result that very little time was available for reconnaissance.

The line eventually allotted to the 169th Infantry Brigade was on the ridge immediately to the west of the Préseau-Valenciennes road, with its right a few hundred yards northwest of the Château de Préseau in touch with troops of the 11th Division, and its left in touch with the 168th Infantry Brigade, at the cross-roads about a mile east of Aulnoy. The relieving troops were ordered to take over as follows: The 2nd Londons on the right, relieving the right of the 7th West Riding Regiment (49th Division), and a portion of the front held by the battalion on their right; the Queen's Westminsters, in the centre, taking over the centre of the 7th West Riding Regiment, with the Kensingtons on their left. The Commanding Officers of the three battalions assembled at the Headquarters of the 7th West Riding Regiment (a cellar measuring about 7 feet by 8 feet), where details about guides and the relief in general were arranged.

Meanwhile the Queen's Westminsters were on the move from Maing to Caumont Farm, where guides were to meet them at 7.0 p.m. The Battalion arrived at the appointed hour but there was no sign of a guide until about 9.0 p.m. The two hours' interval was spent in unloading the Lewis guns and fighting kit, and in issuing the Battalion ammunition and the next day's rations. It seemed, during the last year of the war, to be the Battalion's fate to be issued with rabbits when engaged in active operations. Rabbits were the ration at Gavrelle on March 28th, on the advance to the Bullecourt operations in August, and again on November 3rd, 1918. For the latter date the issue was particularly unfortunate, as the cooks had been on the march all day, and there was barely time to skin the rabbits, let alone cook them ; in the end they had to be issued to the men nearly raw !

When the guides did arrive, they were not very encouraging. All of them were exhausted, and inasmuch as they had only been over the country once and then only in the ranks of their battalion, they had somewhat vague ideas of the routes. The guides for the support and reserve companies were the more confident, and they managed to get their companies into position; but those for the forward companies said frankly that they had not the vaguest idea how they had come back from the front line, or how to get there again. The company commanders preferred to find their way to the front line by compass rather than trust to a bad guide. The Battalion Headquarters personnel were led in a complete circle by their guide, and at the end of two hours' wandering found themselves back again at Caumont Farm, whence they had started. Eventually at 1.0 a.m. on November 3rd, the relief was successfully completed. The Battalion (B Company on the right, D on the left) was now holding the sunken Préseau-Marly road south-west of Saultain. C Company was in support in a sunken road about 800 yards in rear, with A Company in reserve, in a bank by the Rhonelle River, some 1,200 yards further back. Battalion Headquarters were in L'Ancien Moulin on the same river, and shared three mattresses in a minute cellar with the 2nd London Headquarters Officers, two gunner officers, and four civilians (one man, two boys, and a girl).

Marly, a suburb of Valenciennes, was held by the Canadians who were gradually encircling the city.

All was ready for the advance, but many officers were on leave during what proved to be the final week of the war. The expected long stay at Haute Avesnes had been thought to be a good time for as many as possible to get their leave over before the start of what was hoped would be the final "push"; but this had come much sooner than had been expected, with the result that the Queen's Westminsters found themselves without their regular second-in-command, adjutant, quartermaster, and intelligence officer, and with only one company commander. Their deputies, however, made good use of their opportunities, and carried on in their place with complete success. The officers who took part in the operations were: Commanding Officer, Lieut.-Colonel S. R. Savill, D.S.O., M.C.; A/2nd-in-Command, Captain J. B. Baber, M.C.; A/Adjutant, Lieutenant W. H. Gatfield, M.C.; Transport Officer, Captain B. L. Miles; A/Quartermaster, 2nd Lieutenant J. A. N. Webb, M.C.; A Company, Lieutenant V. G. Rayner, M.C. (commanding); Lieutenant I. P. Mcewan; B Company, Lieutenant J. B. Malthouse, M.C. (commanding); Lieutenant E. Coaker and 2nd Lieutenant P. I. Worthington; C Company, Lieutenant O. A. M. Eaton, M.C. (commanding); 2nd Lieutenant S. F. Simonds; D Company, Captain F. E. Whitby, M.C. (commanding); 2nd Lieutenants F. H. B. Moore and H. R. Smith, M.C.

The original intention had been for the 56th Division to carry out an attack on the 4th November, in conjunction with the 11th Division on its right, and the 4th Canadian Division on its left, the final objectives being given as the Aunelle River and the high ground beyond it. Brigade Orders for the attack arrived at Battalion Headquarters before dawn on November 3rd, and several hours were spent in preparing Battalion orders for the operations. These, however, were destined for the waste-paper " sandbag," for the enemy did not wait to be attacked.

The Battalion spent an unpleasant night after the relief; rain fell in torrents, the sunken roads speedily resembled small rivers, and there was a fair amount of long-range shelling. The men had been on the move for over twenty hours, and it was rather unfortunate that, with the strenuous days in front of them, they were not able to get any real rest. But the events which followed soon made everyone forget his discomforts.

At 9 a.m., November 4th, a sentry of the 2nd Londons noticed a mounted German ride up to a hedge and hand a piece of paper to someone on the ground. The recipient appeared to return an envelope to the messenger, who rode off, and in a few moments men carrying a machine gun began to leave the hedge. The officers in the front line immediately sent out patrols to investigate, and a patrol from D Company, under Sergeant Law, was sent by Captain F. E. Whitby to Saultain.

Reports were sent back, and the Commanding Officer and Second-in-Command at once went forward to the front line, with a party of runners and signallers. A visual signal station was established to link up with L'Ancien Moulin, where the Acting-Adjutant was in touch with Brigade Headquarters by telephone. Colonel Savill fortunately met the officer commanding the Kensingtons, in the front line, and it was decided that the two battalions and the 2nd Londons should advance on the frontages already allotted to them for the attack which had been planned for the next day, as far as the first objective. Here they were to check again, and get into touch with each other. This was signalled back and all the companies advanced on a one-company frontage, D leading, followed by B, C and A.

In the meantime the Division, having been informed that the enemy had already withdrawn on the front of the 4th Canadian Division on the left, had issued orders that the 168th and 169th Infantry Brigades were to push forward strong patrols to make good the ridge between Curgies and Estreux, from the cemetery to the Ferme du Moulin, and then to press forward to the " Red Line " which was on the high ground running north-east from Curgies. These orders had, therefore, been anticipated by the subordinate commanders on the spot.

Sergeant Law's patrol reached Saultain unopposed, and great was their astonishment, as they moved down the main street in patrol formation, to see doors and windows flung open and to be greeted, not by the harried but ferocious enemy, but by the civilian population. The latter were hysterical with joy at the arrival of British troops so close on the heels of the enemy who, they said, had gone half an hour earlier. The women seized the N.C.O.'s rifle, kissed him and any soldier they could, and pressed on them luxuries they could ill afford in the form of coffee and cakes which had been supplied by the American Relief Fund. French and Belgian flags were produced in a most miraculous fashion, and the town was soon wild with excitement, no one paying any attention to the German " heavies " which now commenced to fall among the houses. One old lady, whose property caught fire and burned for hours, refused to accept any commiseration, saying it was nothing if she lost everything as long as she lost the Bosches as well. The excitement was contagious, and the men were eager to push on. But, shortly before noon, Brigade orders arrived that Saultain was to be handed over to the 2nd Londons, who were to advance on the whole Brigade front, and that the Queen's Westminsters were to assemble south-west of the town in their support, pending further instructions.

The 2nd Londons met with very little opposition until they reached the " Red Line " about 6.0 p.m. Here further progress was stopped by hostile machine-gun fire. Touch was obtained on both flanks and the line was consolidated for the night.

Colonel Savill had been directed in the morning to return to Battalion Headquarters to receive, on the telephone, the Brigadier's orders for the next day. These orders came at 4.30 p.m. By them, the Queen's Westminsters were ordered to move forward to the ridge about 400 yards east of Saultain, which had been occupied by the 2nd Londons, whilst the latter were continuing their advance to the " Red Line." By the time that the necessary orders had been conveyed to the Battalion, it was dark and the relief had to be conducted without guides in a strange area. As the companies moved forward the shelling became intense, and remained so on their new stations throughout the night. Sleep for a second night was again impossible, but fortunately there were only one or two casualties, although the shelling was both heavy and accurate. Battalion Headquarters were established in Saultain.

The XXII Corps decided to resume the advance at 6.0 a.m. on the following morning (November 4th), covered by mounted troops who were to move forward half an hour earlier so as to secure the crossings of the Aunelle River. The infantry divisions were to operate independently of each other, the Bavai-Hensies road, about seven miles distant, being given as the final objective.

Brigade orders for this attack arrived at Battalion Headquarters at midnight. The Queen's Westminsters, supported by the L.R.B., were ordered to pass through the 2nd Londons, the latter Battalion then becoming the Brigade reserve. The attack was arranged in the expectation that the enemy would continue his retirement on the approach of the British troops ; and the immediate rôle of the Queen's Westminsters was to advance immediately in rear of the squadron of cavalry which formed the protecting screen, and to support them instantly when necessary. No artillery barrage was arranged, as the position taken up by the enemy after leaving Saultain was unknown, but a battery of R.H.A. was to be attached to the Battalion, and it was to be placed under the order of the Commanding Officer. One Company of machine guns, and R.E. and pioneers for bridging were also to be attached.

The Battalion orders provided that the advance was to be made on a two-company frontage ; A and C Companies leading, with D and B Companies, respectively, in support. The companies were to advance in diamond formation of platoons, so that one platoon, from each of the leading companies, formed the spear-head, as it were, of the advance. These orders were delivered personally to the Company Commanders at Battalion Headquarters, and specific instructions were given, by the Commanding Officer, that the leading companies were to commence their advance at zero hour (6.0 a.m.) even if the cavalry had not then come up. Time was short, but the Company Commanders managed to give hurried orders to their men, and the Battalion was assembled ready to move off by zero hour.

For some reason or other, probably owing to the long march up to the front, the other troops on the Brigade frontage had not arrived by 6.0 a.m., and the Queen's Westminster Rifles had to advance alone, in co-operation with troops of the 11th Division on the right and of the 168th Infantry Brigade on the left. The cavalry squadron, which was to have preceded the Battalion, arrived shortly after zero, but by that time the leading companies had come under distant machine-gun fire, and the cavalry had to dismount before they could overtake the infantry. Mounted troops took no further part in the operations on the front of the Queen's Westminsters, and, to this extent, the statement in the War Diary of the 56th Division, that "the advance of the 169th Infantry Brigade was preceded by cavalry," is incorrect. The guns and machine guns attached to the Battalion reported to the Commanding Officer shortly after zero, but could not get up for several hours owing to transport congestion on the roads. This delay, however, probably had little or no influence on the day's operations, as no favourable targets presented themselves during the early stages of the advance.

The Battalion advanced into Sebourg under long-range machine-gun fire and intermittent shelling, but with slight loss. Sebourg, a big village, was quite undamaged by shell-fire when the Queen's Westminsters entered it. A number of Germans still remained there, but they did not show much fight, and they were mostly hiding until a favourable opportunity arose for their surrender. As at Sauchy Cauchy the Battalion was too weak to do its own "mopping up," and this was left to the L.R.B. in support. The civilians in Sebourg were as enthusiastic as those at Saultain. The platoons all received a very hearty welcome, one officer having a rosette, with appropriate wording, pinned on to his tunic. The usual offers of coffee had perforce to be refused, as the troops pressed through the village.

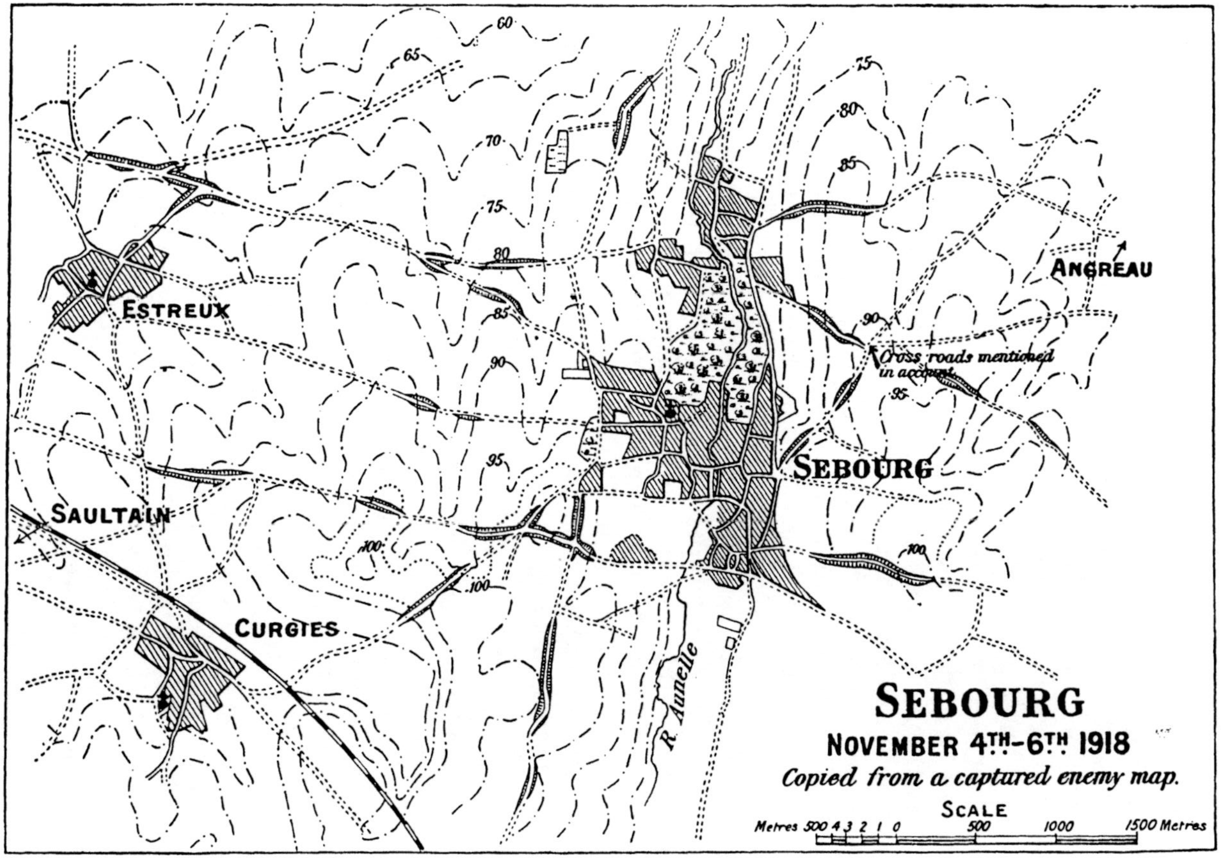
SEBOURG
NOVEMBER 4TH-6TH 1918
Copied from a captured enemy map.
SCALE
Metres 500 4 3 2 1 0 500 1000 1500 Metres
ANGREAU
Cross roads mentioned in account
SEBOURG
ESTREUX
SAULTAIN
CURGIES
R. Aunelle
60
65
70
75
80
85
90
95
100

The streets of Sebourg did not run parallel with the line of advance, and considerable difficulty was experienced by the various parties in keeping formation and direction. Lateral communication was almost impossible. The bridges over the Aunelle River had been mined, but, by great good fortune, the mines had not been detonated, and the Battalion was able to effect the actual crossing of the river without much difficulty. As the rear platoons passed through the village, the enemy barrage fell heavily on it, and steadily increased in density.

At 9.15 a.m. Sebourg was reported clear of the enemy. Up to this time the casualties had been slight, and an estimated number of 50 prisoners had been sent to the rear by the Battalion. The escort, however, was killed, and the prisoners were eventually collected by other units.

The real troubles of the Battalion began when the advance was made on the first objective, a ridge running north and south about 700 yards to the east of Sebourg. The disorganisation caused by traversing the village was intensified by the crossing of the river, and reorganisation, before a further advance, was rendered impossible by violent machine-gun fire from the ridge, particularly from a knoll shown on the map by the 100-metre contour, just beyond the right boundary of the Battalion. In face of this fire delay was out of the question, and a hurried assault was made on the ridge, which was rushed and captured by C Company on the right and A Company on the left. The little platoons, of an average strength of only twelve men, had been quite unable to search the ground on a broad front between the village and the ridge, and the captured position proved a veritable death-trap. Machine guns sprang up from nowhere, and the troops were subjected to an annihilating fire at point-blank range from their front, their rear, and their right flank. The Lewis-gunners, exhausted as they were by a long advance with their heavy loads, strove with the utmost gallantry to keep down the enemy's fire, but their efforts were unavailing. No fresh troops had succeeded in reaching the ridge, and neither flank of the Queen's Westminsters was in touch with the adjoining units.

Casualties mounted up very rapidly, and both flanks were forced back on to the two sunken roads, leading from the northern and southern ends of Sebourg, which met at the cross-roads somewhat on the right of the Battalion's front. The result was that, instead of holding a more or less straight line along the crest of the ridge, the Battalion was on its western slope and holding two sides of a triangle. The steep banks of the roads were manned, and the Lewis-gunners continued to act with the greatest devotion. To show their heads above the top of the banks was to court instant death, but they carried on undaunted. The number of empty magazines and damaged guns and dead men found on the road the next day, was a glorious testimony to the valour of their resistance.

The enemy made an unexpectedly stubborn stand, and fought with great courage. Under cover of machine guns a party of them seized the cross-roads forming the apex of the triangle held by the Queen's Westminsters, whence they directed a devastating enfilade fire on the men lining the banks. The enemy attempted to rush the roads, but they were stopped after a brisk fight in the course of which Sergeant Gillett, D.C.M. (the acting C.S.M. of A Company), was hit by a revolver shot. A few minutes later Sergeant Stinchcombe was killed by rifle fire at point-blank range, whilst gallantly leading a counter-charge. 2nd Lieutenant F. H. B. Moore (D Company) then tried to bring up reinforcements and he, too, was killed charging with his men. Slowly the enemy succeeded in widening the gap in the centre. The left companies were pressed back nearly as far as the houses on the outskirts of Sebourg, and the right companies to within three hundred yards of the village. Here they held their ground, throwing out semicircular screens of skirmishers astride the two roads. In the meantime the L.R.B., some of whose companies had been placed at the disposal of the Battalion, had pushed their way through the village under furious shell-fire, and, closely supporting the Queen's Westminster Rifles, had reinforced the men in the sunken roads. They also lined another road along the eastern boundary of the village which formed the base of the triangle of roads.

It was now late in the afternoon. Intercommunication and reorganisation were both practically impossible owing to the intensity of the artillery and machine-gun fire, and all that could be done was to hold the position and keep the enemy in check. The L.R.B., however, had established touch with the Brigade of the 11th Division on the right. This Division had gained the high ground to the south-east of Sebourg, and in the afternoon, word was passed down that it was being counter-attacked and further that the enemy appeared to be massing for a counter-attack along his whole front. But, although the shelling increased in intensity on the front of the Queen's Westminsters, no counter-attack developed, and the position was maintained until nightfall. The Queen's Westminsters were then relieved by the L.R.B., and withdrew to a field to the west of Sebourg. Here they reorganised and called the roll.

On the credit side of the day could be counted an advance of two miles, some forty to fifty prisoners, and the capture of Sebourg, but the losses were very heavy in proportion to the small fighting strength of the Battalion. One officer (2nd Lieut. F. H. B. Moore) and 20 other ranks were killed, and 52 other ranks were wounded. By a sad coincidence, amongst the killed were the five other ranks who had been elected to serve on a Committee organised only three days previously by the Reverend K. N. Crisford (the Padre), to assist him as company representatives. One of them, Corporal Groom, had behaved with the very greatest gallantry. On two occasions, on the second of which he was killed, he rescued wounded men under conditions which seemed to invite certain death. Lieut.-Colonel S. R. Savill gives the following account of his heroism : " During the fighting in the sunken roads, in front of Sebourg, a wounded man was heard calling in the field in front. This man had tried to crawl back to the road, but was unable to do so. In spite of the many machine guns which opened at once on any individual movement, Corporal Groom walked out and carried the man in. Later, when our troops were forced to withdraw down the road, another man was hit. The only possible way to withdraw appeared to be by crawling down the ditch, and again machine guns were firing directly down the road. Corporal Groom picked up the man and carried him on his back. To do this he had to walk upright down the centre of the road. As was inevitable, Corporal Groom was killed before he could get his comrade to cover, but the man for whom he gave his life was saved."

At the end of the day's attack, the enemy, on the front of the 56th Division, were holding the high ground to the east of the Aunelle River in force ; on the right, the 11th Division had been driven by a counter-attack off the high ground which they had captured, and pushed back to the eastern outskirts of Sebourg. On the left, the 4th Canadian Division was held up outside the village of Rombies, thus exposing the left flank of the 56th Division to heavy enfilade fire. The 56th Division War Diary sums up the general situation as follows : " It was apparent that no further progress could be made without an organised attack in co-operation with the Divisions on either flank."

This attack was ordered to begin at 5.30 a.m. on November 5th.

The task of the 169th Infantry Brigade was to capture the

high ground midway between Sebourg and Angreau, and to establish an outpost line along the line of the sunken road west of Angreau. The L.R.B. were to lead the attack, with the Queen's Westminsters in close support to them, and the latter were to carry the attack forward, if necessary.

The Battalion was reorganised and rations and ammunition were issued, while the Company Commanders were receiving their orders at Battalion Headquarters. As soon as the orders had been explained to the men it was time to move off, and the third successive night brought no rest for weary troops.

The enemy, however, had retired during the night, and the L.R.B., meeting with little opposition, west of Angreau, were ordered to push on to the railway east of the Bois de Beaufort. By 7.30 a.m. they were across the Angreau River and had established a bridgehead to the east of it. The situation at that time is recorded in the War Diary of the 169th Infantry Brigade in the following terms: " Enemy machine guns and snipers very active from the wooded ground east of the river. Northern part of Angreau under heavy and close machine-gun and rifle fire from Angreau and from the area immediately south of it. Heavy artillery fire on Angreau. The 168th Infantry Brigade well back on our left flank. L.R.B. displayed great energy in getting their light trench mortars and machine guns into action, and succeeded in improving our position in the north of Angreau, dealing with considerable opposition."

At 11.0 a.m. the L.R.B. were ordered to halt on a line east of Angreau, until further orders reached them. In the meantime the Queen's Westminsters had moved forward to the sunken roads, to the west of Angreau, ready to support the L.R.B., if required. The enemy's shelling made it impossible to remain on the roads, and the men lay out all day in the open fields in a steady downpour of rain. It was here that Lieutenant H. R. Smith was killed. The Battalion suffered its last officer casualty during the war under rather tragic circumstances. Lieutenant Smith had taken a patrol to secure touch between the L.R.B. and the 168th Infantry Brigade, and, having accomplished a dangerous mission with great skill, he had returned to Battalion Headquarters to report on the result. There he was told, by the Commanding Officer, that he had been awarded a Military Cross for his good work at Sauchy Cauchy. He then returned to his company in the sunken road, but had barely reached them when he was hit by a shell, both legs being so badly shattered that he died on arrival at the Field Ambulance. He had done much splendid work, and it must be some consolation to his relatives to know that he met his death amongst the men with whom he had fought so well, and with the knowledge that his services had met with the recognition that they justly merited.

The Queen's Westminsters remained in the neighbourhood of the sunken roads through the night of November 5th. The conditions were again appalling, the men being wet through to the skin, but they were cheered by the good news contained in every " intelligence summary," and the thought that a victorious end to the war was rapidly and really approaching. The Brigade had now advanced $6\frac{1}{2}$ miles in three days, and had crossed the Belgian frontier between Sebourg and Angreau. From every Army came reports of similar advances, of the capture of villages, prisoners, guns and booty, of the steady decline of the enemy's moral, and also of the frantic joy of the liberated civilians. This joy was in striking contrast to the hatred they showed for their former conquerors. Of this, the following picture recorded by Colonel Savill is a poignant example : " At a cross-roads near the transport lines at Saultain an old man sat, day and night, watching the stream of German prisoners. He carried a murderous-looking knife and scanned the face of every prisoner as he passed, looking for the German officer who had been billeted in his house. What wrong he had suffered was not known, but the look on his face and his evident determination to seek revenge, indicated that it was a serious one."

The attack on the front of the 169th Infantry Brigade was continued at 5.30 a.m. on November 6th, by the L.R.B. and the 2nd Londons, with the Queen's Westminster Rifles in support. The 168th Infantry Brigade on the left and the 11th Division on the right attacked simultaneously. The objective was Montignies.

The two leading battalions crossed the Grande Honnelle River shortly after zero, and, after overcoming very considerable enemy opposition on the east bank, the L.R.B. and a number of the 2nd Londons succeeded in reaching the sunken road on the north-eastern edge of the Bois de Beaufort. This was the first objective. The enemy, however, rallied rapidly, and by a heavy counter-attack, drove the attackers back to their original jumping-off line. Both battalions suffered heavily, but it was reported that their Lewis-gunners had been offered excellent targets during the counter-attack, and had made good use of their opportunities.

The Queen's Westminsters had moved up into Angreau,

but, when it was decided not to press the attack, A and D Companies were withdrawn to their previous position west of the village, B and C Companies remaining forward. At the close of the day the 56th Division held Angreau and Angre, and the west bank of the Grande Honnelle River at Angre. During the evening, the 168th Infantry Brigade crossed the river, and, without meeting any opposition, established itself on the high ground to the east. The 169th Infantry Brigade was now withdrawn from the line.

The attack was taken up on November 7th, by the 167th Infantry Brigade, with the 11th and 63rd Divisions co-operating on the flanks. Montignies was captured, and at the end of the day the line ran along the Bavai-Hensies road, east of Autreppe, the western outskirts of the Bois de Rampemont, and east of Montignies.

From now onwards there was a rapid and practically unopposed advance. Owing to the destruction of bridges and other communications, and the resulting difficulty in forwarding supplies for the pursuing troops, the 169th Infantry Brigade did not advance further than Angreau. The advance of the 167th Infantry Brigade was practically unopposed. By nightfall on November 9th, the 167th Infantry Brigade had reached the line of the Mons-Maubeuge road, and on the following day patrols entered Harmignies.

On November 11th the Armistice was signed.

The experiences of the Queen's Westminsters, after being withdrawn from the fight, are best told in Colonel Savill's own words, written shortly after the Armistice :—

" That evening (November 6th) the 167th Infantry Brigade took over the front, and the Queen's Westminster Rifles withdrew to Sebourg for a well-earned sleep. So ended what is hoped is the last battle for the Queen's Westminster Rifles in the war of 1914-18. The Peace is not yet signed, but the hope does not seem unduly optimistic. The Battalion came out of its last battle, as it went into its first, with ' it's tail up.'

" The civilians in the village were delighted to be able to offer hospitality to the Q.W.R., the first troops to enter the village three days before, and thus the first British troops they had seen since August 24th, 1914.[1] Fires were made in the yards of billets next morning for the men to dry their saturated clothing, and the usual reorganisation and over-

[1] The 4th Cavalry Brigade were at Sebourg from 4.0 a.m. until 1 p.m. on August 24th, 1914.

THE FINAL ADVANCE

2 NOVEMBER — 11 NOVEMBER 1918

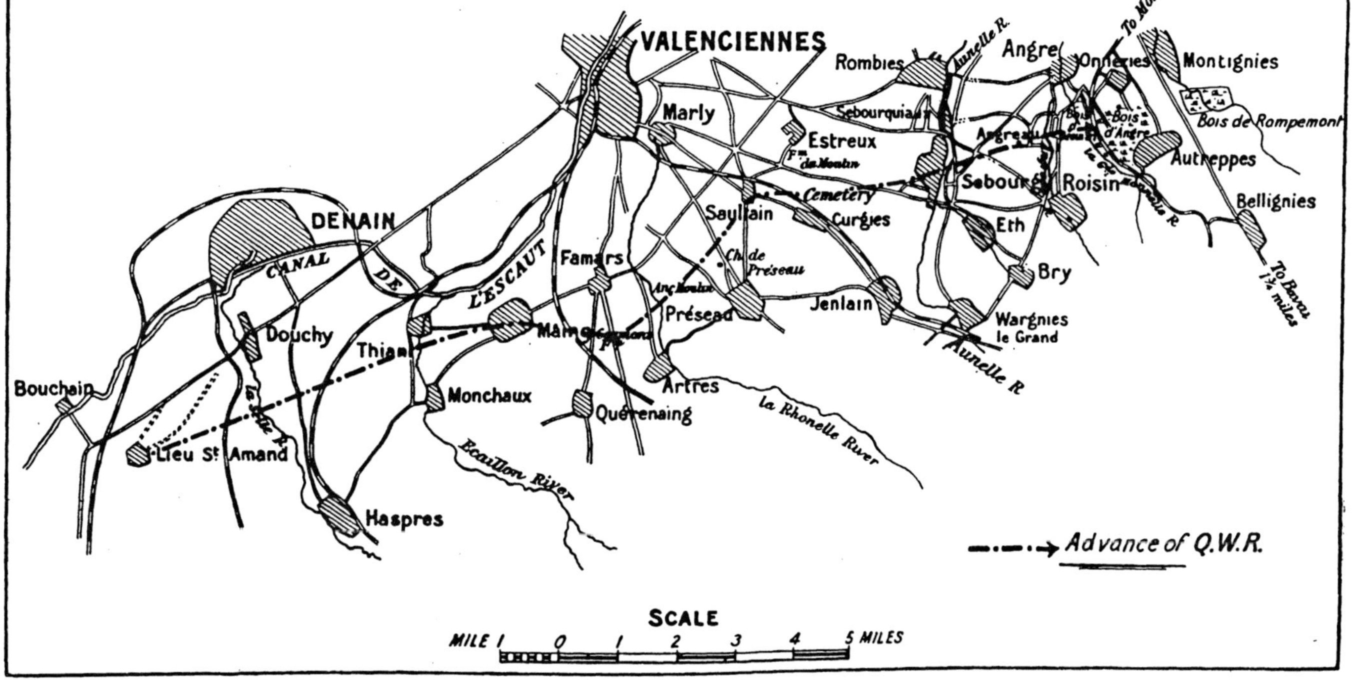

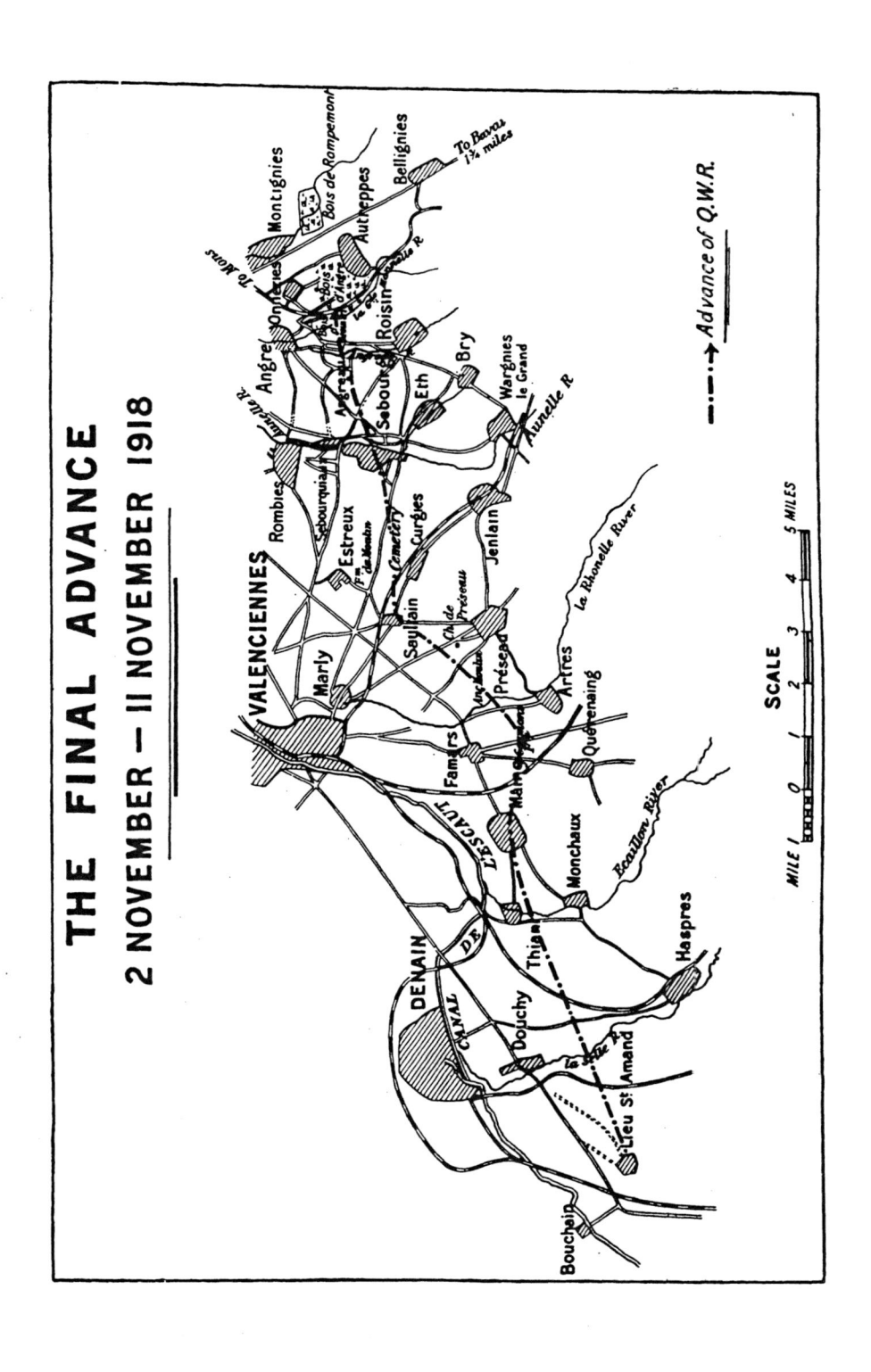

haul of kit were taken in hand. The Brigadier came round to Battalion Headquarters bringing the news that the enemy was retiring rapidly, that the 167th Infantry Brigade could barely keep touch with him, that the whole line was advancing, and that it was thought that Germany would soon crave an armistice. The next day the Battalion advanced to Angreau, with instructions that it would move forward again on the following day. The move on November 9th, however, did not take place, as the Brigade, although now a long way in rear of the 167th Infantry Brigade, could not be fed if it advanced further. The enemy had destroyed every bridge in a land intersected by numerous rivers, and blown in every possible cross-road. Trains could not run at all, and lorries only in small numbers and with the greatest difficulty.

" The Divisional Commander came to see the Battalion, and he told us that the German delegates had come through the lines further south, and that they had been given until 11.0 a.m. on the 11th of the month to accept the Allies' conditions for an armistice. He added that the fighting still continued and the 167th Infantry Brigade was still pursuing the enemy.

" In view of the necessity of opening up the roads, all available men of the Battalion were sent off on working parties for that purpose. On November 9th, the Battalion moved to Athies where it was to stay until November 26th.

" On that memorable day, the 11th November, 1918, the whole Battalion[1] was engaged on road-clearing when the news came through that the Armistice was signed, and that to all intents and purposes the war was over. While everyone must have felt a great relief to think that the hardships of over four years were at an end, the glad news caused no demonstration; everybody appeared too tired to take it in anything but a philosophic manner.[2] The exuberance displayed in London was not imitated in Athies, but perhaps the relief felt was just as great.

" The billets in the village were very comfortable, the houses being absolutely undamaged, in fact one had to walk some way to find a shell hole. The civilians there seemed to have suffered less than many others under the German

---

[1] The total strength of the Battalion at the conclusion of hostilities was 25 officers and 493 other ranks.

[2] The entry in the Battalion War Diary is as follows : " Armistice signed at 11.00 hours. Complete lack of demonstration on the part of the men, who carried on just as though they were in rest billets. Inhabitants observed, in several instances, digging up money, clothes, etc., out of their gardens."

occupation. They still had cattle and fowls and a few horses, and many of their possessions, which had been buried in their gardens, were soon dug up by their owners.

"They were most hospitable, and it was no uncommon sight to see them helping the troops who were working on the roads. Their kindliness and generosity was reminiscent of the friendly feeling shown by the inhabitants of Houplines, in the early days of the war; a very different state of affairs from that to which the Battalion later became accustomed behind the British lines."

This concludes the story of the 1st Battalion Queen's Westminster Rifles during the period of hostilities. Only slight reference has been made in these pages to those who worked so untiringly behind the lines with the transport and in the Quartermaster's department. It is true that they escaped the discomforts of trench life, and much of the danger, but their work was indispensable. The Battalion owes them a debt of gratitude for all their unflagging zeal and devotion to duty, very often in most difficult circumstances. The men in the trenches never lacked anything that was humanly procurable, and everything possible was done for their comfort, both in and out of the line. Many looked upon the actual journey to and from the trenches as a more unpleasant experience than the average tour in the line; yet this journey had to be made every night, frequently along shell-swept roads, by those who brought up the rations, ammunition and stores of every description. The Transport invariably made it a point of honour to bring the rations and supplies as close up to the firing line as they possibly could, and in so doing they saved the carrying parties from the trench garrisons an immense amount of very fatiguing work.

During any period of active operations, and particularly during any advance, the work of keeping the troops supplied with necessaries was always a matter of considerable, and sometimes almost insurmountable, difficulty; but throughout the whole war the Quartermaster's department and the transport never once failed the fighting line. That in itself is sufficient tribute to their work.

Lieutenant-Colonel R. Shoolbred was a great lover of horses, and, during his period of command, always took great pride in the Regimental transport. His care for all the four-footed members of the Battalion was proverbial, and this tradition was maintained by those who succeeded him. The work of 2nd Lieutenant (afterwards Colonel) S. G. L. Bradley and, from September, 1915, to the end of the war, of Captain B. L. Miles, as transport officers, and of the N.C.O.'s and men who served under them, is worthy of all praise.

Of the work of the Quartermasters in France, both of Lieutenant (afterwards Captain) J. H. Kelly, and of Lieutenant (now Captain) E. W. N. Jackson, T.D., it would be difficult to write too appreciatively. Reference has already been made to Captain J. H. Kelly and his work as Adjutant of the 3rd (Reserve) Battalion[1] and the name of " Peter Jackson " is a household word amongst all Queen's Westminsters. The latter joined in 1887 as a rifleman, and ever since has devoted the greater part of his spare time for the good of the Regiment. At the outbreak of war he was Colour-Sergeant of the original C Company, and was promoted Battalion-Quartermaster-Sergeant shortly before the Battalion sailed for France.

In particular, the writer of this history owes him a great personal debt of gratitude for his help, in pre-war days, as colour-sergeant of the company which he (the writer) had the honour to command.

[1] Captain J. H. Kelly is now secretary of the Queen's Westminster Association.

CHAPTER XXI

PEACE

VERY little remains to be told. Soon after the Armistice was signed, the Battalion was warned that it was to take part in the general advance to the Rhine. The march was to commence on November 17th, and the work required to prepare for a triumphant entry into Germany, served as a complete antidote to the reaction which might naturally be expected to follow the sudden cessation of war. All ranks threw themselves heartily into the task of restoring the appearance of the 1st Battalion Queen's Westminster Rifles to that of a peace-time unit. Limbers, bicycles and steel helmets were all repainted, and large quantities of blanco and metal polish were ordered from England to smarten up the equipment.

Some disappointment was felt when the move of the Battalion towards Germany was cancelled, and orders were received that the rest of the winter was to be spent in Belgium; but as events turned out the Battalion had no cause to regret the change. The stay in Belgium was a thoroughly happy one in every way.

On November 15th, the First Army Commander (General Sir H. S. Horne) made his official entry into Mons, and the Battalion sent three officers and eighty other ranks to take part in an historic ceremony. The Battalion remained at Athies until November 26th, occupying the time with road-mending and football; it then moved to Bougnies, and arrived at Genly, outside Mons, on the 29th. It remained in this village until March 23rd, 1919.

Arrangements for the comfort of the troops were taken in hand at once, with the courteous assistance of the Mayor and the inhabitants; a sergeants' mess, canteens for the corporals and the men, and reading, writing, lecture and company dining-rooms were soon equipped, and a small theatre in the village was placed at the disposal of the Battalion.

The following account of the experiences of the Queen's Westminsters during the winter has been obtained from Colonel Savill. The stay at Genly lasted for four months, and, though everything was so unsettled, it was a happy time. No one knew exactly when they would be going home, and there were frequent changes in the individuals holding appointments. These changes were unsettling, but the Queen's Westminster Rifles managed to overcome their difficulties as usual. During this period the reduction to Cadre commenced by the demobilisation of men on leave and continued steadily all the time.

The amusements consisted of Rugby and Association football, dancing, visits from the " Bow Bells," "Capital C's" and the Divisional Band, and a number of lectures organised by the higher military authorities. Work consisted almost entirely of educational training, and the men were able to polish up their knowledge of various subjects such as book-keeping, French, Spanish or drawing, or to commence fresh studies. Unfortunately this scheme had to be discontinued after a month or two, owing to the demobilisation of all available instructors.

Great efforts were made to celebrate Christmas with full traditional rites and ceremonies, and they were very successful. Captain F. E. Whitby, M.C., arranged the decorations of all the regimental institutes, with materials procured from Mons and Etaples. Christmas Day started with a short service at 9 a.m., and at 1.0 p.m., in the dining-halls which were gay with holly and other decorations, the men sat down to a real old English Christmas dinner of roast turkey and sausages and plum pudding. The officers and sergeants acted as waiters, and washed up after the meal, the latter performance not being so successful as the former. The next item on the programme was a party given to the children of the village at 3.0 p.m. in the concert and dining-hall. Every child received a personal invitation, and the Mayor and twenty civilians gave willing help to make the afternoon a success. For over an hour games were played by the children and they were instructed in the rules of Blind Man's Buff and other games, by officers and men alike. A harlequinade, too, was an immensely popular feature of the entertainment. Tea was served to the children in the dining-hall, and then came the *pièce de résistance,* a huge Christmas-tree, loaded with presents and bright with many candles. The children gathered round it, and Corporal Gigly, disguised as Father Christmas, distributed the toys.

This happy scene was followed by the reading, by a little girl dressed in white, of the following address, which expressed in graceful and touching terms, the feeling of the civilians, who for four years had experienced the harsh tyranny of a barbarous invader:—

"Monsieur le Commandant,
    Messieurs les Officiers,
        Messieurs,

Au déclin de cette belle journée à jamais inoubliable pour la population de Genly, je serai certainement l'interprète de tous les habitants de la commune, et en particulier des enfants ici réunis, pour vous remercier de tout cœur de la bienveillante générosité, avec laquelle vous avez organisé en notre faveur, cette fête magnifique. Merci pour la gracieuse réception que vous nous avez réservée, merci pour les beaux objets que vous nous avez offerts. Nous y attachons le plus grand prix et nous les conserverons soigneusement dans la famille, comme un précieux souvenir de votre heureux passage à Genly.

  Messieurs,

Vous avez acquis tous les droits à la gratitude éternelle de la Nation Belge; vous avez largement contribué à delivrer notre chère patrie des troupes ennemies qui l'avaient injustement envahie. Votre glorieuse intervention restera gravée en lettres d'or dans les annales de la Belgique. Soyez remerciés à jamais pour cet insigne bienfait. Qu'en retour, la Providence daigne exaucer les vœux que nous formons pour le bonheur et la prosperité de la grande Nation Anglaise. Et à vous, Messieurs, reconnaissance inaltérable pour la joie que vous nous avez procurée en ce beau jour de fête.
    Vive la Nation Britannique! Vive l'Armée! Vive le Roi!"

In the absence of Lieut.-Colonel Savill, who was on leave, the address was suitably answered by the senior officer present (Major H. F. Grizelle, M.C.). The Christmas festivities closed with a "high tea" for the men, followed by a most successful dance in the evening to which all the village maidens were invited.

On Boxing Day, there was a Brigade League football match in which the Battalion defeated a team from Brigade Headquarters and the Trench Mortar Battery, and in the evening there was a most successful concert arranged by Lieutenants H. J. Simpson and T. H. Jenkins. From now onwards the Battalion dwindled steadily day by day. Life seemed a series of good-byes for those who were not yet going home. Every morning at 10.30 the mess cart collected, at the orderly room, the kits of the party going to the concentration camp, *en route* for dispersal and civilian clothes. Every day more well-known pillars of the Battalion, officers, N.C.O.'s and men, left for home, and by the end of March, 1919, the 1st Battalion Queen's Westminster Rifles was reduced to Cadre strength, having dispatched all retainable men and volunteers to the Army of Occupation.

We will leave the Cadre checking the stores and equipment, and waiting more or less patiently until they can take them to England and follow their comrades into " civilian life."

On March 23rd, 1919, the Cadre left Genly and moved to Quaregnon on the Condé Canal.

The following letters, published in Battalion Orders of March 25th, show that the 1st Battalion Queen's Westminster Rifles had succeeded in maintaining the traditions of the Regiment to the very end of its existence as a mobilised unit.

(1) From D.A.P.M., 56th Division, to H.Q., 56th Division:—
" The village of Genly, recently evacuated by the 1-16th London Regiment (Q.W.R.), was visited on the 23rd inst. by my police, for the purpose of recovering any articles of Government property left behind, and to execute perquisitions upon inhabitants in case of necessity. Billets were entered and the *Maire* was visited. In no case was there any article found, all billets were left scrupulously clean, the streets were all swept and left tidy. The *Maire* expressed his great satisfaction at the condition in which the villages had been left.

" The fact that in other villages large quantities of material have been recovered by the police, and the entire absence of any material in Genly, reflects the greatest credit upon the O.C., Q.W.R., and I wish to express my admiration of the manner in which this Battalion has done its work here."

(2) From B.G.C., 169th Infantry Brigade, to the Commanding Officer : " I note with great satisfaction, that the Q.W.R. are determined to maintain to the last the very high standard of smartness and discipline which this Battalion has always shown."

In publishing these two letters the Commanding Officer added : " The above reflects great credit on all concerned, and especially on the Quartermaster's Department, which has always carried out its duties with the greatest efficiency and energy."

On April 20th, Brigadier-General E. S. D'E. Coke, on relinquishing command of the 169th Infantry Brigade, wrote the following letter to Lieut.-Colonel S. R. Savill :—

" On leaving the Brigade, after having commanded it for over three years of such stirring times, I want to express to you my very high appreciation of your Battalion. The gallantry of London Territorials is well known, and the units of the 169th Infantry Brigade have more than maintained the standard. But no less admirable have been the discipline and conduct. The absence of crime, the thoughtful consideration for the inhabitants and the excellent spirit that has existed among all ranks have been most praiseworthy. . . . Good luck to you all."

The spirit of a commander is reflected in the conduct of those he commands. To General Coke the Queen's Westminsters offer their heartfelt thanks. His leadership, his care for the men who served under him, and his unfailing help in times of difficulty, inspired all ranks with confidence, and called forth the display of the very qualities of which he writes.

The Cadre arrived in London on June 2nd, 1919, and marched, with Lieut.-Colonel S. R. Savill at their head, to Regimental Headquarters. Many old friends were there to greet them, and wish them success on their return to civil life. Amongst the many letters received by the Commanding Officer was one from Watford, which was greatly appreciated. It ran as follows :—

" Council Office, 4th July, 1919.

Sir,—On behalf of the people of Watford, I beg to send you and your Battalion our hearty greetings and cordial good wishes.

Watford will never forget those glorious citizen soldiers of London, who came to us in 1914 and 1915. They have given us a memory which will remain with us as an inspiration for national and civic work for many years to come. We shall always remember both their coming and going. We hope that they, too, those who have returned, will not have forgotten us, who, to-day, are proud in their honour.

(Signed) FRED H. GOOLE,
Chairman of the Watford Urban District Council.

To the Officer Commanding,
 Queen's Westminster Rifles."

The 1st Battalion Queen's Westminster Rifles had completed their work in the war. With their brothers-in-arms, of the 2nd Battalion, they leave the good name of the Regiment in the safe keeping of their successors.

In 1921 the Queen's Westminster Rifles were amalgamated with the Prince of Wales's Own, Civil Service Rifles, and the Regiment is now known as "The Queen's Westminster and Civil Service Rifles."

This Regiment inherits and it will preserve the peacetime traditions of the two Territorial battalions which were in existence before mobilisation, and the fighting traditions of the four battalions which served overseas in the Great War. Amongst its most cherished possessions is the memory of its dead.

The names of the Queen's Westminsters who gave their lives are preserved in a Roll of Honour, written by Mr. E. Graily Hewitt. This Roll is kept at the Regimental Headquarters, and will form part of a memorial which is being erected in the Drill Hall.

Two other memorials of their fallen have been dedicated by the Queen's Westminster Rifles. One, a window in the Parish Church at Leverstock Green; the other, a window in Westminster Abbey. The latter bears the inscription :—

> "To the Glory of God and in memory of the Officers, Non-commissioned Officers and Private Riflemen of the Queen's Westminster Rifles, who died in the War, 1914-1918. Honour all men, Love the Brotherhood, Fear God, Honour the King."

ITINERARY

1st BATTALION QUEEN'S WESTMINSTER RIFLES

AUGUST 4TH, 1914, TO JUNE 2ND, 1919

Italics denote that the Battalion was actually engaged in active operations, or was in their immediate vicinity.
The words trenches or sector indicate (except where otherwise shown) that the Battalion was in the front line.

IN ENGLAND

1914. August 4th to November 1st, 1914.

August	4th	Mobilisation. Battalion H.Q., 58, Buckingham Gate.	2nd London Division.
,,	14th	Leverstock Green.	4th Infantry
November	1st	Embark Southampton.	Brigade.

IN FRANCE

November 2nd, 1914, to June 2nd, 1919.

November	3rd	Land at Havre.	B.E.F.
,,	6th	St. Omer.	Army Troops.
,,	10th	Hazebrouck.	
,,	11th	Bailleul.	
,,	12th	Erquinghem.	

ARMENTIÈRES.

November	17th	Gris Pot.	III Corps,
,,	18th	"A" company in front line.	6th Division. 18th Infantry
,,	24th	Battalion in front line south of Rue du Bois.	Brigade.
December	5th	L'Armée.	
,,	9th	Trenches facing Wez Macquart.	
,,	19th	Chapelle d'Armentières.	
,,	23rd	Chapelle d'Armentières Sector.	

HOUPLINES.

1914.	December	26th	Houplines
1915.	January	1st	Houplines Sector.
	May	28th	Bailleul.

Second Army,
III Corps,
6th Division,
18th Infantry
Brigade.

YPRES SALIENT.

[Front line trenches :—East of Potijze.
Support and Reserve positions :—Potijze, St. Jean, Ypres, Canal Bank, Brielen.
Divisional Reserve, etc. :—Poperinghe.]

1915.			
May	30th	Wippenhoek.	
,,	31st	Potijze.	
June	4th	Potijze Sector.	
,,	8th	Ypres.	
,,	16*th*	*First attack on Bellewaarde. (In support trenches north of Ypres-Roulers Railway.)*	
,,	18th	Poperinghe.	
,,	25th	Potijze Sector.	
July	3rd	Support trenches.	
,,	11th	Poperinghe.	
,,	19th	Potijze Sector.	
,,	26th	Ypres.	
August	2nd	Poperinghe.	
,,	9*th*	*Action of Hooge.*	
,,	10th	Poperinghe.	
,,	23rd	Canal Bank, Potijze and St. Jean.	
September	2nd	Potijze Sector.	
,,	9th	Poperinghe.	
,,	16th	Brielen.	
,,	21st	Kaaie Salient.	
,,	27th	Potijze Sector.	
October	4th	Poperinghe.	
,,	11th	Potijze and St. Jean.	
,,	17th	Canal Bank.	
,,	20th	Potijze Sector.	
,,	23rd	Poperinghe.	
,,	29th	Potijze Sector.	
November	11th	Poperinghe.	
,,	16th	Potijze Sector.	
,,	18th	Poperinghe.	
,,	19th	Houtkerque.	
December	9th	Potijze.	
,,	14th	Potijze Sector.[1]	
,,	19*th*	*German gas attack.*	

[1] From December 14th, 1915, to February 1st, 1916, the Battalion was continuously responsible for part of the Potijze sector. The Battalion found its own reliefs and the companies were located in the front line, and at Potijze, on the Canal Bank at Poperinghe.

ITINERARY, 1916

PREPARING FOR THE OFFENSIVE.

1916.	February	10th	Huppy.	Third Army,
	March	12th	Gezaincourt.	VI Corps,
	May	7th	Halloy.	56th Division,
	June	3rd	Bayencourt.	169th Infantry
	,,	5th ⎫	Dig new Front Line east of	Brigade.
	,,	6th ⎭	Hébuterne.	VII Corps
	,,	9th	Trenches east of Hébuterne.	(May 7th).
	,,	16th	Bayencourt.	
	,,	21st	Halloy.	
	,,	27th	St. Amand.	

THE BATTLES OF THE SOMME, 1916. (1ST JULY TO 18TH NOVEMBER.)

July	1st	Attack on the Gommecourt Salient.	
,,	2nd	Bayencourt.	
,,	3rd	St. Amand.	
,,	6th	Fonquevillers - Bienvillers Sector.	
,,	13th	Raid.	
,,	22nd	St. Amand.	
August	7th	Bienvillers.	
,,	15th	Fonquevillers - Bienvillers Sector.	
,,	20th	Sus St. Leger.	
,,	22nd	Villers l'Hôpital.	
,,	23rd	Domvast.	
September	3rd	Corbie.	Fourth Army,
,,	4th	*Happy Valley (north-west of Bray).*	XIV Corps.
,,	6th	*Maricourt.*	
,,	7th	*Favières Wood.*	
,,	9th	*Leuze Wood.*	
,,	11th	*Citadel (near Bray).*	
,,	13th	*Hardecourt.*	
,,	15th	*Falfemont Farm and Angle Wood Valley.*	
,,	18th	*Leuze Wood.*	
,,	19th	*Angle Wood Valley.*	
,,	20th	*Leuze Wood.*	
,,	23rd	*Falfemont Farm.*	
,,	24th	*Maricourt.*	
,,	26th	*Méaulte.*	
,,	30th	*Lesbœufs (Front Line).*	
October	3rd	*Citadel (near Bray).*	
,,	7th	*Trones Wood.*	
,,	8th	*Lesbœufs (Front Line).*	
,,	10th	*Trones Wood.*	

NEUVE CHAPELLE.

1916.	October	11th	La Chaussée sur Somme.	X Corps.
	,,	21st	Huppy.	
	,,	23rd	Berguette.	First Army,
	,,	24th	Calonne sur la Lys.	XI Corps.
	,,	27th	Lestrem.	
	,,	29th	Bout de Ville.	
	November	3rd	Neuve Chapelle Sector.	
	,,	10th	Croix Barbée.	
	,,	15th	Neuve Chapelle Sector.	
	,,	22nd	Pont du Hem.	
	,,	27th	Robermetz.	
	December	9th	Pont du Hem.	
	,,	15th	Neuve Chapelle Sector.	
	,,	21st	Pont du Hem.	
	,,	27th	Neuve Chapelle Sector.	
1917.	January	3rd	Bout de Ville.	

LAVENTIE.

	January	13*th*	*Posts* (in Fauquissart Sector.)
	,,	14th	Fauquissart Sector and *Posts*.
	,,	20th	Laventie.
	,,	26th	Fauquissart Sector and *Posts*.
	February	1st	Laventie.
	,,	7th	Fauquissart Sector.
	,,	14th	Laventie.
	,,	20th	Fauquissart Sector.
	,,	25th	Laventie.

THE MOVE TO THE ARRAS FRONT.

March 1st, Laventie; (2nd), Bout de Ville; (3rd), Cornet Malo; (4th), Floringhen; Third Army, (5th), Œuf; (6th), Lez Quesnoy; (7th), VII Corps Simencourt. (Distance marched: 100 (March 7th.) miles.)

THE GERMAN RETREAT TO THE HINDENBURG LINE.

(14th March–5th April, 1917.)

	March	14th	Achicourt.
	,,	18*th*	*Beaurains.*
	,,	19*th*	*Preussen Weg Sector.* (Beaurains - Neuville Vitasse Road.)

ITINERARY, 1917

1917.	March	25th	Support trenches north-east of Beaurains.	
	,,	30th	Preussen Weg Sector.	
	April	1st	Monchiet.	

BATTLES OF ARRAS, 1917.
(9th April to 4th May.)

	April	7th	Achicourt.	
	,,	8th	Achicourt and Beaurains.	
	,,	11th	Cojeul Switch Line.	
	,,	12th	Wancourt Line.	
	,,	13th	Wancourt Tower Ridge.	
	,,	14th	Attack Cherisy.	
	,,	15th	Beaurains.	
	,,	20th	St. Amand.	
	,,	24th	Wanquetin.	
	,,	26th	Berneville.	Third Army,
	,,	28th	Telegraph Hill.	VI Corps.
	,,	29th	Guémappe - Wancourt Area.	
	May	1st	Wancourt Line.	
	,,	3rd	Front Line facing Cavalry Farm.	
	,,	6th	Wancourt Line (Reserve).	
	,,	8th	Front Line.	
	,,	11th	Tilloy.	

THE DIVISION AT REST.

	May	19th	Duisans.	
	,,	24th	Agnez les Duisans.	
	June	8th	Telegraph Hill.	
	,,	9th	Front Line north of Cherisy.	
	,,	21st	Achicourt.	
	July	2nd	Gouy en Artois.	VII Corps.
	,,	3rd	Sus St. Leger.	
	,,	24th	La Commune (north of St. Omer).	Fifth Army, V Corps.
	August	6th	Wippenhoek.	II Corps.

BATTLES OF YPRES, 1917.
(31st July to 10th November.)

	August	11th	Château Segard.
	,,	12th	Glencorse Wood.
	,,	15th	Half Way House.
	,,	16th	Glencorse Wood and Tunnel on Menin Road

1917.	August	18*th*	*Wippenhoek.*	
,,		24th	Moule.	

ON THE CAMBRAI FRONT.

	September	1st	Bancourt.	Third Army,
	,,	5th	Lebucquière.	IV Corps.
	,,	6th	Demicourt-Boursies Sector.	
	,,	13th	Lebucquière.	
	,,	21st	Demicourt-Boursies Sector.	
	,,	28*th*	*Patrol fight.*	
	,,	29th	Lebucquière.	
	October	7th	Demicourt-Boursies Sector.	
	,,	9*th*	*Patrol fight.*	
	,,	15th	Lebucquière.	
	,,	23rd	Demicourt-Boursies Sector.	
	,,	27*th*	*Patrol fight.*	
	,,	29*th*	*Patrol fight.*	
	November	1st	Lebucquière.	
	,,	6th	Demicourt-Boursies Sector.	
	,,	16th	Lebucquière.	

BATTLE OF CAMBRAI, 1917.

(20th November to 3rd December.)

	November	20*th*	Old British Line.
	,,	22nd	*Capture of Tadpole Copse.*
	,,	30*th*	*Hindenburg Line* (*Mœuvres*). *German Counter-Attack.*
	December	1st	Lebucquière.
	,,	2nd	Bancourt.

IN THE GAVRELLE SECTOR.

	December	3rd	Berneville.	XIII Corps.
	,,	5th	Marœuil.	
	,,	8th	Ecurie Wood.	
	,,	14th	Gavrelle Sector.	
	,,	20th	Roundhay Camp.	
	,,	24th	Gavrelle Sector.	
	,,	28th	Aubrey Camp.	
1918.	January	1st	Gavrelle Sector.	
	,,	3rd	Marœuil.	
	,,	5th	Caucourt.	
	,,	24th	Roclincourt.	
	February	1st	Frevillers.	
	,,	7th	St. Aubin.	
	,,	8th	Gavrelle Sector.	
	,,	13th	Roundhay Camp.	
	,,	17th	St. Aubin.	
	,,	21st	Gavrelle Sector.	
	,,	27th	Roundhay Camp.	

ITINERARY, 1918

1918.	March	11th	Gavrelle Sector.	
	,,	18th	Roundhay Camp.	
	,,	25th	Gavrelle Sector.	
	,,	26*th*	*Raid.*	
	,,	28*th*	Gavrelle (*First Battle of Arras*, 1918).	
	,,	29th	Roundhay Camp.	

TELEGRAPH HILL.

	March	30th	Mont St. Eloy.	First and then
	April	8th	Dainville.	Third Army.
	,,	14th	Ronville Caves, Arras.	XVII Corps.
	,,	19th	Telegraph Hill Sector.	
	,,	28th	Arras.	
	,,	30th	Arras and St. Sauveur Caves.	
	May	4th	Blangy support trenches.	
	,,	15*th*	*Dig new Front Line.*	
	,,	21st	Arras.	
	,,	23rd	Dainville.	
	,,	30th	Telegraph Hill Sector.	
	June	17th	Dainville.	
	,,	25th	Telegraph Hill Sector.	
	July	2nd	Blangy support trenches.	
	,,	8*th*	*Raid.*	
	,,	9th	Telegraph Hill Sector.	
	,,	15th	La Comté.	
	,,	25th	Telegraph Hill Sector.	
	,,	30th	Caucourt.	
	August	1st	Telegraph Hill.	
	,,	16th	Berneville.	
	,,	17th	Liencourt.	
	,,	19th	Arras.	

BATTLE OF THE SCARPE, 1918.
(August 26th to 30th.)

	August	20th	Noyelle Vion.	
	,,	21st	Bavincourt.	To VI Corps,
	,,	23rd	Bailleulval.	noon 21.8.18.
	,,	24*th*	*Boyelles Reserve Trench.*	Third Army,
	,,	26*th*	*Attack Croisilles.*	XVII Corps,
	,,	28*th*	*Attack Bullecourt.*	2 p.m.
	,,	29*th*	*Attack Bullecourt.*	
	,,	30*th*	*Hindenburg Line.*	
	,,	31*st*	*Boisleau au Mont.*	

VIS EN ARTOIS.

	September	7th	Vis en Artois.	First Army,
	,,	8th	Drocourt - Quéant Switch Line.	XXII Corps.

1918: September 16th   Outposts Ecourt St.
                        Quentin-Lecluse.
   ,,   18th   Guémappe.
   ,,   20th   Vis en Artois.

BATTLE OF THE CANAL DU NORD.
(September 27th to October 1st.)

       September 26th   Villers lez Cagnicourt.
   ,,   27th⎫ *Crossing of the Canal du*
                      Nord; Capture of
   ,,   28th⎭ *Sauchy Cauchy; Advance from Sauchy*
                      Cauchy.
   ,,   29th   Sauchy Cauchy.

"NE PLUS ULTRA" LINES.

       October 2nd   North of Bois du
                        Quesnoy.
   ,,   5th   Rumaucourt.   First Army.
   ,,   11th   Aubencheul au Bac.   Canadian Corps.
   ,,   13th   *Covering bridging and crossing of Sensée Canal.*
                       (Attack on Aubigny au Bac.)
   ,,   14th   Sauchy Cauchy.
   ,,   16th   Haute Avesnes.

THE ADVANCE TO VICTORY.
BATTLE OF VALENCIENNES.   BATTLE OF THE SAMBRE.
PASSAGE OF THE GRANDE HONNELLE.

       October 31st   Lieu St. Amand.   XXII Corps.
       November 2nd   *Caumont Farm.*
   ,,   3rd   *Capture of Saultain.*
   ,,   4th   *Capture of Sebourg.*
   ,,   5th   Angreau.
   ,,   6th   *La Grande Honnelle.*
   ,,   8th   Angreau.
   ,,   9th   Athies.

AFTER THE ARMISTICE

       November 26th   Bougnies.
   ,,   29th   Genly.
1919. March   19th   Quaregnon.
       June   2nd   Cadre disperses at Battalion H.Q., Buckingham Gate.

QUEEN'S WESTMINSTER MEMORIAL
WINDOW, WESTMINSTER ABBEY

ROLL OF HONOUR

1st BATTALION QUEEN'S WESTMINSTER RIFLES

This Roll contains the names of those who gave their lives in the war, 1914–1918

Abbott, H. W.	Rifleman	Bailey, J.	Rifleman
Abrahams, F. A.	Rifleman	Bailey, W. T.	Rifleman
Abrahams, S.	Rifleman	Baily, W. H.	Rifleman
Acourt, A.	Rifleman	Bain, F. W.	Rifleman
Adams, J. R.	Rifleman	Baird, A. S.	Rifleman
Addicott, W. H.	Rifleman	Baker, A. C.	Rifleman
Agate, H.	Captain	Baker, E.	Rifleman
Aguller, W. D.	Rifleman	Baker, G. E.	Rifleman
Ainsley, A.	Rifleman	Baker, L. E.	Rifleman
Aldridge, A. M.	Rifleman	Baker, T. S.	2nd Lieutenant
Aldridge, E. W.	Rifleman	Baker, V. S.	Rifleman
Aldridge, T. G.	Rifleman	Ball, G.	Rifleman
Alexander, A. M.	2nd Lieutenant	Ball, H.	Sergeant
Allen, C. L.	Rifleman	Ball, J.	Rifleman
Allen, C. R.	Rifleman	Balmer, T. F.	Corporal
Allen, F. L.	Rifleman	Banner, W. W.	Rifleman
Allen, M.	Rifleman	Bannester, J.	2nd Lieutenant
Amey, W.	Rifleman	Barfield, A. J.	Rifleman
Amsden, H. L.	Rifleman	Barfield, E. J.	Rifleman
Anderson, H. J.	Rifleman	Barfield, H. J.	Rifleman
Anderson, H. L.	Rifleman	Barker, H. C.	Rifleman
Anwell, B.	Rifleman	Barker, L. P.	Lance-Corporal
Apergis, T. S.	2nd Lieutenant	Barley, A. C.	Rifleman
Appleby, W. V.	Rifleman	Barnes, C. D.	Rifleman
Archer, H.	Rifleman	Barnett, H.	Rifleman
Argles, S.	Lance-Corporal	Barrett, E. H.	Rifleman
Armitage, W. M.	Rifleman	Barry, J.	Rifleman
Arnold, H. O.	Corporal	Barwell, F. L.	Captain
Arthur, H.	Rifleman	Bass, A. E.	Rifleman
Asquith, J.	Rifleman	Bassett, J. R.	Rifleman
Attwood, F.	Rifleman	Bastian, L.	Lance-Corporal
Ayliffe, R. G.	Rifleman	Batch, R.	Rifleman
		Batchelor, N. V.	Rifleman
Babbs, J.	Rifleman	Bathurst, N. S.	Lance-Corporal
Backhurst, J. A.	Rifleman	Batten, R. H.	Rifleman
Bacon, S. R. C.	Rifleman	Bayliss, J. C.	Rifleman
Bailey, A. G.	Rifleman	Beaumont, C. L.	Lance-Sergeant
Bailey, A. W.	Rifleman	Beavis, H. J.	Rifleman
Bailey, H.	Lance-Corporal	Beckett, F. H.	Rifleman

1st QUEEN'S WESTMINSTER RIFLES

Beckman, A. J.	Rifleman	Boyes, G. R.	Rifleman
Beeching, A. E.	Rifleman	Brackley, J. H.	Rifleman
Beer, A. J.	Rifleman	Bradbury, A.	Lance-Corporal
Beer, D. S.	Rifleman	Bradfield, L.	Lance-Corporal
Beham, J.	Rifleman	Bradford, B.	Rifleman
Bell, L. P.	Rifleman	Bradley, A.	Rifleman
Bell, W. S.	Lance-Corporal	Bradley, F.	Rifleman
Bennett, D. B.	Rifleman	Bradley, F.	Rifleman
Bennett, F. C.	Rifleman	Bradley, S. V., *M.M.*	Rifleman
Bennett, G. H.	Rifleman	Brand, A.	Rifleman
Bennett, S. F.	Rifleman	Brannan, A. C.	Rifleman
Bentley, S. R.	Rifleman	Brant, R. D.	Rifleman
Benton, A. V., *M.M.*	Rifleman	Branwhite, E. R.	Rifleman
Benton, S. W.	Rifleman	Brauer, A.	Rifleman
Bernhard, D.	Rifleman	Brett, L. G.	Rifleman
Berry, A. H.	Rifleman	Brewer, W. A., *M.M.*	
Beszant, W. H.	Rifleman		Lance-Corporal
Bevan, A.	Rifleman	Bridges, E. J.	Rifleman
Beville, A. G.	2nd Lieutenant	Briggs, E. W.	Rifleman
Bickford, T.	Corporal	Brightman, A.	Rifleman
Billing, H.	Rifleman	Brocklesby, V. G.	Rifleman
Billing, S. A.	Rifleman	Brockwell, E. J.	Rifleman
Billington, H.	Rifleman	Brook, H.	Rifleman
Bingham, C. H.	Lance-Corporal	Brookes, L.	Rifleman
Bint, H. C.	Rifleman	Brookman, H. G. W.	Rifleman
Bishop, D.	Rifleman	Brooks, G.	Rifleman
Blanch, R. W.	Rifleman	Brooks, R.	Rifleman
Blasby, J. L.	Rifleman	Brooks, R. C.	Rifleman
Bloomfield, E.	Rifleman	Brooman, A. D.	Rifleman
Bloor, C. C.	Rifleman	Brooman, H. D.	Rifleman
Blowers, H. V.	Rifleman	Brown, F. E.	Rifleman
Blunn, C. R.	Rifleman	Brown, F. H.	Rifleman
Bluntach, W. B.	Rifleman	Brown, F. J.	Rifleman
Bodenham, J. E. C.	Rifleman	Brown, H.	Rifleman
Bodle, C. R.	Rifleman	Brown, J. L.	Rifleman
Bolt, A. J.	Rifleman	Browne, F. H.	Rifleman
Bond, S. G.	Rifleman	Bruce, W.	Rifleman
Bonser, N.	Rifleman	Brumage, F. W.	Lance-Corporal
Boothby, A.	Rifleman	Bryan, J. W.	Rifleman
Bottel, P. J.	Rifleman	Bryen, E. F.	Rifleman
Boucher, F. H.	Corporal	Bryon, M. C.	Rifleman
Boughey, F.	Rifleman	Buckley, R. W.	Rifleman
Bounds, H.	Rifleman	Buckley, T.	Rifleman
Bovill, E. H.	Lieutenant	Bucknall, B. J.	Rifleman
Bowditch, A. E.	Rifleman	Bull, R. J. H.	Captain
Bower, A. W.	Rifleman	Bullock, A. A.	Rifleman
Bowie, D. J.	Rifleman	Burbridge, C. T.	Rifleman
Bowman, F. H.	Rifleman	Burford, H.	Rifleman
Bowran, H.	Rifleman	Burgess, F. N.	Rifleman

ROLL OF HONOUR

Burke, T.	Rifleman		Clark, P. L.	Rifleman
Burnham, H. E.	Rifleman		Clarke, A.	Lance-Corporal
Burridge, R. G.	Lance-Corporal		Clarke, A. J.	Rifleman
Burrough, H. J.	Rifleman		Clarke, E. E.	Rifleman
Burrows, H. R.	Lance-Sergeant		Clarke, H. G.	Rifleman
Burtenshaw, G. H.	Rifleman		Clarke, H. R.	Rifleman
Burton, A. W.	Lance-Corporal		Clarke, H. T.	Rifleman
Bushell, W. T.	Rifleman		Clarke, T. H.	Rifleman
Bussell, F. P.	Rifleman		Cleave, O.	Rifleman
Butcher, J. A.	Corporal		Clement, W. T.	Rifleman
Butler, F. L.	Rifleman		Cockerill, G. E.	Captain
Butler, S.	Captain		Cocks, W. H.	Rifleman
Butler, W. J.	Rifleman		Cole, J.	Sergeant
Bye, L. L.	Rifleman		Coleman, H.	Rifleman
			Coleman, S. M.	Lance-Corporal
Cammetta, G.	Rifleman		Collinson, H. C.	Rifleman
Campbell, H. J.	Rifleman		Coltman, N. C.	Rifleman
Campbell, J.	Rifleman		Connor, L. J.	Rifleman
Canavan, A. F.	Rifleman		Cooley, L.	Rifleman
Cane, H.	Rifleman		Cooper, A. W.	Rifleman
Canham, G. H.	Rifleman		Cooper, F. G.	Rifleman
Cannan, B. J.	Rifleman		Cooper, H. H.	Rifleman
Capper, T. J.	Rifleman		Cooper, S. J.	Rifleman
Carlisle, H. T.	Rifleman		Cooper, W.	Rifleman
Carly, G. H.	Rifleman		Corben, A.	Sergeant
Carsberg, A.	Rifleman		Corcoran, W.	Rifleman
Carter, A. E.	Rifleman		Cordery, G. C.	Lance-Sergeant
Carter, A. J.	Rifleman		Corlett, J. H. T.	Sergeant
Carter, H. L.	Rifleman		Corley, F. C.	Rifleman
Case, W. N.	Rifleman		Cornell, C. W.	Lance-Corporal
Castle, E. W. K.	Rifleman		Cornish, F. V.	Rifleman
Caudwell, A. C.	Rifleman		Cornish, R. A.	Rifleman
Caudwell, T.	Captain		Cosmelli, L. C.	Lance-Corporal
Cavell, J. R.	Rifleman		Cottis, A. T.	Rifleman
Chamberlain, J.	Rifleman		Cottrell, C. R.	Sergeant
Chandler, H.	Rifleman		Couper, H. W., *M.M.*	
Chapman, H.	Rifleman			Company-Sergeant-Major
Chapman, H. C.	Sergeant		Couper, W.	Rifleman
Chapman, J. H.	Rifleman		Court, A. G.	Sergeant
Chapshew, C. D.	Rifleman		Coventry, V.	Rifleman
Childs, R.	Rifleman		Coventry, V. C.	Rifleman
Chilman, A. W.	Rifleman		Cox, H. P.	Rifleman
Chilton, E. J.	Corporal		Cox, T.	Rifleman
Chivers, W.	Rifleman		Coxon, R. H.	Rifleman
Christmas, C. A.	Rifleman		Cranfield, H. T.	Rifleman
Ciclitira, J. P.	Rifleman		Crate, H. J.	Rifleman
Clack, H.	Corporal		Crawford, F. T. E.	Rifleman
Clark, A.	Lance-Corporal		Crawford, L.	Rifleman
Clark, A. E., *M.M.*	Sergeant		Creighton, G. R.	Rifleman

1st QUEEN'S WESTMINSTER RIFLES

Croager, B. H.	Rifleman	Duncan, G. P.	Rifleman
Crompton, C. T. A.	Rifleman	Dunn, C.	Rifleman
Crook, E.	Rifleman	Durree, R. E.	Rifleman
Crook, J. T.	Rifleman	Dutton, C. E. F.	Rifleman
Cropley, T. R.	Sergeant	Dye, P. R.	Rifleman
Cross, A. H.	Rifleman	Dyson, A. S.	Rifleman
Cross, J. W.	Rifleman	Dyson, S. C.	Rifleman
Crundell, T.	Lance-Sergeant	Dyson, W. H.	Lieutenant
Cudd, L.	Rifleman	Dyster, A. E.	Rifleman
Cumber, H. R.	Rifleman		
Cunnington, J.	Rifleman	Eastman, C. H.	Rifleman
Curtis, A.	Rifleman	Eastwood, J. E.	Rifleman
Curwen, G. C.	2nd Lieutenant	Eatonshore, J. M.	Rifleman
		Edwards, A.	Rifleman
Daking, E. A.	Rifleman	Edwards, C. G. A.	Rifleman
Dando, J. E.	Lance-Corporal	Edwards, C. J.	Rifleman
Dangerfield, H. J.	Rifleman	Edwards, F. A.	Rifleman
Daniels, A. C. E.	Rifleman	Edwards, H. E.	Rifleman
Davaux, P. A.	Lance-Corporal	Edwards, H. J.	Rifleman
David, J.	Rifleman	Edwards, S. E.	Rifleman
Davies, A. F.	Rifleman	Edwards, W. H.	Lance-Corporal
Davies, J.	Rifleman	Ell, L. V.	Rifleman
Davis, E. S.	Rifleman	Ellen, W.	Rifleman
Davis, W. C.	Rifleman	Ellis, E. J.	Rifleman
Davison, R. E.	Rifleman	Elmslie, G. B.	Rifleman
Dawes, R.	Rifleman	Elsey, A. S.	Rifleman
Daws, W. W.	Rifleman	Elsom, F. D.	Lance-Sergeant
Deakin, S.	Corporal	Engall, J. S.	2nd Lieutenant
Dealey, W. A.	Rifleman	English, H.	Rifleman
Dean, G. E.	Rifleman	Erlebach, H. W.	Rifleman
Dean, J. H.	Rifleman	Evans, A. G.	Rifleman
Dear, G. A.	Lance-Corporal	Evans, H. W.	Rifleman
Delay, E. W.	Rifleman	Evans, W. H.	Rifleman
Denning, F. G.	Rifleman	Everett, A. F.	Rifleman
Dennis, S. W.	Rifleman	Ewen, C. A.	Rifleman
Devoil, B. T.	Rifleman	Exelby, C. R.	Sergeant
Dexter, A. K.	Rifleman	Eyett, W. T.	Rifleman
Dickinson, R. S.	Captain		
Dinham, G. H.	Rifleman	Fagan, H. A., *M.M.*	Sergeant
Dival, R.	Rifleman	Fairbrother, P.	Rifleman
Dodd, W.	Rifleman	Fairclough, L.	Rifleman
Doggett, F. S.	Lance-Corporal	Farren, J.	Rifleman
Donovan, T. S.	Rifleman	Favatt, F. H.	Rifleman
Dornan, H. E.	Rifleman	Fea, A. W.	Rifleman
Dowden, W. T.	Rifleman	Fellows, W. B.	Rifleman
Drown, M. F.	Rifleman	Fentiman, L. W.	Rifleman
Druett, P. A. L.	Sergeant	Fenton, E. F.	Rifleman
Duce, C. E.	Sergeant	Finch, S. A.	Rifleman
Dunbar, A. G.	Rifleman	Finlayson, V. B.	Sergeant

ROLL OF HONOUR

Firth, T. R.	Rifleman	Glover, H. A.	Rifleman
Fitch, C. F. D.	Rifleman	Glover, N. J.	Lance-Corporal
Fittall, G. R.	Rifleman	Goadby, J. C.	2nd Lieutenant
Fitzgerald, J.	Rifleman	Goble, H.	Rifleman
Flake, G.	Rifleman	Godfrey, C. A.	Rifleman
Fleck, J. A.	Rifleman	Goffin, F.	Rifleman
Fleming, R.	Rifleman	Goffin, H. C.	Sergeant
Folland, A.	Rifleman	Goldsmith, E. F.	Rifleman
Ford, A. S.	Rifleman	Goodall, F.	Rifleman
Ford, R. E.	Rifleman	Gooding, R. C.	Rifleman
Forrester, W. B.	Rifleman	Goodwin, W. T.	Rifleman
Fox, E. C.	Rifleman	Goodyear, A. A.	Rifleman
Francis, B.	Rifleman	Gooson, O.	Rifleman
Franklin, J. G.	Rifleman	Gordon, A. J. M.	Captain
Freeman, W.	Rifleman	Gore, C.	Rifleman
French, C. C.	Rifleman	Gorwill, J. H.	Rifleman
French, J.	Rifleman	Gosling, A. S.	Rifleman
Froome, C. W., *D.C.M.*	Company-Sergeant-Major	Gostellow, A. C.	Rifleman
		Graham, K. F.	Rifleman
Frostick, H. J.	Rifleman	Graham, W.	Rifleman
Fryer, E. W.	Rifleman	Grainger, F. T.	Rifleman
Fullbrook, R. B.	Rifleman	Granger, E.	Rifleman
Fuller, L. E.	Rifleman	Grant, J. W.	Rifleman
Fullerton, F. J.	Rifleman	Gray, C. K.	2nd Lieutenant
Furniss, A.	Corporal	Green, A. J. E.	Rifleman
		Green, C. G.	Corporal
Gale, H. A.	Lance-Corporal	Green, J. A.	Captain
Gallop, A. M.	Rifleman	Green, W.	Rifleman
Gammon, N. E.	Corporal	Green, W. J.	Rifleman
Gapes, A. W.	Rifleman	Green, W. L.	Sergeant
Gardiner, D. R.	Rifleman	Greenway, G. H.	Rifleman
Gardner, W.	Rifleman	Gregory, N. E.	Rifleman
Garvic, T.	Rifleman	Griffin, N.	Rifleman
Gaskins, R. W.	Rifleman	Griffiths, C. E.	Rifleman
Gatfield, R. A.	Lieutenant	Griffiths, S.	Rifleman
Gedge, F. H.	Rifleman	Griffiths, W.	Rifleman
Geleit, K. A.	Rifleman	Groom, F. W. J.	Corporal
George, S. A.	Rifleman	Gruitt, V. J.	Rifleman
Gibelli, G. A.	Rifleman	Gudge, R. C.	Rifleman
Gibson, A. H. S.	Rifleman		
Gibson, E.	Lance-Corporal	Hagger, J. W.	Rifleman
Giddons, W.	Rifleman	Haigh, A. D.	Rifleman
Girling, A.	Rifleman	Hainton, R.	Rifleman
Gissing, W. L.	Rifleman	Hall, A. H.	Rifleman
Glaister, H. S.	Rifleman	Hall, F. C.	Rifleman
Glasier, P. M., *D.S.O.*	Lieutenant-Colonel	Hall, S.	Rifleman
		Hall, V.	Rifleman
Glen, H.	Rifleman	Halsey, A. R.	Rifleman
Glenister, V. H.	Rifleman	Hambrook, F. G.	Rifleman

1st QUEEN'S WESTMINSTER RIFLES

Hammond, J. W.	Rifleman	Higgins, M.	Rifleman
Hankard, C.	Rifleman	Hill, G. W.	Rifleman
Hanley, W.	Rifleman	Hill, J.	Corporal
Hardcastle, J. W.	Rifleman	Hill, J. W.	Rifleman
Harding, C. W.	Rifleman	Hill, R. E.	Rifleman
Harding, J.	Rifleman	Hillsdon, F. R.	Rifleman
Hardy, E. R.	Lance-Corporal	Hinde, G. C.	Rifleman
Hardy, H.	Rifleman	Hinds, G.	Rifleman
Hargreaves, R. P.	Rifleman	Hines, R. W.	Corporal
Harley, R. M.	Rifleman	Hitchens, G.	Rifleman
Harlock, W.	Rifleman	Hobbs, A. W. S.	Rifleman
Harman, G. H.	Rifleman	Hodges, A. T.	Rifleman
Harmer, G. F.	Rifleman	Hogg, J. T.	Rifleman
Harper, H. C.	Rifleman	Holdron, R. E.	Rifleman
Harris, J. A.	Rifleman	Holland, F.	Rifleman
Harris, R. R. G.	Lance-Corporal	Hollingham, C. P.	Lance-Corporal
Harris, S. W.	Lance-Corporal	Holloway, P. E.	Rifleman
Harris, S. W.	Rifleman	Holloway, W. G.	Rifleman
Harrison, F. H.	Rifleman	Hollyman, H. E.	Rifleman
Harrison, G.	Rifleman	Holme, H. A.	Rifleman
Harrison, S. E.	Rifleman	Holmes, H. R.	Rifleman
Harrow, L. P., *D.C.M.*	Lieutenant	Holroyd, C. B.	Rifleman
Hart, W. T. C.	Rifleman	Holt, F. W.	Rifleman
Harvey, T. S.	Rifleman	Homewood, W. L.	Rifleman
Haselton, F. D.	Rifleman	Hood, A. E.	Rifleman
Haskey, G. T.	Rifleman	Hood, G. C.	Rifleman
Hatcher, A. G.	Rifleman	Hooper, J. H. M.	2nd Lieutenant
Hatton, H. T. J.	Rifleman	Hooper, T.	Rifleman
Hawker, R.	Rifleman	Hooper, T. E.	Rifleman
Hawkins, W. E.	Sergeant	Hopewell, P. A.	Rifleman
Hayden, J.	Sergeant	Horne, J. A.	Lieutenant
Hayes, S. F.	Rifleman	Hornsby, C. H.	Rifleman
Haygreen, E. H.	Rifleman	Horrill, E. J.	Rifleman
Hayley, J. R. B.	Rifleman	Hosking, F. J.	Rifleman
Hayward, J. K.	Rifleman	Hoskins, A.	Rifleman
Hayward, S.	Rifleman	Houghton, C. W.	Rifleman
Hazell, E. W.	Rifleman	House, A. E.	Rifleman
Heard, R. C.	Acting-Corporal	Howell, C. E.	Rifleman
Heath, J. E.	Rifleman	Hudson, L.	Corporal
Helps, F. B.	Rifleman	Hudson, W.	Rifleman
Hemmings, R. H.	Rifleman	Hughes, A. E.	Rifleman
Henderson, C. W.	Rifleman	Hughes, A. L.	Rifleman
Henderson, H. P.	Rifleman	Hughes, F. A.	Rifleman
Herne, A. R.	Rifleman	Hughes, F. T.	Rifleman
Herne, G. H.	Company-Sergeant-Major	Hughes, M. B.	Rifleman
		Hughes, R. J.	Rifleman
Heywood, H. A.	Rifleman	Huleux, A. M. H.	Rifleman
Heyworth, H. H.	Rifleman	Hull, J.	Lance-Corporal
Hicks, A. H.	Sergeant	Humphrey, G. H.	Sergeant

ROLL OF HONOUR

Humphrey, M. J.	Rifleman	Jones, W. S.	Rifleman
Hunt, E. W.	Rifleman	Jones, W. W.	Lance-Corporal
Hunt, S. H. J. A.	Rifleman	Jordan, H. R.	Rifleman
Hurley, H. W.	Rifleman	Jupp, A. H.	Rifleman
Hurley, J.	Rifleman		
Hurry, J. W.	Rifleman	Keep, L. J.	Rifleman
Hurst, P. H.	Rifleman	Kell, H. W.	Rifleman
Hussey, E. W.	Lance-Corporal	Kellcher, P.	Rifleman
Hussey, P. J.	Rifleman	Keller, A. J.	Rifleman
Hutchinson, D. H.	Lieutenant	Kemp, W.	Lance-Corporal
		Kemp, W. R.	Rifleman
Ibberson, W.	Rifleman	Kench, R. W.	Rifleman
Ilott, W. H.	Rifleman	Kent, E. T.	Rifleman
Ims, R. T.	Rifleman	Kentszinsky, P. W.	Rifleman
Ineson, B. C.	Rifleman	Kerl, W. A.	Rifleman
Ingram, J. D.	Rifleman	Kew, H. C.	Rifleman
Inns, W. H.	Rifleman	Keywood, H. A.	Lance-Corporal
Ireland, W. A.	Rifleman	Kidby, G. F.	Rifleman
Issacs, E. F.	Rifleman	Kidman, F. H.	Rifleman
Ives, V. G.	Rifleman	Kidner, F. E.	Rifleman
		Kilby, C. P.	Lance-Corporal
Jaccey, S. J.	Rifleman	Killick, C. J.	Rifleman
Jackson, A. C.	Rifleman	King, J. W.	Rifleman
Jackson, F. H.	Rifleman	King, L. F.	Sergeant
Jackson, F. W.	Rifleman	Kington, P. F.	Rifleman
Jackson, J.	Rifleman	Kirton, W.	Rifleman
Jackson, J. R.	Rifleman	Knott, R. M.	Rifleman
Jackson, W.	Rifleman	Knowles, F.	Rifleman
Jacob, H. W. T.	2nd Lieutenant	Kronenberger, P. C.	Rifleman
Jacobs, C. H.	Lance-Corporal	Kyte, A. A.	Sergeant
Jakins, H.	Rifleman		
Jarrett, W. T.	Rifleman	Lacey, F. H. P.	Rifleman
Jarvis, A. F.	Corporal	Laird, W. J.	Rifleman
Jeffrey, C.	Rifleman	Lambert, R. W.	Rifleman
Jeffries, V. M.	Rifleman	Lancaster, E. E.	Rifleman
Jenkins, T.	Rifleman	Lanchbery, T. H.	Rifleman
Jennings, R.	Rifleman	Lane, E. B.	Rifleman
Johns, L.	Rifleman	Langdale, W. J.	Rifleman
Johnson, A. T.	Rifleman	Langrish, L. A.	Rifleman
Johnson, F. G.	Corporal	Lasham, W. B.	Rifleman
Johnson, F. H. J.	Corporal	Latreille, A. Y.	Lance-Corporal
Johnston, E. F.	2nd Lieutenant	Laver, A.	Rifleman
Jolley, S. J.	Rifleman	Law, S. C.	Rifleman
Jones, A. E.	Rifleman	Lawrence, W. E.	Rifleman
Jones, E. A. O.	2nd Lieutenant	Layzell, G. F.	Rifleman
Jones, H. S.	Sergeant	Leach, W. A.	Rifleman
Jones, J.	Rifleman	Learoyd, J.	Rifleman
Jones, J. D. B.	Rifleman	Ledger, C. H.	Rifleman
Jones, P.	Rifleman	Legg, W. H.	Rifleman

Y

1st QUEEN'S WESTMINSTER RIFLES

Leggett, H.	Rifleman	Marshall, W. D.	Rifleman
Letzer, S. C.	Rifleman	Martin, J. G.	Rifleman
Lewin, P. V.	Rifleman	Martyn, J.	Rifleman
Lewis, E. G.	Rifleman	Mascard, A.	Rifleman
Lewis, J. M.	Rifleman	Mason, F. G.	Rifleman
Libby, H. G.	Rifleman	Masson, H. M.	Company-Sergeant-Major
Light, P. T.	Sergeant		
Lipscombe, A.	Rifleman	Masters, N. G.	Rifleman
Littlechild, H.	Rifleman	Matterson, T. P.	Rifleman
Lloyd, D. H. L.	Rifleman	Matthews, G. W.	Rifleman
Lloyd, F. G.	Rifleman	Matthews, T. T. B.	Lance-Corporal
Lloyd, R. C.	Rifleman	Mawson, W. F.	Rifleman
Loader, H. W.	Rifleman	May, R. J.	Rifleman
Lobley, D. L.	Rifleman	Mead, J. J.	Rifleman
Lockwood, R. D.	Rifleman	Mears, W. J.	Rifleman
Lofthouse, L.	Rifleman	Meedy, E. J.	Rifleman
Long, A.	Rifleman	Meek, G.	Rifleman
Long, H.	Rifleman	Meikle, A. D. B.	Rifleman
Longman, F. W.	Rifleman	Mellor, L.	Rifleman
Love, V. J.	Rifleman	Mendham, W.	Lance-Corporal
Lovegrove, G.	Rifleman	Mercer, W. C.	Rifleman
Loynes, E. F.	Rifleman	Mighall, C. C. N.	Sergeant
Luscombe, R.	Rifleman	Mileman, G. H.	Rifleman
Luxford, R.	Lance-Corporal	Miles, A.	Rifleman
		Miles, G.	Rifleman
Mabbott, A. L.	Rifleman	Miles, J. H.	Rifleman
McClurg, W. A.	Rifleman	Millem, H.	Rifleman
McConachie, H.	Rifleman	Miller, F.	Rifleman
McDonald, A. P.	Rifleman	Mills, C. G.	Lance-Corporal
MacDonald, F. P.	Rifleman	Mills, C. P.	Rifleman
McGillivray, F.	Rifleman	Minshall, J. W.	Rifleman
McGillivray, J. R.	Rifleman	Minuto, T. J.	Rifleman
McIntyre, L.	Rifleman	Mitchell, C.	Rifleman
McKenna, N.	Lance-Corporal	Mitchell, L.	Rifleman
MacKinnon, C. A.	Rifleman	Mitchenall, W. E.	Rifleman
Mackle, A. M.	2nd Lieutenant	Moase, J.	Rifleman
Macrae, W. C. M.	Captain	Mobey, A., *D.C.M.*	Rifleman
Makins, H.	Captain	Mockett, W. E.	Rifleman
Malcolm, J. P.	Rifleman	Moody, T. J.	Rifleman
Males, W.	Rifleman	Moorat, A.	Rifleman
Maltby, F. C.	Rifleman	Moore, F. H. B.	2nd Lieutenant
Manning, J. S.	Rifleman	Moore, S.	Corporal
Mansell, J. E.	Rifleman	Morgan, A. J.	Rifleman
Mansell, W. M.	Lance-Sergeant	Morgan, C. H.	Rifleman
Markmoss, T. J.	Rifleman	Morley, E. G.	Rifleman
Marriner, A. E.	Rifleman	Morley, H.	Rifleman
Marsh, A. L.	Corporal	Mosley, F.	Rifleman
Marshall, D. G.	Rifleman	Moss, M. J. T.	Rifleman
Marshall, F. F.	Rifleman	Mothen, F. F.	Rifleman

ROLL OF HONOUR

Mott, H.F., *M.C.*	Captain	Oliver, J. L.	Sergeant
Mott, W. J.	Rifleman	Oram, A. E.	Rifleman
Mullins, F. J.	Lance-Corporal	Orchard, J. H., *M.M.*	
Mullins, H. J.	Rifleman		Lance-Corporal
Mullins, J.	Rifleman	Osmond, G. F.	Corporal
Musgrove, W. M.	2nd Lieutenant	Ousey, J. A.	Rifleman
Naddermier, A. J. J.	Rifleman	Paling, A. C.	Rifleman
Napper, G. S.	Rifleman	Pallett, G. W.	Rifleman
Nash, A.	Rifleman	Palmer, J. A.	Rifleman
Nash, F. R.	Corporal	Pangbourne, G.	Rifleman
Neale, H. W.	Rifleman	Parish, W. T.	Rifleman
Needham, J. L.	Lance-Corporal	Parker, C.	Regt.-Sergeant-Major
Negus, A. G.	2nd Lieutenant	Parkhouse, A. G.	Rifleman
Nelhams, S. C.	Rifleman	Parr, J.	Corporal
Nelson, J.	Rifleman	Parsley, R. J.	Rifleman
Nevard, C. R.	Rifleman	Parsons, H.	Rifleman
Newbury, R.	Rifleman	Parsons, W. P.	Rifleman
Newby, J. R. T.	Lance-Corporal	Pascell, W. G.	Rifleman
Newcombe, E.	Captain	Patten, C. W.	Rifleman
Newell, A. F.	Rifleman	Payne, S.	Lance-Corporal
Newham, H. F.	Rifleman	Payne, W.	Rifleman
Newland, H.	Rifleman	Pearce, G. A.	Lance-Corporal
Newman, A. H.	Rifleman	Pearce, W. R.	Lance-Corporal
Newman, A. V.	Rifleman	Pearson, B.	Rifleman
Newman, E.	Lance-Corporal	Penfold, H. C.	Rifleman
Newnham, H. J.	Rifleman	Penn, C. W.	Rifleman
Newton, D.	Lance-Corporal	Percy, C.	Rifleman
Nicholls, K. H.	Rifleman	Perkins, A. E.	Rifleman
Nicholls, W. M.	Rifleman	Perry, E. C.	Rifleman
Nichols, E.	Rifleman	Perry, F. P.	Rifleman
Nichols, R. E.	Rifleman	Perry, L. W.	Rifleman
Nightingale, N. A. B.		Pert, E. R.	Rifleman
	Lance-Corporal	Petersen, C.	Rifleman
Nightingale, S.	Rifleman	Petzsche, R. A.	Rifleman
Noble, R. E.	Rifleman	Philip, W., *M.M.*	Lance-Corporal
Noding, D. H.	Corporal	Phillips, C. H.	Rifleman
Norman, H.	Rifleman	Phillips, J. R.	Rifleman
Norrington, R.	Rifleman	Phillips, T.	Rifleman
North, S.	2nd Lieutenant	Phipps, H. E.	Rifleman
Norton, A.	Rifleman	Pickworth, A. W.	2nd Lieutenant
Nutley, C. E.	Rifleman	Pilgrim, E. J.	Rifleman
Nye, F.	Rifleman	Pitt, R. J.	Rifleman
		Pittet, L.	Corporal
O'Connor, J.	Rifleman	Pocock, M. W.	Rifleman
Oldham, F.	Rifleman	Pomeroy, W. G.	Corporal
Oldham, H. L.	Rifleman	Poole, A. R.	Rifleman
Oldham, W. J.	Rifleman	Pope, T. C.	Rifleman
Olive, R. E.	Rifleman	Poppmacher, J. H. M.	Rifleman

Potter, A. W.	Sergeant	Ridley, C. E.	Rifleman
Potts, D. E.	Rifleman	Ridley, R.	Rifleman
Potts, E.	Rifleman	Ridley, R. P.	Rifleman
Powell, A. W.	Musician	Ridout, F. W.	Sergeant
Poynor, F. J. R.	Rifleman	Riminton, P. H.	Rifleman
Prescott, F. W. J.	Rifleman	Risbridger, H. G.	Rifleman
Prestage, W. J.	Rifleman	Risley, O. W.	Corporal
Priest, R.	Sergeant	Ritchings, A. A. W.	
Prince, E. N.	Rifleman		2nd Lieutenant
Prior, R. C.	Rifleman	Rivett, A. J.	Rifleman
Prowse, F. G.	Rifleman	Roberts, S.	Rifleman
Pulford, S. A.	Rifleman	Robertshaw, J. H.	Lance-Corporal
Pullen, G. E.	Rifleman	Robertshaw, J. H.	Rifleman
Pullin, G. H.	Rifleman	Robertson, C. H.	Rifleman
Punchard, A. D.	Rifleman	Robinson, F. J., *M.M.*	Rifleman
Purdue, F. J.	Rifleman	Robinson, H.	Rifleman
		Robinson, R. R.	Rifleman
Quinney, T. E. A.	Rifleman	Robson, R.	Rifleman
		Roche, R. de R.	Corporal
Radcliffe, S. H.	Rifleman	Rodwell, C. A.	Rifleman
Randles, G. P.	Rifleman	Rogers, F. A.	Corporal
Rands, F.	Rifleman	Rogers, H. D.	Rifleman
Ransom, R. J.	Rifleman	Rogers, M. S.	Sergeant
Ranson, R. G.	Rifleman	Rolfe, A. D.	Rifleman
Ratcliffe, F. C.	Rifleman	Rolff, S. T.	Rifleman
Raven, C. H.	2nd Lieutenant	Rollo, A. W.	Rifleman
Rayner, E. J.	Rifleman	Rolls, E. A.	Rifleman
Read, J. D.	Rifleman	Roper, H. E.	Lance-Corporal
Read, T. C.	Rifleman	Roser, S.	Rifleman
Reading, H. T.	Lance-Corporal	Ross, C. W.	Rifleman
Reed, F. C.	Rifleman	Rossignol, Le, L.	Rifleman
Reeks, E. F.	Rifleman	Rothen, F. F.	Rifleman
Reeve, E. J.	Rifleman	Routley, H. W. J.	Rifleman
Reeves, A. W.	Rifleman	Rowe, H. S.	Rifleman
Regeaux, F. C.	Lance-Corporal	Rowe, J. H.	Lance-Corporal
Reid, A. F.	Corporal	Rowland, C. H.	Rifleman
Reid, P. G.	2nd Lieutenant	Rowson, D.	Rifleman
Restall, F.	Rifleman	Rowson, J. E.	Rifleman
Reuter, G. E.	Rifleman	Rudall, W. H.	Rifleman
Reynolds, E. W. E.	Rifleman	Rush, E. W.	Corporal
Reynolds, H.	Lance-Corporal	Russell, C. A. P.	Bugler
Richard, G.	Rifleman	Russell, F. W., *M.C.*	Lieutenant
Richards, A. G.	Lance-Sergeant	Russell, W. G.	Corporal
Richards, T. S.	Lance-Corporal	Ryan, A. S.	Rifleman
Richardson, D.	Rifleman	Ryan, J.	Rifleman
Richardson, R. J. G.	Rifleman	Ryce, W. E.	Rifleman
Richens, R. I.	2nd Lieutenant		
Ridden, W. L.	Rifleman	Saddington, H. J.	Rifleman
Rider, W. T.	Rifleman	Sainsbury, G. B.	Rifleman

ROLL OF HONOUR

Salmon, W.	Rifleman	Smith, H. B.	Rifleman
Salmon, W. J.	Rifleman	Smith, H. S.	Rifleman
Salt, H.	Rifleman	Smith, T. F.	Lance-Sergeant
Samuels, W. P.	Corporal	Smorthwaite, R.	Rifleman
Sanders, H. J.	Rifleman	Soars, J.	Corporal
Sarch, F. S.	Rifleman	Somers, J. H.	Rifleman
Saunders, A. P.	Rifleman	Sowden, L.	Rifleman
Saxton, H. H.	Rifleman	Spaan, J. H.	Rifleman
Scamell, H. M.	Rifleman	Sparge, F. A.	Lance-Corporal
Scheidlowsky, F. A.	Rifleman	Spark, B. E.	Rifleman
Schooling, G. H.	Rifleman	Spence, G.	Rifleman
Schultz, W. E. T.	Rifleman	Spencer-Smith, M.	2nd Lieutenant
Sclanders, C. M.	Lieutenant	Spotswood, T. A.	Rifleman
Scott, F. J.	Rifleman	Spragg, F.	Lance-Corporal
Scowcroft, J.	Rifleman	Spry, A.	Rifleman
Scruby, A. C.	Rifleman	Squire, W. J.	Lance-Corporal
Seaker, F. A.	Corporal	Squires, W. F.	Lance-Corporal
Sellwood, W. H.	Rifleman	Stace, A.	Lance-Corporal
Senior, E. B.	Rifleman	Stacy, S.	Rifleman
Sergeant, A. O.	Rifleman	Stanford, H.	Rifleman
Seymour, G. M.	Lance-Corporal	Stanley, F. B.	Rifleman
Sharp, E. G.	Rifleman	Stanton, C. T. R.	Rifleman
Sharp, T.	Rifleman	Starke, D. R. B.	Rifleman
Sharpe, W. A.	Rifleman	Stebbins, H. G.	Rifleman
Shattock, M. M.	Captain	Stedeford, H. K.	Lance-Corporal
Shepherd, D. A. M.	Rifleman	Stein, C. E.	Sergeant
Shepley, H.	Rifleman	Stentiford, J.	Rifleman
Sheppard, C.	2nd Lieutenant	Step, F. H.	Sergeant
Sheppard, F. G.	Rifleman	Stephens, D. H. H.	Rifleman
Sherlock, L. W.	Lance-Corporal	Stephens, H. J.	Rifleman
Shutte, L. A.	Sergeant	Stevens, F.	Sergeant
Sillitoe, J. T.	Rifleman	Stevenson, H.	2nd Lieutenant
Silvester, A. F.	Rifleman	Stinchcombe, E.	Sergeant
Simmons, A.	Rifleman	Stitt, I. d'A. S.	2nd Lieutenant
Simpson, J.	Rifleman	Stone, E. A.	Rifleman
Simpson, S. J.	Rifleman	Stone, G.	Rifleman
Sims, M. H. M.	Rifleman	Stonhold, H. W.	Rifleman
Singleton, E. J.	Rifleman	Strachan, A. L.	Rifleman
Small, K. G. W.	Rifleman	Straker, S. C.	Lance-Corporal
Small, R.	Rifleman	Stratton, G. O.	Rifleman
Smart, W. G.	Corporal	Streeton, J. R.	Lance-Corporal
Smart, W. J. E.	Rifleman	Streeton, T. G.	Rifleman
Smeathers, C. H.	Rifleman	Stroud, E.	Rifleman
Smee, J. D.	Lance-Corporal	Stubbs, A. J.	Rifleman
Smith, A. B.	Rifleman	Summers, F. C. J.	Rifleman
Smith, A. G.	Rifleman	Sutch, F. W.	Rifleman
Smith, A. R.	Lance-Corporal	Swaffield, T.	Rifleman
Smith, E. J.	Rifleman	Swainson, F. G., *M.C.*	Captain
Smith, F. J.	Rifleman	Swaisland, F. E.	Rifleman

1st QUEEN'S WESTMINSTER RIFLES

Taffs, W. C.	Rifleman	Tucker, R.	Rifleman
Tait, L. S.	Rifleman	Tucker, T. J., *M.M.*	Sergeant
Tanner, H.	Rifleman	Tuckey, H. V.	Rifleman
Tarsey, E. D.	Rifleman	Tunstall, W. H.	Rifleman
Tassell, B. T.	Rifleman	Turnbull, R.	Rifleman
Tatham, F.	Rifleman	Turner, E. E.	Rifleman
Tavendale, J.	Rifleman	Turner, G.	Rifleman
Taylor, C.	Rifleman	Turner, L. G.	Rifleman
Taylor, R. E.	Rifleman	Turtle, C. L.	Rifleman
Taylor, R. G. R.	Rifleman	Tuttle, F.	Rifleman
Taylor, W. G.	Rifleman	Tyler, L. J.	Lance-Corporal
Tebbutt, R.	Rifleman	Tynan, J.	Rifleman
Temple, L. F.	Lance-Corporal	Tyrrell, C. E.	Rifleman
Tenbrocke, Q. L.	Rifleman	Tyrwhitt, N. B.	Major
Tennant, L.	Rifleman		
Theys, A.	Rifleman	Vann, H. G.	Rifleman
Thomas, C. A. W.	Rifleman	Venning, W. J. S.	Rifleman
Thompson, A. G.	Rifleman	Vernon, R. M. J.	Corporal
Thompson, C. F.	Corporal	Vince, G. L.	Lance-Corporal
Thompson, C. R.	Rifleman	Vince, J.	Lance-Corporal
Thompson, F. W.	Rifleman	Vincent, J.	Rifleman
Thompson, H. W.	Rifleman	Vize, G. D.	Rifleman
Thomson, L.	Rifleman	Voller, J. R.	Lance-Corporal
Thorley, H. N.	Rifleman		
Thornborrow, J. D.	Rifleman	Wacher, W. G.	Sergeant
Thorndyke, E.	Rifleman	Waddington, W. J.	Rifleman
Thornton, E. G.	Rifleman	Wagstaff, C. E.	Rifleman
Thornton, V.	Lance-Corporal	Waind, A.	Rifleman
Throuvenot, M. E.	Rifleman	Walker, A.	Rifleman
Thynne, L. G.	Rifleman	Walker, R. W.	Rifleman
Thynne, S.	Rifleman	Wall, W. L. J.	Rifleman
Tibbels, P. J.	Rifleman	Wallace, D. C.	Rifleman
Tibbs, P. H.	Rifleman	Wallace, L.	Rifleman
Tolliday, S. B.	Rifleman	Waller, C. D.	Rifleman
Tompkins, H.	Lance-Corporal	Waller, W.	Rifleman
Tong, W. J.	Rifleman	Walter, E. A.	Rifleman
Tooke, G. E.	Rifleman	Ward, H., *M.M.*	Rifleman
Tope, A. F.	Rifleman	Ward, R. J.	Rifleman
Townley, C. N.	Rifleman	Wareham, B.	Rifleman
Townley, H. L.	Rifleman	Warner, W. H.	Rifleman
Townley, H. W.	Rifleman	Warren, C. G.	2nd Lieutenant
Townsend-Green, H. R.	Captain	Waterhouse, J.	Rifleman
Trace, J.	Rifleman	Waterman, G. S.	Rifleman
Treffry, R. H.	Rifleman	Waterson, E.	Rifleman
Tressadern, R. R.	Rifleman	Watkins, W. W.	Rifleman
Treuge, A.	Rifleman	Watkinson, H.	Rifleman
Trewin, F. L.	Rifleman	Watson, C., *M.M.*	
Trigg, A. C.	Corporal	Compy.-Quarterm.-Sergeant	
Tucker, A. C.	Rifleman	Watson, P. G.	Rifleman

ROLL OF HONOUR

Watson, S. A.	Rifleman	Williams, S.	Rifleman
Watson, S. F., *M.M.*	Lance-Corporal	Williamson, A.	Rifleman
Waymark, C. W.	Lance-Corporal	Willis, C. G.	Rifleman
Wearn, R. R.	Rifleman	Willoughby, W. E.	Rifleman
Weatherhead, H. K.	Rifleman	Willsher, A. C.	Rifleman
Weaver, J. G.	Rifleman	Wilshin, E.	Rifleman
Webb, A. C. W.	Rifleman	Wilson, C. H.	Rifleman
Webb, F. L.	Rifleman	Wilson, C. S.	Sergeant
Webb, J.	Lance-Corporal	Wilson, C. S. C.	Sergeant
Webb, M. M.	Captain	Wilson, E.	Rifleman
Webber, G.	Rifleman	Wilson, E. B.	Rifleman
Webster, T. W.	2nd Lieutenant	Wilson, H.	Lance-Corporal
Welbank, H.	Rifleman	Wing, B.	Sergeant
Weller, C.	Rifleman	Wingfield, A. W.	Rifleman
Weller, C. G.	Rifleman	Winkley, A.	Rifleman
Wells, G. A.	Rifleman	Winn, S. E. W.	Rifleman
West, A. H.	Rifleman	Winstanley, A.	Rifleman
West, E. H.	Lance-Corporal	Winter, H. L.	Rifleman
Westbury, E. L.	Rifleman	Winter, H. W.	Rifleman
Westcott, W. R.	Rifleman	Winterton, C. A.	Rifleman
Weston, F. G.	Company-Sergeant-Major	Witney, H. H.	Sergeant
		Wood, F.	Rifleman
Weston, J. C.	2nd Lieutenant	Wood, R. A.	Lance-Sergeant
Weston, T. C.	Rifleman	Wood, W.	Rifleman
Wharhirst, F.	Rifleman	Wood, W. J.	Rifleman
Wheatcroft, A. E.	Rifleman	Woodbridge, W. A.	Rifleman
Wheatley, L. A. R.	Rifleman	Wootton, J. W.	Rifleman
Whelbourn, F. W.	Lance-Corporal	Wray, W. T.	Rifleman
Wherrett, F. J.	Sergeant	Wright, A. E.	Rifleman
Whiddett, W. C. F.	Rifleman	Wright, A. K. T.	2nd Lieutenant
Whiskin, E. C.	Compy.-Quarterm.-Sergeant	Wright, E. C. B.	Rifleman
		Wright, F. H.	Rifleman
White, H. J.	Rifleman	Wright, R.	Rifleman
White, R. W.	Rifleman	Wright, W. G.	Rifleman
White, S.	Rifleman	Wylde, G.	Rifleman
White, W. D. F.	Rifleman	Wyles, W. G.	Rifleman
Whitehouse, H.	Rifleman		
Whittle, H. F.	Rifleman	Yates, A. G. V.	2nd Lieutenant
Wild, F. B.	Rifleman	Yeates, S. C.	Lieutenant
Wiles, W. E.	Rifleman	Yetton, W. V.	Rifleman
Wilkinson, E.	Rifleman	Yewer, P. H.	Rifleman
Wilkinson, W. R.	Rifleman	Young, J. R.	Rifleman
Williams, A. V.	Rifleman	Young, P. R.	Rifleman
Williams, E. G.	Rifleman	Young, S. Y.	Rifleman
Williams, E. S.	Rifleman		
Williams, S.	Corporal	Zeims, A.	Rifleman

HONOURS AND AWARDS
1st BATTALION QUEEN'S WESTMINSTER RIFLES
1914–1919

[The ranks shown are those held at the date of the award or of the first mention in despatches]

I. OFFICERS

(a) For Services Overseas

COMPANION OF THE ORDER OF ST. MICHAEL AND ST. GEORGE

Lieut.-Colonels

R. Shoolbred, T.D., D.I..   J. Waley Cohen, D.S.O., T.D.

COMPANION OF THE DISTINGUISHED SERVICE ORDER

Lieut.-Colonels

S. G. L. Bradley, M.C., D.C.M.   S. R. Savill, M.C.
P. M. Glasier.

Major J. Waley Cohen, T.D.

OFFICER OF THE ORDER OF THE BRITISH EMPIRE

Colonel P. E. Harding, M.C.
Captain E. G. S. Waley.

BAR TO THE MILITARY CROSS

Captains

N. T. Thurston, M.C.   F. E. Whitby, M.C.

MILITARY CROSS

Captains

J. B. Baber.
S. G. L. Bradley, D.C.M.
H. F. Grizelle.
P. E. Harding.
G. A. N. Lowndes.
H. F. Mott.
S. R. Savill.
F. G. Swainson.
N. T. Thurston.
F. E. Whitby, M.C.
R. L. Whittle.

Captain and Adjutants

H. J. Flower.   H. S. Price.

MILITARY CROSS—*continued*
Lieutenants

O. A. M. Eaton.
W. H. Gatfield.
C. R. Jacomb.
J. B. Malthouse.

C. E. Moy.
W. G. Orr.
V. G. Rayner.

Second Lieutenants

F. W. Russell.
H. R. Smith.
J. A. N. Webb.

W. H. Ormiston.
D. F. Upton.

FRENCH CROIX DE GUERRE
Lieut.-Colonel J. Waley Cohen, C.M.G., D.S.O., T.D.

MENTIONED IN DESPATCHES
Lieut.-Colonels

R. Shoolbred, C.M.G., T.D., D.L. (2).

P. M. Glasier, D.S.O. (4).
S. R. Savill, D.S.O., M.C. (2).

Majors

J. Waley Cohen, D.S.O. (4).

N. B. Tyrwhitt.

Captains

J. B. Baber, M.C.
S. G. L. Bradley (4).
H. J. Flower, and *Adjutant* K.R.R.C.
H. F. Grizelle.

P. E. Harding.
W. M. Henderson-Scott.
B. L. Miles.
H. S. Price.
N. T. Thurston.

(b) For Services at Home

COMMANDER OF THE ORDER OF THE BRITISH EMPIRE
Lieut.-Colonel E. G. H. Cox.

OFFICER OF THE ORDER OF THE BRITISH EMPIRE
Major G. H. Lambert, T.D.

BREVET MAJOR
Captains

E. G. H. Cox.

O. P. L. Hoskyns.

MENTIONED IN DESPATCHES AT HOME
Lieut.-Colonels

E. G. H. Cox (2).

G. H. Lambert (2).

Captains

J. H. Kelly (2).

O. P. L. Hoskyns (1).

HONOURS AND AWARDS

II. Warrant Officers and Non-Commissioned Officers and Riflemen

BAR TO DISTINGUISHED CONDUCT MEDAL
Company Sergeant-Major C. L. Ives.

DISTINGUISHED CONDUCT MEDAL
Regimental Sergeant-Major A. H. Davis.

Company Sergeant-Majors
C. W. Froome.
J. B. Hill.
C. L. Ives.
H. Lintott.
W. H. Musselwhite, M.M.
J. E. Plumridge.
S. J. Turnbull.

Sergeants
H. R. Casey.
A. G. Fulton.
L. P. Harrow.
L. H. Jenks.
J. R. Jones.

Lance-Sergeants
A. W. G. Frost.
E. W. Gillett.

Corporals
H. Lewis.
S. C. Tomlinson.

Lance-Corporals
J. Clamp, M.M.
A. W. Lance, M.M.

Riflemen
E. Bryant.
J. Denison.
F. A. Mobey.
J. H. Pouchot.
F. Scotney.

BAR TO THE MILITARY MEDAL
Sergeants
F. D. Peake, M.M.
E. Yarnold, M.M.

Lance-Sergeant R. R. Bulford, M.M.
Corporal A. C. Dormand, M.M.
Lance-Corporal A. W. Lance, M.M.

MILITARY MEDAL
Company Sergeant-Major H. W. Couper.

Company Quartermaster-Sergeants
W. H. Musselwhite.
C. Watson.

1st QUEEN'S WESTMINSTER RIFLES

MILITARY MEDAL—continued

Sergeants

J. H. Atkins.
G. W. Avens.
A. V. Benton.
W. R. Berry.
A. Carey.
F. R. Davis.
J. W. Davis.
H. A. Fagan.
A. Finbow.
A. Fursee.
A. Goy.
C. E. Green.
C. C. Hall.
M. A. Johnson.
R. Kett.
W. Law.
L. Mabbett.
E. E. Matthews.
G. R. Membery.
F. B. Peake.
J. H. Smith.
R. F. Townsend.
S. Tucker.
T. J. Tucker.

Lance-Sergeants

R. R. Bulford.
H. J. Cartmell.
E. Yarnold.

Corporals

J. Archer.
G. Bristowe.
J. Clamp.
J. R. Cocking.
A. C. Dormand.
H. S. Floyd.
F. Francis.
T. Hayward.
A. D. Hicks.
C. F. Higgins.
R. Knight.
K. M. Marshall.
W. H. Royden.
S. V. Russel.
T. A. Skeate.
B. T. Taylor.
J. Taylor.
W. E. Wright.

Lance-Corporals

W. A. Brewer.
A. E. Clarke.
H. W. Cozens.
F. Garrett.
R. A. Green.
H. G. Hale.
W. G. Harris.
J. E. Knox.
A. W. Lance.
C. F. Parker.
S. Rundle.
H. Sheffield.
J. D. Smith.
W. E. Upfold.
C. V. Vane.
S. F. Watson.
E. E. West.
F. Williams.

Riflemen

J. Barker.
S. V. Barlow.
F. W. Barnes.
R. Barrow.
S. V. Bradley.
A. H. Broome.
A. E. Clapham.
R. Cotton.
F. Daley.
W. D. Dealey.
G. Donning.
S. Eveleigh.
L. French.
S. W. Geer.

HONOURS AND AWARDS

MILITARY MEDAL—*continued*

S. H. Goater.
G. Hinley.
O. S. Hollocks.
J. W. Hutchings.
A. H. Jarvis.
M. E. Kramer.
S. Leah.
E. D. Long.
R. W. Lowman.
F. Masters.
W. Ogden.
J. H. Orchard.
W. Phillip.
J. G. Pilkington.
F. Roberts.
F. J. Robinson.
W. Sheldon.
F. C. Skinner.
R. G. Smith.
J. W. Sunderland.
C. J. Tedman.
E. Trowbridge.
H. G. Tuke.
P. E. Walter.
H. Ward.
W. A. Williams.
A. M. Wingfield.
G. A. Winter.
T. W. Woodall.
J. E. Wright.

MERITORIOUS SERVICE MEDAL

Regimental Sergeant-Major A. H. Davis, D.C.M.

Company-Quartermaster-Sergeants

A. Finbow, M.M.
A. J. Nutting.

Company Sergeant-Major W. Essam.

Sergeants

W. H. Cole.
F. G. Fisher.
W. B. Green.
G. O. Meech.

Riflemen

F. E. Eddowes.
J. H. James.

MENTIONED IN DESPATCHES

Regimental Quartermaster-Sergeant E. W. N. Jackson.
Regimental Sergeant-Major A. H. Davis.
Acting Staff-Sergeant-Major A. E. Harvey.

Company Sergeant-Majors

H. M. Masson.
F. G. Weston.

Company Quartermaster-Sergeant E. P. Loveland.

Sergeants

E. W. Adams.
H. Fagan.
G. Hinley.
M. A. Johnson.
A. Maas.
W. H. Musselwhite.
E. Sandewell.
C. Watson.

Lance-Sergeants

G. C. Cordery.
W. M. Mansell.

MENTIONED IN DESPATCHES—continued

Corporals
A. T. Gardiner.
R. de R. Roche.
E. Yarnold.

Lance-Corporal P. P. Wheaton.

Riflemen
R. W. Lowman.
C. J. Tedman.
D. H. Tibbs.
G. Warren.
A. J. Wakefield.
A. M. Wingfield (2).

ROYAL VICTORIA MEDAL
Sergeant A. J. Nutting.

FRENCH MEDAILLE MILITAIRE
Sergeant P. N. McCready.
Rifleman D. J. Gander.

BELGIAN CROIX DE GUERRE
Sergeant C. H. Ashdown.

RUSSIAN MEDAL OF ST. GEORGE (2nd Class)
Sergeants
H. R. Casey.
E. W. Adams.

RUMANIAN MEDAILLE BARBATIC ST. CREDINTA (3rd Class)
Rifleman W. T. Morris.

TOTAL HONOURS AND AWARDS

C.M.G.	2
C.B.E.	1
D.S.O.	4
O.B.E.	3
Bar to M.C.	2
M.C.	25
Bar to D.C.M.	1
D.C.M.	24
Bar to M.M.	5
M.M.	110
M.S.M.	10
Mentioned in Despatches	59
Other Honours	10
Grand Total	256

OFFICERS WHO SERVED OVERSEAS, 1914–1919

1st BATTALION QUEEN'S WESTMINSTER RIFLES

[Except where otherwise stated appointments at home, extra-regimental and temporary appointments, are not shown. The ranks are permanent ranks.]

Lieut.-Colonel R. Shoolbred, C.M.G., T.D., D.L. (commanding).
Colonel P. E. Harding, O.B.E., M.C., T.D. (in command).
T/Lieut.-Colonel P. M. Glasier, D.S.O. (commanding).
Lieut.-Colonel S. R. Savill, D.S.O., M.C. (commanding).
Lieut.-Colonel J. Waley Cohen, C.M.G., D.S.O., T.D. (2nd in command).
Lieut.-Colonel G. H. Lambert, O.B.E., T.D. (commanding 3rd Reserve Battalion).
Lieut.-Colonel E. G. H. Cox, C.B.E., T.D.
Lieut.-Colonel S. G. L. Bradley, D.S.O., M.C., D.C.M.

Majors

J. Q. Henriques, T.D. (2nd in command).
S. Low, T.D. (2nd in command, 3rd Reserve Battalion).
N. B. Tyrwhitt, T.D. (2nd in command).
J. B. Whitmore, T.D. (2nd in command).

Captains

C. R. W. Attenborough.
J. B. Baber, M.C.
F. L. Barwell.
R. J. H. Bull.
J. E. M. Carvell.
L. S. Challis, T.D.
G. E. Cockerill.
P. C. Coote.
H. D. Corlett.
H. J. Flower, D.S.O., M.C., K.R.R.C. (Adjutant).
A. J. M. Gordon.
J. A. Green.
H. F. Grizelle, M.C.
W. M. Henderson-Scott.
L. W. G. Henshaw.
O. P. L. Hoskyns (Brevet-Major).
C. R. Jacomb, M.C.
J. H. Kelly (Adjutant 3rd Battalion).
L. C. Lauchland.
W. C. M. Macrae (A.S.C.).
J. H. Martin.
B. L. Miles.
H. F. Mott, M.C.
W. G. Orr, M.C. (attached).
A. R. Z. Porter.
H. S. Price, M.C. (Adjutant).
E. Ridehalgh.
P. Spencer-Smith.
N. T. Thurston, M.C. (a/Adjutant).
H. R. Townsend-Green.
S. L. Townsend-Green.
M. E. Trollope.

1ST QUEEN'S WESTMINSTER RIFLES

Captains—continued

R. H. Wagner.
E. G. S. Waley, O.B.E.
H. F. Waters, M.C.
M. M. Webb.

F. E. Whitby, M.C.
R. L. Whittle, M.C.
S. Williams.

Lieutenants and 2nd Lieutenants

H. Agate (a/Captain).
C. W. Anderson.
T. S. Apergis.
S. E. Arber.
G. W. Avens, M.C., M.M.

T. S. Baker.
R. A. Bassham.
E. Bawtree.
D. C. Beadel.
H. L. Bell.
V. Bell.
J. Betteridge.
A. G. Beville.
A. G. Bird (a/Captain).
W. T. W. Birts.
E. H. Bovill.
E. Brimelow (a/Captain).
A. C. Brooke.
R. H. Brown.

R. R. Calkin.
T. Caudwell (a/Captain).
A. D. C. Chadbourn.
F. L. Chamberlain.
A. H. Chaplin.
G. Chilton.
A. E. Clapham, M.M.
E. Coaker.
A. C. Cooper.
G. W. Cranmore.
W. E. Crawford.
E. L. Crompton.

G. Daniel.
F. R. A. Dansey.
H. Davies.
S. F. Dean.
G. Delaforce.
R. S. Dickinson (a/Captain).
F. Dixon.
F. G. Douthwaite.

C. H. Dudley-Ward (D.S.O., Major, Welsh Guards).
W. H. Dyson.
O. A. M. Eaton, M.C.
A. Edwards.
E. E. Ellis.
J. S. Engall.
C. A. English.

J. H. Falconer.
F. A. Farley.
G. J. Farmer.
F. H. Favell.
F. Fisher.
E. S. Foley.
A. C. C. Fraser.
L. W. Friend.
H. J. Furminger.

W. H. Gatfield.
R. A. Gatfield, M.C. (a/Captain).
F. H. Geary.
J. C. Goadby.
A. P. T. Godly.
J. E. S. Goulding.
W. H. Graham.
C. K. Gray.

W. F. Hall.
H. T. Harper.
R. Harrison.
L. P. Harrow, D.C.M.
E. C. Hayes.
R. Herring.
J. L. Hewitt.
F. A. Hitchings.
D. Hoare.
H. J. Holland.
J. H. M. Hooper.
J. A. Horne.
E. A. Hudson.
T. F. Hudson.

Lieutenants and 2nd Lieutenants—continued

W. Hull.
R. C. Hurst, M.M.

C. C. Iveson (a/Captain).

R. S. Jackson.
E. H. Jarvis.
T. H. Jenkin.
E. F. Johnston.
E. A. C. Jones.
W. E. S. Jotcham.

J. P. D. Kennedy.
H. A. Kilburn.
V. H. Kirkby.
C. A. F. Knapp.

B. C. Lewall.
G. L. Lloyd.
G. A. N. Lowndes, M.C. (a/Captain).
H. Luscombe.

M. McBean.
I. P. McEwan.
A. M. Mackle.
E. W. G. Malcolm.
J. B. Malthouse, M.C.
S. L. Mann.
A. M. Manson.
W. B. Marsh.
C. S. H. Melhado.
F. H. B. Moore.
W. E. Morgan.
H. K. Moulton.
C. E. Moy, M.C. (a/Captain).
W. M. Musgrove.

A. G. Negus.
S. North.

E. G. T. Okill.
C. J. Oppitz.
W. H. Ormiston, M.C.

K. Palmer.
P. Palmer.

R. C. Palmer.
A. J. Philip.
P. Pickles.
J. R. Plunket.
A. E. Pollard.
O. M. Power.
J. C. B. Prince.
T. W. R. Procter.

F. A. Rankin.
C. H. Raven.
V. G. Rayner, M.C.
T. L. Relton.
C. W. Renton.
R. I. Richens.
A. A. W. Ritchings.
F. W. Rouse.
A. B. Russell.
F. W. Russell, M.C.
W. J. Ryan.

J. A. A. Scott.
C. Sheppard.
S. F. Simonds.
H. J. Simpson.
A. M. Smith.
A. T. B. Smith.
E. W. Smith.
F. E. Smith.
H. R. Smith, M.C.
S. H. Smith.
W. D. Smith.
L. G. Speck.
M. Spencer-Smith.
H. Stevenson.
W. A. Stilwell.
I. d'A. Stitt.
W. E. Strange.
C. A. Stubbs.
F. G. Swainson, M.C. (a/Captain).

C. C. Tabberer.
H. J. D. Talling.
F. S. Thomas (a/Captain)
W. J. Thomas.
E. W. Thompson.

1st QUEEN'S WESTMINSTER RIFLES

Lieutenants and 2nd Lieutenants—continued

W. E. Todd.
S. E. Trotter.

D. F. Upton, M.C.

T. J. M. Van der Linde.

J. W. Waddington.
B. Wade.
C. G. Warren.
F. Warwick.
J. A. N. Webb, M.C. (a/Captain).

T. W. Webster.
J. J. Westmoreland (a/Captain).
G. F. Westwood.
H. J. Wetherall.
F. R. Wilson.
S. L. Wilson.
P. I. Worthington.

A. G. V. Yates.
S. C. Yeates.
W. F. D. Young.

Quartermasters

Q.-M. and Hon. Major A. S. Pridmore, T.D. (in England).

Q.-M. and Hon. Captain J. H. Kelly.
Q.-M. and Hon. Captain E. W. N. Jackson.

Medical Officers—R.A.M.C. attached

Captains

M. A. S. Murray.
A. Ramsbottom, M.C.
D. Rees.
E. Williams.

R. Barnwell Rhett (U.S.A. Army).
J. Beadel.

Chaplains

Rev. T. Tiplady.
Rev. H. C. Read.
Rev. J. R. Temple.

Rev. K. N. Crisford, M.C.
Rev. H. C. Lewis.

INDEX

Abbéville, 15
Abeele, 167, 170, 176
Abergavenny, 2
Achicourt, 140, 142, 143, 159, 160, 163, 164, 238, 239
Adams, Lt., 64
Agache, River, 266, 271, 272
Agate, H., Capt., 64, 115, 155
Agnez les Duisans, 280, 281
Ailly, 77
Ainslie, H. S., Lt.-Col., 50
Aldershot, 2
Allenby, Sir E. H. H., General, 145
Ambrose, Sgt., 183
American Army, 210, 246
Amiens, 247, 248
Amiens, Battle of, 248
Anglewood Valley, 121, 123
Angre, 296
Angreau, 294, 295, 296
Angreau River, 294
Apergis, T. S., 2/Lt., 116, 118
Arleux, 277, 279
l'Armée, 30
Armentières, 18, 32, 44
Armistice, 296, 297
Army Education Scheme, 214, 215, 240, 301
Arnold, A. E., Lt., 279
Arras, 159, 217, 233, 234, 238, 239, 240, 246, 247, 281
Arras, Battle of, 1917, 145
Arras, First Battle of, 1918, 209
Arthur, G. S., Lt., 93
Ashdown, Sgt., 176, 334
Athies, 297, 300
Atkins, J., Sgt., 225
Aubencheul-au-Bac, 277, 279, 280
Aubigny-au-Bac, 279, 280
Aulnoy, 284
Aunelle, River, 286, 288, 291, 293
Autreppe, 296
Avens, G. W., Lt., 267, 270, 272, 331

Baber, J. B., Capt., v, 13, 28, 78, 267, 283, 286, 329, 330
Bailleulval, 246, 249

Baker, T. S., 2/Lt., 135, 155
Bancourt, 177
"Bantams," 103
Bapaume, 180
Barlow, Rfmn., 276
Barly, 164
Barret, E. F., Rfmn., 149
Barrow, R., Bugler, 70
Barwell, F., 2/Lt., 12, 22, 80
Battalion :
   equipment of, with new rifles, 11
   first under fire, 22
   proceeds overseas, 12
   reorganisation of, 18
   sports, 79, 80, 164, 165, 245
   strength of, 54, 84, 265
Battalions, Infantry :
   Camerons, 6th Bn., 246
   Cheshire, 1/5th (Pioneer) Bn., 91, 93, 98, 123, 178, 220, 240
   Coldstream Guards, 2nd Bn., 252
   Duke of Cornwall's L.I., 6th Bn., 56, 140
   Duke of Wellington's,
     2/4th Bn., 216
     7th Bn., 284
   Durham L.I.,
     2nd Bn., 19, 21, 31, 32, 58, 59, 60
     6th Bn., 150, 151, 152, 153
     8th Bn., 150, 151, 152, 153
   East Yorkshire, 1st Bn., 21, 23, 25, 49, 52, 58, 59, 64
   Essex, 11th Bn., 64, 66
   H.A.C., 17, 123
   King's (Liverpool),
     1st Bn., 202, 203
     9th Bn., 254, 257
     Scottish, 14, 56
   K.O.Y.L.I., 6th Bn., 67
   K.R.R.C.,
     2nd Bn., 8
     7th Bn., 175
   Lancashire Fusiliers, 2nd Bn., 223, 225
   Lincolnshire,
     5th Bn., 105
     7th Bn., 107

INDEX

Battalions, Infantry:
  London Regt.,
    1/1st Bn., 74, 238, 241
    1/2nd Bn., 74, 76, 82, 117, 119, 120, 140, 141, 146, 147, 157, 158, 171, 172, 173, 175, 199, 203, 208, 213, 216, 219, 220, 228, 229, 244, 245, 249, 251, 253, 254, 255, 257, 260, 264, 266, 268, 271, 272, 275, 280, 284, 287, 288, 295
    2/2nd Bn., 81
    1/3rd Bn., 74
    1/4th Bn., 74, 103, 173, 214, 221, 256
    1/5th Bn. (London Rifle Bde.), 74, 76, 87, 88, 95, 98, 102, 113, 114, 119, 120, 121, 122, 123, 124, 126, 135, 136, 137, 142, 146, 147, 148, 150, 152, 156, 157, 158, 172, 173, 175, 182, 198, 205, 217, 219, 220, 221, 225, 249, 250, 251, 253, 254, 255, 257, 258, 259, 260, 288, 289, 292, 294, 295
    8th Bn. (Post Office Rifles), 108
    1/9th Bn. (Queen Victoria's Rifles), 74, 78, 87, 88, 91, 98, 105, 107, 114, 116, 123, 125, 130, 131, 132, 147, 148, 149, 150, 151, 152, 157, 158, 160, 166, 169, 170, 171, 172, 174, 179, 182, 183, 184, 185, 186, 187, 194, 196, 215, 216
    12th Bn. (Rangers), 74, 142
    13th Bn. (Kensingtons), 6, 15, 74, 126, 132, 246, 270, 271, 273, 287
    14th Bn. (London Scottish), 6, 74, 158, 160, 198, 199, 208, 252, 260
    15th Bn. (Prince of Wales's Own, Civil Service Rifles), 6, 305
    22nd Bn. (Queen's), 108
    23rd Bn. (Queen's), 108
    24th Bn. (Queen's), 108
    28th Bn. (Artists Rifles), 6, 17
  Loyal Regt., 1st Bn., 263
  Machine Gun, 56th Bn., 228
  Middlesex,
    1/7th Bn., 74, 170, 261, 264, 277
    1/8th Bn., 74, 208, 230, 240, 242, 250, 251, 275
    15th Bn., 61

Battalions, Infantry:
  North Stafford,
    1st Bn., 46
    4th Bn., 184
    1/5th Bn., 47
  Queen's Westminster Rifles,
    2nd Bn., 8, 43, 61, 305
    3rd Bn., 7, 70, 73
  Rifle Brigade,
    2nd Bn., 31
    3rd Bn., 54
    5th Bn., 54
  Royal Berkshire, 6th Bn., 170
  Royal Fusiliers, 1st Bn., 33, 35
  Royal Scots,
    2nd Bn., 177
    8th Bn., 17
    10th Bn., 50
  Royal Sussex, 9th Bn., 64
  Scottish Rifles, 1/5th Bn., 37
  Sherwood Foresters, 2nd Bn., 21; 48, 49, 58, 59, 60, 63, 64
  Shropshire L.I., 1st Bn., 27
  Somerset L.I., 6th Bn., 159
  South Lancashire,
    2nd Bn., 169
    2/4th Bn., 257, 258
    1/5th Bn., 48
  Suffolk, 9th Bn., 124
  Warwickshire, 1/7th Bn., 48
  West Yorkshire,
    1st Bn., 21, 27, 29, 49
    1/5th Bn., 137
  Canadian,
    5th Bn., 280
    15th Bn., 44
    16th Bn., 245
Batteries R.F.A., XXIV, 32, 63
Bavincourt, 246
Bayencourt, 8, 82, 103
Bazentin-le-Petit, 103, 111
Beaucamp, 201
Beaumetz, 156, 164
Beaurains, 140, 141, 144, 156, 159
Bell, H. L., 2/Lt., 118
Bell, V., 2/Lt., 155
Bellacourt-Wailly, 140
Bellewaarde, 11, 53, 62
Bennett, Rfmn., 276
Berguette, 128
Berles, 156
Berneville, 156, 209, 238, 240, 246
Berry, W. R., Sgt., 258, 259
Berthen, 52

INDEX 341

Betteridge, J. H., 2/Lt., 135, 155
Beville, A. G., 2/Lt., 144
Bienvillers, 103, 107
Bishop, Rfmn., 118
Bisley, 2
Blackdown, 2
Blairville, 249
Boeschepe, 52
Boiry Becquerelle, 248
Bois de Beaufort, 294, 295
Bois Grenier, 22, 23
Bois du Quesnoy, 275, 277
Bois du Vert, 160
Boisleux-au-Mont, 249
Bougnies, 300
Bouleaux Wood, 112, 119, 120, 129
Bouquemaison, 166
Bourlon, 191, 193, 202
Bourlon Hill, 181, 190
Boursies, 177, 179, 181, 192, 194
Bout de Ville, 130, 131, 133
Bovill, E. H., Lt., xv, 92, 97, 98, 99
" Bow Bells," 133, 159, 165, 181, 186, 282, 301
Bowden, Sgt., 282
Boyelles, 248
Bradley, S. G. L., Col., 5, 13, 65, 73, 298, 329, 330
Bray, 110
Bridgeford, R. J., Brig.-General, 73
Brielen, 64
Brigades, Infantry :
  4th, 6
  6th, 202
  9th, 52, 53
  12th, 48
  16th, 22, 57, 61, 62
  17th, 32, 46, 50, 57
  18th, 21, 23, 32, 35, 38, 50, 52, 53, 57, 58, 61, 64, 67, 176
  41st, 61
  42nd, 68
  43rd, 56
  53rd, 170, 171
  85th, 8
  92nd, 209
  109th, 186, 192, 194, 195
  117th, 170
  150th, 151
  154th, 209
  167th, 86, 90, 106, 120, 127, 133, 155, 170, 221, 240, 248, 249, 250, 256, 275, 279, 296, 297

Brigades, Infantry :
  168th, 82, 86, 87, 96, 103, 127, 154, 248, 256, 259, 266, 274, 275, 279, 284, 287, 289, 294, 295, 296
  169th, 74, 75, 76, 82, 86, 87, 94, 96, 100, 104, 113, 114, 120, 124, 127, 137, 139, 146, 147, 150, 157, 158, 170, 171, 173, 191, 195, 199, 209, 210, 228, 249, 250, 254, 258, 259, 260, 261, 274, 284, 287, 289, 293, 294, 295, 296
  186th, 216
  " The Grey," 6, 11, 15
Brimelcw, E., Capt., 172, 175
Bristowe, G., Cpl., 204, 332
Broadbent, Sgt., 219
Brooks, R., Rfmn., 27
" Buckingham Palace," 39
Buckley, Rfmn., 133
Bullecourt, 252, 254, 256, 261
Bunkers Farm, 6
Burnell, Major, 157
Byng, Hon. Sir J., General, 177, 207, 229

Calkin, R. R., Lt., 251, 255
Calonne sur la Lys, 128
Calvert Farm, 22
Cambrai, 170, 180, 217, 264, 265, 278
Cambrai, Battle of, 1917, 189, 233
Cambridge Road, 53
Campbell, G., Lt.-Col., 143
Canal du Nord, 177, 180, 189, 190, 193, 194
Canal du Nord, Battle of, 263, 265
Cane, F., Cr./Sgt., 12
Captures (prisoners and material), 198, 275, 280, 291
Casualties, 36, 43, 47, 49, 50, 53, 54, 56, 60, 61, 64, 67, 68, 69, 70, 73, 99, 114, 116, 118, 122, 125, 127, 129, 144, 153, 154, 175, 176, 185, 198, 205, 224, 230, 241, 244, 252, 261, 262, 268, 274, 276, 280, 292
Caucourt, 214, 245
Caudwell, T., Capt., 184, 195, 196, 202, 204, 205
Caumont Farm, 284, 285
Chamberlain, F. L., Lt., 221, 226
Chaplin, A. H., 2/Lt., 246

INDEX

Chapman, H. W., Sgt., 13
Château de Préseau, 284
Château Segard, 170, 176
Chemin des Dames, 157, 247
Cherisy, 146, 147, 148, 149, 157, 159
Christmas Day, 1914, 34
Citadel, The, 128
Clamp, J., L./Cpl., 225, 226, 331, 332
Clapham, A. E., Rfmn., 115, 332
Clark, A. E., Rfmn., 92
Clark, Gordon, C. A., Lt.-Col., 7, 166
Clark, Mrs. Gordon, 37
Cockerill, G. E., Capt., xv, 88, 90, 99, 107
Cohen, J. Waley, Lt.-Col., 3, 12, 66, 73, 329, 330
Cohen, Mrs., 10
Coigneux, 81
Cojeul River, 160
Coke, E. S. D'E, Brig.-General, 75, 105, 158, 160, 187, 207, 282, 303
Combles, 119, 120, 124, 129
Commune, La, 165, 166
Comté, La, 244
Congreve, C. R., Capt., 65
Congreve, W. N., Maj.-General, V.C., 21, 25, 50, 51, 61
Cooper, Sgt., 72
Corbie, 110
Cordery, G. C., Sgt., 118
Corlett, H. D., 2/Lt., 13
Corner Farm, 6
Corps, German XIX (2nd Saxon), 29
Cotton, R., Rfmn., 274, 332
Couper, H.W., C.S.M., 95, 331
Courtenay, A. D. H., C.Q.M.S., 101, 102, 151
Courtrai, 43
Cox, E. G. H., Lt.-Col., xiv, 5, 12, 18, 22, 330
Cranmore, G. W., 2/Lt., 118
Crisford, K. N., Rev., 293
Croisilles, 156, 248, 249, 250, 251, 253
Croix Barbée, 131
Crump Farm, 69
Curgies, 287
Cuthbert, G. J., Col., 6

Dainville, 159, 238, 239, 242, 243
Davidson, Rfmn., 64
Davis, A. H., R.S.M., 12, 180, 333
Davis, R. F., Sgt., 82, 197
Davis, W. J., L./Sgt., 276
Dealy, W. E., L./Cpl., 277, 332

Defences, German, at Gommecourt, 86
Defences, German, at Cambrai, 190
Delbe, Professor, 108
"Dells, The," 7
Delville Wood, 111, 119
Demicourt, 177, 179, 192, 194
Dennison, J., Rfmn., 277
Desplanque Farm, 33
Devil's Wood, 245
Dickins, Lt.-Col., 114
Dickinson, R. S., Capt., 12, 22, 63
Divisions :
  Guards, 248, 249, 251
  2nd, 202
  2nd London, 3, 5, 6, 10
  3rd, 53, 157, 160, 177
  5th, 113, 124
  6th, 21, 50, 51, 56, 63, 72, 120
  8th, 171, 199
  11th, 265, 268, 270, 284, 286, 289, 292, 293, 295, 296
  14th, 56, 145, 146, 157, 159, 175
  15th, 241, 243
  16th, 114
  18th, 171
  20th, 120
  21st, 147
  30th, 145, 146
  36th, 85, 193, 195, 196, 200
  46th, 85, 87, 94, 99, 123
  47th, 202
  49th, 284, 293
  50th, 147
  51st, 205
  52nd, 249, 250, 255, 258, 263
  56th, 72, 85, 86, 94, 99, 105, 113, 114, 119, 129, 136, 137, 145, 146, 157, 171, 193, 194, 202, 205, 220, 229, 231, 232, 234, 235, 241, 244, 247, 248, 249, 253, 258, 259, 261, 265, 266, 268, 269, 270, 274, 277, 278, 286, 289, 296
    Composition of, on formation, 75
    Queen's Westminsters join, 76
  57th, 209, 253, 254, 257, 260
  63rd, 263, 296
Divisions, Canadian :
  1st, 244
  2nd, 241
  3rd, 220
  4th, 221, 228, 229, 230, 235, 286, 287, 293

INDEX

Divisions, German:
  2nd Prussian Guard Reserve, 91
  23rd, 218
  41st, 234
  75th Reserve, 234
  83rd, 234
  187th, 234
  214th, 244
  219th, 218
  240th, 234
Doignies, 178, 179, 181, 182, 194
Domvast, 108, 109
Doran, W., Brig.-General, 32
Du Biez Farm, 31
Dudgeon, F. A., Maj.-General, 75, 206, 235
Duisans, 159, 161, 163
Dunn, R., Sgt., 13
Dury, 263
Dyson, W. H., 2/Lt., 104

Eaton, O. A. M., 2/Lt., 221, 330
Eaucourt l'Abbaye, 125
Ecourt St. Quentin, 264
Ecurie Wood, 209, 213
Edmead's Farm, 50
Edwards, H. E., Rfmn., 93
Ellis, E. E., 2/Lt., 175
Emanuel School, Wandsworth, 38
Endowed Schools, 4, 5
Engall, 2/Lt., 99
English, C. A., 2/Lt., 155
l'Epinette, 29, 46
Erquinghem, 18, 21
Estreux, 287
Eveleigh, S., Rfmn., 203, 204, 332

Fairclough, Rfmn., 93
Falfemont Farm, 112, 114, 120
Famars, 282
Farley, L./Cpl., 72
Faucourt, 124
Fauquissart, 134
Favière Wood, 113
Fergusson, Sir C., Lt.-General, Bt., 238, 249, 262, 263
Firth, J. C. B., 2/Lt., 220, 223
Fisher, F., 2/Lt., 221
Flower, H. J., Capt., 7, 8, 12, 56, 73, 329, 330
Fonquevillers, 85, 103, 105, 107
Fontaine, 193
Fontaine lez Croisilles, 251, 252
Francis, D., Cpl., 149, 153

Fraser, Rfmn., 95
Frelinghien, 38, 39, 42, 44, 46
Fremicourt, 209
French, Sir John, Field-Marshal, 8, 16, 50, 57
Fressies, 279
Frohen, 108
Froome, C.S.M., 13, 92, 99, 331
Frost, Sgt., 272, 331
Fulton, A. G., Sgt., 2, 11, 13, 28, 331
Fulton, G. E., Sgt., 2, 11

Gallipoli, 81
Gander, D. J., Rfmn., 152, 334
Gatfield, W. H., Lt., 260, 261, 284, 286, 330
Gavrelle, 156, 209, 210, 211, 212, 218, 220, 223, 224, 226, 274
Gay, C., Cr./Sgt., 12
Genly, 300, 303
German Regiments:
  107th, 35
  179th, 29
  358th, 244
Gezaincourt, 77
Gigly, Cpl., 301
Gillett, E. W., Sgt., 257, 292, 331
Ginchy, 112, 119, 120
Glasier, P. M., Lt.-Col., 13, 54, 89, 163, 167, 172, 186, 198, 226, 241, 242, 245, 329, 330
Glencorse Wood, 168, 170, 172, 173, 175, 176
Goadby, J. C., 2/Lt., 215, 243, 261, 262
Godley, Sir A. J., Lt.-General, 263, 277
Gommecourt, 81, 82, 84, 86, 89, 94, 97, 99, 105, 164
Gonnelieu, 189
Goole, F. H., Esq., 304
Gordon, A. J. M., Capt., 185, 196
Gorhambury Park, 10
Gouy-en-Artois, 164
Gouzeaucourt, 201, 265
Graincourt, 180, 194
Gray, C. K., 2/Lt., 155
Green, J. A., Capt., 12, 22, 115, 122, 142
Gris-pot, 22, 24
Grizelle, H. F., Major, 115, 243, 302, 330
Grocers' Federation, 38

INDEX

Groom, Cpl., 293
Guémappe, 147, 156, 157, 158, 264
Gueudecourt, 119
Guillemont, 112

Haig, Sir D., Field-Marshal, 67
Haking, Sir R. C. B., Lt.-General, 133, 136
Haldane, Sir J. A. L., Lt.-General, 248
Hale, L./Cpl., 276
Hales, J. E., Cpl., 152
Hall, C. C., Sgt., 204, 332
Halloy, 80, 82
Hamilton, Sir Ian, General, 9
Happy Valley, 110
Hardecourt, 119
Harding, P. E., Lt.-Col., 13, 36, 81, 127, 128, 130, 131, 163, 329, 330
Harper, H. T., 2/Lt., 184, 220
Harris, Cpl., 204
Harrison, R., 2/Lt., 123
Harrow, L. P., Lt., 92, 141, 256, 261, 331
Haute Avesnes, 281, 285
Havre, 14, 15
Havrincourt, 190
Hawker, D. G., Sgt., 96, 100
Hawkins, Sgt., 131
Hayward, F. E., Cpl., 93
Hazebrouck, 17
Hébuterne, 81, 82, 84, 85, 102
Hem, 111
Hendecourt, 254, 256, 257, 258, 259
Henderson-Scott, W. M., Capt., 12, 41, 73, 330
Héninel, 146, 149
Henriques, J. Q., Major, 12, 18, 335
Henshaw, Capt., 60
Hewitt, E. Graily, Esq., 305
Heyworth, F. J., Col., 6
Hicks, Sgt., 104, 332
Hill 60, 52
Hindenburg, Von, Field-Marshal, 234
H.M. the King, 29, 65, 132, 231
Hobbs Farm, 50
Honnelle, River, 295
Hooge, 52, 53, 56, 60
Hooper, J. H. M., 2/Lt., 202, 205
Horne, Sir H. S., General, 145, 245
Horne, J. A., 2/Lt., 72, 92, 93, 97, 99
Hoskyns, O. P. L., Bt.-Major, 7, 13, 330

Houplines, 35, 37, 38, 42, 43, 44, 48
Houplines, Curé of, 49
Houtkerque, 67, 68
Hull, Sir C. P. A., Maj.-General, 75, 83, 163
Hull, W., 2/Lt., 155
Humphries, Rfmn., 203
Huppy, 76, 128
Hurst, Sgt., 246
Husey, R. H., Lt.-Col., 225
Hutchinson, D. M., Lt., 60

Ide, W. C., Cpl., 93
Inchy en Artois, 191, 193
Infantry Regiments (*see* Battalions):
  American, 2/213th, 246
  German,
    Prussian Guards, 18
    49th Res., 174
    55th Res., 98, 105
    107th, 35
    120th Res., 185
    179th, 29
    358th Res., 244
    414th, 184
Ing, Sgt., 133
Ingouville-Williams, E. C., Brig.-General, 22, 25
Inverness Copse, 168
Iremonger, H. E., Sgt., 94
Ives, C. L., C.S.M., 228, 331

Jackson, Lt.-Col., 243
Jackson, E. W. N., Capt., 12, 299, 333
Jacomb, C. R., Capt., 252, 255, 257, 258, 259, 267, 330
James, C. de B., Lt., 13
Jelf, R. J., Capt., 8
Jenkins, T. H., Lt., 302
Jenks, Sgt., 183, 331
Johnson, Sgt., 176
Johnston, E. F., 2/Lt., 115, 116, 118
Jones, E., 2/Lt., 121, 123
Jones, Goring-, Lt.-Col., 70
Jones, R. T., Major, 123
Jones, C.S.M., 198
Jones, Sgt., 223
Jones, L./Cpl., 104

Kaaie Salient, 62, 69
Keir, J. L., Maj.-General, 21
Kellett, J. P., Lt.-Col., 228

INDEX

Kelly, J. H., Capt., v, 12, 73, 299, 330
Kemp, G. C., Lt.-Col., 21
Kennedy, J. P. D., 2/Lt., 160, 187
Kilburn, H. A., 2/Lt., 185
King's Langley, 10
"Kingsaps Swimming Bath," 179
Kitchener, Lord, 10

L'Ancien Moulin, 285, 287
La Chapelle d'Armentières, 32, 33
La Flamanderie Farm, 22
La Houssoie, 23, 25
Lakeman, Rfmn., 95
Lambert, G. H., Lt.-Col., 13, 18, 73, 330
Lancaster, Rfmn., 151, 153
Lance, A. W., L./Cpl., 276, 331
Laventie, 130, 135, 136, 137
Law, Sgt., 286, 287, 332
Lea, Rfmn., 276
Le Bizet, 48
Lebucquière, 177, 181, 182, 184, 185, 194, 205, 209
Lecluse, 264
Legh, H. C., Lt.-Col., 7
Lesbœufs, 119, 124, 125, 127
Lethern, Sgt., 238
Le Touquet, 48
Leuze Wood, 112, 114, 115, 119, 120, 121, 124, 129
Leverstock Green, 6, 7, 9, 10, 16, 305
Lewall, B. C., 2/Lt., 134, 155
Lewis, H., Cpl., 228, 331
Liencourt, 246
Lieu St. Amand, 282
Lintott, H., C.S.M., 225, 226, 331
Lloyd, Sir Francis, Maj.-General, 10
Lloyd, Lady, 10
Lloyd, G. L., 2/Lt., 205
Lockley, E. W., 2/Lt., 117
Long, E. D., Rfmn., 97
Long, J. W., Capt., 117
Longueval, 105, 111
Louverval, 182, 185, 194, 200
Loveland, C.Q.M.S., 181, 333
Low, S., Capt., 12, 18, 22, 47
Lowman, R. W., Rfmn., 63, 334
Lowndes, G. A. N., Capt., 121, 187, 211, 220, 221, 222, 329
Ludendorff, General, 234
Ludgate Hill, 39
Lys, River, 35, 38, 41, 48
Lys, Battles of, 236, 247

Mabbett, Sgt., 227, 231, 332
McCarthy, A. C., Rfmn., 154
McCracken, Sir F. W. N., Maj.-General, 228, 230
McEwan, J. P., Lt., 286
Mackle, A. M., 2/Lt., 133, 134, 153, 175
Macnamara, J. J., Cr./Sgt., 13
Macrae, W. C. M., Capt., 273
Maidan, s.s., 14, 56
Maing, 283, 284
Makins, G., Capt., 8
Makins, H., Capt., 67
Malthouse, J. B., Lt., 286, 330
Maltz Horn Farm, 111, 114
Mann, S. L., 2/Lt., 243
Maple Copse, 58
"Mappin Terraces," 39
Maresches, 283
"Margate Pier," 39
Maricourt, 113, 123
Marly, 285
Marœuil, 209, 214
Marquion, 268, 269, 281
Marshall, K. M., L./Cpl., 198, 332
Maslin, W. H., Rfmn., 258
Masson, H. M., C.S.M., 13, 94, 99, 333
Masson, L. G., Sgt., 13
Matheson, T. G., Maj.-General, 235
Maxwell, Lt.-Col., 169
May, Rfmn., 72
Mearns, D. J., Capt., 258
Méaulte, 124
Menin, 43
Menin Gate, 56
Merville, 131
Messines Ridge, 168
Miles, B. L., Capt., 44, 182, 286, 299, 330
Miller, Sgt., 223
Minster, Island of Sheppey, 2
Miraumont, 176, 177
Mobilisation and Training, 1–13
  Strength of Battalion on, 3
Mœuvres, 180, 190, 191, 194, 195, 200, 202, 265
Monchaux, 77, 128
Monchiet, 142, 164
Monchy le Preux, 157, 159, 218
Mondicourt, 81
Monro, C. C., Maj.-General, 5
Mons, 300
Montignies, 295, 296
Mont St. Eloy, 237

INDEX

Moore, F. H. B., 2/Lt., 286, 292, 293
Morgan, W. L., 2/Lt., 118
Morland, T. L. N., Maj.-General, 5
Morval, 111, 119, 124
Mott, H. E., Capt., 89, 90, 99, 100, 101, 329
Moulle, 176
Moulton, H. K., 2/Lt., 186, 205
Moy, C. E., 2/Lt., 118, 330
Mullins, Rfmn., 104
Murchiston College, 61
Murray, H., Lt., 12
Musgrove, W. M., 2/Lt., 155
Musselwhite, R.S.M., 198, 256, 331, 333

Nameless Farm, 86, 90, 91, 92, 97
Negus, A. G., 2/Lt., 92
Nelson, L./Sgt., 242
Neuve Chapelle, 46, 47, 130, 131, 132
Neuville Vitasse, 141, 142, 145, 146, 154
Newnham, E., Sgt., 121
Newton, D., L./Cpl., 92
Nicholls, Stretcher-bearer, 100
Nicholls, W. G., Rfmn., 70
Nicholls, Sgt., 95
North, S., 2/Lt., 175
Noyelle Vion, 246

Oder Houses (*see* Stink Houses), 63
Oisy le Verger, 267, 268
Okill, E. G. T., 2/Lt., 118
Oliver, Sgt., 159
Oppy, 218
Orchard, J. L., Rfmn., 91
Ormiston, W. H., 2/Lt., 183, 195, 199, 330
Orr, W. G., Capt., 151, 152, 154, 155, 195, 196, 197, 202, 205, 330
Ouderdom, 170

Page, Lt., 82
Palluel, 275, 279
Palmer, P., 2/Lt., 155
" Pancake," 6
Partridge, H. H., L./Sgt., 93
Pattenden, H., L./Cpl., 231
Pelling, G. A., Rfmn., 149
Perenchies, 43
Perham Down, 3
Pettit, Cpl., 223
Phelp, W., Rfmn., 175

Philip, A. J., Lt., 34, 255
Pickles, H., 2/Lt., 132, 155
Pike, Cpl., 224
Pinnell, Rfmn., 95
Ploegsteert Wood, 32
Plumer, Sir H., General, 61, 72
Plumridge, C.S.M., 159, 272, 331
Plunkett, J. R., Lt., 268
Pollard, L. C., 2/Lt., 260
Polygone Wood, 52, 172, 173
Pommier, 156
Pont Ballot, 50
Pont du Hem, 131
Pont Remy, 76, 128
Poperinghe, 52, 55, 61, 62, 64, 66, 67
Porter, M. L., Capt., 8
Potijze, 52, 61, 62, 64, 68
Potter's Crouch Farm, 6
Pouchot, Rfmn., 40, 331
Power, O. M., 2/Lt., 252
Prémesques, 43
Price, H. S., Capt., 81, 102, 329, 330
Pridmore, A. S., Major, 4
Prince of Wales, xiv, 29
Princess Mary's Gift Box, 35
Pronville, 190

Quadrilateral, 86, 87, 93, 94, 96
Quaregnon, 303
Quéant, 190

Ramsbottom, A., Capt., 102, 103, 118
Rankin, 2/Lt., 132
Ratcliffe, L., Cpl., 91, 92
Raven, C. H., 2/Lt., 221, 230
Rawlinson, Sir H., General, 128, 219, 221
Rayner, V. G., Lt., 243, 286, 240, 330
Reinforcements, 43, 54, 61, 81, 103, 108, 161, 215, 237
Relton, Capt., 160
Rhett, R. B., Capt., 227
Rhonelle, River, 283, 285
Richens, R. I., 2/Lt., 155
Richmond Park, 2
Riencourt, 254, 260
Ritchings, A. A. W., 2/Lt., 274
Robermetz, 131
Roberts, Lord, 1, 19
Roche, R. de R., Cpl., 2, 28, 40, 334
Roclincourt, 215
Rogers, Sgt., 33
Rombies, 293
Ronville, 238

INDEX

Roper, Rfmn., 72
Rosenberg, W. F. H., Cr./Sgt., 13
Rouen, 15
Royal Engineers:
  416th Field Coy., 279
  185th Tunnelling Coy., 215
Rue du Bacquerot, 137
Rue du Bois, 31, 33
Rumaulcourt, 277, 278
Rundle, S., L./Cpl., 196
Russell, F. W., Lt., 184, 221, 226, 227, 228, 252, 330
Russia, Collapse of, 209

St. Albans, 6
St. Amand, 83, 89, 103, 105, 107, 108, 186
St. Aubin, 216, 237
St. Jans Cappel, 52
St. Jean, 61, 62, 64
St. Omer, 15, 16, 17, 166
Sailly-Saillisel, 112
Salmon, Rfmn., 72
Sambrin, 164
Samson, L. H., Cr./Sgt., 12
Samuels, L./Cpl., 231
Sanctuary Wood, 56, 57, 58, 59, 60, 170
Sauchy Cauchy, 266, 267, 271, 272, 273, 275, 276, 277, 280, 289
Sauchy Lestrée, 265, 266, 271
Saultain, 285, 286, 287, 288, 289
Savill, S. R., Lt.-Col., 12, 22, 234, 242, 250, 251, 252, 256, 258, 259, 269, 271, 276, 286, 287, 288, 293, 295, 296, 300, 304
Savy, 214, 216
Scarpe, Battle of, 1917, 156
Scarpe, Battle of, 1918, 246, 247
Sebourg, 289, 291, 292, 293, 294, 295, 296
Secretan, Mr., 7
Sensée Canal, 279
Sensée River, 147, 274, 275, 278
Sharp, Rfmn., 23
Shattock, M. M., Capt., 13, 18, 40
Sheldon, W., Rfmn., 276, 333
Shells, Restrictĕd use of, 27
Sheppard, C., Lt., 273
Shoolbred, F., Esq., 10
Shoolbred, R., Lt.-Col., 3, 12, 56, 62, 66, 67, 77, 83, 97, 99, 105, 114, 117, 128, 150, 165, 166, 298, 329, 330, 335

Shoolbred & Co., Ltd., 4
Simencourt, 139
Simonds, S. F., 2/Lt., 286
Simpson, H. J., Lt., 302
Skeate, Cpl., 171, 332
Sloan, D., Capt., 280
Smith, H. R., Lt., 279, 280, 286, 294, 330
Smith, L. G., Rfmn., 277
Smith, W. D., Maj.-General, 75
Smith, W. D., 2/Lt., 175
Snow, Sir T. D'O., Lt.-General, 83, 85
Spencer-Smith, M., 2/Lt., 118
Spencer-Smith, P., Lt., xv, 78, 93, 107
Steenstraade, 52
Stein, C. E., L./Cpl., 152
Step, Sgt., 104
Stevenson, H., 2/Lt., 118
Stillwell, W. A., 2/Lt., 221
Stinchcombe, Sgt., 292
Stink Houses (*see* Oder Houses)
Stitt, I. d'A., 2/Lt., 186, 218, 220, 224, 230
Stow, F. H., Rfmn., 93
Strange, Lt., xv, 90
Strauss, Lt., 63
Sus St. Leger, 108, 164, 165
Swainson, F. G., Capt., xv, 13, 63, 64, 69, 88, 92, 99
Sykes, H. C., Pte., 118

Tadpole Copse, 189, 190, 191, 193, 194, 195, 197, 198, 201
Talbot, N., Rev., 33
Tal-y-Maes, 2
Tanks, 119, 193
Taylor, A. K., Rfmn., 231
Taylor, P. C., 2/Lt., 117
Telegraph Hill, 146, 156, 159
Thiepval, 111
Thilloy, 124
Thurston, N. T., Capt., 121, 122, 226, 227, 329, 330
Tibbs, P. H. A., Rfmn., 40, 334
Tilloy, 241, 253
Tinques, 215
Toovey, C.S.M., 268
Tower of London, 5
Townsend, R. F., Cpl., 93, 332
Townsend-Green, H. R., Capt., 13, 18, 45
Townsend-Green, S. L., Lt., 13
Towsey, F. W., Lt.-Col., 53

INDEX

Towy Post, 212, 221, 222
Transloy, Le, 124
Transloy Ridges, 124
Trench feet, 31
Trescault, 201
Trollope, C., Capt., 165
Trollope, G. H., Col., vi, xiii, 10
Trollope, M. E., 2/Lt., 12, 32, 36
Trones Wood, 111, 127, 128
Trotter, S. E., 2/Lt., 155
Trowbridge, Rfmn., 276, 333
Tyrwhitt, N. B., Major, 12, 18, 29, 70, 335
Tucker, S., Sgt., 64, 332
Turnbull, E. J., Cr./Sgt., 13, 331

Upton, D. F., 2/Lt., 92, 97, 98, 330

Valenciennes, 282, 283
Vandenbussche, Edouard, 24
Velu Wood, 191
Verlorenhoek, 55, 63
Villers lez Cagnicourt, 267
Villers l'Hôpital, 108
Vimy, 212, 218
Vimy Ridge, 168, 231, 233, 235
Vincent, Sir C. E. Howard, xiii
Vincent, Lady Howard, vi, 10, 37
Vis en Artois, 157, 159, 263, 264, 267
Vlamertinghe, 52

Wagner, Lt., 82
Wailly, 164
Waley, E. G. S., Capt., 13, 329
Wallis, H. R., Rfmn., 95, 115
Wancourt, 145, 146, 147, 150, 154, 156, 264
Wanquetin, 156
Ward, H., Rfmn., 204
Warlencourt, 124
Warlus, 156, 244
Warren, C. G., 2/Lt., 261, 262
Warwick, 2/Lt., 121
Waterlot Farm, 112
Watford, 10, 304
Watten, 167
Watts, F. J., Rfmn., 154

Webb, J. A. N., 2/Lt., 257, 286, 330
Webb, M. M., Capt., 82, 115, 117, 121, 122, 123
Webster, T. W., 2/Lt., 125
Welling, C.S.M., 223
Werner, Cpl., 96
Wernham, Rfmn., 82
"Westminster Bridge," 39, 40, 41
Westminster, City of, xiii, 236
Westminster Abbey, 5, 305
Westminster, 1st Duke of, xiii
Westminster, 2nd Duke of, xiv
Westmoreland, Lt., xv, 82, 91, 267
Westridge Farm, 6
Westwick Hall Farm, 6
Westwick Row Farm, 6
Whitby, F. E., Capt., 169, 170, 175, 196, 202, 251, 257, 258, 286, 301, 329
Whitmore, J. B., Major, 13, 335
Whittle, R. L., Capt., 172, 175, 221, 225, 329
Wilberforce, Archdeacon, 5
Willcox, J. N., L./Cpl., 119
Willeman, 139
Williams, Rfmn., 169, 170, 175, 333
Wimbledon, 2
Wimbledon Collegiate School, 38
Wingfield, A. M., Rfmn., 70, 333, 334
Wippenhoek, 52, 167, 176
Wizernes, 166, 176
Woollacombe, Sir C. L., General, 182
Worthington, P. T., 2/Lt., 286
Wright, F. E., L./Cpl., 95
Wright, H. E., L./Cpl., 119

Yarnold, E., Sgt., 171, 223, 331, 332, 334
Yates, A. G., 2/Lt., 92, 99
Yeates, S. C., Lt., 155
Yeomanry Post, 170
Young, W. F. D., Lt., v
Ypres, 18, 19, 39, 52, 61
Ypres, Battles of, 1917, 168

Zillebeke Lake, 170
Zouave Wood, 56, 58

Printed in the United States
151284LV00001B/11/A